STORY
AND
STRUCTURE

STORY
AND
STRUCTURE

A COMPLETE GUIDE

~~~~~~~~~~~~~

LEON CONRAD

illustrated by Jason Chuang

the
SQUEEZE
PRESS

This edition published in Great Britain in 2022 by the Squeeze Press, an imprint of Wooden Books Ltd. Glastonbury, Somerset
www.woodenbooks.com

9 8 7 6 5 4 3 2 1

British Library Cataloguing in Publication Data
Leon Conrad.
Story and Structure

A CIP catalogue record for this book may be obtained from the British Library

ISBN-13: 9781-906069-25-4

Introductory epigraph from The 'Nasadiya Sukta' or 'Hymn of Creation' from *The Rigveda*, translated by Stephanie Jamison and Joel Brereton (New York: Oxford University Press, 2014), Vol. 3, 10:129, 1607–1609. Text in square brackets adapted by Leon Conrad.

Designed and typeset by Studio Monachino. Printed in India by Replika Press on 100% sustainable papers.

In memoriam
GEORGE SPENCER-BROWN

Who really knows? Who shall here proclaim it?—
from where was it born, from where this creation?
The gods are on this side of the creation of this (world).
So then who does know from where it came to be?
This creation—from where it came to be, if it was produced or if not—
[s/]he who is the overseer of this (world) in the furthest heaven,
[s/]he surely knows. Or if [s/]he does not know . . . ?

CONTENTS

ACKNOWLEDGEMENTS

This book would never have appeared without the help and support of many friends and colleagues who contributed their time, skill, and energy so generously to helping me realise it. I owe them a great deal. Firstly, I'd like to thank Giles Abbott for kindly sharing his early work on story structure with me. The nine story structures he came up with, which predate Christopher Booker's work, were instrumental in my quest to find out how story works. Next, a huge thank you to my wonderful students, who have engaged so enthusiastically with the ideas outlined in the book and have used them successfully to create stories, essays, and chapter books, allowing these ideas to be tried and tested, revised, and reformulated. If they can use them, anyone can. I'd also like to thank Shonaleigh Cumbers for her insights into her living tradition of oral storytelling, and the Temenos Academy for being a continuous source of inspiration and light – in particular, Stephen and Genevieve Overy for their work behind the scenes organising inspiring lectures by speakers such as storyteller Martin Shaw, and Sinologist Sandra Hill, whose insights helped inform and shape this work. A big thank you to Yura Senokossov and Lena Nemirovskaya for giving me the opportunity to share my ideas with the students and alumni of the School of Civic Education at their seminars, particularly during two unforgettable trips to the Republic of Georgia.

My music teachers influenced me in ways they could never have imagined. I'd like to thank Christine Croshaw, the piano teacher who taught me the importance of creating the illusion of an unbroken line of music with no downbeats; my harpsichord teacher, Maria Boxall, whose fingering techniques filled baroque music with the joy of dance; Kenneth van Barthold, for fuelling my interest in bar structure; and my theory teacher, George Kinnear, who first introduced me to Schenkerian musical analysis. My thanks also goes out to the many musicians who provided me with gateways to inspiration: Gary Branch, Maria Callas, Nelson Freire, Rhiannon

Giddens, Philippe Jaroussky, Jakub Józef Orliński, Alex Penda, Joan Sutherland, and the late, sorely missed Julie Felix – among so many others. Words cannot convey how much you helped me!

I'm humbled by and very grateful to Teresa Monachino whose creative approach to the design and layout of this book has made it sing; and to Jason Chuang (jasonchuangart.co.uk) for his skilful work in illuminating the space around the words and ideas, adding depth and bringing out the fun in the work so well.

I'm also grateful to Alette Willis and Elizabeth Mannion for their work on copy and line editing early drafts of the work, to Hannah Bouhamdi for her help in reviewing appendix 1, and to Elizabeth Mannion for indexing. I've done my best to follow their advice. Any shortfalls are due to a lack of attention on my part, which I'll happily put right where I can.

I owe a particular debt of thanks to the many friends and colleagues who read through various drafts of the work and gave me valuable feedback on them, including Juan Acevedo, Christopher Bemrose, Gary Branch, Christopher Chilton, Randolph Dible II, Rodion Garshin, Simon Heywood, Hoc Ling Duong, André Kleinbaum, Bernie Lewin, Phil McDermott, David Pinto, Alessandro Scafi, Adam Tetlow, Alexander Tsigkas, Jacob Watson, and my wife Tanya and my daughter Katya.

Three final thank yous: to John Martineau at The Squeeze Press/ Wooden Books for his invaluable insights and advice throughout the publishing process; to Liz Dubelman for her marketing advice; and last but not least, to the late Professor George Spencer-Brown, whose work inspired mine.

To explore the ideas outlined in this book further, visit my website (www.leonconrad.com), sign up to my mailing list and follow The Unknown Storyteller Project on social media channels.

PREFACE

What is necessary for the story of Cinderella to be the story of Cinderella?
... This is a question that can never be answered with precision.

H. PORTER ABBOTT
The Cambridge Introduction to Narrative[1]

Where do stories come from? Why do stories exist? And while we're on the subject ... how does story work? What makes it what it is?

These aren't easy questions to answer. If we're going to find satisfactory answers to them, we'll need to go right back to the very source of story.

The process is rather like being a moth in flight trying to watch itself flying. You might just manage to catch a reflection out of your peripheral vision while keeping your focus straight ahead. You might just manage to slow down time and stretch past the boundaries of space to touch infinity, where there's no beginning and no end, and observe the infinitesimal changes that occur within that state of infinity.

It's a bit like trying to hear music that exists potentially in silence, or trying to catch a thought in flight without confining it or changing its course in any way.

To make sense of anything we come across or realise, we need to tell some kind of a story. Every thing we say or do is either a story or part of one. And the way to make sense of the mystery of story is to become story – and be storied by story – in a living process. It's a bit like an embryo trying to hear the beat of the heart it's yet to develop.

We don't ask to be born, but as human beings, we're called to fulfil our potential, to realise our vocation, to respond to our calling. Sometimes we can get in our own way; sometimes life presents us with challenges. And sometimes, there are those moments of clarity which allow us to catch a glimpse of what's possible. Story shapes all of those experiences.

Story shapes the story spinner ... the story spinner's story ... and how the story spinner develops their story. And when a story spinner becomes aware of that, story recognises itself.

In this book, I invite you to rethink your idea of story. Rather than classifying stories based on content and saying that myths and legends are stories but essays and adverts aren't, I invite you to see story in a different way: like a necklace.

Necklaces are a combination of the discrete and the continuous: beads and the filament on which they're strung. Stories are no different: they feature discrete moments or events arranged sequentially like beads and a dynamic of relationships through which events are linked forming a string that links them together. Story is the ultimate necklace – a necklace that can form itself, restring and refashion itself again and again and again in countless narrative patterns that conform to a far smaller number of story structures.

Looking at story this way, we can observe how and why events in stories are linked, a process which will lead us to identifying the structures that lie under the surface of any story.

We use these story structures far more often than when we just tell stories – we use them throughout our everyday '9-to-5, Monday-to-Friday, weekend-break, 4-weeks-of-holiday-a-year' lives. As human beings, we're uniquely positioned to reflect on this. Once we get to know the story structures and understand how they work, we'll be far more empowered to solve problems we come across in 'everyday life'. We'll start to see parallels between the story structures and the habitual patterns of thinking and acting we use. Some are typically helpful; some less so. Learning to appreciate their differences will help us think more clearly and live our lives more effectively, more purposefully. The good news is that there's a way we can do that which is both easier and more intuitive than it ever has been before.

We know that stories can be classified under different headings: 'Cinderella' stories, for instance, are referred to as 'Rags to Riches' stories; 'Snow White' and 'Sleeping Beauty' stories as 'Death and Rebirth' stories. You may be familiar with Vladimir Propp's 31 functions, Georges Polti's 36 dramatic situations, Joseph Campbell's 'monomyth' popularly referred to as 'the hero's journey', or Christopher Booker's 'seven basic plots'. These writers all focus primarily on content in their work. And that makes it more difficult for us to match our own stories to the patterns they've defined. In order to capture the pulse—or heartbeat—of story, we need to go beyond the content and we need an easy way to chart the patterns that appear at this deep level.

Some people have tried to use algebraic symbols to map the shapes of stories – Claude Levi-Strauss is one example. Some (like Kurt Vonnegut) have used squiggly lines or graphs. Others have used tables, charts, or diagrams. There are word-based descriptions for different kinds of motifs, and numbers for different tale types. Many of these are explored in appendix 2. Nevertheless, despite our long history of telling stories, we still need a simple, easy, intuitive way of visualising how stories work. And that's precisely what the system outlined in this book provides.

It's inspired by the work of Professor George Spencer-Brown whose book, *Laws of Form*, was first published in 1969. I had the privilege of studying it with him towards the end of his life. To date, Spencer-Brown's work has been applied mainly in the fields of mathematics, logic, and social theory. Its application to literary analysis and narrative studies has been minimal. While there have been attempts to apply his work in the field of literary analysis, this is the first time his work has been systematically applied to analysing story structure in its broadest sense.[2] Based on only six symbols, Spencer-Brown's approach is remarkably simple. It's visually intuitive, easy to understand, and extraordinarily powerful.

Using his six simple symbols allows us to get fresh insights into how story works, how and why story structures differ, and why story really is a much wider phenomenon than most people have taken it to be up to now. It has the potential to take us right to the heart of what makes story work, to make us better problem solvers, and – perhaps most importantly – to help us understand ourselves better.

This book introduces 18 distinct story structures:

Quest
Transformation
Rags to Riches
Death and Rebirth
Trickster
Revelation
Call and Response (Variation 1)
Call and Response (Variation 2)
Trickster Variation
The Chinese Circular Structure
Dilemma
Ki-Shō-Ten-Ketsu
Open-Ended Ki-Shō-Ten-Ketsu
Koan
Riddle
Voyage and Return
Perpetual Motion
Creation Myth

It shows that story structures can be classified in four distinct ways – by the quality of how the stories unfold based on the quality of the first step in a character's story line; by key elements that can be found in the middle (Threshold/Non-Threshold structures); by what happens at the end (Open-Ended/Closed structures); and finally, by quality, acknowledging the two aspects of story outlined above (Linear and Dynamic), linking to the ideas of the discrete lines of 'beads' and continuous 'stringing' that the necklace of story uses to create its patterns. While every bead is different, all beads fit into common families of shapes – spheres, cylinders, teardrops, for instance. Every static bead, however, depends on a unifying string to hold it in place as part of the dynamic structure which is a necklace.

Although the approach is based on Spencer-Brown's work, don't worry if you aren't familiar with it. All you need is laid out right here in this book, pitched in a readable, easy-to-understand way. You probably instinctively know much of this already. It's just hasn't been described in this way before.

Even though the approach is based on only six primary symbols, it allows for unlimited expansion, without any additional symbols being needed. It's like a mandala – the kind in which small fractal elements scale up to form a whole that's larger than the sum of its parts.

I've found Spencer-Brown's minimalistic system not only beautiful but a joy to work with.[3] Using it has allowed me to answer H. Porter Abbott's question (quoted at the beginning of this section) about what makes the story of Cinderella the story of Cinderella … with precision.

The pattern of that story structure (the Rags to Riches structure)—and those of the 17 other story structures outlined in this book—can be traced back centuries – back to some of the earliest written records, which means they existed as part of oral culture well before that. And we're still using the very same story structures to create stories today! There clearly are *laws of story*. The methodology presented here works in harmony with them.

When we look at how structures compare, deep relationships appear – giving us new insights into the relationships between story structures. Understanding how the Quest structure is nested in the more compressed Transformation structure, for instance, leads to a deeper understanding of how we process emotions – and that can help us manage anger more effectively. It can also show us how we can avoid being pulled in to emotional traps laid for us by unscrupulous advertisers. That's just one of many fascinating insights and applications that emerge.

This book clearly demonstrates how different story structures can be distinguished … more precisely than ever before, but also why Comedy and Tragedy are structure neutral; it shows how these can be applied to *any* story structure, and presents the argument that they exist to bring us into a better state of balance. Moreover, it shows that our innate yearning for balance *is* the energy that drives story. If there's any bias to be detected in the work, it'll be found to align with principles common to Daoist and Perennial Philosophy and the kind of rationalism advocated by J M Robertson.[4]

The stories I've drawn on as examples come from a range of cultures and eras – from China, Japan, Europe, North, West and South East Africa, North America, India, Persia, the Middle East, and others. They go back to ancient Egyptian times, to ancient Israel and Babylonia, ancient Greece and Rome, and on through the Middle Ages, the Renaissance, and the early modern period to the present day. They're all relevant.

I've based my examples on stories which are well known and well loved – Brer Rabbit and Simple Jack stories, riddles from *The Old English Riddle Book*, classics like Beowulf, stories from Ovid's *Metamorphoses*, Greek tragedies and extracts from literary works such as Kipling's *The Just So Stories*. I've also drawn on some lesser-known examples such as a tale about a cuckolded husband from *The Arabian Nights*. In addition, I've included jokes, West African dilemma tales, oriental Ki-Shō-Ten-Ketsu stories, koans, and a story from Malawi about *The Moon and His Two Wives* (a rare example of a Perpetual Motion structure story), tales from Russia, China, the Middle East, and extracts from Chinese literary classics.

I also draw on a range of poetry in regular forms, including a limerick about Kim Kardashian by Salman Rushdie, haikus by Bashō and Buson, a Shakespearean sonnet, a ghazal by Wali, and a collection of landays from Afghanistan.

I look at why some story structures feature more commonly in songs or poems than they do in stories ... all this to get closer to finding the source of story than we've managed to get previously.

This way of looking at story demands we see with our eyes, hear with our ears, but experience with our soul. It requires embodied engagement – it calls for thoughts and feelings to work together in a balanced way. It requires a new way of looking. Individual journeys will differ. The book has one goal: to bring story to life in you.

If, as I argue here, story structures arise in and from human awareness, and reflect aspects of human awareness related to a yearning for balance, then one has to ask why ... what purpose do they serve? The only satisfying answer I've come to so far is that they point to a deep need for the voice of The Unknown Storyteller to be heard. We achieve this through being open to story storying within us – to story storying us.

In the prologue, I present some key definitions. In chapter 1, I introduce a brief basic overview of the methodology outlined in this book, which I expand on in the subsequent three chapters. In chapters 5 to 18, the individual story structures identified are presented in turn, showing how they differ, following which, in chapters 19 onwards, I explore some of the implications of the methodology. In chapters 21 and 22, I introduce insights that the approach can bring to the appreciation of literary forms such as narrative and poetry, pending a more in-depth work showing how the methodology can be applied in the practice of writing.

Some of the best story spinners are poets. Poets know how story works better than anyone – they create in the moment, while also being storied as living, breathing beings caught up in the awe-inspiring mystery of a living, breathing cosmos.

The greatest of these poets have left us treasures – Farīd ud-Dīn 'Attâr, whose quotes frame the work, for instance and the great poets behind the text of the *Rigveda* whose words take us as close as I think we can get to the source of story.

We start and end this journey with their works, which point to a starting point and destination for our exploration of story which lies just beyond us ... until we re-discover it all around us, and within ourselves. Once that happens, it becomes easier to see that life lifes; story stories. Story lifes. Life stories. Story = life; life = story. Story and life are one-and-the-same. Realising that gives us the potential to achieve a more finely tuned sense of balance – both in relation to ourselves and in relation to others.

I hope this book will help you tell life's story and help you to story your life by living your life story in harmony ... with story.

NOTES

1   H. Porter Abbott, *The Cambridge Introduction to Narrative* (Cambridge: Cambridge University Press, 2021), 21.

2   Spencer-Brown's work has been seen – at least potentially – as providing an answer to what Bouissac calls the 'Saussurean unfinished agenda' (Paul Bouissac, "Saussure's Legacy in Semiotics," in *The Cambridge Companion to Saussure*, edited by Carol Sanders, 240–260 (Cambridge: Cambridge University Press, 2006), at 256, 260). Ingo Berensmeyer ("'Twofold Vibration': Samuel Beckett's Laws of Form," *Poetics Today* 25 (3): 465–495), Bruce Clarke (*Posthuman Metamorphosis: Narrative and Systems* (New York: Fordham University Press, 2008)), and Don Kunze ("Triplicity in Spencer-Brown, Lacan, and Poe," in *Lacan and the Nonhuman*, edited by Gautam Basu Thakur and Jonathan Michael Dickstein, 157–176 (Cham: Palgrave Macmillan, 2018)) are, to my knowledge, the only narrative scholars to have drawn on Spencer-Brown's work in print to date. A detailed analysis of the ways in which they have applied Spencer-Brown's work in this field can be found in my paper, "Laws of Form – Laws of Narrative – Laws of Story," in *Laws of Form: A Fiftieth Anniversary*, Series On Knots & Everything. Vol. 72, edited by Louis H. Kauffman, Fred Cummins, Randolph Dible, Leon Conrad, Graham Ellsbury, Andrew Crompton, and Florian Grote, 785–806. Singapore: World Scientific, 2022.

3   While the Chinese Circular Structure can be easily mapped with Spencer-Brown's six primary symbols, I've added five further 'nice to have' symbols for visual clarity.

4   Rt Hon John Mackinnon Robertson, *Letters on Reasoning*, 2nd ed., revised with additions (London: Watts, 1905). The important influence that Robertson's work had on George Spencer-Brown's is explored in Leon Conrad, "Roots, shoots, fruits: William Blake and J M Robertson: two key influences on George Spencer-Brown's work and the latter's relationship to Niklas Luhmann's work," *Kybernetes* 51, no. 5 (2022): 1879–1895.

PROLOGUE

COMING TO TERMS WITH STORY

Whosoever desires to explore The Way—
Let them set out—for what more is there to say?

'ATTÂR, TRANS. UNKNOWN, *Canticle of the Birds*[1]

Let's begin with a few definitions. I use story; stories, a story, the story; and narrative(s) to stand for the three levels that are found together in every narrative.

Story

> I use the word 'story' to mean two things which are linked: firstly, the relatively static ways in which events in a chronological sequence are linked; and secondly, the dynamic impulse that links these events. The combination of these is what makes story 'story'.

Stories, a story, the story

> Stories come into being when someone initiates or communicates a series of events which are (or are capable of being) meaningfully related to each other.[2]

I use the terms stories, a story, or the story to mean a linked arrangement of events that's easily recognisable, regardless of how a/the story is told.

Because there are many ways of telling a story, we end up with different narratives.

Narrative(s)

By narrative(s), I mean (a) particular version(s), or telling(s) of a story.

A narrative is the static, finished form that results from an interpretation of a story.

A book can be made into a screenplay that's made into a film, then adapted for theatre, and retold in the form of a graphic novel. The graphic novel might be remade as a film and its plot could be summarised as a spoiler on a review site on the internet, or retold among friends in a social setting. Each of these is an example of a narrative based on the same key source: a story.

For instance, *West Side Story* (a film) is based on Shakespeare's stage play, *Romeo and Juliet*, which could have been based on the poem by Arthur Brooke (1562), and/or the prose narrative by William Painter (1580), either of which could have been based on the earlier Italian prose version by Luigi da Porto, written in the 1520s, and published in various editions from 1531 onwards, which may have been based on an earlier version from an oral tradition.[3] These are all narratives based on 'a single, common core story' recognised as the story of the 'star-crossed lovers'. Folklorists have estimated that there are over 1,500 Cinderella stories, for instance,[4] all of them recognised by the similarity in their key content as being based on 'a single, common core story' which could be described as the 'Rags to Riches' story. Each of these stories can be told in a variety of narrative ways, which leads us to interpretations.

Interpretation(s)

Different (re)presentations of a work or performances of a production come about as a result of a dynamic process of engaging with a narrative.

> An interpretation is a dynamic process through which a narrative unfolds over time.

Within any narrative, each character has their own story line.

Story line(s)

> Story lines map the moment-to-moment sequence of events each character experiences. Story lines always follow (a) particular story structure(s).

Story structure

> I use story structure to mean the minimum number of related events we need for a unified whole we can recognise as being common to a particular group of stories with the qualities of distinctive 'single, common core stories' or 'masterplots', as Porter Abbott calls them.[5]

Joseph Campbell has argued, in *The Hero with a Thousand Faces*, that the 'hero's journey' masterplot can be traced through a wide range of narratives. He describes their story structure as having three main stages (separation, initiation, return), each stage containing several subsections.[6]

By starting from a narrative, then following each character's story line, identifying the distinctive narrative units which unfold through these story lines, arranging them in chronological order, reducing them to the minimum number of units required to tell the 'bare bones' of a story, and then seeing how the characters' story lines interlink, we identify the story which underpins the narrative. We can then analyse the relationship between the story and the story structure(s) which it follows to understand the role that story plays in that context – both in the story and in our engagement with it. The approach develops and builds on the work of many narrative theorists and writers, and I am particularly indebted to the work of Mieke Bal, Roland Barthes, Joseph Campbell, Gerard Genette, A. J. Greimas, Claude Levi-Strauss, Georges Polti, Vladimir Propp, Philip Pullman, Arielle Saiber, Ferdinand de Saussure, and John Yorke.[7]

Plot pattern

> **Plot pattern deals with how a story is told and the order in which the sequence of events is narrated.**

Story unfolds in both space and time, but they're treated differently at different levels. Story structures emphasise time – they map sequences of events in the order in which they happen, moment to moment. Plot patterns, however, emphasise space. Think of where a narrator is positioned, for instance. Usually, shifts in a narrator's position indicates a scene change and takes us from place to place in the story – but not necessarily in chronological order.

Story			
Story spinner			
Plot pattern		Story structure	
Space	Time	Space	**Time**
Narrative			

Other terms will be defined as we come to them. In homage to Spencer-Brown, the quirky injunctive style he uses to introduce definitions in his book *Laws of Form* is invoked here when structures are defined.

By defining terms, or story structures, we fix them – temporarily. It's more useful, however, to see the structures in particular as flexible, responsive building blocks, which can merge, and develop variant forms in context and yet still follow recognisable structural patterns. Often the story seeker's interpretation will influence how a character's story structure is determined. The detailed analysis presented in appendix 1, which complements and develops the basic overview of the structures as presented in the main part of this work, provides an example of this.

NOTES

1 The last lines of the poem (lines 4482–4483), as quoted in Clarissa Estes' introduction to Joseph Campbell, *The Hero with a Thousand Faces* (Princeton and Oxford: Princeton University Press, 2004), xxix.

2 There are useful definitions to be found in the glossary in H. Porter Abbott's *Cambridge Introduction to Narrative* (Cambridge: Cambridge University Press, 2021), 243–263, particularly those for 'entity', 'event', and 'story' on pages 248, 249 and 261 respectively.

3 For the film, see Jerome Robbins and Robert Wise, directors, *West Side Story* (Los Angeles: United Artists, 1961); the play, William Shakespeare, *Romeo and Juliet*. In *The Arden Shakespeare, Third Series*, edited by René Weis (London: Bloomsbury, 2012), 1125–1158; the poem, Arthur Brooke, "Romeus and Juliet." *Shakespeare Navigators*, 1 February, 2021, https://www.shakespeare-navigators.com/romeo/BrookeIndex.html; the prose narratives, William Painter, "Romeo and Juliet," *The Palace of Pleasure: Elizabethan Versions of Italian and French Novels from Boccacio, Bandello, Cinthio, Straparola, Queen Margaret of Navarre, and Others*. Vol. 2, Tome 2, edited by Joseph Jacobs, 3 January, 2011, Project Gutenberg, http://www.gutenberg.org/files/34840/34840-h/34840-h.htm#novel2_25; Luigi da Porto, Matteo Bandello, and Pierre Boaistuau, *Romeo and Juliet Before Shakespeare: Four Early Stories of Star-crossed Love* (Toronto: Centre for Reformation and Renaissance Studies, 2000); and Luigi da Porto, *Romeo and Juliet*, translated by Maurice Jonas (London: Davis & Orioli, 1921), https://archive.org/details/romeojulietphoto00dapo/page/n9.

4 Marian Roalfe Cox, *Cinderella; three hundred and forty-five variants of Cinderella, Catskin, and Cap o'Rushes, abstracted and tabulated, with a discussion of mediaeval analogues, and notes* (London: David Nutt for the Folk-Lore Society, 1893), https://archive.org/details/cinderellathreeh00coxmuoft/; Anna Birgitta Rooth, *The Cinderella Cycle*, (New York: Arno, 1980); Alan Dundes, ed., *Cinderella: A Folklore Casebook* (New York: Garland, 1982); Russell A. Peck, "The Cinderella Bibliography", in *A Robbins Library Digital Project*, accessed 16 November, 2018, http://d.lib.rochester.edu/cinderella. According to Heidi Anne Heiner, 'Sources disagree about how many versions of the tale exist, with numbers conservatively ranging from 345 to over 1,500.' "History of Cinderella," 1998–2021, https://www.surlalunefairytales.com/a-g/cinderella/cinderella-history.html. Heiner elsewhere states that

'the general consensus is that well over 1,000 variants, with a conservative estimate of over twice that amount, have been recorded as part of literary folklore.' *Cinderella Tales from Around the World*, (n.p.: SurLaLune Press, 2012), 1.

5   For the definition of 'masterplots' as 'recurrent skeletal stories', see Abbott, *Cambridge Introduction*, 254–255 and further references listed therein. See also Christopher Booker, *The Seven Basic Plots: Why We Tell Stories* (London and New York: Continuum, 2005). Italics mine.

6   See Joseph Campbell, *The Hero with a Thousand Faces*, 2004, 28–36, and chapter 18 of this work, where I compare Campbell's views on the 'navel of the world' and the Chinese Circular Structure.

7   Mieke Bal, *Narratology in Practice* (Toronto, Buffalo, London: University of Toronto Press, 2021), *Narratology: Introduction to the Theory of Narrative*, 4th ed. (Toronto: University of Toronto Press, 2017), *On Storytelling: Essays in Narratology* (Sonoma, CA: Polebridge, 1991); Roland Barthes, "An Introduction to the Structural Analysis of Narrative," in *New Literary History: On Narrative and Narratives* 6, no. 2 (Winter 1975): 237–272, https://doi.org/10.2307/468419; Joseph Campbell, *The Hero with a Thousand Faces*, 2004; Gerard Genette, *Narrative Discourse* (Oxford: Blackwell, 1979); Algirdas Julien Greimas, "Elements of a Narrative Grammar," in *Diacritics* 7, no. 1 (Spring 1977): 23–40; Algirdas Julien Greimas, and François Rastier, "The Interaction of Semiotic Constraints," in *Yale French Studies: Game, Play, Literature* 41 (1968): 86–105; Georges Polti, *The Thirty-Six Dramatic Situations*, translated by Lucile Ray (Franklin, OH: James Knapp Reeve, 1924), https://archive.org/details/thirtysixdramati00polt/page/n4; Vladimir Propp, *Morphology of the Folktale*, 2nd ed. (Austin, TX: University of Texas Press, 2005), and Levi-Strauss' commentary on his work therein; Philip Pullman's "Poco a Poco," in *Daemon Voices: Essays on Storytelling* (Oxford: David Fickling, 2017), 150–173; Arielle Saiber, *Giordano Bruno and the Geometry of Language: Literary and Scientific Cultures of Early Modernity*, (Aldershot and Burlington, VT: Ashgate Publishing Company, 2005); Charles Bally, Albert Riedlinger, Ferdinand de Saussure, and Albert Sechehaye, *Course in General Linguistics* (London: Duckworth, 1983); Carol Sanders, *The Cambridge Companion to Saussure* (Cambridge: Cambridge University Press, 2004) and especially the chapter therein by Bouissac entitled "Saussure's Legacy in Semiotics," 240–260; and John Yorke, *Into the Woods: How Stories Work and Why We Tell Them* (London: Penguin, 2013).

1

THE BASICS
IN BRIEF

The poet … must familiarize *himself with the* secrets *of his calling, the great and inviolable* laws *and the lesser and breakable* rules *of his* discipline *or* craft.

GEORGE SPENCER-BROWN, WRITING AS JAMES KEYS, *Only Two Can Play This Game*[1]

Just as a farmer ploughs a field before starting to sow, or a builder lays foundations before putting up a building, in this chapter, I lay out the foundations of the methodology. With the foundations in place, we'll be able to build on them in more detail. We start with some key ideas.

Assumptions and conventions

Story implies the presence of a story spinner. The story spinner communicates information to a story seeker.

Story emerges from a sense that something is out of balance with respect to a specific character – a sense that something (from their perspective) either should be, but isn't; or a sense that something isn't, but should be.

Story is based on a series of events that can be classified as 'backward and forward steps' (the 'heartbeat' of story, the pulsing beats of which being 'counted' when the story is 'recounted' or 'told') within a character's story line.[2]

Story lines always relate to a particular character in a particular situation.

Stories involve one or more characters' story lines unfolding.

This emergent unfolding of a related series of events is how story 'stories'.[3]

The events are (or are capable of being) meaningfully related to each other in relation to the initial state in which a character (concrete or abstract)[4] starts out and to the state in which they end up, taking the character from one point in space and/or time to another.

The events are either seen as 'fortunate' and/or 'unfortunate' relative to the perceived state of imbalance to which they relate.[5]

At the level of story structure, the sequences of steps always follows the chronological order in which the events unfold in time.

The order in which these steps occur at the level of plot pattern in the narrative telling of a story need not be chronological.

The minimum number of events, and the order in which these events unfold distinguish different story structures.

Notation

George Spencer-Brown's calculus, which inspires this work, is based on a single mark (⌐) which represents a token of the first distinction, resulting from a self-realised 'act of crossing'.[6] Its presence implies an unmarked state which stands for the space in which the mark appears, 'in the form' (⌐).[7] The unmarked state contains unlimited potential for the emergence of new marks – just as we have unlimited potential for ideas to appear in and from our minds. When ideas are expressed, the expressions can expand (→) and contract (←).[8] Where the movement has potential to expand or contract, but the result is (as yet) undetermined, the double barb is used (⇌).[9] Finally, 'the snake eating its own tail' is introduced – the mark of recursion, or re-entry into the form – to deal with memory, time, and other looping or indeterminate forms such as the principle behind the square root of minus 1. Until one option is chosen, it can either be -1 or +1. It's indeterminate (⊔).[10] These six simple symbols, along with the absence of form, are the only elements we need to map the deep structure of story. They're applied as follows:

Events	Symbols	As used by George Spencer-Brown	As used in this work
Openings/ Closings	⊐	Recursion or re-entry. Introduces time, memory and second-order forms, like the principle behind the square root of minus 1.	The mark of recursion or re-entry is used to symbolise openings and closings of stories. These typically set up and resolve cognitive dissonances in space-time (e.g., 'Once upon a time', which treats time as a bounded region of space on which something can be placed, rather than something flowing, moving and constantly in motion; and 'they lived happily ever after', which treats the extent of characters' lives as indefinite rather than definite). This applies to all story structures.
Initial/final situations	⌐	Mark of indication. Performs a pointing function. Stands for the marked state.	The mark is used to symbolise a 'who, when, and where': a character in a particular point in space and time at the start and end of a story. This applies to all story structures.
Empty space		Absence of form. This indicates the unmarked state. In relation to the first distinction, it signifies 'nothing'; 'mystery'; the void from which, and in which, form emerges.	The only structure in which a blank space appears, indicating the absence of a mark, is the Open-Ended Linear Koan structure. Here, I focus on the comparatively static aspect of the symbol, and link it to a transcendent, awe-inspired 'WOW!' state.
Backward step	←	Act of condensation, cancellation. Retracing	The backward barb symbolises an event which poses a problem for a character or hinders them from resolving it. In this context, meetings are interpreted as backward steps.
Forward step	→	Act of confirmation, compensation. Tracing	The forward barb symbolises an event which helps a character resolve the problem they face, or propels them towards realising their destiny.

Events	Symbols	As used by George Spencer-Brown	As used in this work
Events involving cognitive dissonance	⇌	Potential for expansion or contraction, as yet unrealised, thus indeterminate.	As will be described, the double barb symbolises an event which involves a 'mistake' of some kind – specifically, an Aristotelian categorical cognitive dissonance often in the form of defeated expectation in the quality of the interaction between two characters.[11] This could be: (i) an active intention to dupe (Trickster step and its resolution in a Transformational Twist), (ii) a comic outcome (Comic step, based on a simile-based category mistake and its resolution in a Transformational Twist), or (iii) a surprising outcome (Trickster Awe step, based on an interjection-like perception of dissonance between categorematic and syncategorematic qualities of being (Huh?!) and the resolution of that perceived sense of dissonance (Ah!) in a Transformational Twist). The double barb typically appears either singly (⇌), not (⇌ ⇌), or as a pair framing a backward step (⇌ ← ⇌).

Although I introduce an extra set of secondary symbols in chapter 13 to map the dynamic movement of the energy in a story in relation to the Chinese Circular Structure for convenience, the steps can still be notated in a basic manner using Spencer-Brown's marks of indication (⌐) and cancellation (⌐) alternately.

Treatment of steps and step sequences

Sequences of *the same* step type can expand and contract as follows:

A double (← ←) sequence of steps can contract to a single (←) step.
A double (→ →) sequence of steps can contract to a single (→) step.

A single (⟵) step can expand to a double (⟵ ⟵) sequence.
A single (⟶) step can expand to a double (⟶ ⟶) sequence.

Sequences of *different* step types can expand and contract as follows:

A triple (⟵ ⟶ ⟵) sequence of steps can contract to a single (⟵) step.
A triple (⟶ ⟵ ⟶) sequence of steps can contract to a single (⟶) step.
A triple (⇌ ⟵ ⇌) sequence of steps can contract to a single (⇌) step.

Contrariwise, as Tweedledee might say:[12]

A single (⟵) step can expand to a triple (⟵ ⟶ ⟵) sequence.
A single (⟶) step can expand to a triple (⟶ ⟵ ⟶) sequence.
A single (⇌) step can expand to a triple (⇌ ⟵ ⇌) sequence.

Call this the expansion and contraction of steps.

Process of working
With the basic principles outlined above in mind,
1.   Select a story to analyse.
2.   Note the source version, where relevant.
3.   Summarise the story in 'bare bones' form.
4.   Note the story opening and closing, stated or implied.
5.   Identify the main characters and their initial situation (who, when, where, and in what condition).
6.   Identify the problem(s) which caused the story to emerge for each of these characters – these are typically resolved (but sometimes left unresolved) at the end of the story.
7.   Identify the main structural parts of the story (beginning, middle, end, and any subsections).
8.   Arrange the events related to each character's story line in chronological order.
9.   Within these story lines, look for pairs of 'unfortunate'/ 'fortunate' steps which relate to the ebb and flow of the story structure. The terms 'unfortunate' and 'fortunate' are relative

to the solution of the character's initial problem. Ask yourself, 'Where does the tide of the story's flow change?' 'Which elements of the story flow forward and help the character on their journey towards solving their problem?' 'Which elements of the story relate to a reversal of the flow, that delay or distract a character on their journey?' Are there any outliers? Are there any single steps that don't fit into a pair? Note these. Analyse them. What do they point to?

10. Identify the quality of each element using the appropriate symbol:

   Opening, Closing: Oscillatory Step (⊐)
   Character: Mark (⌐)
   Forward step: Forward barb (→)
   Backward step: Backward barb (←)
   Meetings are always interpreted as backward steps in this approach to the analysis of story structure, as they stop the character in their tracks and delay or distract the character from continuing on their journey.
   Trickster, Dupe, Comic, Transformational Twist, Trickster Awe steps: Double barb (⇌). These steps signify an interaction between two characters which involves a defeated expectation or cognitive dissonance of some kind.[13]

11. Can you condense (← ←) or (← → ←), to (←); (→ →) or (→ ← →) to (→) and/or (⇌ ← ⇌) to (⇌) without losing essential information? If you can, then do.

12. Analyse the overarching structure of the entire story based on the dominant pattern which results, using the 18 story structures currently identified as a guide.

13. Note any questions or variations that result from your analysis when compared to the 18 story structures currently identified.

Application

For the purpose of demonstration, we'll be using the story of *The Gigantic Turnip*.[14] It's a cumulative story in which the main character (the grandfather, in Afanas'ev's version, analysed below) starts with a problem, goes through a sequence of events that, after many failed attempts, leads to him overcoming the hindrance that lies in the way, with the help of his family and friends, which results in his problem being solved. In the following analysis of his story line, each step is assigned an appropriate symbol.[15]

Analysis of the grandfather's story line in the story of *The Gigantic Turnip*

Steps	Symbols	Structure	Outline of content
1	☐	Opening	[Implied]
2	⌐	Initial situation	Grandfather planted a turnip.
3	←	Problem	When the time came to harvest it, he couldn't pull it up.
4	→	Journey	He called for help.
5	←	Meeting with ...	A character came over ...
6	→	... friend/helper	... and tried to help him harvest it, but the attempt failed. *Loop back to step 3 in a series featuring grandmother, granddaughter, a dog, five beetles.*
7	←	Meeting with ...	The fifth beetle, adding its strength to the cumulative build-up ...
8	→	... enemy/ hindrance	... helped them pull up the turnip ...
9	⌐	Final situation (outcome/resolution)	... enabling the grandfather to harvest it.
10	☐	Closing	[Implied]

When the 'friend/helper' characters join the story, they're simply that – friends/helpers. As soon as their attempts to help fail, they share in the grandfather's problem and their story lines and his merge. The final iteration (relating to the fifth beetle) allows the story structure to resolve. The story structure is then revealed to be a standard Quest structure, outlined in full in chapter 5, the typical steps of which are shown in the column marked 'Structure' above.

Classification of story structures
(a) Linear and Dynamic story structures

16 story structures involve barbs in their notation – whether these relate to backward steps (←), forward steps (→), or steps involving a categorical cognitive dissonance of some kind, indicated by (⇌). All of these 16 story structures are Linear structures.

Two story structures start off, as the Linear structures do, with an opening step (⊐) and a mark for the character (⌐). From there, an alternation between marked (⌐) and unmarked (⌐̄) states unfolds, the number of such steps, and their qualities distinguishing the structures and giving them their individuality. These story structures are the Chinese Circular Structure and the Revelation structure. They're identified as Dynamic story structures. Dynamic story structures symbiotically underpin Linear story structures.

> **Call the Chinese Circular Structure and the Revelation structure Dynamic story structures. Call the remaining structures identified Linear story structures.**[16]

Each step in the Chinese Circular Structure or Revelation structure relates to one or more steps in a Linear story structure. Steps in Dynamic story structures are notated using the following three symbols (⊐), (⌐), (⌐̄), which, in the context of Dynamic story structures, are used to denote the following:

Events	Symbols	As used by George Spencer-Brown	As used in this work
Oscillation	⊐	Recursion or re-entry. Introduces time, memory and second-order equations.	In Dynamic story structures, the mark of oscillation symbolises a qualitative change in the relationship between knower and known. The change is from either a marked or an unmarked state to an oscillatory state.

Events	Symbols	As used by George Spencer-Brown	As used in this work
Marking	⌐	Mark of indication. Performs a pointing function. Stands for the marked state.	In Dynamic story structures, the mark of indication symbolises a qualitative change in the relationship between knower and known. The change is from either an oscillatory or an unmarked state to a marked state. Elsewhere, I refer to this as a state which gives rise to a statement (the declarative mood).
Unmarking	⌐‖	Mark of cancellation. Cancels a mark of indication, or stands for the unmarked state. Equivalent to the blank piece of paper on which it is written. In relation to the first distinction, it signifies 'nothing'; 'mystery'; the void from which, and in which, form emerges.	In Dynamic story structures, the mark of cancellation symbolises a qualitative change in the relationship between knower and known. The change is from either an oscillatory or a marked state to an unmarked state. Elsewhere, I refer to this as a state which gives rise to a wish or prayer (the optative mood).

(b) Threshold and Non-Threshold structures

The 18 story structures can be classified according to whether a character crosses a threshold between transcendent (metaphysical or supernatural) and immanent (physical) dimensions of being, with the Creation Myth structure straddling both:

Threshold structures	Non-Threshold structures
Transformation	Quest
Trickster Variation	Trickster
Death and Rebirth	Ki-Shō-Ten-Ketsu
Rags to Riches	Open-Ended Ki-Shō-Ten-Ketsu
Revelation	Dilemma
Call and Response (2 Variations)	Riddle
Chinese Circular Structure	Voyage and Return
Koan	Perpetual Motion

Creation Myth

Threshold structures typically feature fairy godmothers, angels, demons, etc. It may be useful to distinguish between concepts and percepts here – we experience trees with our senses; we experience tree spirits with our mind … until they cross a threshold and manifest in physical form. In the Creation Myth structure, both dimensions unite.

Linear story structures can also be classified according to (c) the quality of a character's initial step and (d) the quality of the ending.

(c) Classification by initial step

The mark (⌐) stands for a character in a particular time and place. It can be followed by any of the other 5 primary symbols used in the methodology:

⌐	⌐⌐	←	→	⇌
Revelation	The Chinese Story Structure	Quest Transformation Death & Rebirth Trickster Call and Response (2 Variations) Trickster Variation Dilemma Voyage & Return Perpetual Motion	Ki-Shō-Ten-Ketsu Open-Ended Ki-Shō-Ten-Ketsu Creation Myth	Riddle Koan

(d) Classification by endings

Closed	Open-Ended	No clear ending
Quest Transformation Rags to Riches Death and Rebirth Trickster Trickster Variation Call and Response (2 Variations) Ki-Shō-Ten-Ketsu Voyage and Return	Dilemma Open-Ended Ki-Shō-Ten-Ketsu Koan Riddle	Perpetual Motion Creation Myth

NOTES

1 James Keys, *Only Two Can Play This Game* (Bath: Cat Books, 1971), 37.

2 One exception is the Creation Myth structure, although this can be expressed as the first contraction and release that generate the heartbeat of all of the other story structures. Another could be the Chinese Circular Structure, which exhibits a similar contraction/expansion pattern – the ebb and flow of *qi*.

3 The principle is behind a game used in storytelling, improvised theatre, and theatre warm-up contexts. It has inspired two books: Remy Charlip, *Fortunately* (New York: Aladdin, 1993), and Michael Foreman, *Fortunately, Unfortunately* (Minneapolis, MN: Andersen, 2011). More recently, it has appeared as a 'texting game': Simon Hill, "The best texting games," in *Digital Trends*. 15 July, 2019. https://www.digitaltrends.com/mobile/best-texting-games/.

4 Abstract concepts are often personified as fictional characters; mathematical proofs are an example of stories which feature abstract propositions as characters.

5 The terms 'unfortunate'/'fortunate' are intended as props to help bridge the gap of unfamiliarity with the symbolic methodology, to be swiftly discarded once familiarity with the methodology is acquired.

6 George Spencer-Brown, *Laws of Form* (London: George Allen and Unwin, 1969; Leipzig: Bohmeier Verlag, 2011), 3. Citations refer to the Bohmeier edition unless stated otherwise. In Spencer-Brown's work, all acts (and thus marks) of distinction are taken to be tokens of the first distinction.

7 Spencer-Brown, *Laws of Form*, 5.

8 Spencer-Brown, *Laws of Form*, 7–10.

9 Spencer-Brown, *Laws of Form*, 10. In Spencer-Brown's work, the $\rightleftharpoons$ is used this way, but is not expanded on further. It plays a key role in the analysis of story structure in this methodology.

10 Spencer-Brown, *Laws of Form*, 53; Louis H Kauffman, "Laws of Form and Form Dynamics," in *Cybernetics & Human Knowing* 9, no. 2 (2002): 49–63 at 58; André Reichel, "Snakes all the Way Down: Varela's Calculus for Self-Reference and the Praxis of Paradise," in *Systems Research and Behavioral Science* 28, no. 6 (2011): 646–662, https://doi.org/10.1002/sres.1105. In conversations with me, Spencer-Brown referred to this as the 'if' function.

11 The dissonance relates to Aristotle's 10 Categories of Being, summarised in chapter 9 of this work. See Aristotle, "The Categories," translated by Harold

P. Cooke, in *The Categories; On Interpretation,* translated by Harold P. Cooke and Hugh Tredennick (Cambridge, MA: Harvard University Press, 1962).

12 Lewis Carroll, *The Annotated Alice: The Definitive Edition,* illustrated by John Tenniel, edited by Martin Gardner (London: Penguin, 2001), 180.

13 These are explained in detail in the main body of this work. See especially chapters 6, 12, 14, and 15.

14 My analysis is based on the version in Aleksandr Afanas'ev, *Russian Fairy Tales,* translated by Norbert Guterman (New York: Pantheon Books, 1945), 26–27.

15 A step-by-step analysis of this story is outlined in a presentation I gave entitled "The Unknown Storyteller," (PowerPoint presentation, LoF50, 'Laws of Form' 50th anniversary conference, Liverpool, 10 August, 2019), YouTube: GZJdlhG0z78.

16 A mapping of the links between Dynamic and Linear story structures can be found in chapter 18 and is explored further in Leon Conrad, "The Chinese Circular Structure," 2 parts, unpublished manuscript, last modified 18 and 2 June 2020 respectively.

2

WHAT MAKES A STORY ... A STORY?

... the poignant question strikes a spark to the engine that ignites the heart. This starts up the energy of the story; it rolls the story forward. The mythic tale unfolds in response to that single igniting question.

CLARISSA ESTES, *What Does the Soul Want?* [1]

When we come across something we think is different, something unusual, or something that makes us stop and ask questions, a story appears. Our ability to spot subtle changes in our environment—and our drive to make sense of these changes—are innate instincts on which the deeply embodied frameworks which story uses to story are fashioned.

Firstly, within the story spinner, a story emerges as a result of a causative spark. That spark shapes—and links—a chronological sequence of events. Without it, there can be no story.

Take this sequence of events, for example ... is it a story?

I woke up yesterday morning.
The sun was shining.
I had breakfast and went out.
I sat in the park.
I got hungry.
I went to the park café.
It started raining.
I had lunch.
It had stopped raining when I started my journey home.
I met Janet on the way.
We talked for a bit.
We parted.
I had a quiet supper at home.
I went to bed and slept through the night.

It could be a story – there's potential there, but at the moment, it's simply a sequence of events.

But what if those events were presented like this … ?

> I woke up yesterday morning and saw that the sun was shining, so I decided to have a quick breakfast and take a walk. I went where my feet led me and ended up sitting in the park around 12 o'clock, by which time I was hungry, so I walked over to the café by the lake. I'd just chosen something to eat when it started to pour down. Luckily, I was inside, so I avoided getting wet. It took a while for the rain to clear, and when it did, the world looked fresh and clean. The rain had given me an opportunity to focus on clearing my mind, sorting out some stuff, and I started home with a clearer head. It took me about half an hour to walk back. Just as I turned the corner into my road, I met Janet and stopped to chat with her. We talked for a bit – I found out about what had been going on with her and shared some of the stuff I'd been thinking about. It brought us closer together somehow. Then we parted. As I prepared a light supper at home, I reflected that I was better off for having shared something of my life with another human being and hoped that she felt the same. I think she might have. When my head hit my pillow that night, I ended up sleeping better than I'd slept for a long time.

Although it's definitely not Booker prizeworthy, the events in this version are woven together more meaningfully than they are in the first version. They hang together better. They're explicitly related both chronologically and causally rather than simply being listed chronologically. They open up more possibilities: What did the protagonist need to sort out? And why? … Who was Janet? … What was their relationship? … Is romance likely? … Why had the protagonist been sleeping poorly by comparison to how they slept after their day out? Is this just one story? Or are there many? You're the story spinner … you get to decide. They're your stories. Story emerges in a general sense – not just the stories mentioned here, but all stories – because something sets off a sequence of events at the level of story. Come across something unusual, or something that makes you stop and ask questions ... a story is born.

What ignites the process for one person may well be different to what ignites it for someone else. Nevertheless, the stories which flare up will usually be connected to some form of unresolved question or perceived state of imbalance. This book argues that stories exist for a purpose. They help us restore unrestricted flow. Stories help us bring things back to a state of balance. Through the power of story, stories help us realise the Oneness-of-Being.[2] Being is one, so logically, story facilitates the manifestation of a fully formed entity that unfolds step by step through time, yet is fundamentally unified.

Our relationship to this fundamental unity is supported by the coming together of three universal principles: truth, goodness, and beauty (harmony, or proportion) – an idea that goes at least back to Plato,[3] who identified these as 'goodness, symmetry, truth'.[4] When we're out of balance, story helps bring us back into balance. As we'll see in the chapters on Comedy, Tragedy, and Riddles, story also depends on the embodied ways in which we make sense of the world around us, first categorised, as far as I know, by Aristotle, in the 4th century BCE.[5]

If Janet and the protagonist had failed to meet; if there'd been no mention of them being together, could the story of their evolving relationship ever be told? If the overriding questions are about who the protagonist is, what kind of person they are, or why they did what they did, the questions open up a back story for them, a story that begs to be told.

We're predisposed to respond to our environment, and we respond in particular ways to imbalances in that environment. We can't help responding to change. When an unresolved question is involved, a story invariably emerges ...

Imagine you're in a familiar spot – the room you spent the most time in as a child, where you were happiest. Imagine that out of the corner of your eye, you see a shadow ... a shadow that shouldn't be there ...

Hold that thought … let it develop …
What happens?

Where did it happen?
  What's really happening?
  Is a story being set up?
  Probably.
  So, what's setting up the story?
  My guess is that it's not the shadow, but something else. Shadows are part of the environment, after all. Perhaps it's that a particular shadow *shouldn't be there*. The imbalance we perceive in relation to our environment sets up … the story.

Stories are linked to perceived imbalances in our environment, and stories are ways of making sense of—and resolving—those imbalances.

In his *Poetics*, Aristotle describes changes in state and perception (changes that flow naturally, or changes that involve reversal and recognition) which drive story forward.[6] You might prefer to use terms such as 'inciting incidents', 'problems', 'mythic questions', or 'conflicts' – the essence is the same. Flow and balance are essential to story. They go back to the birth of story, well before the first written theories on how story works appeared, and well before 'problems' emerged.

Stories are set up as a result of imbalances which can manifest in several forms.

That shadow that appeared as an imbalance because it shouldn't be there is one kind of imbalance. It shouldn't be there, but it is. Defeated expectation stops us in our tracks; it 'blocks flow'.

But what about this?

Imagine that you're just about to walk into a place that's very familiar to you. As you enter, you notice that a particular piece of furniture is missing.

It should be there, but it isn't. Or is it the other way round?

Is it that there should be an absence of a shadow in that particular place in the first of these two scenarios, but there isn't? And is it that there shouldn't be an absence of that piece of furniture in the second one, but there is?

Is—Isn't—Is—Isn't—It could be thought of as rather agonising, couldn't it?

I'd be hard pressed to think of any other way to frame an imbalance – either we feel something should be and it isn't, or it shouldn't be and it is. Either way, the flow is blocked; the block is unhelpful because flow is necessary.

So how can flow be restored?

Should we try to solve problems? Or give up hopelessly? Should we find someone or something that can help? If so, then who or what can help put things right? How can we know what the right thing to do is? How can we find the best way to solve a problem? Can we ever?

I could ask: What makes the difference? What sets up these responses? Story happens because these responses emerge. Without the responses, we wouldn't have story, but we do – and one of the clues to understanding how story works can be found embedded deep in the story of how story is born ...

NOTES

1   Joseph Campbell, *The Hero with a Thousand Faces*, xlviii.

2   The thesis that as all things participate in Being, in that sense, they are all paradoxically 'one and the same' can be traced at least as far back as Parmenides, if not earlier, and onwards through Plato and Aristotle. It is central to Spencer-Brown's work.

    For references, see Parmenides' "Fragment 8": 'A single story of a route still / Is left: that [*it*] *is*; on this [route] there are signs / Very numerous: that what-is is ungenerated and imperishable; / Whole, single-limbed, steadfast, and complete,' in Parmenides of Elea, *Fragments*, translated by David Gallop (Toronto: University of Toronto Press, 1991), 64–75, at 8.1–4, 64.

    Plato describes three states of Being united as one – 'the Being which is indivisible and remains always the same and the Being which is transient and divisible in bodies' and a compound, all blended together 'into one form': *Timaeus*, 35a, from *Plato in Twelve Volumes*, Vol. 9, translated by W.R.M. Lamb (Cambridge, MA: Harvard University Press; London: W. Heinemann Ltd. 1925), https://www.perseus.tufts.edu/hopper/text?doc=Perseus:text:1999.01.0180:text=Tim.:section=35a.

    For Aristotle, 'Unity is nothing distinct from Being.' *The Metaphysics*, translated by Hugh Tredennick, Vol. 1. (London: W. Heinemann; New York: G. P. Putnam's Sons, 1933) 4.1003b, 150–151.

    On 'The Oneness-of-Being' (*waḥdat al-wujūd*) in the Sufi tradition, see René Guénon, *The Essential René Guénon: Metaphysics, Tradition, and the Crisis of Modernity*, edited by Ed Herlihy (Bloomington, IA: World Wisdom, 2009), 125–126; Seyyed Hosein Nasr, "Scientia Sacra," in *The Underlying Religion: An Introduction to the Perennial Philosophy*, edited by Martin Lings and Clinton Minnaar, 114–140 (Bloomington, IN: World Wisdom, 2007), 120n13; and Muhammad Ali Aziz, *Religion and Mysticism in Early Islam: Theology and Sufism in Yemen. The Legacy of Ahmad Ibn 'Alwān* (London and New York: I.B. Tauris, 2011), 69.

3   Plato, *The Republic of Plato*, translated by Allan Bloom (New York: Basic Books, 1991). Truth and measure are covered at 6.486d, 166; exemplary philosophic practice is defined as integrating being, truth, goodness, and the ability to apprehend the harmony or relationship between them at 6.501d, 181; truth and goodness (with knowledge of them implying harmony) at 6.508d, 188–189. See also Seth Benardete, *Socrates' Second Sailing: On Plato's "Republic"* (Chicago, IL: University of Chicago Press, 1992), 157–177.

In his book *On the Divine Names*, Pseudo-Dionysius, in the late 5th or early 6th century CE, drawing on revelation 'from the Oracles' and on inspiration from philosophers such as Aristotle and Plato, lists among his names for the Nameless: Being, One, Truth, Goodness, and Beauty: Dionysius the Areopagite, *On the Divine Names and the Mystical Theology*, translated by Clarence Edwin Rolt (London: Society for Promoting Christian Knowledge, 1920), https://archive.org/details/dionysiusareopag00dion/page/n5 at 1.5–6, 59–62; 2.11, 78–81; 3.1, 81–83; and 5.1, 131–132 respectively. He discusses the Platonic link between the Universals (in his terms, the 'divine names') and light in chapter 4, 86–130.

4   Plato, *Philebus*, from *Plato in Twelve Volumes*, Vol. 8, translated by Harold N. Fowler (Cambridge, MA, Harvard University Press; London, W. Heinemann Ltd. 1925), 64e–65a and ff, https://www.perseus.tufts.edu/hopper/text?doc=Perseus:text:1999.01.0174:text=Phileb.:section=64e. See also Plato's *Seventh Letter*, in Hans Joachim Krämer, *Plato and the Foundations of Metaphysics: A Work on the Theory of the Principles and Unwritten Doctrines of Plato with a Collection of the Fundamental Documents*, edited and translated by John R. Catan (Albany, NY: SUNY Press, 1990), 342d, 196 and Plato, *Symposium*, from *Plato in Twelve Volumes*, Vol. 3 translated by W. R. M. Lamb (Cambridge, MA, Harvard University Press; London, William Heinemann Ltd. 1925), Diotima's speech, 205e ff, especially 210e–212a, where the discourse soars from the physical realm, through the metaphysical realm to transcend both. Symmetry is variously translated as proportion, harmony, balance, or beauty, https://www.perseus.tufts.edu/hopper/text?doc=Perseus:text:1999.01.0174:text=Sym.:section=205e.

5   Aristotle's 10 Categories of Being are summarised in chapter 9 of this work. See Aristotle, "The Categories," translated by Harold P. Cooke, in *The Categories; On Interpretation*, translated by Harold P. Cooke and Hugh Tredennick (Cambridge, MA: Harvard University Press, 1962), 1–111, and especially at 4.1b25–1b26, 16–19.

6   *Aristotle: On Poetics*, translated by Seth Bernardete and Michael Davis (South Bend, IN: St Augustine's Press, 2002) 1452a, 29.

3

THE BIRTH OF STORY

SYMBOL 1 (□):

STORY OPENINGS AND CLOSINGS

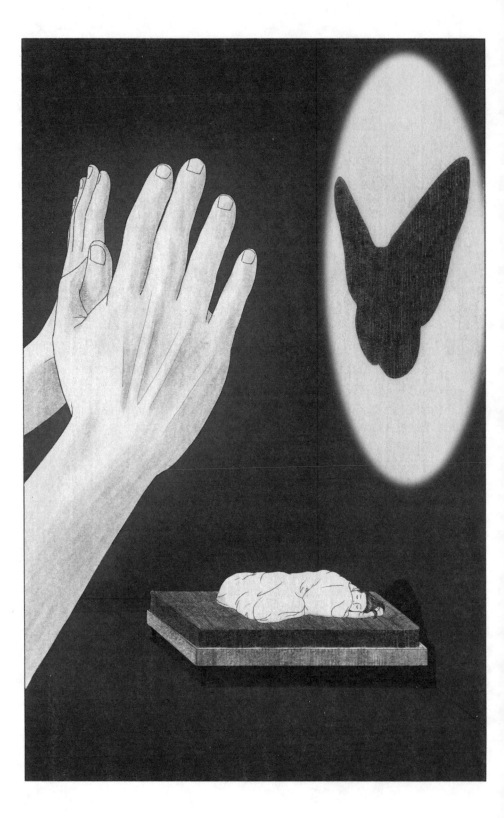

En ma fin git mon commencement. (In my end lies my beginning.)

MOTTO USED BY MARY QUEEN OF SCOTS[1]

In my beginning is my end.

T. S. ELIOT, *Four Quartets: East Coker*[2]

How does a story start?
One possibility is:

'Once upon a time …'

'Once upon a time …' confounds our sense of space-time. It deliberately sets up a cognitive dissonance. We may not be fully aware of it when we hear it, but it has a hypnotic quality that calms us down, whispering soothingly, 'We're about to enter a different realm … the realm of story. Are you ready? Here we go …' The quality is common to story openings found in many cultures all around the planet.[3]

'Once upon a time …' is a strange phrase. The word 'once' indicates an instance, but not necessarily the only time (think of 'once again …' or 'once and for all …'); an instance in the past. How long ago? It's not clear – deliberately unclear, it would seem. Then we have 'upon' – which implies something being put on top of something else. But how can anyone put anything on 'a time', let alone do it 'once'? And then we have the indefinite article: 'a', which allows us to point to something specific, but still keeps it vague: 'a time' … but which time is that, exactly?

'Once upon a time …' sets up a blank slate which is separate from—yet part of—our experience of our environment. It's like saying, 'Take a piece of paper …' or 'Imagine this …'.

'Once upon a time ...' is one of many invocations that allow something different to emerge – something with its own rules and frameworks ... invocations that herald the mysterious emergence of ... story.

From there, 'a story' can unfold – like an emergent origami creation in the mind, through a series of folds and marks which divide the field, so 'something' can emerge, often through a revelatory process. The origami creation then unfolds, a folded paper aeroplane previously launched out into the open is unfolded, and the blank slate reappears, its return celebrated with a ritualistic, 'Imagine that!' or '... and they lived happily ever after', leaving the piece of paper ready to be refolded, reused, or recycled in some way ... leaving behind ... a story.

Would you be willing to try a thought experiment?

Let go of the notion of there being any question to answer. Let go of any notion of a command to fulfil ...
    'Once upon a time ...'

In the expectancy that follows, if you listen closely, you may well hear the voice of story.

This organic unfolding of story can be hard to spot, especially when we start to tell a story that's well known. The ritualistic words 'Once upon a time ...' can seem mere formalities, mere social contracts that frame a social interaction that introduces a well-known tale ... 'Once upon a time there were three little pigs ...' or 'Once upon a time, in a land far, far, away, an old woman baked a gingerbread man which she left on a ledge to cool ...' These kinds of lines can launch a series of events so familiar that they rattle off the tongue without a second thought. They take us into the world of story, in which the story unfolds. It reaches a natural end. We experience a state of equilibrium, a sense of balance; then, with a verbal puff of smoke, the characters return to 'storyland' where they can '… live happily ever after', ready to emerge once more to take part in another story and we return, the same, but different, to the dimension of being in which our 'everyday lives' unfold.[4]

> **Story lives within us, along with the basic rules and frameworks for story. When we invoke story, we also invoke the potential for the rules of story to be revealed.**

The revelation—if we allow ourselves to invite story to work through us in this way—can help us find ways to help us restore ourselves to a better state of balance from a state of relative imbalance.

Am I really saying that by being more aware of how story works, we might be able to live more fulfilled lives? Yes, and other people have expressed similar thoughts. Joseph Campbell, for one, believed that we have much to learn from the particular kind of story he identified as the monomyth.

He identified a process of separation—initiation—return and considered it 'the nuclear unit' of both rites of passage and of this kind of story.[5] I'd argue it goes further – back to the birth of story. Campbell's link between the 'hero's journey' (as the monomyth has come to be known) and rites of passage goes right to the heart of what story can do, why story exists, and how story works.

Story and stories are symbiotically linked. However, story— rather than stories—is the main focus of this work. As will be clear in the following chapters, the focus will lead to a close exploration of story structures. The act of following the train of thought of story may take a bit of getting used to, but as it's part of each and every one of us – part of how we think, how we make sense of the world – I can assure you it'll become second (or even first) nature.

At the end of a story, when order is restored, the imaginary piece of origami paper returns to its source, once again becoming one with it, allowing once upon a time to live happily ever after.[6] Rather than emerging from our being, I invite you to see stories as originating in our non-being. How can we mark this mysterious process of origination from non-being into being, and reabsorption from being into non-being?

There's a symbol which is central to Spencer-Brown's work that's ideally suited to this purpose. It's the first of the six primary symbols we'll be using to analyse stories. It looks like this: ⊐ .[7] Spencer-Brown introduces it as a 'mark of recursion' when he talks about oscillation and memory, two things which appear in and through time. It's been linked to the ouroboros symbol, traditionally depicted as a snake eating its tail – the snake, in feeding on itself, sustains itself.[8] I see the same thing in the image of a baby chewing on its toes – the baby, in experiencing itself, senses itself; in sensing itself, it recognises itself; in recognising itself, it realises itself.

As the openings and closings of stories share the same quality of circularity, of an emergence from and return to the ground of story, use this 'mark of recursion' (⊐) to symbolise both the 'Once upon a time …'-type opening step at the beginning of a story and the closing step in which the story returns into the state of being in which and from which it emerged.

A state of cognitive dissonance is common to both transformational steps. We'll come back to this in chapter 6, but first we need to look at what happens in between the opening and closing of a story.

So far in this chapter, I've mainly focused on the birth or emergence of story and only secondarily with stories. Once a story is born, if we put content to one side and concentrate rather on the transcendent (or rather, foundational) view of story evoked above, how can we map what story does – at that level? What's the basic pattern on which the unfolding of story depends?

NOTES

1   Letter from Nicholas White to Sir William Cecil dated 26 February 1569, transcribed in full in Mary Queen of Scots, *Letters of Mary Queen of Scots and Documents Connected with her Personal History*, edited by Agnes Strickland. Vol. 2 (London: Henry Colburn, 1843), 304–311, at 310, https://archive. org/details/lettersofmaryque02mary/page/310/. The motto is discussed in the wider context of 16th Century emblem culture in Peter M. Daly, *The English Emblem and the Continental Tradition* (New York: AMS Press, 1988), 21–24.

2   The opening sentence of T. S. Eliot's "East Coker," No. 2 of *Four Quartets*, June 2000, http://www.davidgorman.com/4Quartets/2-coker.htm

3   See the list of story openings in Herrick Jeffers, *Once Upon A Time, They Lived Happily Ever After*, Melbourne Village, FL: Herrick Jeffers, 1997.

4   The level indicated here is equivalent to the level of a story.

5   Campbell's work links to Arnold van Gennep's work on rites of passage. See Arnold van Gennep, *Rites of Passage* (Chicago, IL: Chicago University Press, 1959).

6   The link between opening and closing is explicit in the title of Jeffers' work on story openings and closings: *Once Upon A Time, They Lived Happily Ever After* referenced in note 3, above.

7   Spencer-Brown, *Laws of Form*, 53; Kauffman, "Laws of Form and Form Dynamics," 58; Reichel, "Snakes all the Way Down", 652.

8   The link between snake and creator god in Ancient Egypt is explored in Marshall Clagett, *Knowledge and Order*, Vol. 1, Tome 1 of Ancient Egyptian Science: A Sourcebook (Philadelphia: American Philosophical Society, 1989), 290–292; 382–383n27.

4

HOW DOES
STORY WORK?

'FORTUNATELY', 'UNFORTUNATELY'

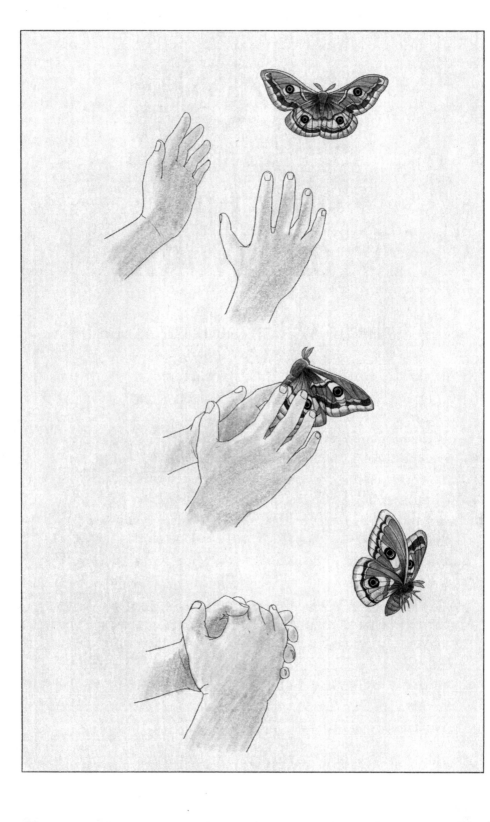

First of all, [life] "times" itself. The moves of life in their constructive ontopoietic patterns time life. Life throughout its advancing interrogative steps of constructive/destructive becoming times itself.

ANNA-TERESA TYMIENIECKA, *The Fullness of the Logos in the Key of Life – Book I: The Case of God in the New Enlightenment*[1]

Stories are based on a series of 'fortunate' and/or 'unfortunate' steps.

The words 'fortunate' and 'unfortunate' appear in inverted commas for a reason. In this context, they're used specifically in relation to the initial state of imbalance, or block in flow, which gives rises to a story. From this state of imbalance, a series of meaningfully linked steps emerges.

This emergence of a series of steps is how story stories.[2]

The minimum number of steps and the order in which they come distinguish different story structures.

In order to work out the minimum number of steps in a story structure, we need to figure out what's happening underneath the content of a story. We need to look at story in a particular way. We need to learn to look past a story to get to the story structure which underpins it and work out how story is unfolding through it. If we're going to successfully identify the steps which make up the story behind a narrative, we have to engage with the story both subjectively and objectively, so we can connect with story through the story.

I'd like to demonstrate the approach using a simple narrative version of *The Three Little Pigs*, following the step-by-step methodology laid out in chapter 1:

1. Select a story to analyse.

The Three Little Pigs

2. Note the source version, where relevant.

The Three Wee Pigs Source: School of Scottish Studies. Hamish Henderson, from Bella Higgins. Heard from her mother.

3. Summarise the story in 'bare bones' form.

Three pigs (Dennis, Biddy and Rex) lived together with their mother. The house was overcrowded, so the mother decided to send the three eldest pigs out to 'find their fortunes for themselves'. On their journey, they had to shelter from the rain, but this allowed them to meet people with a cart of straw, a cart full of slats of wood, and a lorry with a load of bricks. The men each agreed to give some of their materials to the pigs to build houses with. Biddy built a house of straw; Dennis, one of wooden slats; Rex, one of bricks. A hungry wolf came to call on Biddy and, failing to trick Biddy into letting him in, blew her house in. Biddy escaped and ran to Dennis's house. The wolf followed and, failing to trick either pig into letting him in, blew Dennis's house in. Both pigs escaped and ran to Rex's house. The wolf followed and, failing to blow the brick house in, was about to get in through the chimney, but the pigs had some straw to put on the fire which blazed up and burnt the wolf to death, … allowing the pigs to cook him and eat him for supper. The pigs lived together safely there until eventually they ended up being taken 'to the old people's houses' where they died.

4. Note the story opening and closing, stated or implied.

'There was once a pigs' house where they were getting thick on the ground.'

'But there are no houses up in the wood now, for the pigs were all taken to the old people's houses, and there they died.'

5. Identify the main characters and their initial situation (who, when, where, and in what condition).

Mother pig with pigs 'getting thick on the ground'; Biddy, Dennis, Rex, in the way of 'a younger family' ('Dennis had trod on one of the wee piglets by mistake'); wolf, hungry (condition implied).

The story's opening (⊐) is implied in 'There was once …'. After the main characters are identified, we need to establish whether each character's initial situation is 'fortunate' or 'unfortunate'. We start with the three pigs' story lines.

6. Identify the problem(s) these characters have – typically resolved (but sometimes left unresolved) at the end of the story.

They need to 'find their fortunes' but also find shelter from the wind, snow, and rain.

7. Identify the main structural parts of the story (beginning, middle, end, and any subsections).

The pigs' story lines follow similar patterns. They build houses, escape from the wolf, and defeat him at the end in a 'try, try, try again' looping structure.

8. Arrange the events related to each character's story line in chronological order.

9. Within these story lines, look for pairs of 'unfortunate'/'fortunate' steps (the terms 'unfortunate' and 'fortunate' are relative to the solution of the character's initial problem, so meetings are

interpreted as backward steps). Are there any outliers? Are there any single steps that don't fit into a pair? Note these. Analyse them. What do they point to?

A back story is implied in 'Dennis had trod on one of the wee piglets by mistake.' From there, the pigs' story lines unfold as follows:

1. 'Unfortunately' the pigs had to go out into the world, learn to become independent little piggies, and fend for themselves.
2. 'Fortunately' they were able to set out to try to 'find their fortunes'.
3. 'Unfortunately' the weather was stormy and their 'trotters were sore!'
4. 'Fortunately' they were able to rest 'by the roadside, under the shade of a wood'.

A man with a cart of straw comes by. Biddy 'thought she's [sic] build herself a house, if the man would give her some straw.' At this point, the meeting and conversation Biddy has to have with the man stops her story line from flowing forward for a while, which is 'unfortunate'. It may seem unusual to interpret a meeting as a 'backward step', but if you think about it, and allow yourself to 'go with the flow' of (the) story, you'll probably find it natural. I think of the backward and forward movement in the ebb and flow of the story as being a bit like the swing of a pendulum, or the movement of a seiche tide, where the wind builds up pressure on an enclosed body of water, causing the water to oscillate back and forth for a while before reaching a climax and then calming back down again.

Back to the story – at the point of meeting, we don't know what the outcome will be. The pig's story line flows backward for a while.

5. 'Unfortunately' Biddy couldn't build herself a house unless she had something to build it with.
6. 'Fortunately' the man agreed to give her some of the straw he was carrying.

In the story, the people carrying supplies play minor supporting roles. I could plot each of their story lines along with the story lines for each element of the story, including the supplies and the houses built from them. However, if I did so, it would add nothing of value to the analysis, so I'm limiting myself to the main characters' story lines.

The sequence repeats for Dennis' and Rex's story lines.

7. 'Unfortunately' a wolf came knocking at each of the pigs' doors.
8. 'Fortunately' Biddy and Dennis managed to escape from the wolf, and – together with Rex – managed to defeat him.

Those are the bones of the story, but not quite the 'bare bones'. As we progress, we'll see how we can apply appropriate symbols to each step. But for now, let's see how we can get down to the bare bones. Steps 3, 4, and 5 can be compressed without loss of essential features. Thus, we can identify the minimum number of steps that make up the story as follows:

1. 'Unfortunately' the pigs had to go out into the world, learn to become independent little piggies, and fend for themselves.
2. 'Fortunately' they were able to set out to try to 'find their fortunes'.
3. 'Unfortunately' they were unable to build themselves houses without materials.
4. 'Fortunately' helpful men agreed to give them different materials which allowed them to build three houses.

5. 'Unfortunately' a wolf came knocking at the pigs' respective doors.
6. 'Fortunately' Biddy and Dennis managed to escape from the wolf, and – together with Rex – managed to defeat him.

The core structure is made up of six steps which are remarkably similar to an outline for a story-based intervention devised by Mooli Lahad which has been used successfully with trauma victims, particularly children suffering from the traumatic effects of war. Lahad calls the approach the 6-part Story Method (6PSM).[3] The six parts cover the following elements:

1. A main character and where they live.
2. Their mission or task.
3. Who or what can help the main character.
4. Who or what obstacle stands in the way of his/her carrying out the mission/task.
5. How he/she copes with this obstacle.
6. What happens.

Lahad's structure has an underlying sense of backward and forward movement to it. However, Lahad's view of the underlying structure differs from mine in three key ways:

Firstly, Lahad assumes, but doesn't state, that there's an initial state of imbalance. After all, why would a character in a story start out on a mission unless they had a problem to solve?

Secondly, Lahad doesn't interpret meetings as 'unfortunate' steps. These two points probably result from the context in which Lahad works. In practice, Lahad—rightly or wrongly— may have chosen to focus on 'fortunate' 'forward steps' rather than 'unfortunate' 'backward steps' in terms of the unfolding of therapeutic stories.

Last but not least, Lahad assigns little, if any, importance to openings and closings, whereas for me, they're integral to story.

In analysing stories as I propose, it's important to remember that we're aiming to reduce the basic steps in a narrative to the minimum number of steps needed to tell the story. I think you'll agree that this is achieved in the final compressed version of the pigs' story lines in the narrative version of *The Three Little Pigs* outlined above.

If this seems overly complex now, I assure you it'll soon get simpler. It's important to feel how the story ebbs and flows as it unfolds. It's easy to get distracted by the narrative content – any part of a story can be expanded and explored in minute detail to form a narrative.[4] Take the opening scene of Andrew Lang's version of *The Three Little Pigs*.[5] We're introduced to each of the pigs in turn … their names, their characters, their behaviours … their wishes for houses which their mother ultimately grants them … (we're 678 words in, and he's still describing the initial situation) … before she dies. (That's the inciting event which leaves them in an 'unfortunate' situation.) They each go off and live in the houses they have chosen … (and the story flows forward) … when each pig's peace and quiet is 'unfortunately' disturbed by … who knows?! They suspect it might be the wolf, but they're not sure.

In *Little Red Riding Hood*, her first meeting with the wolf in the forest delays her. At that point in the unfolding of story, Red is 'unfortunately' stopped in her tracks, and is 'fortunately' allowed to proceed. The meeting generally leads to the wolf eating her grandmother up, but we can't skip forward in the story when we're at the level of story. At that moment, at the level of story, Red doesn't know what will happen. Following the flow of story every 'fortunate' and 'unfortunate' step of the way is to feel the rhythm, the flow in our veins, feeling story come alive within us–being born, for the first time, in us, all over again.

Story unfolds chronologically, but we don't need to tell stories chronologically. There are hundreds, perhaps thousands of possibilities for narrative treatments. We'll take a very brief look at these plot patterns, as I call them, in chapter 21. We can follow a story through flashbacks, or through a gradual unveiling of a series of events – the latter is how detective novels work. In the main part of this book, however, I'll be looking at story at a more fundamental level.

As a story spinner, I've found that if I allow myself to *feel* story emerging, if I *first* allow myself to feel story pulse and flow within me through its 'unfortunate' and 'fortunate' steps (as I described in the analysis of *The Three Little Pigs* above) and *then* engage with the narrative content to craft my telling of a story, it's much easier for me to connect with story when I spin the story – as opposed to connecting with 'a story' or with narrative when I'm telling. I've also found that getting in touch with how story moves 'a story' along brings the purpose and function of that story to light. Moreover, using the approach outlined in this book to analyse narratives in terms of the story structures on which they're based can provide illuminating insights into what makes those narratives effective or ineffective. But there's far more to this than what we've covered so far.

Feeling our way through a story is all very well, but writing out the steps the story takes in words, as I did with the analysis of *The Three Little Pigs* above, is a rather long-winded process.

In the version of *The Three Little Pigs* we analysed, there are essentially three 'unfortunately/fortunately' pairs framed within an initial setting and final outcome. These, in turn, are framed within an opening (☐) and a closing (☐). Using words to describe this is cumbersome.

If there's any hope of us grasping what's happening in terms of story structure as intuitively and as easily as possible, we need something else. We need an easy way of symbolising what's happening, so we can take in the shape of a story at a glance. We need an easy visual key to use to map what's happening. I'd like to propose just such a key in the next chapter, in which we'll look at the next three primary symbols from the set of six we'll be using to analyse stories.

NOTES

1   Anna-Teresa Tymieniecka, *The Fullness of the Logos in the Key of Life: Book 1. The Case of God in the New Enlightenment*, Vol. C of Analecta Husserliana: The Yearbook of Phenomenological Research (Dordrecht: Springer, 2009), 11.

2   See Remy Charlip, *Fortunately* (New York: Aladdin, 1993), and Michael Foreman, *Fortunately, Unfortunately* (Minneapolis, MN: Andersen, 2011). 'Fortunately, Unfortunately' is often used as a game in storytelling, improvised theatre, and theatre warm-up contexts, and, as noted previously (chapter 1, note 3), it has more recently appeared as a 'texting game' (Simon Hill, "The best texting games," 2019). The events usually come in pairs, but there are exceptions which are discussed in detail later in this work. See, in particular, chapter 8 (Rags to Riches), chapter 13 (Chinese Circular), and chapter 17 (Creation Myth) structures.

3   Mooli Lahad, "Story-making: An Assessment Method for Coping with Stress," in *Dramatherapy: Theory and Practice 2*, edited by Sue Jennings, 150–163 (London: Routledge, 1992), 157; Lahad, Mooli, and Ofra Ayalon. "BASIC Ph: The Story of Coping Resources," in *Community Stress Prevention. Vol. 2* (Israel: Kiryat Shmona, Community Stress Prevention Centre, 1997), 126–127.

4   Besides the link between Barthes' analysis of Ian Fleming's writing (Barthes, "An Introduction to the Structural Analysis of Narrative", 253), parallels with music and philosophy seem to me to be noteworthy here. Schenkerian musical analysis reduces a piece of tonal music to a short sequence of notes in relation to a major or minor scale in which it's composed. The short sequence conveys the essential 'fingerprint' of the piece. In philosophy, the relationship between extension and intention in the so-called 'Tree of Porphyry' where an increase in intension (from genus to species, for example – e.g., tree to oak) is associated with a decrease in extension (as if moving from a wide shot to a close up, which restricts the frame of vision, and vice versa).

5   Andrew Lang, *The Green Fairy Book* (New York: A. I. Burt, n.d.), 101–106, https://archive.org/details/greenfairybook00langiala/page/100/. A paper outlining a comparative analysis of this and one other version of *The Three Little Pigs* is forthcoming.

5

SCRIBING THE SHAPE OF STORY

SYMBOLS 2–4 (⌐), (←), (→);

THE QUEST STRUCTURE

Each novel or story is a path ... that goes through a wood. ...
the wood ... is the sum of all possibilities.

PHILIP PULLMAN, *The Path through the Wood* [1]

In chapter 3, we looked at a way of visualising how story materialises and dematerialises using this mark (⬜). But what about the initial situation that follows on from the opening, the setting up of the 'who, when, where' of the story—the characters that feature in it, and the environment and time frame they're in?

And what about the ending (the final resolution) which precedes the closing, allowing a particular group of characters to move from the final 'who, when, where' states to living 'happily ever after'?

And what about the marks for the 'fortunately'/'unfortunately' steps?

There are three symbols from George Spencer-Brown's work which fit these three elements perfectly. In terms of analysing story, the character in the initial situation is always presented in neutral terms. The function of this part of the story is simply to introduce the characters.

For both the initial situation which follows the opening and the final situation which precedes the closing, use Spencer-Brown's symbol for the 'mark' (⌐). [2]

In Spencer-Brown's work, this is a 'mark of indication'. [3] In simple terms, it indicates that something can be distinguished from its surroundings. Again, because the initial and final situations that characters find themselves in within stories both mark stable points of reference, we use the same symbol for both situations. While in terms of content, at the level of a narrative, they may be different, in terms of story as form, they perform the same function.

Thus, what we have so far is:

Symbolic rendition of story structure: 'The story so far'

Steps	Symbols	Structure
1	□	Opening
2	┐	Initial situation
3	...	...
4	┐	Final situation
5	□	Closing

The sequence is scribed thus:

□ ┐ ... ┐ □

Once we're introduced to the 'subject', the 'predicate' follows, through which we find out the particular attribute of the subject that moves the character's story line 'forward' or 'backward' directly following the opening and initial situation within the story depending on whether their initial situation is 'fortunate' or 'unfortunate'.[3]

Between the initial and final situations, for the sequence of 'fortunately'/'unfortunately' steps, use the following symbols: (⇀) for 'fortunately', and (↽) for 'unfortunately'.[4]

Thus, the story structure which underlines the minimal 'bare bones' version of the three pigs' joint story line in *The Three Little Pigs* analysed above is scribed as follows:

□ ┐ ↽ ⇀ ↽ ⇀ ↽ ⇀ ┐ □

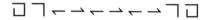

With only four symbols, we've mapped the entire structure of the story.

Call this the Quest structure.

Here's how it applies to the 'bare bones' outline:

Steps	Symbols	Structure	The three pigs' story lines ('bare bones')
1	⊐	Opening	[Implied]
2	⌐	Initial situation (who, when, where)	Family of pigs (mother and three older pigs being the main characters).
3	←	Problem	The pigs had to go out into the world, learn to become independent little piggies, and fend for themselves.
4	→	Journey	They were able to set out to try to 'find their fortunes'.
5	←	Meeting with ...	They were unable to build themselves houses without materials.
6	→	... friend/ helper	Helpful builders agreed to give them different materials which allow them to build three houses.
7	←	Meeting with ...	A wolf came knocking at the pigs' respective doors.
8	→	... enemy/ hindrance	Biddy and Dennis managed to escape from the wolf, and – together with Rex – managed to defeat him.
9	⌐	Final situation (outcome/ resolution)	The pigs lived together safely there until eventually they ended up in old people's houses where they died.
10	⊐	Closing	[Implied]

The pigs' story lines clearly follow a Quest structure, which other characters' story lines in many other stories also follow ... take this simple narrative version of the story of *Nasr-el-Din Hodja* (also known as Goha) *and the Walnut Tree*, for instance ...[5]

Analysis of Nasr-el-Din Hodja's story line in Ashliman's narrative of
The Story of Nasr-el-Din Hodja and the Walnut Tree

Steps	Symbols	Structure	Outline of content
1	⊐	Opening	Once upon a time ...
2	⌐	Initial situation	... Nasr-el-Din Hodja lay under a walnut tree to rest.

Analysis of Nasr-el-Din Hodja's story line in Ashliman's narrative of
The Story of Nasr-el-Din Hodja and the Walnut Tree

Steps	Symbols	Structure	Outline of content
3	←	'Unfortunately'	While his body was at rest, his mind was troubled. He couldn't understand why Allah, in His infinite wisdom had paired a big, strong tree and small, light walnuts.
4	→	'Fortunately'	Hodja had an idea – he thought that it would be far better for large pumpkins to grow on sturdy trees, and small walnuts on the slender stems of creeping plants.
5	←	'Unfortunately'	Sleep came to him before he could follow this train of thought further.
6	→	'Fortunately'	A walnut fell on him from the tree and woke him up.
7	←	'Unfortunately'	He realised that if the world had been constructed according to his scheme, he would have been killed.
8	→	'Fortunately'	He then realised that there was a good reason why things were the way they were rather than the way he thought they should be.
9	⌐	Final situation	And he never questioned the wisdom of Allah ...
10	☐	Closing	... ever again.

The Three Little Pigs is different to *Nasr-el-Din Hodja and the Walnut Tree*. The two stories feature different characters. The characters' story lines differ in terms of content. The resolutions are different. And yet, their story lines can be seen to share the same underlying structure. The pigs sought stability and prosperity and found it. Nasr-el-Din Hodja sought peace of mind and found it. The Hodja's problem was his lack of clarity and understanding which is resolved when things are finally clarified. The pigs' problem was their lack of self-sufficiency and independence, which they solved when they ended up living together in a brick house strong enough to protect them, using their wits and resourcefulness to defend themselves against threats and predators. While the different starting points set off different sets of causal events in terms of content, the underlying structure is *identical* for both stories. There's an uncanny inevitability about it. In both cases, the story starts because of a lack of harmony, and a sense of there being some kind of imbalance in the environment. By the end of the story, balance is typically restored. The minimum number of steps needed for this to happen is for there to be three 'backward-forward' pairs with clear common features, as outlined in the structure.

At this point, a couple of reminders may be useful: Firstly, meetings are seen as (←) steps in this approach. Secondly, journeys are seen as (→) steps.

Up to now, I've used the terms 'fortunately'/'unfortunately' as stopgaps. It's time to get rid of them. Meetings aren't always unfortunate, and journeys don't always happen for fortunate reasons. What matters is the energetic pulse of story as it works itself out, underneath 'a story', to get from a state of imbalance to one of balance ... the (← →) or (→ ←) steps which story takes, in the process of working out the unrealised solution to its own problem, thus ultimately bringing about its own end in the telling of a story.

If a character experiences a problem (←), the im-pulse of story compels them to go off on a mission to try to find a solution (→).
    Conversely, if everything is hunky-dory (→) at the start of a story, it's almost certain that an event will soon occur which has story propel their story line backward (←).[6]

Taking away the 'fortunate'/'unfortunate' crutches allows us to see the story structure which underpins stories more clearly, and to trace the action of story through different characters' story lines.

It also opens up an exciting and rewarding means of analysing story structures across narrative genres, providing surprising insights into the commonality across genres. For example, the Quest structure provides the basic story structure for many academic papers:

Outline of a typical academic paper

Steps	Symbols	Structure	Outline of content
1	⊐	Opening	Title
2	⌐	Initial situation	Introduction – the topic, and context
3	←	Problem	Problem
4	→	Journey	Methodology
5	←	Meeting with ...	Experiment/thesis (3 points?)
6	→	... friend/helper	Result/support
7	←	Meeting with ...	Objections/antithesis (3 points?)
8	→	... enemy/ hindrance	Refutation/synthesis
9	⌐	Final situation (outcome/ resolution)	Conclusion (definitive or provisional)
10	⊐	Closing	Implications, recommendations for future research

There's a popular structure in the US education system called 'the five-part essay structure' or 'the five-paragraph essay'.[7] It's composed of (1) introduction and statement of thesis; (2–4) three annotated supporting pieces of evidence, each in its own paragraph; and (5) a final paragraph that links the evidence and the thesis in a conclusion. The five-part essay structure is an extended version of a paragraph structure taught in the English educational system, memorably named the PEE paragraph (Point, Evidence, Explanation), in which the 'Explanation' should show how the 'Evidence' supports the 'Point'.

Recently, authors have resorted to writing entire volumes to try to get educators not just to teach their students how to structure, but how to develop critical thinking skills as well.[8] Instinctively, they sense that the five-paragraph essay follows a Quest structure, but misses two crucial steps: steps 7 and 8: the meeting with the enemy/hindrance and the resulting outcome.

Outline of a five-paragraph essay

Steps	Symbols	Structure	Outline of content		The 5 parts
1	⊐	Opening	Title		
2	⌐	Initial situation	Introduction – the topic and context		①
3	↼	Problem	Problem		
4	⇀	Journey	Thesis		
5	↼	Meeting with ...	Evidence	*Steps 5 and 6 loop three times*	②–④
6	⇀	... friend/helper	Analysis		
7	↼	Meeting with ...	Not present		
8	⇀	... enemy/ hindrance	Not present		
9	⌐	Final situation (outcome/ resolution)	Conclusion		⑤
10	⊐	Closing	[Implied]		

What they propose instead generally follows the lines that academic papers follow, as outlined above:[9]

Revised outline of a five-part US essay structure

Steps	Symbols	Structure	Outline of content
1	⊐	Opening	Title
2	⌐	Initial situation	Topic sentence
3	↼	Problem	The thesis
4	⇀	Journey	The intended approach to exploring the thesis
5	↼	Meeting with ...	Arguments in favour of the thesis[10]

Revised outline of a five-part US essay structure

Steps	Symbols	Structure	Outline of content
6	⇀	... friend/helper	Supporting evidence for the arguments for the thesis
7	↽	Meeting with ...	Arguments against the thesis
8	⇀	... enemy/ hindrance	Refutation of the arguments against the thesis
9	⌐	Final situation (outcome/ resolution)	Conclusion
10	⊐	Closing	Implications and close

It doesn't matter whether the character here is the researcher or enquirer, the personified topic, or the personified relationship between the knower and the known, the same structure applies. Every student whom I've taught to plan essays this way has found it empowering. It teaches both the importance of structure and the importance of critical thinking. Students I've taught typically find that using the Quest structure to plan and write academic essays makes their work easier, more effective, and more intuitive. It's hardly surprising. Why? This commonly used essay structure is such an effective way of outlining the academic quest for knowledge <u>because</u> the approach builds on pre-existing knowledge of the many Quest structure stories in most—if not all—cultures across the world. Students are invariably familiar with stories in which characters follow the Quest structure, as the pigs do in the story of *The Three Little Pigs*. The intuitive natural flow of the Quest structure links them directly to the power of story. When they see how new knowledge links to existing knowledge, they often find learning more exciting.

Can an academic essay be classified as a story? Why ever not?! If exactly the same story structure underpins an academic essay as the story structure that underpins *The Three Little Pigs*, then we definitely need to re-examine our idea of exactly what a story is and expand the meaning of the term 'event' in the definitions provided to indicate any distinction in thought. Both cases are covered by the definition provided in the introduction. In Spencer-Brown's terms, this is a 'mark of distinction'.[11] Any mark can generate an expression through a process of expansion and contraction. Any step of the process will have the same value in the form,[12] so why not see both *The Three Little Pigs* and an academic essay as stories that share the same story structure?

Key to a successful academic essay is the character of 'the wolf' – in that context, they're the arguments against a point of view that are defeated by sound reasoning. Given the importance of the wolf's character, let's take a look at the wolf's story line in the version of *The Three Little Pigs* in the next chapter.

NOTES

1   Philip Pullman, "The Path through the Wood," in *Dæmon Voices: Essays on Storytelling*, 85–106, (Oxford: David Fickling, 2017), 87.

2   Spencer-Brown, *Laws of Form*, 2.

3   While Spencer-Brown starts from 'a point of such degeneracy as to find that the ideas of description, indication, name, and instruction can amount to the same thing' (*Laws of Form*, 67), I use 'distinction' to refer to 'the first distinction' and 'indication' to tokens of the first distinction. Story flows 'forward' through time. The 'backward' and 'forward' steps are relative to the ideal (potential) condition that impels an individual character's story line.

4   Spencer-Brown, *Laws of Form*, 7–10, 30.

5   D. L. Ashliman, "Nasreddin Hodja: Tales of the Turkish Trickster," *Folklore and Mythology Electronic Texts*, 16 May, 2009, https://pitt.edu/~dash/hodja.html#walnuts.

6   The exception is the Creation Myth structure, but to what extent can that extend forward indefinitely?

7   Examples of works which focus on this one structure include David S. Dye, *How to Teach the Five-Paragraph Essay* (Mesquite, NV: Model Citizen Enterprises, 2005), Martin M. Rojas, *How to Write Like a College Student*, (n.p.: CreateSpace Independent Publishing Platform, 2014), and Susan Van Zile, *Mastering the 5-Paragraph Essay: Mini-Lessons, Models, and Engaging Activities That Give Students the Writing Tools They Need to Tackle—And Succeed On—The Tests* (New York: Scholastic, 2006).

8   Examples include Kimberley Hill Campbell, and Kristi Latimer, *Beyond the Five-Paragraph Essay* (Portland, ME: Stenhouse, 2012) and John Warner, *Why They Can't Write: Killing the Five-Paragraph Essay and Other Necessities* (Baltimore, MD: Johns Hopkins University Press, 2018).

9   See, for instance, Paul Graham, "A Version 1.0," *PaulGraham.com*, October 2004, http://paulgraham.com/laundry.html; and "The Age of the Essay," *PaulGraham.com*, September 2004, http://paulgraham.com/essay.html.

10 While presented as 'friendly/helpful' arguments in support of the thesis, it isn't until the evidence for them is examined that we can fully evaluate their usefulness.

11 'We take as given the idea of distinction and the idea of indication, and that we cannot make an indication without drawing a distinction. We take, therefore, the form of distinction for the form.' Spencer-Brown, *Laws of Form*, 1.

12 '…the first distinction, the mark, and the observer are not only interchangeable, but, in the form, identical.' Spencer-Brown, *Laws of Form*, 63.

6

TRICKSTER TALES

SYMBOL 5 ($\rightleftharpoons$):

THE TRICKSTER STRUCTURE

"El-ahrairah[1] is a trickster," said Buckthorn,
"and rabbits will always need tricks."
"No," said a new voice from the further end of the hall,
beyond Cowslip. "Rabbits need dignity and, above all,
the will to accept their fate."

RICHARD ADAMS, *Watership Down*[2]

Perhaps the most popular stories are those known as 'Trickster Tales'. They typically involve characters like the scheming Brer Rabbit; the wily Reynard the Fox; the cunning Coyote; the Greek gods Hermes and Dionysus; or Loki in the Norse sagas – commonly seen as fickle, changeable, amoral, Mercurial characters. But what elicits those behaviours? What makes a trickster a trickster?

In a Quest story, a 'friend or helper' is clearly a 'friend or helper' and the 'enemy or hindrance' clearly an 'enemy or hindrance'. However, in a Trickster story, someone or something usually appears in the role of a 'friend or helper' but turns out to be an 'enemy or hindrance' (the wolf, in *The Three Little Pigs* knocking on the door, pretending to be a well-meaning visitor but turning out to be a predator out to kill; the huntsman telling the evil queen he's done what she asked him to do and killed Snow White for her, although he's really let Snow White go; the wizard Jafar posing as a long-lost family member and grooming Aladdin to do his dirty work for him; the tar baby seeming friendly, but actually being a trap to catch Brer Rabbit). On the other hand, someone or something can appear in the role of an 'enemy or hindrance' but turn out to be a 'friend or helper' (For instance, Brer Fox meaning to kill Brer Rabbit by throwing him in the briar patch after Brer Rabbit confesses his 'greatest fears' to him of dying by being thrown in the briar patch – behaving as an enemy would behave – and by doing so, allowing Brer Rabbit to escape his clutches … tragically and unwittingly duped yet again).

Disguise, dissemblance, distortion, deliberate deceitfulness, and gullibility are qualities that depend on a dynamic between two parties: the trickster and the dupe. It's this dynamic that distinguishes the Trickster structure from the Quest structure.

The Quest structure is scribed like this:

$$\square\,\sqsupset\, \hookleftarrow \rightarrow \hookleftarrow \rightarrow \hookleftarrow \rightarrow \sqsupset\, \square$$

Just as Propp noted in his book, *Morphology of the Folktale*, in the Quest structure, both the 'friend/helper' and the 'enemy/hindrance' characters appear, they fulfil particular functions and then they disappear.[3] In the Trickster structure, these characters act differently: they take on trickster functions because they're on missions or quests of their own which generally conflict with another character's quest.

In a Quest structure, when the main character meets a 'friend or helper' (←), the 'friend or helper' typically helps them solve a particular problem, restoring a state of balance (→). When the main character meets the 'enemy or hindrance (←), they come face to face with an obstacle or challenge that they have to overcome (→). In a Trickster structure, the meeting steps remain the same, but the subsequent results involve a reversal of some kind.

In *Laws of Form*, George Spencer-Brown uses the (⇌) symbol to indicate the expansion and/or contraction of expressions.[4] In the context of that work, it has an indeterminate, Mercurial quality – the movement could go either way, which is why I use it here to indicate steps associated with the Trickster structure. It's the penultimate symbol I've drawn on from his work to analyse stories.[5]

This is the story structure that the wolf's story line in *The Three Little Pigs* analysed previously follows:

The wolf's story line in the story of *The Three Little Pigs*

Steps	Symbols	Structure	Outline of content
1	⊓	Opening	[Implied]
2	⌐	Initial situation (set-up: who, when, where – two characters on conflicting quests)	A wolf ...
3	←	Problem	... was hungry [implied] ...
4	→	Journey	... so he went off in search of food ... [implied]
5	←	Meeting between ...	... and when he was brought short by a door behind which he could sense pig ...
6	⇌	... the two characters (one is tricked or duped by the other)	... he dissembled, and asked Biddy to 'Just let me in and have a news [sic] with you.'
7	←	Meeting between ...	Biddy replied ...
8	⇌	... the two characters (the previously duped character tricks the other)	... 'Oh, no, I'll not let you in,' – hardly appropriate behaviour (from the wolf's perspective). His story line loops back to step 3.
3a	←	Problem	He was still hungry [implied] and the door was in his way.
4a	→	Journey	He went on an internal journey to seek the resources he needed to solve the problem [implied].
5a	←	Meeting between ...	He found and deployed the resources.
6a	⇌	... the two characters (one is tricked or duped by the other)	He blew Biddy's house in. 'But just as he got in at the front door,' ...[6]
7a	←	Meeting between ...	... and was about to catch Biddy [implied] ...
8a	⇌	... the two characters (the previously duped character tricks the other)	... 'Biddy ran out at the back'.

Steps 3a–5a which form a triplicity of different symbols in the form (← → ←) can condense to a single step (←) and steps 6a–8a (⇌ ← ⇌) to (⇌). Moreover, the sequence repeats. This allows us to compress the wolf's extended story line to the following elements:

The wolf's story line in the story of *The Three Little Pigs*

Steps	Symbols	Structure	Outline of content
1	⧠	Opening	[Implied]
2	⌐	Initial situation (set-up: who, when, where – two characters on conflicting quests)	A wolf ...
3	⟵	Problem	... was hungry [implied]
4	⟶	Journey	... so he went off in search of food ... [implied]
5	⟵	Meeting between ...	... and when he was brought short by three doors in turn, behind which he could sense increasing numbers of pigs ...
6	⇌	... the two characters (one is tricked or duped by the other)	... he dissembled at the first two, and asked to be let in.
7	⟵	Meeting between ...	But the first two ...
8	⇌	... the two characters (the previously duped character tricks the other)	... refused, and the last was too solid to give way, so ...
9	⟵	Meeting between ...	... he blew the first two houses in, but ...
10	⇌	... the two characters (one is tricked or duped by the other)	... failed to catch Biddy and Dennis, and decided to try to enter the third house by stealth through the chimney.
11	⟵	Meeting between ...	He came up against burning straw ...
12	⇌	... the two characters (the previously duped character tricks the other)	... and met an unexpected and painful death.
13	⌐	Final situation (outcome/resolution)	He was a threat to the pigs no longer.
14	⧠	Closing	[Implied]

The story structure can be compressed further, for steps 5–8 and 9–12 follow the same pattern. If these are reduced to one iteration, the wolf's story line can be reduced to the following 'bare bones' elements:

The wolf's story line in the story of *The Three Little Pigs*

Steps	Symbols	Structure	Outline of content
1	☐	Opening	[Implied]
2	⌐	Initial situation (set-up: who, when, where – two characters on conflicting quests)	A wolf ...
3	←	Problem	... was hungry [implied] ...
4	→	Journey	... so he went off in search of food ... [implied]
5	←	Meeting between ...	... and when he was brought short by three doors in turn, behind which he could sense increasing numbers of pigs ...
6	⇌	... the two characters (one is tricked or duped by the other)	... he dissembled at the first two, and asked to be let in; and tried to get into the third via the chimney.
7	←	Meeting between ...	Although he blew the first houses in, almost managed to eat the first two pigs and almost managed to gain entry to the third house, ...
8	⇌	... the two characters (the previously duped character tricks the other)	... the three pigs always managed to get the better of him ...
13	⌐	Final situation (outcome/ resolution)	... and he met a tragic end which allowed the pigs to live out their lives in peace and quiet.
14	☐	Closing	[Implied]

In linear form, the story structure is scribed like this:

$$☐\ ⌐\ ←\ →\ ←\ ⇌\ ←\ ⇌\ ⌐\ ☐$$

Call this the Trickster structure.

In the Trickster structure, two characters follow individual quests, the aims of which conflict with each other in some way. Call this Conflicting Quests.

In the Trickster structure, two characters on Conflicting Quests interact, and one intentionally tricks or dupes the other. Call this a Trickster step ($\rightleftharpoons$).

In the Trickster structure, where a pair of Trickster steps subvert and restore order in turn. Call this Transformational Twists.

In stories that follow Trickster structures, the Conflicting Quest relationship between the Trickster and the 'dupe' is key. Here's a story from India about a dhobi (a washerman) and his ass.[7] The 'bare bones' of the story are as follows:

A childless washerman and his wife, believing a mullah (a religious teacher) can literally transform donkeys into human beings, pay him to transform their donkey to a son they can pass on their savings to, who'll perform the last rites for them when they die. The mullah agrees, after negotiating a handsome fee. He tells them to return in a year and a day. Knowing that they'll return, he prepares a ruse in order to get his own back on a rival – a qazi (a judge) in a nearby town. When they arrive, he tells them they've just missed seeing their son take up the position of qazi and that they should take his feed bag and halter and show them to him. He assures them the qazi will recognise them and be reunited with them not as donkey but as their son. The qazi, who's taken aback by their public behaviour, receives them in private and understands that they've been duped. Rather than burst their bubble, he plays along with the ruse. All he asks is for them to keep his story secret. In exchange, he promises to fulfil his duties towards them as a son and perform the last rites for them. As a result, they leave him all their wealth. The qazi benefits; the mullah loses out.

The story involves three main characters: the mullah; the couple (whose individual story lines run in parallel, so we'll treat them as a single character); and the qazi. In the analysis which follows, we'll focus on the couple's story line. The first section above the horizontal dividing line in the table below maps the Trickster structure which covers the interaction between the couple and the mullah; the second, below the dividing line, maps the Trickster structure which covers the interaction between the couple and the qazi. We'll look at the second part of this story in a bit more detail in chapter 12.

Analysis of the couple's story line in a narrative version of the story of *The Washerman and His Ass*[8]

Steps	Symbols	Structure	Outline of content
1	⊐	Opening	Once upon a time ...
2	⌐	Initial situation	... an elderly couple with no children of their own overhear a mullah say he can change asses into men.
3	←	Problem	The couple have no children to pass on their savings to who would perform the last rites for them ...
4	→	Journey	... so, they decide to ask the mullah to change their ass into a boy they can raise as their son.
5	←	Meeting between ...	They approach the mullah ...
6	⇌	... the two characters (one is tricked or duped by the other)	... who tells them that he will effect the transformation if the couple leave him the ass and a thousand rupees. The couple do so and are told to return on a particular day at a particular time when the job will be complete.
7	←	Meeting between ...	When the couple return, ...
8	⇌	... the two characters (one is tricked or duped by the other)	... they're told the transformation has been effected and the man has left to become a qazi in Jaunpur.
9	←	(3) Problem	The washerman and his wife are left neither with their original ass nor the transformed one.
10	→	(4) Journey	They decide to go to Jaunpur to visit the transformed qazi.
11	←	(5) Meeting between ...	Arriving at Cawnpore Court, the couple find their way to the mosque where the qazi's holding court.

Analysis of the couple's story line in a narrative version of the story of
The Washerman and His Ass[8]

Steps	Symbols	Structure	Outline of content
12	⇌	(6) ... the two characters (one is tricked or duped by the other)	They wave the rope and nosebag at him as they'd been instructed to do by the mullah, but the qazi doesn't respond as they'd expected he would.[9]
13	↼	(7) Meeting with ...	He wants to find out why they were behaving in such a strange way ... so he calls a member of the congregation to bring them to him so he can get to the bottom of the matter.
14	⇌	(8) ... the two characters (the previously duped character tricks the other)	When he hears their story, he realises what has happened ... and decides to play a trick on the mullah, going along with the story, while swearing them to secrecy ...
15	⌐	(9) Final situation (outcome/ resolution)	... which ends in the qazi's reputation remaining unscathed, with them being buried respectfully when they die, with the qazi inheriting their wealth, and with the mullah being very disappointed.
16	⊐	(10) Closing	[Implied]

How do Conflicting Quests, Trickster steps and Transformational Twists work in the story?

Following the numbering in the leftmost column, at stage 6, we find the couple on a quest to gain a child and the mullah on a quest to seek financial gain. While he agrees to help them, he does so with the sole aim of benefiting from their gullibility.

At stage 8, the couple's quest remains the same; the mullah, however, has a new quest. He wants to get revenge on the qazi and the couple act as his agents; the mullah's story line and the couple's join to run in parallel here.

At stage 12, the couple act as unwitting tricksters. They have no intention of embarrassing or humiliating the qazi, but that's exactly what they end up doing in carrying out the mullah's instructions. The qazi has absolutely no idea why they're behaving in this way.

However, at stage 14, the qazi turns the tables on the mullah, taking on the role of trickster, with the mullah becoming the duped party.

Trickster steps subvert order but they're typically balanced out through Transformational Twists. For example, stage 6, in which the mullah seeks financial gain dishonourably is balanced with a Transformational Twist in stage 14, in which the qazi is the one who gains financially as a result of the mullah's actions, and he does so more honourably. At stage 8, the mullah's goal is to humiliate the qazi by advising the couple to wave the rope and nosebag at him in public. This is balanced with a Transformational Twist in stage 12, where the couple's actions merely serve to arouse the qazi's curiosity. Because he reacts calmly and curiously, he suffers no damage to his reputation.

The success of a Trickster step is dependent on the gullibility of the duped party. This gullibility is usually founded on some kind of misunderstanding, commonly based on a false assumption. For example, the wolf, in *The Three Wee Pigs*, mistakenly believes that by blowing down the first two pigs' houses, or gaining entry to the third house through the chimney, he'll successfully end up with a tummy full of pig. In stage 6 of the story analysed above, the couple believe that the mullah can transform an ass into a human through education. At stage 8, they believe that the eminent qazi will respond positively to an implied association with an ass's rope and nosebag.

At stage 12, a Transformational Twist occurs when the potential humiliation the mullah had put in place at stage 8, which he assumed would work, is neutralised by the qazi's calm reaction. The qazi sees the situation as curious rather than personally humiliating, thus neutralising the threat. At stage 14, a similar step occurs. While the qazi accepts the ruse set up at stage 12 and asserts that the couple's interests are 'his interests', nothing could be further from the truth. All he's concerned with is neutralising the threat to his reputation. As a result, he's willing to continue to support the couple in their belief in the miraculous transformative power of the mullah's educational methods. Despite the trickery, it works out for them.

At the end, when the qazi performs the last rites for them, he acts as their friend and helper, with a nested structure implied. At first, I thought it was a Quest structure. The last two steps (let's call them 14a (←) and 14b, (→)) involve the qazi performing the last rights for the couple. I found that I could interpret these as a 'meeting with … enemy/hindrance' from the couple's point of view. The 'enemy/hindrance' is the event of dying without anyone to perform the last rites for them. They avoid this with the help of the qazi. Their story line can be interpreted as a Quest which involves the following numbered steps from the outline:

1	2	3	4	13	14	14a	14b	15	16
⨐	⎤	←	→	←	→	←	→	⎤	⨐	.

However, step 14 in the qazi's story line is a Trickster step, as he's intentionally duping the couple in accepting their story that he used to be an ass, and this demands a balancing step at 14b to provide the Transformational Twist:

1	2	(9)	(10)	11	12	14a	14b	15	16
⨐	⎤	←	→	←	⇌	←	⇌	⎤	⨐	.

But … if the couple's story line follows a Quest structure, and they're dead by step 14a, who or what is involved in the Conflicting Quest that gives rise to the Transformational Twist in step 14b?

The question shed a totally new light on the story and revealed hidden depths to it. At the end of the story, the mullah's material greed for wealth, which is in direct contrast with – and transgresses against – his spiritual duty, is balanced by a final act of retribution in the story structure in which the qazi's respect for the couple's spiritual values leaves him better off in financial terms. The qazi's reputation remains intact; the mullah loses out. With this insight, we reach the heart of the story, which the analysis of the story structure shows is about spiritual wealth, not material wealth.

This methodology has the potential to reveal new insights into the deep meaning or links in a story and to elicit a deeper appreciation for what makes story work in us than we may have had previously. This is particularly so in stories with multiple characters and parallel plot lines. These stories have connections which are often difficult to see and to track. However, the methodology and intuitive visual approach outlined in this book have the potential to make it far easier to track these connections, particularly when tracing the story structures that individual characters' story lines follow.[10] In the table below, implied steps are shown in brackets. Steps 3 and 4 for the mullah cover the reasons why he set up his school; steps 9 and 10 for the qazi cover the reasons behind why this 'doctor of Mohammedan law' is addressing the congregation after prayer outside the mosque that Friday. The entire story structure can be encapsulated in 16 parts, using only 5 symbols. Grey highlights show connections between the Mullah's story line and the qazi's.

Analysis of the principal characters' story lines in a narrative version of the story of *The Washerman and His Ass* (symbols only)

Characters	1	2	3	4	5	6	7	8	9	10	11	12	13	14	15	16
Mullah[11]	□	⊓	(←	→)	←	⇌	←	⇌							⊓	□
Couple	□	⊓	←	→	←	⇌	←	⇌	←	→	←	⇌	←	⇌	⊓	□
Qazi	□	⊓							(←	→)	←	⇌	←	⇌	⊓	□

The analysis shows that the story clearly follows two main sequential Trickster structures. On one level, little changes. The mullah continues to deceive; the couple still die without a child of their own. The qazi's reputation remains intact, and the conflict between the mullah and the qazi remains unresolved. Cartoons

like Hanna and Barbera's *Tom and Jerry* (MGM, USA) or Kandel,
Khait and Kurlyandsky's *Well, Just You Wait!* (Russian: *Ну, погоди!*
[*Nu, pogodi!*]) (Soyuzmultfilm, Russia) are typical of the genre. The
characters are trapped in trickster loops – it's as if the goal of each
character's existence is to trick each other.

On another level, the couple's real aim in having a son – that of
having someone perform the last rites for them – is fulfilled when
the qazi takes on that duty for them. It's no coincidence that the
couple's part is comic here: there's often a serious undercurrent to
Comic steps. The relationship between the Trickster step and the
Comic step will be explored in chapter 9.

> The Trickster structure is a useful teaching tool. If you're in
> control, like Brer Rabbit is, and use your trickster powers of
> wit and guile to escape a sticky situation, fine – but it would be
> unwise to go back for more. There's more to life – much, much
> more. Move on. Live it – to the full.

How can we avoid the 'trickster trap'? Two ways spring to mind:
one way of avoiding being tricked is to hone our ability to think
critically, to develop a healthy level of scepticism. Trust is great. We
need to trust each other. But blind trust never did anyone a blind
bit of good. We need to cultivate the kind of mutual trust, based
on truth, that will allow us to achieve balance and flow. Another
option, however, is to stop and think: What's the other character's
problem? What if, instead of pretending to be each other's friends
and helpers and only ending up getting in each other's way, we
thought about how we might help each other? What goals might
we share? What might we be able to work on together? The qazi
avoids falling into the trap the mullah has laid for him. Instead, he
goes on a nested Quest to find a solution to the problem he faces
and benefits from the solution.

The Quest structure can help us break out of a trickster loop if we find ourselves in one. Then, we need to draw on our powers of reasoning, our sense of shared values, and see them as our inner friends and helpers. We also need to be alert to them acting as 'false friends'. We're not immune to carrying inner tricksters around. The way to deal with them is to acknowledge them, listen to them, and find out what they need. Not all tricksters know they're tricksters!

Where the pair of Trickster steps ($\rightleftharpoons$) appears, the first step of the pair can often be seen as a transgression which is restored to order by the second step of the pair. The principle of a transgression against—or imbalance in—the natural order, followed by a restoration of balance is a key feature of the Transformation structure, which features in the next chapter.

NOTES

1   El-ahrairah is the rabbit folk hero. The name (Elil-hrair-rah) means "Enemies-Thousand-Prince" = the Prince with a Thousand Enemies.

2   Richard Adams, *Watership Down* (New York: Scribner, 2005), 101.

3   Vladimir Propp, *Morphology of the Folktale*, 2nd ed. (Austin, TX: University of Texas Press, 2005), 84.

4   Spencer-Brown, *Laws of Form*, 12.

5   Later on in this work, the ($\rightleftharpoons$) symbol is used to denote other steps which create cognitive dissonance based on one or more of Aristotle's categories. These are summarised in chapter 9 of this work. See Aristotle, "The Categories," in *The Categories; On Interpretation*, translated by Harold P. Cooke and Hugh Tredennick (Cambridge, MA: Harvard University Press, 1962), 1–111, and especially at 4.1b25–1b26, 16–19.

6   Here, the interaction involves an inner trickster for the wolf – his misguided belief that the strategy he's chosen will be effective in helping him reach his goal.

7   D. L. Ashliman, "The Education of an Ox," *Folklore and Mythology Electronic Texts*, 1999–2014, story 5, https://www.pitt.edu/~dash/type1675.html.

8   The numbers in the left-hand column relate to the steps in the story. The numbers in brackets in the third column mark the numbers of the steps in relation to the individual Trickster structures which make up the story.

9   We'll revisit this story when we explore the Trickster Awe step, in chapter 12.

10 See appendix 1 for an example. Further examples of in-depth analyses are forthcoming.

11 After step 6, there's a quest implied for the mullah, who knows he has a year to come up with an explanation for his ruse. His explanation involves a Trickster step which targets the qazi, in the hope that the couple will realise for him in steps 11 and 12. The Transformational Twist at the end (steps 13, 14) resolves the Conflicting Quest in this part of the mullah's story line. It also points to an implied 'history' or 'back story' of envy in terms of position, social status, achievement, and intelligence which explains the historic enmity behind the mullah and the qazi that drives the second half of the story forward.

7

THE EXPANSION AND CONTRACTION OF STEPS

THE TRANSFORMATION STRUCTURE

If you want to shrink something,
you must first allow it to expand.

LAOZI, TRANS. STEPHEN MITCHELL, *Tao Te Ching*, CHAPTER 36[1]

Many stories share common underlying masterplots: Snow White and Sleeping Beauty are both examples of 'Death and Rebirth' stories; Cinderella, a 'Rags to Riches' story.[2] These, as we'll see, all have nested Quest structures within them. Both of these masterplots nest within them Quest structures; a number of them also have nested Trickster structures in one or more of the characters' story lines. Many of the story structures found in Ovid's *Metamorphoses*, however, are more compressed.

The *Metamorphoses* dates from around the beginning of the Common Era. One of the earliest collections of stories, it contains many highly compressed stories of how 'bodies' are 'changed into new forms' told in 'a continuous thread of words, from the world's first origins to [Ovid's] own time', a thread that extends beyond his time, to ours.[3] Take this narrative version of Ovid's story of Cornix's metamorphosis into a white crow, for example:

Once when I [Cornix] was walking slowly as I used to do along the crest of the sands by the shore the sea-god [Neptune] saw me and grew hot. When his flattering words and entreaties proved a waste of time, he tried force, and chased after me. I ran, leaving the solid shore behind, tiring myself out uselessly in the soft sand. Then I called out to gods and men. No mortal heard my voice, but the virgin goddess [Minerva] feels pity for a virgin and she helped me. I was stretching out my arms to the sky: those arms began to darken with soft plumage. I tried to lift my cloak from my shoulders but it had turned to feathers with roots deep in my skin. I tried to beat my naked breast with my hands but found I had neither hands nor naked breast.

I ran, and now the sand did not clog my feet as before but I lifted from the ground, and soon sailed high into the air. So I became an innocent servant of Minerva.[4]

My analysis of the story structure which underpins this narrative is as follows:

Outline of the story of Cornix from Ovid's *Metamorphoses*

Steps	Symbols	Structure	Outline of content
1	☐	Opening	[Implied]
2	⌐	Initial situation	Cornix (C), Neptune (N) initially; Minerva (M) later.
3	←	Problem (N)	Neptune sees Cornix.
4	→	Journey (N)	Neptune approaches Cornix.
5	←	Problem (C) / Meeting with ... (N)	They meet face to face.
6	→	Journey (C)	She uses her powers of resistance;
		... friend/helper (N)[5]	he uses his powers of seduction.
7	←	Meeting with ... (C, N)[6]	He tries to use force.
8	→	... friend/helper (C)[7]	She runs away, crying for help; he chases after her,
		... enemy/hindrance (N)[8]	but she evades him.
9	←	Problem (M)	Minerva hears Cornix's cry.
10	→	Outcome/resolution (M)	Minerva intervenes.
11	←	Meeting with ... (C)	Minerva's intervention reaches Cornix.
12	→	... enemy/hindrance (C)[9]	Cornix is transformed.
13	⌐	Final situation (outcome/resolution)	Cornix becomes Minerva's servant; for Neptune and Minerva, business continues as usual.
14	☐	Closing	[Implied]

The story lines can be mapped out as follows:

Analysis of the story of Cornix from Ovid's *Metamorphoses*

Characters	Steps													
	1	2	3	4	5	6	7	8	9	10	11	12	13	14
Neptune	⊔	⌐	←	→	←	→	←	→					⌐	⊔
Cornix	⊔	⌐			←	→	←	→			←	→	⌐	⊔
Minerva	⊔	⌐							←	→			⌐	⊔

In the above table, Neptune and Cornix's story lines clearly follow a Quest structure. But what about Minerva's story line? Should her story line follow a Quest structure too? After all, in order to help Cornix (a problem she feels she needs to solve), she has to come to a decision (an inner journey), draw on her power (a meeting of sorts), and send it out (as her friend/helper). The power has to reach Cornix (a meeting) and transform her (overcoming the enemy/hindrance in the process).

But how essential are these steps to the story? It's almost as if there isn't enough time to include them. In *The Three Little Pigs*, the wolf needs time to draw on his powers. The narrative telling becomes more and more exciting the longer the huffing and puffing go on. In the story of Cornix, Minerva's intervention seems to take no time at all. Minerva sees and acts. Done. In a sense, steps 9 and 10 and steps 11 and 12 can easily be superimposed: steps 9 and 11 could take place at the same time; so could steps 10 and 12. The more instantaneous and miraculous the transformation here, the more dramatic the narrative becomes.

When I asked myself whether I could reduce the story further, I found that I could:

Outline of Minerva's story line from the story of Cornix from Ovid's _Metamorphoses_

Steps	Symbols	Outline of content
1	⊐	Opening: Once upon a time ...
2	⌐	... Minerva ...
3	↼	... heard Cornix's cry for help ...
4	⇀	... and transformed her ...
5	⌐	... into a white crow. [Cornix lived like that ...
6	⊐	... from then on.]

It works for Cornix's story line:

Outline of Cornix's story line from the story of Cornix from Ovid's _Metamorphoses_

Steps	Symbols	Outline of content
1	⊐	Opening: Once upon a time ...
2	⌐	... Cornix ...
3	↼	... was chased by Neptune ...
4	⇀	... but saved by Minerva ...
5	⌐	... who transformed Cornix into a white crow. Cornix lived like that ...
6	⊐	... from then on.

It works for Neptune's story line:

Outline of Neptune's story line from the story of Cornix from Ovid's _Metamorphoses_

Steps	Symbols	Outline of content
1	⊐	Opening: Once upon a time ...
2	⌐	... Neptune ...
3	↼	... was enamoured by Cornix ...
4	⇀	... but had his desires thwarted by Minerva ...
5	⌐	... who transformed her into a white crow. [Cornix lived like that ...
6	⊐	... from then on.]

When scribed, the minimal structure looks like this:

Call this the Transformation structure.

The Transformation structure is common to most of the stories in Ovid's *Metamorphoses*. It's the most compressed story structure I know of. It's as if the com-pressed structure *demands* that the content be im-pressive. It's *because* the structure is so com-pact that it lends itself so well to conveying interactions between the divine and the human realms. Moreover, as far as I can see, the major 'steps' typically revolve around an act of transgression against the natural order and a violent act of retribution that restores equilibrium – but things are never ever the same after the intervention.

The steps typically link to elements with the following features:

The Transformation structure

Steps	Symbols	Structure
1	⊓	Opening
2	⅂	Initial situation (set-up: who, when, where – character and setting)
3	⌐	Transgression against the natural order
4	→	Restoration of natural order
5	⅂	Final situation (outcome/resolution)
6	⊔	Closing

In each of the characters' story lines, a transgression against the natural order occurs in step 3, and a restoration of the natural order in step 4. Each story line follows the same structure.

The Transformation structure also drives the story of Narcissus forward: Narcissus transgresses against love by turning his feelings inwards rather than outwards; as a result, he's forced to gaze lovingly at his reflection for ever, after being changed into a flower.[10]

It drives the story of Arachne forward: Arachne transgresses against Pallas Minerva by consistently refusing to acknowledge the source of her gift, by refusing to recognise the goddess's skill, by choosing to compete against the goddess, and by choosing to flagrantly depict divine acts of transgression on the tapestry she weaves.[11] Although Minerva finds no technical fault whatsoever in Arachne's work, she still hits Arachne 'three or four times, on the forehead'—one for each transgression, perhaps?—and consigns her to a fate of spinning webs in dark corners and across the flight paths of flies in perpetuity. The same theme of transgression and restoration is common to the stories that Ovid describes in relation to Minerva's tapestry.[12]

Is this structure limited to Ovid's *Metamorphoses*?

It could be argued that the ($\leftarrow$ $\rightarrow$) steps are the basis of all of the story structures we've covered so far. After all, *Nasr-el-din Hodja and the Walnut Tree*, outlined in the previous chapter could be analysed, in bare bones form, as an expanded Transformation structure story:

Analysis of Nasr-el-Din Hodja's story line in *Nasr-el-Din Hodja and the Walnut Tree* as a Transformation structure story

Steps	Symbols	Structure	Outline of content
1	☐	Opening	Once upon a time
2	⌐	Initial situation (set-up: who, when, where – character and setting)	Nasr-el-Din Hodja lay under a walnut tree to rest.
3	$\leftarrow$	Transgression against the natural order	He transgressed by doubting the wisdom of Allah ...
4	$\rightarrow$	Restoration of natural order	... and was sent a serendipitous wake-up call ...
5	⌐	Final situation (outcome/ resolution)	... to remind him that things are made the way they are for a reason ...
6	☐	Closing	... and he never questioned the wisdom of Allah ever again.

But as soon as we do this, the perspective changes. We're no longer looking at Nasr-el-Din's story line from his point of view. He has no idea he's transgressing against anything. By compressing the story structure from Quest to Transformation, we've phase-shifted from a story line which unfolds in a mortal dimension of being to one which unfolds in a different dimension – it has something of the divine force of nature, the Oneness-of-Being about it.

From this insight, we can see what happens when, flowing with story, we compress a (← → ←) sequence of steps to a single (←) step and a (→ ← →) sequence of steps to a single (→) step. Contrariwise, as Tweedledee[13] might say, a single (→) step can expand to a (→ ← →) sequence and a single (←) step to a (← → ←) sequence, and an inverse phase shift will result.

Call this the expansion and contraction of steps.

The table below provides a visual comparison of the Transformation and Quest structures, illustrating a vital link between them.

The expansion and contraction of steps in Transformation and Quest structures

Structures	Steps									
Transformation	1	2	3			4		5	6	
	□	⌐	←			→		⌐	□	
Quest	1	2	3	4	5	6	7	8	9	10
	□	⌐	←	→	←	→	←	→	⌐	□

When expanded, step 3 of the Transformation structure – which symbolises a 'transgression against the natural order' – allows steps 3, 4, and 5 of the Quest structure to unfold. These three steps are: the problem, the journey, and the first meeting, respectively. The 'transgression against the natural order step' in the Transformation structure, therefore, can be seen as *generating* the momentum that propels the protagonist on their journey in a Quest structure story. The expanded form also contains within it the revelation or appearance of the 'friend or helper' character. While the character forces the protagonist to stop, delaying their progress towards the resolution of their problem, their function is to help the protagonist in some way. Whether the protagonist accepts their help is another matter. When step 3 of the Transformation structure expands, the strength of the Transformation structure's 'transgression against the natural order' is diminished and is reduced to a problem—a problem that contains within itself the seed of its own (dis)solution. All it has to do is open up a bit, allow story to flow, and a bit of transformative magic is released. How else can the 'friend or helper' character appear?!

Step 4 of the Transformation structure provides the counter-balance to this expansion. The step indicates the divine intervention which restores order. When this step expands, two 'positive' moves appear: the result of the meeting with the 'friend or helper' character and the 'defeat of enemy or hindrance' (steps 6 and 8 of the Quest structure, respectively); but the expansion also brings forth the very obstacle which needs to be defeated (step 7). There's a subtle *yin/yang*, concord/discord balance to the relationship, which is sustained in and exists to sustain harmony.

The Transformation structure often functions as a bridge between divine and mortal states of being. It's also the domain of heightened emotional states – of extreme actions that are conceived and realised in the moment. Whenever we lash out instantly and reactively with a swear word or a blow in a fight response; whenever we make a swift, instinctive retreat, or experience a sudden feeling of being gutted in a flight response, we're probably following a Transformation structure. The structure has great potential for being used to appeal to the emotions. It can also help us manage our emotions. It's no surprise to find that it's a common structure used in advertising – the kind of advert designed to make one think, 'It's a crime against the natural order not to own this brand of skin cream; car; item of clothing ...' or 'This celebrity wears this brand of clothing, and you don't – that's a crime against the natural order'. Advertisers can spin the story. We don't have to buy into it. If we see through their ruse, we can quickly change the dynamic. Instead of seeing ourselves as playing our parts in their Transformation structure story, we can use a nested Quest structure story to find our way. In doing so, we'll need to slow down and call on our inner friends and helpers – our powers of reasoning, our powers of critical thinking. A state of emotional imbalance is trumped by wisdom. One of the main ways of making this happen is by expanding a Transformation structure to a Quest structure, as shown above. On the other hand, the uncertainty of over-thinking is trumped by love (contracting a Quest structure to a Transformation structure). Through the process of expansion and contraction outlined here, we can see how one can easily transition from one structure to another to achieve a better sense of balance. We engage in the same process when we take time to cool things down, rather than lash out in anger. The ultimate state of balance, of course, is one in which no transgression against the natural order occurs, and life just flows. There's a story structure which is a perfect example of this. I call it the Creation Myth structure. We'll come to it in chapter 15.

The initial 'backward' step (←) is a key element of both Transformation and Quest structures, but this doesn't hold for all story structures. In the next chapter, we'll look at a story structure that starts with a different initial step.

NOTES

1   Laozi, *Tao Te Ching: A New English Version*, translated by Stephen Mitchell (New York: Harper & Row, 1988).

2   The structures which underpin these stories are outlined in chapter 8.

3   Ovid, *The Metamorphoses*, translated by Anthony S. Kline, 2000, 1.1, 9 http://ovid.lib.virginia.edu/trans/Ovhome.htm#askline.

4   Ovid, *Metamorphoses*, 2.566–595, 63.

5   Neptune's ability to flatter, and entreat, are his 'friends and helpers'.

6   I see the contact as being more physical, more immediate here. This provides the pivotal force for a change in direction of flow.

7   Cornix's ability to run from Neptune is her 'friend and helper'.

8   Neptune's inability to catch Cornix is his 'enemy or hindrance'.

9   As a result of the transformation, which arrived like a bolt out of the blue, Cornix (who is now a crow) is now able to overcome the 'enemy or hindrance' (the limitations of her human frame), escape Neptune's advances, and solve her problem. She asked for help. She got it. She wanted to preserve her virginity. She stayed a virgin. As I point out further on in the chapter, in Transformation structure stories, order is restored, but things are never the same as they previously were.

10 Ovid, *Metamorphoses*, 3.339–510, 91–95.

11 Ovid, *Metamorphoses*, 6.1–145, 157–160.

12 Ovid, *Metamorphoses*. Arachne's punishment is covered in 6.129–145, 160; Minerva's creations in 6.70–128, 158–160. By contrast, Arachne chooses to weave depictions of stories in which gods rape exceptionally beautiful young women. The starting point of 'an excess of goodness' will be discussed in chapter 11 in relation to the Call and Response structure.

13 Lewis Carroll, *The Annotated Alice: The Definitive Edition*, edited by Martin Gardner, illustrated by John Tenniel (London: Penguin, 2001), 180.

8

THE EXPANSION
OF STORY

THE RAGS TO RICHES, AND DEATH AND
REBIRTH STRUCTURES

Form is the envelope of pulsation.

TANTRIC APHORISM, QUOTED BY ROBERT LAWLOR IN
Sacred Geometry: Philosophy and Practice[1]

Many Cinderella stories follow the Rags to Riches structure; many Snow White and Sleeping Beauty stories follow the Death and Rebirth structure. The structures share common features. They both have nested Quest structures, and some versions have nested Trickster structures. But similarities aside, they differ in one very important way. The first steps in both Quest and Transformation story structures outlined in the preceding chapters 'flow backward' (←). The Death and Rebirth structure also starts with a backward step (←). The first step of the Rags to Riches structure, however, is positive (→). It 'flows forward'. It's this key feature that makes the Cinderella story recognisable as following a Rags to Riches structure. The analysis of the two main story lines in a simple narrative version of Cinderella below shows a key connection found in both structures. Let's look at how it works in the Rags to Riches structure first.

Analysis of a simple narrative version of *Cinderella*

Cinderella's story line				The prince's story line
Steps	Symbols	Structure	Outline of content	Symbols
1	☐	Opening	Once upon a time ...	☐
2	☐	Initial situation (set-up: who, when, where – character and setting)	... a family ...	
3	→	Positive condition	... live together happily, until ...	

Analysis of a simple narrative version of *Cinderella*

Cinderella's story line				The prince's story line
Steps	**Symbols**	**Structure**	**Outline of content**	**Symbols**
4	↶	Problem (that usually comes 'out of the blue') resulting in a state of **subversion**	... the mother dies, the father remarries (and in some versions dies himself). A state of **subversion** leaves (the orphaned) Cinderella to be treated badly by her stepmother and two ugly stepsisters.	
5	→	Journey	Meanwhile, a prince, needing a wife, decides to invite all eligible young women in the realm to a ball to choose a royal bride.	⌐ ↶ →
6	↶	Journey thwarted, meeting with ...	The family are invited, but Cinderella's stepmother and stepsisters refuse to allow her to attend.	
7	→	... friend/helper (*positive transformation often achieved by means of an external, often supernatural being*)	By means of an external force (fairy godmother, magical animal, etc.), she experiences a temporary positive transformation and is able to get to the ball, where she and the prince fall in love ...	
8	↶	***Reversion*** to previous state <u>in an altered state of consciousness</u> *Nested Quest structure involving a Saviour character starts*	... but it doesn't last, and she **reverts** to her previous state <u>in an altered state of consciousness</u> – she's back amongst the cinders. This time, though, she has the memory and experience of having been at the ball and having danced with the prince. She's left an item behind, however, which sets up a problem for the prince who's lost the woman of his dreams. He wants to find her, but all he has to go on is this item.	↶

Analysis of a simple narrative version of *Cinderella*

Cinderella's story line				The prince's story line
Steps	Symbols	Structure	Outline of content	Symbols
9	➡	*Nested Quest structure involving a Saviour character ends*	The prince goes on a quest to find the mysterious guest, using the item to help him, which ultimately (despite the machinations of the stepmother and stepsisters) ...	→ ← → ← →
10	┐	Final situation (outcome/ resolution)	... restores Cinderella to her happy state and (in some versions) punishes the evildoers who wanted to pervert the course of natural justice ...	┐
11	⛶	Closing	... enabling the couple to live happily ever after.	⛶

Steps 8 and 9 symbolise the quest that the Saviour character (the prince in the Cinderella story) goes through. His quest includes all of the classic steps of the Quest structure, prefixed by an additional pair of steps (steps 3 and 4 below). When these expand, they produce an unresolved initial Quest structure ...

Analysis of a simple narrative version of *Cinderella* (The prince's story line)

Steps	Symbols	Structure	Outline of content
1	⛶	Opening	The structure emerges *in response to* or perhaps *prior to* Cinderella's need.
2	┐	Initial situation (set-up: who, when, where – character and setting)	The prince ...
3	←	Problem 1	... lacks a bride.
4	→	Journey 1	He holds a ball (nested Quest implied) which Cinderella attends. They fall in love ...

Analysis of a simple narrative version of *Cinderella* (The prince's story line)

Steps	Symbols	Structure	Outline of content
5	⤙	Problem 2	… he loses her, but she leaves behind a shoe … (this is the problem which sets off his quest to find her).
6	→	Journey 2	He goes on a journey … on which …
7	⤙	Meeting with …	… the shoe helps him eliminate …
8	→	… friend/helper	… countless candidates who are not Cinderella until …
9	⤙	Meeting with …	… he finds her …
10	→	… enemy/ hindrance	… and finally tries the shoe on her foot. It fits (resolving both Quest structures) …
11	⌐	Final situation (outcome/ resolution)	… they marry …
12	⊐	Closing	… and live happily ever after.

Steps 3–5 (⤙ → ⤙) can be condensed to a single (⤙) step, giving the minimal 'bare bones' Quest structure of the Prince's story line.

Reduced to its minimal number of steps, this simple version of *Cinderella* can be scribed as follows. In the sequence below, the nested Quest structure the Saviour character follows is highlighted in grey:

$$\square \; \urcorner \rightarrow \; \llcorner \; \rightarrow \; \llcorner \; \rightarrow \; \llcorner \; \rightarrow \; \urcorner \; \square$$

Call this the Rags to Riches structure.

Four features make the Rags to Riches structure distinctive:
1. The initial step is 'positive'.
2. A character experiences a reversal of fortune which puts them in a state of *subversion*. Typically, they can only solve their problem with the intervention of a metaphysical friend/helper (often an external, supernatural being) and the help of a physical Saviour character.

3. The character *reverts* to their previous state <u>in an altered state of consciousness</u>.
4. The Saviour character's story line which follows on from the *reversion* typically follows a nested Quest structure.

A nested Quest structure is also a key feature of the Death and Rebirth structure, which the stories of *Snow White* and of *Sleeping Beauty* follow.

As in the Rags to Riches structure, in the Death and Rebirth structure, balance can only be restored once a Saviour character has successfully completed a quest, which solves both their problem and the problem that the 'main' character in the story (Sleeping Beauty, Snow White) is typically unable to solve themselves.

To see how this works in a story, let's look at a simple version of *Sleeping Beauty* first:[2]

Analysis of the story lines of the royal couple and of the prince in a simple narrative version of *Sleeping Beauty*

The royal couple's story line				The prince's story line
Steps	Symbols	Structure	Outline of content	Symbols
1	⊐	Opening	Once upon a time ...	⊐
2	⌐	Initial situation (set-up: who, when, where – character and setting)	... a royal couple ...	
3	⤆	Problem (lack)	... lack a child.	
4	⤇	Lack fulfilled	Their wish is granted ... they celebrate ...	
5	⤆	There's a price to pay	... but there's a price to pay ... a curse is laid down.	
6	⤇	There are attempts to avoid paying the price	There are attempts to mitigate the curse ...	⌐

Analysis of the story lines of the royal couple and of the prince in a simple narrative version of *Sleeping Beauty*

Steps	Symbols	Structure	Outline of content	Symbols
The royal couple's story line				The prince's story line
7	←	The attempts fail, the price is exacted, there's a **submersion** *Nested Quest structure involving a Saviour character starts*	... which ultimately fail, leaving them and the princess in a state of **submersion** ...	←
8	→	*Nested Quest structure involving a Saviour character ends*	... which results in a prince undertaking a quest to find the princess, which leads to the characters awakening and the prince and princess ...	→ ← → ← →
9	⌐	Final situation (outcome/ resolution)	... marrying ...	⌐
10	⊐	Closing	... bringing the story to an end ... if not once and for all, at least for now.	⊐

As with any story, we can easily find different versions of *Sleeping Beauty*. However, the basic version of *Snow White* below is underpinned by *exactly the same* structure, outlined above. The key features they have in common—and which make this story structure distinctive—are: the starting point of a lack, a failed attempt to mitigate disaster leading to a state of **submersion**, and a nested Quest structure for a Saviour character.

Analysis of the story lines of the queen, of Snow White and of the prince in a simple narrative version of *Snow White*

The queen/ Snow White's story lines				The prince's story line
Steps	Symbols	Structure	Outline of content	Symbols
1	☐	Opening	Once upon a time ...	☐
2	⌐	Initial situation (set-up: who, when, where – character and setting)	... a queen ...	
3	↞	Problem (lack)	... lacked a child.	
4	↠	Lack fulfilled	She wished for one and her wish was granted ...	
5	↞	There's a price to pay	... but there was a price to pay ... the mother died, the king remarried. Snow White's beauty threatened her stepmother's vanity, and the new queen decided to have Snow White murdered.	
6	↠	There are attempts to avoid paying the price	The huntsman attempted to mitigate the crime by allowing Snow White to escape (nested Trickster structure)...	⌐
7	↞	The attempts fail, the price is exacted, a ***submersion*** follows *Nested Quest structure involving a Saviour character starts*	... but the stepmother managed to get to her (nested structure), and (apparently) kill her, leaving the princess in a state of ***submersion*** ...	↞

Analysis of the story lines of the queen, of Snow White and of the prince in a simple narrative version of *Snow White*

The queen/ Snow White's story lines				The prince's story line
Steps	Symbols	Structure	Outline of content	Symbols
8	⇀	*Nested Quest structure involving a Saviour character ends*	… resulting in a prince undertaking a quest to find the princess, (and defeat the stepmother) which led to them …	⇀ ↽ ⇀ ↽ ⇀
9	⌐	Final situation (outcome/ resolution)	… marrying …	⌐
10	⊐	Closing	… bringing the story to an end … if not once and for all, at least for now.	⊐

The 10 steps above which outline the 'bare bones' structure of *Snow White* clearly fit the same Death and Rebirth framework as *Sleeping Beauty*.

Take the text away, and we're left with …

Call this the Death and Rebirth structure.

The Death and Rebirth structure unfolds when we feel something is lacking. If this were a problem we could solve on our own, a Quest structure would unfold, but it's not that kind of a problem. The lack isn't so much the lack of a child, as in the *Snow White* and *Sleeping Beauty* stories, but rather a lack of what the child represents: the continuation of life. Not just the continuation of life, but the fulfilment of a life well lived.

Four features make the Death and Rebirth structure distinctive:

1. The initial step is 'negative'.
2. A character experiences a reversal of fortune but there's a price to pay.
3. The attempt to avoid paying the price fails and the character experiences a *submersion*, often through the 'negative' intervention of a metaphysical friend/helper (in the form of an external, supernatural being).
4. The Saviour character's story line which follows on from the *submersion* typically follows a nested Quest structure.

While Quest stories revolve around a character with a problem they're perfectly capable of solving by themselves—with a little help from their friend(s), the 'main' characters in Death and Rebirth stories (*Sleeping Beauty* and *Snow White*, for example), are generally rather passive by comparison. In Quest structure stories, the initial problem is usually resolved (or is left tragically unresolved) at the end; in Death and Rebirth structure stories, a lack is resolved early on – usually without the character who suffers the lack needing to do anything. The unfolding of the story then involves the 'main' character (as identified above) having to pay the price.

Both the Death and Rebirth and the Rags to Riches story structures revolve around key themes of life and death, including the subthemes of going through a living death and of dying to live. Both story structures have huge potential for lasting personal transformation. Both involve magical, metaphysical, transcendent forces. Both involve a crucial turning point (a crux). Both depend on a Saviour character going on a nested Quest for their resolution.[3] These features are embedded in and emerge from deep within us.

The Rags to Riches and Death and Rebirth structures don't just apply to fictional stories. They apply to our everyday lives. Much has been written by authors such as Joseph Campbell and

Christopher Booker, among others, about the parallels between archetypes in stories and aspects of our psyche. Sure, we can all imagine having inner fairy godmothers; as we can imagine having inner demons. Among the former could be listed qualities like intuition, contemplation, Keats' 'negative capability'.[4] Among the latter, self-doubt, or Blake's 'selfhood', a quality that separates us from being in a loving relationship to others. Although we can use a mark to indicate these metaphysical characters, their story lines will typically follow a Transformation structure; functionally, they operate dynamically as Spencer-Brown's 'unmarked state'. Their ability to influence us depends on our willingness to trust them – and our awareness of their limits. Perhaps we may need to act as fairy godmothers to others – maybe by invoking a state of 'negative capability' in them when they're coming out of a state of *subversion*. Obviously, we should beware of acting as if we were demons! But the way of looking at story structure outlined in this book goes well beyond this.

These structures both seem to be about living in full awareness of the flow of life. The achievement of a life or a life goal is often the focus of the fulfilment of the initial lack, or the goal towards which the characters are headed – until their flow is blocked in some way. Looking at story in the way we've been doing shows us that life, when blocked in terms of flow, develops within itself the means of its own release. It happens within story. It happens within us. To release the energy of that seed is a process and going through that process, however difficult we find travelling through the stage we're going through, we must never lose hope. We must keep going. We need to challenge the world of rumour, insecurity, doubt, hearsay. We can draw on our inner metaphysical powers – our powers of contemplation, or insight, of imagination, anything that can link us to the transcendent, to the things that make life worth living. It may well be why art, music, poetry exist – our ability to connect to these is one of the ways in which our internal 'fairy godmother' characters manifest. And we can outwit our inner 'demons'. Even if they only let us catch a glimpse of what's possible, it can be enough – that glimpse can be all we need to point to a way out, and lead us in the right direction. From there, we all have the power, the strength, the capacity to be our own saviours. It's up to use to connect to our inner saviour character and transform ourselves. This is where reason and action (the powers of our inner saviour characters) come into play.

When I've found myself in a state of *submersion* in a Death and Rebirth story structure, or a *reversion* step in a Rags to Riches structure; when all's seemed lost, I've found it particularly fruitful to meditate on the link outlined earlier on between the Transformation and Quest structures.[5] The last pair of steps in the Death and Rebirth or Rags to Riches structures expands into the nested Quest that the Saviour character follows. It opens out from *submersion*/resolution and *reversion*/resolution states in these structures. So the Saviour character's appearance is already contained as a seed of potential in the *submersion*/*reversion* steps. All we need to do is expand the steps from the first step in a nested Transformation structure (a transgression against the natural order) to a ($\leftarrow \rightarrow \leftarrow$) 'problem, journey, meeting' sequence that starts off a Quest structure. The second part of the Transformation pair (restoration of the natural order) contains nested within it the potential for the defeat of the enemy/hindrance when expanded. By doing so, I was able to connect with the content-free energetic impulses which are the heartbeat of story, I was able to go deeper – beyond the symbolic archetypes of 'fairy godmothers' or 'demons', and connect directly to the things symbolised – the energetic forces which these archetypes represent. I found them to be more complex and nuanced than I previously realised.

While I was working on this chapter, I happened to be helping a talented young dyslexic writer friend shape and edit a young adult novel he was working on. We spent some very enjoyable hours over supper talking about story structure. It was over a meal one evening, after I'd outlined some thoughts I'd had about the Death and Rebirth structure, that he suddenly exclaimed, "You know something? Here in the western world, we've got it all wrong –

we've been telling ourselves the wrong story. We think we're living a Rags to Riches story – where everything is possible – America! The land of opportunity! Anyone can make it there! I know that's not how you see the structure, but it's how most people see it. But we're actually living a Death and Rebirth story! We're in the *submersion* phase – and it's *no wonder* things don't make sense!" He has a point. Aspects of our culture do follow Quest or Creation Myth structures; an increasing number of elements seem to be stuck in the *submersion* stage, waiting for a Saviour character to come along – the wish for continual (unsustainable) economic growth; the mounting ecological problems the planet faces; the use of GDP as the main measure of economic prosperity; the view of technology and computing power as key indicators of progress are all problematic. If we put too much emphasis on them, we risk putting something far more valuable to sleep, something wished for a long while back, but forgotten, something we would benefit from re-membering. The story structure points to the source of the power that will liberate the saviour character within us. The *source* of that power is love – the ultimate balancer that drives life forward, in balance.

The huntsman in *Snow White* is notable in that the queen takes him to be a helper, but he ends up hindering her plan; and from Snow White's view, he starts off by being her enemy, but in releasing her into the woods, he spares her life, thereby acting in the capacity of a friend. What motivates him to act for good rather than evil if not love, and a sense of what is good, true, and will bring harmony and promote the Oneness-of-Being? At least to the extent he feels it's in his power to achieve. He still has to face the queen, who in no way shares his view. What does he do? He wonders how he can trick her – how he can deliberately get her to believe a lie. His story line follows a Trickster structure and is worth exploring in its own right.

While tricksters deliberately set out to trick someone, fools and simpletons rarely intend to trick anyone – and if they do, it usually backfires ... which generally results in comedy, which is what we'll be looking at in the next chapter.

NOTES

1   Robert Lawlor, *Sacred Geometry: Philosophy and Practice* (London: Thames & Hudson, 2002), 71.

2   Another version is discussed in chapter 11, on p. 167.

3   i.e., a crossing, a term central to Spencer-Brown's work.

4   In 1817, Keats, who was then 22 years old, described in a letter to his brothers what he thought 'went to form a Man of Achievement especially in Literature'. He called it 'Negative Capability, that is when a man is capable of being in uncertainties, Mysteries, doubts, without any irritable reaching after fact & reason. ... This, pursued through Volumes would perhaps take us no further than this, that with a great poet the sense of Beauty overcomes every other consideration, or rather obliterates all consideration.' John Keats, *Selected Letters*, edited by Robert Gittings (Oxford: Oxford World's Classics, 2002), 41–42. For a practical exploration of this with reference to the art of writing, see Philip Pullman, *Perverse, All Monstrous, All Prodigious Things* (Sheffield: National Association for the Teaching of English (NATE), 2002), 15–18.

5   See p. 81 – the expansion and contraction of steps.

9

COMEDY

... laughter is dependent on wonder
... wonder cannot be separated from laughter.

VINCENZO MAGGI, *On the Ridiculous*[1]

G iven that laughter is an instinctive act over which we have little or no natural control, why is it that some things make us laugh and others fail to? What is it that 'tricks' us into laughing when we experience something we consider funny?

Funnily enough, there's a subtle relationship between tricksters and comic characters which the application of Spencer-Brown's calculus to the analysis of story structure reveals. It turns out that both Trickster steps and Comic steps depend on cognitive dissonance,[2] which is why I've chosen to symbolise both steps in the same way ($\rightleftharpoons$).[3]

If we compare Trickster steps and Comic steps, we see that by definition, the Trickster step involves a deliberate intention to dupe, but the Comic step, by contrast, doesn't involve a deliberate intention to dupe; rather, something humorous that seems to catch one by surprise. It involves something that seems to be, but isn't.

Where an enemy appears to be a friend but is actually an enemy; or a friend appears to be an enemy but is actually a friend, call this the Trickster step.

Where an enemy's behaviour is like the behaviour of a friend; or a friend's behaviour is like the behaviour of an enemy, call this the Comic step.

The difference lies in whether we experience a form of cognitive dissonance based on something *being* its counterpart or *being like* its counterpart. The Trickster step depends on the apparent friend *being* an enemy, or vice versa – the cognitive dissonance involves the verb *to be*. It's based on metaphor, a pattern in thought where we link two unlike things, based on an underlying commonality, in the pattern '*a* is *b*'. Because the enemy-friend relationship is a diametrically ·oppositional relationship, it's more appropriate to think of it as an oxymoron or paradox (*a* is *not-a*). If we accept *not-a* as *a*, we're being duped, either by an external or an internal trickster. The cognitive dissonance that results in a Comic step depends on the apparent friend *appearing like* an enemy, or vice versa – it's based on simile, (*a* is like *b*); (*a* is as x as *b*) or even (*a* is like *not-a*). We don't laugh at metaphoric constructs; rather, we laugh when constructs are based on similes. The comic potential depends on expectation being unexpectedly defeated. It's like saying (*x* should be like *a*, but it's like *b*) or (*x* should be like *a*, but it's like *not-a*). 'But' is a key connective here.[4] The element of surprise can also be seen as a feature.[5] Along with the element of surprise, the presence of what one *perceives* as being humorous should be noted here.[6]

The link shows a deep connection between the fundamental patterns found in logic, rhetoric, poetry (in the sense of a poietic act) and – at a fundamental level – story. Spencer-Brown's minimal calculus on which this methodology is based is particularly well-suited to exploring these patterns.

Within the story of *Brer Rabbit and the Tar Baby*, the first Trickster step occurs when Brer Rabbit encounters the tar baby and is duped into thinking it's a real person. The Trickster step occurs as a result of Brer Fox's story line intersecting with Brer Rabbit's. Brer Fox knows the tar baby isn't a real baby – it's a trap. It has to be reasonably convincing for it to work as a trap. The tar baby itself has no intention of duping Brer Rabbit; Brer Rabbit has no intention of duping the tar baby.

Brer Rabbit acts towards the tar baby like a friend, but when he does so, he unwittingly acts against his own interests, leading to a series of interactions which land him in a very sticky spot.[7]

While the build-up to a climax helps intensify the drama, and builds suspense, the interaction between Brer Rabbit and the tar baby has comic potential because it's based on a series of Comic steps.

We know the tar baby isn't really a real person – it's designed to look like one. Brer Rabbit fails to see that, which makes us laugh. The laughs increase as Brer Rabbit's interactions with the seemingly neutral tar baby get more and more involved.

When Brer Fox catches Brer Rabbit, Brer Rabbit takes on a trickster role, saying, "Whatever you do, don't throw me in the briar patch!" There's a ($\rightleftharpoons \leftharpoonup \rightleftharpoons$) expansion at this point. The first ($\rightleftharpoons$) comes at the point where Brer Fox is duped by Brer Rabbit. Here, the enemy (Brer Rabbit) appears to be acting in Brer Fox's interests—as a friend would; but Brer Rabbit knows what he's doing. He intends to dupe Brer Fox, who is duped because he takes what Brer Rabbit says at face value. He sees the information as supporting his ends, not going against them. It's a Trickster step in both of their story lines. Where Brer Fox grabs Brer Rabbit ($\leftharpoonup$) and throws him into the briar patch ($\rightleftharpoons$), from our point of view, and from Brer Rabbit's, it's a Comic Transformational Twist; from Brer Fox's point of view, it's a a Transformational Twist with a tragic outcome. In all three cases, cognitive dissonance is involved.

> There are three differences between the Trickster step and the Comic step:
> 1. The presence or absence of an intention to dupe;
> 2. the absence or presence of an element of surprise; and
> 3. whether the basis is in metaphor or simile.

When Brer Fox believes Brer Rabbit, and ends up throwing him in the briar patch, the balancing Transformational Twist becomes a Comic step for us and for Brer Rabbit because the enemy's (Brer Fox's) behaviour not only ends up being like the behaviour of a friend, but he also unwittingly acts against his own interests and is surprised at the result. Rather than destroying Brer Rabbit, he unwittingly delivers him back home. Tragic for him; comic for us.

Previously, we looked at Trickster steps in the context of Trickster structures and touched briefly on the role of the dupe and simpleton in *The Washerman and His Ass*. In this chapter, I'd like to take a closer look at three stories which feature fools and simpletons. While each of these stories comes from a different culture, all of them have Comic steps.

The first is a story from England, called *Lazy Jack*. As Jack Zipes points out in his book, *Speaking Out: Storytelling and Creative Drama for Children*, the Jack character features in a number of stories. He developed gradually over time into the English version of Germany's Simple Hans (or Hansel); Italy's Pietro, Russia's Ivan as well as the character of Giufà from Sicily (Goha in the Middle East), not to mention Appalachian 'Jack Tales', featuring the English Jack's North American distant – or perhaps not too distant – relative in this extended family of wise and lucky fools.

The second is a story about a cuckold husband which is found in several versions from different cultures.[8] These include one collected by the Brothers Grimm, one from India, and another which appears in *The Arabian Nights* (which is the one we'll be looking at below).

The third is a story about Goha (whom we've already met in the guise of Nasr-el-Din Hodja)[9] which appears throughout the Middle East.

First, a narrative version of *Lazy Jack*:[10]

Analysis of Jack's story line in a narrative version of *Lazy Jack*

Steps	Symbols	Outline of content
1	⊐	Once upon a time ...
2	⊐	... Jack lived on a farm with his mother.
3	⟵	Jack's mother was fed up with his laziness and told him to get a job.
4	⟶	Jack went off to get a job the next day.
5	⟵	He met a farmer ...
6	⇌	... who gave him a day's work and paid him with [a shiny coin which he wasted].
7	⟵	When he told his mother what had happened ...
8	⇌	... she gave him some advice, telling him to [put it in his pocket next time].

Analysis of Jack's story line in a narrative version of *Lazy Jack*

Steps	Symbols	Outline of content
	(← ⇌)	Steps 3–8 repeat with milk, cheese, cat, meat. Jack wasted each of these goods, his mother having given him a different piece of advice each time. After he'd wasted the meat and she'd told him he should have carried it over his shoulder ...
9	←	... she sent him off to get a new job.
10	⇀	He went off the next day ...
11	←	... and met a cattle farmer ...
12	⇌	... who employed him and paid him with a donkey, which he carried back over his shoulder.
13	←	Passing through town, he was seen by a supposedly deaf and dumb girl ...
14	⇌	... who burst out laughing at the sight and started to speak.
15	⌐	They ended up married ...
16	⊐	... and lived happily together with Jack's mother from there on.

Taking steps 9–14 as being, in essence, a repeat of steps 3–8, the structure revealed is a Trickster structure:

$$\square\ \urcorner\ \leftharpoondown\ \rightharpoonup\ \leftharpoondown\ \rightleftharpoons\ \leftharpoondown\ \rightleftharpoons\ \urcorner\ \square$$

We'll find both Conflicting Quests and Transformational Twists in the story. Looking at the Conflicting Quests first, Jack's mother is on a desperate quest to give Jack the advice he needs to be self-supporting and independent, but her advice consistently fails to meet the mark; Jack's quest is that he wants to be an obedient son and follow his mother's advice, but whenever he follows her advice, he consistently ends up getting things wrong. Moreover, all the people who pay Jack are trying to support him, but Jack's desire to follow his mother's advice always conflicts with the nature of the goods he's given.

While the structure has all the hallmarks of a Trickster structure, the difference lies in all the characters' *intentions* with respect to their actions. This is what makes us see the (⇌) steps as Comic steps rather than Trickster steps. Jack's mother doesn't intend to give him bad advice. Jack's employers don't intend to cheat him. Jack's intention isn't to waste the goods he has received, nor is to make anyone laugh ... all arguably features which give the story its comic potential.[11]

The Transformational Twists in the story emerge from the way in which the Comic steps balance each other out. Jack consistently wastes the goods he has received as payment for his work (steps 6 and 11) either by following his instincts, or his mother's advice. The final Transformational Twist is a Comic step which restores order (step 13). Jack, still following his mother's advice, although it goes against common sense, unintentionally cures an illness the doctors were unable to cure, gains a wife, and he and his mother go up in the world as a result. The pairs of Comic steps all share (a) the absence of an intention to dupe; (b) the presence of an element of surprise; and (c) a basis in simile, rather than in metaphor.

The second example of a story which contains Comic steps also provides us with an opportunity to take a more detailed look at other aspects of analysis, including implied steps and more complex nested story lines, each of which is always linked to a particular character. The story, which contains both nested Trickster and Quest structures, can be analysed as follows:

Analysis of *The Woman who Humoured her Lover at Her Husband's Expense* from *The Arabian Nights*[12]

Steps	Symbols	Outline of content	Lover	Wife	Husband	Guest	Guests
1	⎕	Once upon a time ...	⎕	⎕	⎕	⎕	⎕
2	⌐	... a merchant, his wife (and unbeknownst to him, her lover) lived in Cairo.	⌐	⌐	⌐	⌐	⌐

Analysis of *The Woman who Humoured her Lover at Her Husband's Expense* from *The Arabian Nights*[12]

Steps	Symbols	Outline of content	Lover	Wife	Husband	Guest	Guests
3	↼	The lover saw two fat geese when he visited the house and coveted them.	↼				
4	⇀	He asked the merchant's wife to cook them for him.	⇀				
5	↼	To do so, the merchant's wife needed to create a ruse to fool her husband …	↼	(↼	(↼		
6	⇀	… so she hatched a plan to make it happen.[13]	⇀	⇀)	⇀) *implied*		
7	↼	When her husband came home …		↼	↼		
8	⇌	… she said she wanted to cook the geese for his friends, and asked him to get some food from the market the next day.		⇌	⇌		
9	↼	He returned with the food.		↼	↼		

Analysis of *The Woman who Humoured her Lover at Her Husband's Expense* from *The Arabian Nights*[12]

Steps	Symbols	Outline of content	Lover	Wife	Husband	Guest	Guests
10	⇌	Having no guests to share the meal with, the merchant's wife told her husband to go to work and bring a friend back for lunch.		⇌	⇌	*(← →) meeting and agree-ment implied*	
11	←	The lover arrived ...	←				
12	→	... and left with the geese.	→				
13	←	The merchant arrived with a friend, as requested ...		←	←		
14	⇌	... but was told one wasn't enough.		⇌	⇌		*(← →) implied*
15	←	This left the guest alone with the wife ...		←		←	
16		... who told him that her husband wanted to castrate him ...		⇌		⇌	
17		... making him run off just as the husband returned with more guests ...		←	←	←	←
18		... to be told the first guest had stolen the geese ...		⇌	⇌		⇌

Analysis of *The Woman who Humoured her Lover at Her Husband's Expense* from *The Arabian Nights*[12]

Steps	Symbols	Outline of content	Lover	Wife	Husband	Guest	Guests
19		... making the husband run off after the first guest ...			↜		
20	⇌	... to get at least one goose back, while that guest thought the merchant wanted one of his balls.			⇌	⇌	
21	⌐	The first guest left town, and the couple and their remaining guests ended up having a simple meal together.	⌐	(↜ ⇌) implied ⌐	⌐	⌐	(↜ ⇌) implied ⌐
22	⊐	As for what happened to the lover and the geese ... well, that's "another story for another time."	⊐	⊐	⊐	⊐	⊐

Each character's story line follows its own sequence of story structures.

The opening, set-up, final condition, and closing (steps 1, 2, 21, 22) apply to all characters' story lines. Within the frame, the lover's story line follows a standard Quest structure (steps 3, 4, 5, 6, 11, 12 in the analysis above). He wants to dine on goose. The wife acts in the role of his friend/helper and the husband in the role of the enemy/hindrance (which the wife deals with). Thus, steps 5 and 6 of the lover's story line—which cover the need to overcome the challenge of the husband not finding out about the wife's plan—

launch the wife's story. Before that, she doesn't have a problem. The pre-existing cuckolding situation, which adds to the comedy as it continues through the story, and persists beyond its conclusion, adds a frisson of tension to the unfolding of the story, but within this story, it's unproblematic.

The wife's story line involves three nested iterations of the Trickster structure. The nested iterations provide cumulative solutions to her problem of needing to create a story with enough credibility to cover up the fact that she'd given the geese she was supposed to be serving up to her husband's guests to her lover instead. Thus, steps 5 and 6, which serve to outline the problem in her story line are shared amongst all three Trickster structures.

The first of the Trickster structures in the wife's story line (consisting of steps 5, 6; 7, 8; 9, 10) involves setting up a dinner party as a ruse. The second of the Trickster structures in the wife's story line (consisting of steps 5, 6; 13, 14; 15, 16) involves duping the guest to think of the husband as his enemy. The final Trickster structure in the wife's story line (consisting of steps 5, 6; 17, 18; [21a, 21b, shown as - = below][14]) involves duping her husband to think of their guest as his enemy.

The husband appears as helper and dupe to his wife. His story line mirrors his wife's. The comedy lies in the false assumptions and beliefs that the husband and the first guest have about each other. There's a pair of implied ($\leftarrow$ $\rightarrow$) steps (shown as - - below) that act as initial steps in his story line just as steps 5 and 6 do in the wife's story line.

The guest's story line involves a structure in which the first pair of steps (where he meets the merchant in the market, gets invited to dinner and travels back with him) are implied (10a, 10b, shown as - - below). These are followed by a Trickster step (16), an implied nested Quest involving his nimble feet and escape route as his friends/helpers, and a Transformational Twist which manifests as a Comic step (20) to do with the need to escape from the husband, who should really be behaving better towards him but is behaving towards him like an enemy who's after his balls. The fact that neither one intends to harm the other, but neither of them realises it, is what gives this step its comic potential.

The guests' story line involves a Trickster structure with the first and last pairs implied. The first pair (14a, 14b, shown as - - below) being where they meet the merchant in the market, get invited to dinner and travel back with him. In step 18, they become the dupes for the wife's ruse meal, with their expectation of a positive outcome playing right into her hand.

Analysis of *The Woman who Humoured her Lover at her Husband's Expense* (Symbols Only)

Characters	Steps																					
	1	2	3	4	5	6	7	8	9	10	11	12	13	14	15	16	17	18	19	20	21	22
Lover	□	⌐	←	→	←	→					←	→									⌐	□
Wife	□	⌐			←	→	←	⇌	←	⇌			←	⇌	←	⇌	←	⇌			⌐̿	□
Husband	□	⌐			-	-	←	⇌	←	⇌			←	⇌			←	⇌	←	⇌	⌐̿	□
Guest	□								⌐₋₋								←	⇌	←	⇌	⌐	□
Guests	□									⌐₋₋					←	⇌					⌐̿	□

The main Conflicting Quests that run through the story are to do with the wife and her lover conspiring against her husband, which gives the conflict between the husband and the first guest its comic potential. The Transformational Twists are mainly based around the ruse meal – and the defeated expectation that runs through the meal the characters actually have in the story, implied in steps 21a, 21b, shown as (- =) above. They're too polite to show their disappointment. We never do find out what happened to the lover or the geese. Perhaps a Transformation structure story lies hidden in there that's yet to be told … either way, it's "another story … for another time."

The third story I'd like to present here is one of the many stories of Goha and his donkey included in George Borrow's collection of Goha stories from Turkey, where he's known as Cogia [Hadji, the title given to a person who has completed the pilgrimage to Mecca known as the Hadj] Nasr Eddin Efendi [Esquire]:

Analysis of Goha's story line in a narrative version of *When Goha Lost His Donkey* [15]

Steps	Symbols	Outline of content
1	⊐	Once upon a time ...
2	⌐	... Goha ...
3	↼	... lost his donkey ...
4	⇀	... so he went to look for it.
5	↼	Meeting a man on the way, Goha asked the man whether he'd seen it.
6	⇌	"I've seen the donkey officiating as a judge," came the reply.
7	↼	Goha processed the response ...
8	⇌	... and answered, "I knew he'd be a Cadi ... when I taught him philosophy, I noticed his ears weren't sewed up."
9	⌐	[The story is left unresolved.]
10	⊐	[The story is left open-ended.] [16]

The structure is a clear Trickster structure, but are the (⇌) steps Trickster steps and Transformational Twists, or are they Comic steps? The subtle difference opens up an aspect of analysis which will be examined in chapter 11, where the relationship between rhetoric and story is explored in more detail. For now, let's look at how the story unfolds.

The story clearly contains Conflicting Quests. Goha is trying to find his donkey. The man Goha meets isn't trying to help him, although he does try to cheer him up by cracking a joke – a Conflicting Quest. Rather than take this in the spirit in which it's meant (as a pun on the stupidity of judges), Goha takes it literally and responds with his own joke – again, in a Conflicting Quest. But is there an intent to dupe? It's not clear.

Goha's response can be seen as a Transformational Twist which balances out his friend's remark, but the Transformational Twist manifests on two levels ... the open-ended, unresolved quality of the ending either leaves us laughing at the way in which the man's humour and Goha's form a kind of unintentional double-crossing that's tricksterish, but funny ... or it leaves us wondering about what the story was about ...

We'll be looking at what happens when stories are left open-ended in terms of structure later; for now, let's look at what might make these steps Comic steps, rather than Trickster steps. After all, both characters – the man and Goha – have something of the trickster about them ... at least, while there could be some doubt about Goha's motivation, the man can be seen as dissembling. But then again, this isn't the only way his actions can be seen. After all, there's something funny about it. So, if the man's intention is to dupe Goha, why might this be a Comic step, rather than a Trickster step?

What seems to give the man's response comic potential is that (a) he appears to be a friend. One would expect a friend to help Goha find his donkey, and he does tell Goha he has seen it. One can just imagine Goha getting excited, getting his hopes up ... and then the man behaves as an enemy would ... and (b) makes a link between the appearance and/or behaviour of a judge and the appearance and/or behaviour of Goha's donkey. It's an intentional step, but the man isn't Goha's enemy; he just chooses to behave that way towards him. The relationship isn't framed as a metaphorical construction (the man's behaviour *is* the behaviour of an enemy); it's based on a simile (the man's behaviour is *like* the behaviour of an enemy), which makes it a Comic step – if we see it that way.

Goha's response is ambiguous. It could be seen as him taking a joke to be literal (what is not true *is* true to him), but it could also be seen in another way. If Goha takes the man's remark as a joke (what isn't true *seems* true to him), then it has comic potential. When Goha builds on the idea and responds with another simile-based construct, he brings in a Transformational Twist: the stereotypically stupid donkey is seen as having the potential to learn philosophy, dissolving the distinction between animal and human, while pointing out not only Goha's belief in the donkey's ability to take in philosophy, but also his related belief that the donkey's behaviour would be *like* the behaviour of an ideal judge and *un*like the stereotypical ass-like behaviour of an inadequate judge. These are the main things which provide the potential for humour here, making this a Comic step. But there's a sense that there's more to this than meets the ear. There's a niggling ambiguity that demands to be resolved.

The ambiguity is something we'll come back to in chapter 12. For now, I'd like to take a closer look at the ambiguity inherent in the relationship between (a) metaphor and simile, and (b) Trickster steps and Comic steps.

'That man is a snake' outlines a relationship based on metaphor. I fail to see anything funny in it.

It involves a 'category mistake' (object A (a man) is object B (a snake)). The word 'category' relates to Aristotle's 10 Categories of Being: 10 embodied categories of thinking through which we make sense of things:

Aristotle's 10 Categories of Being

Nos.	Category	Explanation
1	Substance	The essence of what a thing is: the essence of a bottle, or an orange, for example (animal, vegetable, mineral; living, non-living, abstract).
2	Quality	Attributes that you can't separate from it: colour, shape, sweetness, ripeness, etc.
3	Quantity	Anything you can measure about it: its number, its height, its weight, its circumference, its age.
4	Relationship	What it connects to: its family, its maker, its country of origin, its owner or user, for instance.
5	Where	Where it is – right here, for example.
6	When	Anything related to time – right now, for instance.
7	Being-in-a-position	Is it upright? Lying down? Tilted?
8	Having	What does it have that can be removed from it without it losing any of its essential qualities? The label, clothing, wrapping.
9	Active	What does it do (with inanimate objects, this only applies to the effects they have).
10	Passive	What does it feel, or what is being done to it (with inanimate objects, only the latter applies).

We've established that 'that man is a snake' is a metaphor, so now, let's look at another example drawn from a US-based web page …

A man in a movie theater notices what looks like a snake sitting next to him.

"Are you a snake?" asked the man, surprised.

"Yes."

"What are you doing at the movies?"

The snake replied, "Well, I liked the book."[17]

The joke seems to be based on several category mistakes, all of which seem to hinge on a core simile: this snake's behaviour is *like* that of a man.

That arguably has the potential to make us laugh, while the metaphorical construction doesn't.

But some jokes are based on metaphors ...

Pa asks son how he's getting on with his new maths teacher.

Son replies, "Great, dad. I think she really likes me. She keeps putting little kisses next to all my maths sums."[18]

But what is it that makes us laugh? Is it the metaphor (crosses are kisses)? Or is it the simile (the teacher's placement of crosses next to the maths sums is like a lover's placement of kisses at the end of a love letter)?

I suspect it's the latter.

If your child came home from school and said, "Look! My teacher put little kisses next to all my answers in my maths test!" what would your first reaction be?

I think it would be fair to say that our reactions would be based on how we interpret the relationship between the terms in the context: Metaphor: These crosses are kisses (not funny); Simile: These crosses are like kisses (funny); Oxymoron: These marks of disfavour are marks of favour (bittersweet, the stuff of dark comedy, or psychological imbalance).

While Comic steps are linked to Trickster steps, comic potential, at a fundamental level, is based on a category mistake in the form of a simile linked to a should(n't) be, 'but' is(n't) formula. These types of category mistakes can theoretically be found in any of the 18 story structures identified in this book.[19]

Comedy is structure neutral.

We have little or no control over our laughter, but it clearly has a purpose. It teaches us the importance of seeing things as they are – and making us aware that they're not as they should be.

This chapter opened with a quote by Vincenzo Maggi (1498–1564), who saw a link between laughter and wonder.[20] No wonder we laugh! Laughter invites us to wonder … about how things should or could be. Once we're aware of the underlying dissonance, to resolve the problems that arise in our awareness inevitably involves us going on a quest. There's much that we can learn from doing so.

Laughter is just one reaction we have little or no control over. Another is crying. To what extent does crying relate to the same generative instinct as laughter does? To what extent might we also be able to associate crying with patterns of ideas? What might these patterns be? And how does tragedy differ from other types of story structures? These are the questions we'll be exploring in the next chapter.

NOTES

1 Quoted in Andrew Calder, *Molière: The Theory and Practice of Comedy* (Atlantic Highlands, NJ: Athlone Press, 1996), 19.

2 The kinds of cognitive dissonances which Trickster steps and Comic steps arise from differ from the kind of cognitive dissonance associated with the openings and closings of stories, which takes us into and back out of the world of story.

3 When I was devising the methodology outlined in this book, I did wonder about using (⇌), overlaid with T or C, or some such sign to mark distinctions between Trickster steps and Comic steps, but ended up discarding the idea on the grounds of its irrelevance with regard to story.

4 'Is', 'as', 'like', and 'but' are syncategorematic words–words which don't fit into Aristotle's 10 Categories of Being which are outlined later on in this chapter. Medieval scholastics such as Peter of Spain rightly saw syncategorematic words as revealing something rather magical about the patterns of thought we naturally have embodied within us. For more on categorematic and syncategorematic words, see Peter of Spain, *Syncategoreumata*, translated by Joke Spruyt (Leiden: E. J. Brill, 1992)); Leon Conrad and Aristel Skrbic, "TEDx Talk: The Magic of Words," filmed 3 December, 2013 in London, YouTube: HYit3MYAoqM.

5 The surprise is at the initial encounter. However, one arguably laughs at a familiar joke or clip one hears again or rewatches because the experience triggers the memory of the initial surprise. According to the innovative British physical theatre practitioner, Desmond Jones, this is particularly applicable to physical comedy gags.

6 Compare this with the Trickster Awe Step which is discussed in detail in chapter 12.

7 In Joel Chandler Harris's version (D. L. Ashliman, "The Tar-Baby," *Folklore and Mythology Electronic Texts*, 2014–2018, https://www.pitt.edu/~dash/type0175.html, story 1), the part of Brer Rabbit's story line which covers his interaction with the tar baby follows two nested comic iterations of a Call and Response 1 structure (with an initial Transformation structure). The first is where Brer Rabbit finds the tar baby rude and the second where he first finds himself stuck to the tar baby.

8 Aarne-Thompson-Uther type 1741.

9 In the story of *Nasr-el-Din Hodja and the Walnut Tree*, in chapter 6.

10 This is a story classified under Aarne-Thompson-Uther type 1696:

D. L. Ashliman, "What Should I Have Said (or Done)?" *Folklore and Mythology Electronic Texts*, 2000–2010, https://www.pitt.edu/~dash/ type1696.html#england, story 6; see also Norma J. Livo, *Tales to Tickle Your Funny Bone: Humorous Tales from Around the World* (Westport, CT: Libraries Unlimited, 2007), 3–5.

11   The girl's story line follows a Trickster Variation structure, outlined in chapter 12.

12   This narrative version is based on *The Arabian Nights Entertainments*, edited by Andrew Lang (London, New York and Bombay: Longmans, Green & Co., 1898), 397–400, and D. L. Ashliman, "Trickster Wives and Maids," *Folklore and Mythology Electronic Texts*, 1999–2013, https://www.pitt. edu/~dash/type1741.html, which is essentially the same, but modernised.

13   A nested Quest structure is implied here.

14   The – and = symbols are simply used here to overcome restrictions of space. In the previous table, they're shown with Spencer-Brown's symbols presented in brackets, for ease of visualisation; the brackets aren't essential. They're optional. At the level of narrative, the steps aren't included. As Jewish story spinner, Drut'syla Shonaleigh Cumbers notes, 'As a storyteller, you don't have to tell everything you know, but you do have to know everything you tell.'

15   Nasreddin Hoca, *The Turkish Jester, or the Pleasantries of Cogia Nasr Eddin Effendi*, translated by George Borrow (Ipswich: W. Webber, 1884), 275–276; Project Gutenberg, 2005, http://www.gutenberg.org/ files/16244/16244-h/16244-h.htm.

16   The open-ended nature of this story is addressed in chapter 14 in the context of the discussion of the Dilemma structure. It also features in chapter 12 in the context of the discussion with regards to a particular aspect of the Trickster Variation step.

17   Source: *Snake Jokes*, 2018, http://jokes4us.com/animaljokes/snakejokes. html.

18   Based on a version in Gyles Brandreth, *1000 Jokes: The Greatest Joke Book Ever Known* (London: Carousel, 1980).

19   There are 18 story structures defined, excluding Comedy and Tragedy. Comedy can turn tragedy into tragic-comedy, and Tragedy turn comedy into dark comedy; the point here is that both Comedy and Tragedy are structure neutral.

20   Vincenzo Maggi was one of a group of Italian scholars of the Renaissance who ran something of a fan club for Aristotle through their work at the

University of Padua (Daniel Javitch, "The Assimilation of Aristotle's Poetics in Sixteenth-Century Italy," in *The Cambridge History of Literary Criticism, Vol. 3, The Renaissance*, edited by Glyn P. Norton, 53–65 (Cambridge: Cambridge University Press, 2006), https://doi.org/10.1017/CHOL9780521300087.006, at 55) and through the *Accademia degli Infiammati* [*The Academy of the Burning Ones*] (Richard S. Samuels, "Benedetto Varchi, the Accademia degli Infiammati and the Origins of the Italian Academic Movement," *Renaissance Quarterly* 29, no. 4 (Winter 1976): 599–634, https://doi.org/10.2307/2860034, at 605). Members of the group popularised works by Aristotle and other classic authors by lecturing on them and translating them into the vernacular (Nicholas Cronk, "Aristotle, Horace, and Longinus: The Conception of Reader Response," in *The Cambridge History of Literary Criticism. Vol. 3, The Renaissance*, edited by Glyn P. Norton, 199–204 (Cambridge: Cambridge University Press, 2006) at 201), (Javitch, "Assimilation", 55–56), (Samuels, "Varchi," 608). The Accademia was a serious affair, and it seems that the members took themselves so seriously they invoked mockery and satire, with a new Academy, the *Accademia degli Umidi* [*The Academy of the Humid Ones*] being set up as a parody by a curious eccentric, Giovanni Mazzuoli, in his home. Mazzuoli was known for walking around with skull pendants round his neck, carrying a variety of notebooks. It was the 'wet' academy and not the 'dry' one which evolved into the famous Florentine Academy, which flourished under the patronage of the Medici (Massimiliano Albanese, "MAZZUOLI, Giovanni, detto lo Stradino," in *Dizionario Biografico degli Italiani* (Rome: Istituto della Enciclopedia Italiana, 2008), http://www.treccani.it/enciclopedia/mazzuoli-giovanni-detto-lo-stradino_(Dizionario-Biografico)/).

10

TRAGEDY: THE SPACE WITHIN

*We stand with Oedipus and Hamlet and Lear and confront
the truth and the meaning of life.*

MORTIMER ADLER, *The Meaning of Tragedy*[1]

What makes tragedy tragic?
Mortimer Adler has two views of tragedy, one narrow; one broad. The narrow view focuses on a particular quality of events that take place on the stage—or in films or novels; the broad view focuses on a particular quality of human existence that applies in actual life.[2] The first results in tragic stories. The second results in tragedy. Either way, when tension is resolved, then 'ruin results'.[3] The difference is to do with who the protagonist is. Both types of tragedy, according to Mortimer Adler, involve 'a quality' of events, or of human existence – but what does he mean by this? What creates the potential for tragic stories? What creates the potential for tragedy in life?

Let's explore tragic stories first.

**Tragic stories typically start with a problem the protagonist
has created *unwittingly* that they want to prevent but cannot.**

This is a form of paradoxical category mistake.

Tragedy (as a form), like Comedy, is structure neutral.

Even though I have defined tragedy as structure neutral, tragedy can still be closely linked to a specific story structure. While Comedy involves Comic steps – which are related to Trickster steps and the Trickster structure, Tragedy is most closely related to the Transformation structure. There's a clear link between the transgression against the natural order that initiates a Transformation structure story and the paradoxical category mistake that gives something its tragic quality.

Take, for example, the story of Oedipus—the king who unwittingly kills his father, marries his mother, ends up blinding himself and submits to exile (in Sophocles' version). Where does the story start?

Oedipus' story starts—according to some—when he went to consult the Delphic oracle and was told that it was his destiny to kill his father and marry his mother. He wanted to prevent the tragedy, but failed to stop it from happening. He tried to go as far away as possible from the couple he considered to be his parents, not knowing that he wasn't their biological child and ended up doing exactly what the oracle prophesized he would do.

This state of affairs only came into being—according to others—because his father, Laius, committed a similar *unwitting* act. Laius was the great-grandson of Cadmus, one of the legendary founders of Thebes. Laius was due to rule over Thebes when he came of age, but when Amphion and Zethus captured the city, Laius' supporters, hoping that Laius would be able to return to rule over Thebes, smuggled him out of Thebes to keep him safe.[4] Laius was offered shelter by Pelops, king of Pisa. How did Laius thank Pelops for his hospitality? By abducting Pelops' son, Chrysippus, and raping him. Laius later married Jocasta and was told by the Delphic oracle not to have a child with her. "If you do," the oracle said, "your child will kill you and marry his mother." Laius tried to be good. He really did. But one night, he got drunk, let down his guard, Jocasta's dress, and his principles, and *unwittingly* broke the interdict. However much he wanted to stop the tragedy occurring, he couldn't. Nine months later, Oedipus was born, and *his* tragedy started to unfold.

Both Laius and Oedipus transgress against the natural order. In both cases, an oracle prophesizes a tragic destiny. When we attempt to cheat fate, problems arise. That's never a good idea. Bargain? Perhaps. Embrace? Even better. 'Feel the fear and do it anyway?' That could well be a way to get around it. But to do any of these things, we have to face facts – we have to look them in the face, and the essence of tragedy is the *unwitting* relationship protagonists have towards some aspect of their situation. Eventually, balance in the natural order is restored, but usually, boundaries have been crossed, and things can never ever go back to the way they were. There's clearly a Transformation structure at work here, but there's also something else going on.

If the protagonists in a story *knowingly* transgress, a Transformation structure story is likely to unfold.

In Ovid's version of the story of Medusa and Poseidon, which he has Perseus tell, the gods are fully aware of what is going on:

> "[Medusa] was once most beautiful, and the jealous aspiration of many suitors. Of all her beauties none was more admired than her hair: I came across a man who recalled having seen her. They say that Neptune, lord of the seas, violated her in the temple of Minerva. Jupiter's daughter turned away, and hid her chaste eyes behind her aegis. So that it might not go unpunished, she changed the Gorgon's hair to foul snakes. And now, to terrify her enemies, numbing them with fear, the goddess wears the snakes, that she created, as a breastplate."[5]

The story clearly follows a Transformation structure. Neptune transgresses against the natural order. Minerva, out for revenge, transforms Medusa's extreme beauty into extreme ugliness. Moreover, in his collection of myths and legends, Apollodorus states the following:

> It is affirmed by some that Medousa (Medusa) was beheaded because of Athene (Athena), for they say the Gorgon had been willing to be compared with Athene in beauty.[6]

In these versions of the story, Minerva punishes either Neptune or Medusa for their transgressions. When you realise what she has done, what's your response? Do you want to cry? You might think the punishment excessive, but do you think it's tragic? Don't you think the punishment is well-deserved? After all, Neptune did *knowingly* invite Medusa back to Minerva's temple, where he violated her – an act of *knowing* defilement. And Medusa *knowingly* pitted her mortal beauty against the divine beauty of a goddess.

But consider this … the night is dark. Medusa is lost. She doesn't know where she's going. She and Poseidon find a warm safe place to make love in. They both long to be with each other … After a night, she wakes up, stretches, smiles at the warm, comforting feeling that comes from being loved by a god whom she loves back, looks about … and finds … they're in Athena's temple, having *unwittingly* made love in front of her statue! Then … might one think Medusa's punishment tragic? At least more so than in the original scenario? There's clearly a link to the Transformation structure here, but how strong a link is it? Do all tragedies fit the Transformation structure?

It would seem that the difference between a Transformation structure story and a tragic story is whether an action has taken place wittingly or unwittingly, which is why I propose the following:

Tragedy is based on a paradoxical category mistake.

Earlier on, I proposed that Tragedy, like Comedy, is structure neutral. If so, it should be possible to write a tragedy using any structure – so, to test out the theory, I decided to see if I could create three original tragic stories, each based on one of the structures we have explored in previous chapters (Quest, Rags to Riches, Death and Rebirth). These are the stories I came up with …

Paul's Journey: A tragic Quest story

'I'm not feeling too good today, but it's not worth trying to see a doctor – they're not going to be able to help. I'll deal with it myself. God! What have I done to deserve this? The pain – Oh! F***! Breathe. Just breathe. That's it – in, out, in … take it easy … pause … slowly out … and … it's OK. I'll get through this. I can do it … I *think* … Oh! Why am I doing this to myself? Come on, I can get out of this. I just need to lie down ... find a comfortable position. Why the f*** can't I ... What the f*** ...??? Why can't I find a f***ing comfortable position? I need something to hold – the bed post – no, something softer – the pillow – no, something firmer ...'

He reached under the pillow for the revolver he kept there.

'That's it. Just right ... cold, fitting – at last ... something that feels good to hold ...'

The cold metal against his teeth sent a fresh wave of pain through him.

'Just grip hard ...,' he thought.

His finger curled around the trigger, and squeezed. The pain shattered past his skull, mingling with the blood that dripped down from the bullet hole in the wall behind his lifeless body and in that moment, the opportunity for his life to continue without pain was irrevocably lost. The headlines in the paper that morning were that a local pharmaceutical company had found a simple cure for the extreme migraines that Paul had been suffering from for years.

Analysis of *Paul's Journey*: A tragic Quest story

Steps	Symbols	Structure	Paul's story line
1	⊓	Opening	[Implied]
2	⌐	Initial situation	Paul, not knowing there's now a cure for his extreme migraines, ...
3	⟵	Problem	... is battling with intense pain.
4	⟶	Journey	To try to ease the pain, he decides to lie down.
5	⟵	Meeting with ...	He moves to the bed ...
6	⟶	... friend/ helper (tragic)	... but lying down fails to solve the problem. He finds it hard to get into a comfortable position. He looks for something to grip tightly, as that sometimes helps squeeze the pain away. He finds the bed post too firm and unyielding (loop back to 2) and the pillow too soft (loop back to 2), but the revolver (implied) under the pillow feels just right. The trigger has just the right combination of firmness and flexibility.

Analysis of *Paul's Journey*: A tragic Quest story

Steps	Symbols	Structure	Paul's story line
7	←	Meeting with ...	[Implied] He puts the gun to his head ...
8	→	... enemy/ hindrance (tragic)	... [implied] and puts an end to his pain.
9	⌐	Final situation (outcome/ resolution)	Both Paul's pain and his life escape through the bullet hole he puts in his head ...
10	⊐	Closing (tragic)	... and, in his doing so, the opportunity for his life to continue without pain becomes irrevocably lost.

The Billionaire's Way Out: A tragic Rags to Riches story

'She deletes my texts, won't answer my phone calls. The letters I sent her – handwritten, and cards ... she's sent them all back. What can I do? It's finally got to me.'

You wouldn't have thought it would have. Mark Gates had so much going for him – he was a self-made man, from a poor background, who'd made good – an ideal catch – money, flash car ... he'd even got his own yacht. People who knew of him thought he had it made ... but people who knew him knew that the one thing he didn't have was happiness. Max, his bohemian friend, suggested he try yoga. Mark's secretary found him a guy who charged $300 a session – he didn't get much out of it. He tried breathing, and tantric sex – he felt better for a while, but the chicks who came on to him weren't into it; and although the sex was amazing, nothing really lasted with the tarts – and then one day he met Alice.

With Alice, Mark felt truly happy - for the first time in ages.

They spent six weeks together. Those six weeks were the best weeks of his life. He fêted her like a princess. He worshipped her like a goddess. But for some reason, he just didn't know how to bond with her as a person. She felt like a trophy. He tried to connect – it was as if she was on a different wavelength. She was pure, she was perfect. They got on well enough at first, but he felt unworthy of her. He'd book a table at a 5-star restaurant. He was planning to propose, to give her an allowance, to set her up for life; she was planning to tell him she thought it was time they broke up. She admired him. She didn't love him. She left before the second course. '… no, absolutely nothing wrong with the food … and the pairings were exquisite,' he said, reflecting on the irony as he paid, then left in her wake.

He tried to get her back. He really wanted to make it work. He sent her flowers every day – it didn't work; He wrote letters – they got sent back. He didn't know what to do.

Max suggested he see an astrologer, so he thought, 'Why not? I'll give it a try.' They arranged to meet for a debrief afterwards.

"$500 for a consultation, only to get a charlatan tell me that things might get better at the next solar eclipse? Yeah right!"

Max's girlfriend offered to give him a tarot reading – no luck there; business deals just didn't do it for him any more. He couldn't stop thinking about Alice. He wondered whether he'd ever be happy again.

'Perhaps the Alpha Course that happens in the church across the road from the office on Monday nights … the people coming out of there look really happy …?'

Well, he tried … maybe he had a bad experience, but it turned out that religion wasn't for him – not in that form. He couldn't stand the mass hysteria trading empty dreams.

'Drugs and alcohol are boring and they leave you worse off than when you started; I can't stand my job – I'd rather quit and sit in my bed until I die – I can't try any more – I have no interest in food, or drink – TV's boring – the Internet's full of rubbish – there's nothing left – nothing – well, there's suicide – but that isn't nothing – that's something … it leads to nothing, though … it leads to nothing …'

'After all,' he decided, sitting in his Ferrari, an empty pill canister on the passenger seat beside him, having decided to end it all, 'nothing's got to be better than a life without happiness, don't you think, Alice …?'

There was no answer, no heartbeat, just silence.

Analysis of *The Billionaire's Way Out*: A tragic Rags to Riches story

Steps	Symbols	Structure	The Billionaire's story line
1	⊓	Opening	[Implied]
2	⌐	Initial situation	A young man from a poor background …
3	→	Positive condition	… decides to leave home and become rich and succeeds.
4	←	Problem (that usually 'comes out of the blue') resulting in a state of **subversion**	Despite his success, he's never really happy.
5	→	Journey	He tries yoga, breathing, tantric sex …
6	←	Journey thwarted, meeting with …	… but nothing really works.
7	→	… friend/helper (positive transformation often achieved by means of an external, often supernatural force)	*By means of an external force* (Alice, whom he sees as an idealised, unattainable, perfect, Beatrice-like character) he finds happiness …
8	←	Reversion to previous state <u>in an altered state of consciousness</u> *Nested Quest structure involving Saviour character[7] starts:* Problem	… but it fails to last and he reverts to his previous state <u>in an altered state of consciousness</u>.
9	→	Journey	As a result, he sets out on a quest to try to regain the happiness he's lost.
10	←	Meeting with …	He tries astrology, tarot readings, religion.
11	→	… friend/helper (tragic)	Nothing works.

Analysis of *The Billionaire's Way Out*: A tragic Rags to Riches story

Steps	Symbols	Structure	The Billionaire's story line
12	←	Meeting with ...	He finds no purpose in life and decides to give up. He gives up going in to work. He finds nothing meaningful. He contemplates nothingness as a way out ...
13	→	... enemy/hindrance (tragic) *Nested Quest structure involving Saviour character ends*	... commits suicide ... finally putting an end to his unhappiness ... 'after all ... anything is better than a life without happiness, don't you think, Alice ...?'
14	⌐	Final situation (outcome/resolution)	There was no answer, no heartbeat, just silence.
15	⌷	Closing (tragic)	[Implied]

The Day the Lights Went Out: A tragic Death and Rebirth story

It's ten past two on Friday afternoon and the light breeze that has danced in through the open window of the third-floor apartment on the corner of North 2nd and Fairburn Streets has brought the scent of berries and roses – the incense that rises from the earth as part of the celebration of the high mass of summer – into Jean's bedroom.

Jean, an ample woman in her early forties with dimples in her pale cheeks, high arched eyebrows browner than her naturally wavy blonde hair, deep soul-revealing blue eyes and a hesitant smile, is on the phone to her boss at the homeless shelter. Jean has been off work with depression. It's been a while since she's been able to think positively about anything, let alone about going to work, and they're catching up with where she is. "Yeah – actually, I'm feeling a *lot* better. The doctor gave me some new pills last week, and – touch wood – they seem to be working ... No ... He's signed me off for another week, but I'm planning to be back at work on Monday ... no, no ... it's fine. He said if I felt up to it, it'd be fine to go back ... I know. It's been a while, hasn't it? I miss you guys ... What's that? ... Well, let's see how we go ... I really don't think I'll need to ease back in ... honestly ... You don't say! Well, maybe I will! Whose decision was *that*? ... Oh, that explains it ... well, you can take me through the new system when I see you ... teething problems, huh? Why am I not surprised? It's always the way when IT are involved ..." As the conversation continued, her thoughts took her past her immediate surroundings and she was back at work, at her desk. As she put the phone down, she smiled. She was looking forward to going back.

But she never imagined she'd find it as stressful as she did when she returned to her job at the shelter. 'I never thought it would be this bad,' she told herself. 'I can cope ... I've got to learn to live with my problems, they'll never go away. Others have it much worse.'

It wasn't the big things – dealing with the druggies or the drunks, the fundraising challenges – that got to her. It was the small things ... the unexpected things. She got upset at herself for weeping uncontrollably and irrationally when she found there was no toilet paper in the holder when she needed it ... at first, she took things easy. She asked for a day off, but it didn't make things easier, so she just ended up soldiering on. Finding a dirty spoon in the sink in the morning when she got in to work left her in tears ... she pulled herself together on the loo ... at least there was toilet paper in the holder this time. She was fine for a while after that, but when someone rang and put the phone down on her late one Friday, she just broke down. The last thing she remembered was bursting into tears at her desk. The next thing she knew, she was on a stretcher being wheeled into the emergency ward.

Tests – beeping machinery – sedation ... MRI scans ... "... a what? ... brain tumour? No, that can't be ... what does that mean?" They'd explained the risks associated with the operation. She'd signed the forms. Four hours after the operation, she was still in a coma.

Her fate lay in the balance. The doctors had done their best, but knew her survival was suspect … if only they had worked out that the brain tumour had developed as a rare side effect of the new drug she'd been put on, she might have survived. They never did work it out.

On 20th September, the lights didn't just go out on the ward Jean was on …

Analysis of *The Day the Lights Went Out*: A tragic Death and Rebirth story

Steps	Symbols	Structure	Jean's (outline of content)	The doctors' (symbols)
			Story lines	
1	⊔	Opening	[Implied]	⊔
2	⌐	Initial situation	Jean …	
3	⭠	Problem (lack)	… has been suffering from depression for a while.	
4	⭢	Lack fulfilled	The new pills she has been given have made it possible for her to go back to work …	
5	⭠	There's a price to pay	… but she finds little things irrationally stressful.	
6	⭢	There are attempts to avoid paying the price	She tries to find ways of living with the problem …	⌐
7	⭠	The attempts fail, the price is exacted, there's a **submersion** *Nested Quest structure involving Saviour character starts:* Problem	… which ultimately fail. She ends up in hospital and is diagnosed with a brain tumour …	⭠
8		Journey	… where doctors undertake a quest to try to cure her. They perform an operation …	⭢
9		Meeting with …	… which isn't as successful as they had hoped it would be …	⭠
10		… friend/helper (tragic)	… she goes into a coma …	⭢

Analysis of *The Day the Lights Went Out*: A tragic Death and Rebirth story

Steps	Symbols	Structure	Jean's (outline of content)	The doctors' (symbols)
			Story lines	
11		Meeting with ...	... time passes ...	↼
12	→	... enemy/ hindrance (tragic) *Nested Quest structure involving Saviour character ends*	... the medical staff do their best, ...	→
13	⌐	Final situation (outcome/ resolution)	... but they fail to save her, and Jean dies.	⌐
14	⊐	Closing	[Implied]	⊐

All three of these stories can be seen as tragic. Each of them follows a different structure. Perhaps it could be argued that the tragic steps have an affinity with Trickster steps because they occur at (→) points, but have a (←) quality to them. But in steps 6 and 8 of Paul's story structure, the inanimate objects remain neutral. They don't intend to dupe anyone. There's no clear sense here of there being a pair of Conflicting Quests. Ultimately, they don't—they can't—help him solve his problem, which is what I believe gives the story its tragic potential. The billionaire wants to find love, but money can't buy him happiness. He's his own worst enemy although he's *unaware* of this. The paradoxical category mistake is arguably what gives his story its tragic potential. Similarly, in steps 10 and 12 of Jean's story structure, there's no intention to dupe. There are no Conflicting Quests in the story. All of these steps share the same potential to be seen as tragic. The quality they share – the quality I think Adler was pointing to – is that they're all based on a *paradoxical category mistake*. While each of the characters is duped by an internal trickster, each of the three stories clearly follows a different story structure. The evidence provided above clearly supports the view outlined here that tragedy is structure neutral.[8]

Two things give these stories their tragic potential: firstly, how the stories unfold; secondly, how the stories end. In these stories, the drama unfolds <u>primarily</u> in people's internal worlds. At the end, the initial problems remain unresolved.

The first point relates to a point I raised earlier regarding Greek tragedy:

Tragic stories typically start with a problem the protagonist has created *unwittingly* **that they want to prevent but fail to.**

The tragedy, in all three stories outlined above, comes directly from a main character's inability – for whatever reason – to solve their problem. Sometimes we fail to see the answers to problems either because they're hidden or because they're just not there, even though we think they are. Sometimes the answers are out there, but for some reason, we fail to see them. Either way, it's tragic.

In all three of the stories above, the main characters face internal battles. They all suffer health problems, but I'm not in any way proposing that their health problems are of their own making.

Paul wants to get better, but his problem is that he *chooses* not to go out when he's able to. As a result, he *unwittingly* misses the chance to find a way of defeating the extreme migraines he's suffering from and decides to end his life. He could very well have lived a pain-free life, which is what he *wanted* to do, but *unwittingly* – and tragically – closed off that option. The billionaire is his own worst enemy. He wants to find love, but his problem is that he *thinks* money can buy him happiness – even though he tries to pursue spiritual paths, neither his cynicism nor his materialism allow him to find or maintain a lasting relationship. He could have found fulfilment in any of the pursuits he engaged in by seeking to make any of them meaningful, but *unwittingly* – and tragically – by focusing on the trappings of success, he ended up closing off the path to finding a meaningful existence. As for Jean … she *wants* to get better … her doctors *want* her to get better … they do their best. Jean's problems are due to a reaction to the drugs she's on – her brain tumour arises as an extreme side effect … the tragedy is that *no one* (in the story) *realises it*. What makes these events tragic, as the italicised words in this paragraph indicate, is that the drama unfolds *primarily* in the characters' internal worlds.

There are far more happy endings to wonder tales than there are tragic ones. Sure, even in some of the most uplifting of them, there are curses and problems, but somehow there always seems to be a way to resolve them. It's heartening. Of course, Quest structure stories involve a character's thoughts, decisions, reflections, and feelings. The focus, however, is *primarily* external. An objectively known problem needs to be solved. A character following a Quest structure in their story line is aware of the problem and this drives the story forward. The Quest structure provides the most efficient means of solving the problem which sets it off in the first place. The character typically has the ability to solve it. When they do, we cheer. When they fail to, we find it tragic – whether slightly so or strongly so, the connection remains.

This brings us to the second thing that creates potential for tragedy, which is how tragic stories end.

One could say that the whole story sequence that tragedy follows can be reduced to (□ ⌐ ⤙ ⤚ ⌐ □). You could also say that tragedy leaves problems unresolved and that the whole sequence can be reduced to (□ ⌐ ⤙ ⌐ □), but story works at a deeper level … and tragedy involves more than that.

In the previous chapter, we explored laughter. What about tears?

People cry for a variety of reasons. I've cried from watching films with soppy endings; from pain; as a result of experiencing transcendent beauty – often at the opera, or when struck by a work of art that 'does it' for me; when someone I love has died; when I've been rejected; when I've gone through a transformative experience. I've cried tears of relief and I've cried from laughter.

Why do these very different things make me cry? What do they all have in common?

While tragic stories end at the close of a story structure, tragedy and the release of tears comes after a closure which can occur within an overarching story structure and can provide a cathartic release. Tragedy and tears are related but they differ in their patterns of thought. We've already established that tragedy is based on a paradoxical category mistake. Simile-based category mistakes give things comic potential, and generate laughs. The correction of paradoxical category mistakes gives things tragic potential and generates tears.

We cry when we experience the correction of paradoxical category mistakes.

As my responses are not unique, but are shared by many others who also find the same types of stimuli to be tear-inducing, I'd guess the same mechanisms are probably at work.

When I feel things *should* be one way, and when I'd previously hoped they *could* be that way, but I finally realise either that they *can't* be, I cry. I cry when I feel things *shouldn't* be a particular way, and I'd previously hoped they wouldn't be that way forever, but I finally have to accept that they either *are* or (tragically) *will stay that way* (How likely is it that we'll be able to bring back extinct species or reverse climate change?) – in either case, what generates tears is the *correction* of the paradoxical category mistake. All of the examples I've given previously which are linked to pain, death, rejection have the potential to fit this model, releasing tears of sorrow.

On the other hand, there are tears of joy. When I experience a piece of music that I find particularly beautiful, my sense of perception is expanded. Only afterwards do I realise that for the duration of that experience, my sense of time and space were significantly altered. In the timeless moment, I feel that things *are* as they *should* be (in *contrast* to the way they *were*). As soon as I feel I re-enter time, I realise what I've lost, and I cry. I cry because I feel things are *no longer* as they *should* be (in contrast to the way they *were*) (or vice versa). If the music is still going on, tears might still flow, in response to the subtle irony of experiencing a timeless experience through time, knowing it's fleeting, catching a taste of the eternal without the hope of ever realising it; wanting to believe it's possible to do so, faced with the evidence that it is; knowing that it can never be achieved through an act of will and, having to come to terms with that, having to let go. Tears flow when paradoxical or extreme category mistakes are corrected. Films with soppy endings, transcendental beauty, transformative experiences, sensations of extreme relief all fit this model.

I'm excluding onion chopping here – onion chopping does make me cry, but the mechanism involved is a different mechanism. It turns out that the chemical composition of these tears and the chemical composition of the kind of tears which flow as an expression of emotion are very different.[9] When we experience the correction of a paradoxical category mistake, we cry ... and it's no surprise that the same author that gave us the categories also gave us a definition of tragedy that still holds to this day. In the *Poetics*, Aristotle uses the term *catharsis* within his definition of tragedy as an imitation *(mimesis)* of an action *(praxeôs)* that is of stature and complete, with magnitude, that by means of sweetened speech ... [and] of people acting *(drôntôn)* and not through report, ... accomplishes through pity and fear the cleansing *(catharsis)* of experiences *(pathematôn)* of this sort.[10]

Aristotle describes tragedy here as a self-generated, auto-poietic process, embodied in a structure, rather than a product (a performance, or text) which merely gives it form. As part of this process, Aristotle points out, audiences are moved to feel pity and/or fear, *following which* they're cleansed emotionally, in a kind of soul-cleansing experience.

The pity and fear that Aristotle writes about typically emerge from category mistakes based on irresolvable paradoxes – situations in which we feel things *should* be one way, but they *can't be* or that things *shouldn't* be a particular way, but they *are* ('an orphan *should* have a family, like any other child – an orphan *shouldn't* be deprived of their parents …') ('I *should* feel that poor man has nothing to do with me … it's only an actor on stage, after all, but I keep on thinking, "What if …?"') ('I *shouldn't* feel that situation has anything to do with me, but I do … and what if …?')

But pity and fear alone don't make tragedy, nor do category mistakes alone. Aristotle goes on to describe what he sees as another essential feature of tragedy: actions in and from which there's 'a recognition or a reversal or both'.[11] He explains reversal as 'the change into the contrary of the things being done' and recognition as 'a change from ignorance *(agnoia)* to knowledge *(gnosis)*'.[12]

Both recognition and reversal are based on *category corrections*. Both are based on paradox – on a juxtaposition of contraries. Both are part of an embodied system of being and knowing that works, through story, to help us achieve a sense of balance and harmony in the way in which we live our lives.

It's tragically ironic that we prefer to engage in humour than to engage in tragedy! After all, Comedy is based on category *mistakes*, but we rarely reach beyond the laughter to the sense of wonder that generates it. By comparison, we try to evade tragedy, although tragedy is arguably more restorative. Tragedy, being based on category corrections, brings us closer to the truth, and provokes soul-cleansing catharsis, but we find laughter more pleasant. Facing the truth is often painful—and yet, the pain has healing power.

When we accept things that we thought it would be impossible for us to accept; when we recognise that the things which we held to be correct were false, or that the things which we held to be false were true, we undergo a catharsis; when we experience the kind of change described in the above examples – a change from ignorance to knowledge, we cry, but we can emerge transformed, rebalanced.

Tragedy and Comedy both involve and engage, but they do so in different ways. We laugh *about* things, or laugh them *off*, but we cry things *out*, or cry them *through*.[13] Grief seems to be linked to a sustained state in which an unsustainable paradox persists ('it *can't* be', 'it *shouldn't* be''no, I *can't* accept it' – denial is inevitably involved) – but the tears flow when the paradox is accepted. When we accept what *is*, however paradoxical, we experience catharsis, and catharsis allows us to move on, to flow, and that allows us to 'get on with our lives'.

In the process of writing this book, I found this chapter one of the most difficult to write. Writing it was, in itself, a cathartic process. When, for the first time in my life, I realised, as a result of working through the ideas I've presented here, that there was no distinction between my experience of weeping in response to something I found beautiful and weeping as an act of catharsis on accepting and experiencing a category correction, I wept. I wept because I realised that exactly the same process of inner correction was at work. I experienced balance (or a greater proximation to it) – a kind of balance I seem compelled to seek. I achieved this state of (relative) balance simply by seeing things as they were. It was painful to accept that I was wrong to think of crying 'tears of joy' in response to something I found beautiful as being 'good' and crying 'tears of sorrow' in response to something I found sad as being 'bad'. I realised they were both good. They were both potentially transformative. When I realised my mistake, it was cathartic. I not only understood what George Spencer-Brown meant when he wrote, 'When wrong is done we sometimes laugh, but when right is done we cry',[14] I experienced it. However difficult it might be, I can only wish that this chapter provokes a similar response in you.

Story is born from imbalance, to rebalance a system which is out of balance. It's no surprise that Aristotle devoted most of his *Poetics* to tragedy and identified catharsis (an act of ritual cleansing) as its goal. After all, the word 'poetics' means creativity – a sense which is carried through in terms such as 'autopoiesis' … a fitting term to describe the self-generated and self-sustaining process through which life stories.[15]

While tragedy achieves transformation through catharsis, other forms use other means, which is what we'll be exploring in the next chapter.

NOTES

1   Mortimer J. Adler, *Great Ideas from the Great Books*, Rev. ed. (New York: Washington Square Press, 1969), 137.

2   Adler, *Great Ideas from the Great Books*, 137.

3   Mortimer J. Adler, "Duty," in *The Great Ideas: A Syntopicon of Great Books of the Western World*, Vol. 1, Great Books of the Western World, Vol. 2 (Chicago: Encyclopaedia Britannica, 1952), 364.

4   Robert Graves, *The Greek Myths* (London: Penguin, 2011), 257; on the history of Thebes and its gates, see Aeschylus, *The Seven Against Thebes*, edited by The Rev James Davies (London: Virtue Brothers, 1864), ix–x, https://books.google.co.uk/books?id=Z9oIAAAAQAAJ&pg=PR9.

5   Ovid, *Metamorphoses*, 4.753–803, 129–130.

6   Apollodorus, *The Library of Greek Mythology*, translated by Keith Aldrich, quoted by Aaron J. Atsma, "Gorgones & Medousa," *Theoi Project*, 2000–2017, https://www.theoi.com/Pontios/Gorgones.html.

7   The role of 'supernatural friend/helper' applies just as well to the potential for our 'higher selves' or 'will' to help us access 'higher wisdom' linking us to what ancient Greeks referred to as *sophia* rather than *phronesis* (practical wisdom).

8   I'm consciously using a Quest structure as a way of framing the argument I present in this section.

9   Michael Trimble, *Why Humans Like to Cry: Tragedy, Evolution and the Brain* (Oxford: Oxford University Press, 2012), 43–44.

10   Aristotle, *Aristotle: On Poetics*, translated by Seth Bernardete and Michael Davis (South Bend, IN: St Augustine's Press, 2002), 17–18; 17n46; 1449b, 24–29.

11   Aristotle, *Poetics*, 1452a, chapter 10, 29n74.

12   Aristotle, *Poetics*, 1452a, chapter 11, 30.

13   Here, 'through' (as in 'to see something through') is used metaphorically to reference a cathartic process, as in the following sentence: 'I patted my sister's shoulder and let her cry it through while I surveyed the room' (Gillian Roberts, *Adam and Evil: An Amanda Pepper Mystery*, (New York: Ballantine, 1999), chapter 7, page 4), rather than a reference to an external expanse of space (e.g., 'cry it through the streets' or 'see through a glass, darkly').

14   Spencer-Brown, *Laws of Form*, 115.

15   Poetics is derived from ποίησις (*poiesis*) in Greek, alluding both to an imaginative act of creation generally and to an act of poetic composition specifically.

11

APPEARANCES IN AND FROM STORY

SYMBOL 6 (⊓): THE REVELATION, CALL AND RESPONSE (VARIATIONS 1 AND 2), AND RELATED COMPOSITE STRUCTURES

What is revealed will be concealed,
but what is concealed will again be revealed.

GEORGE SPENCER-BROWN, *Laws of Form*[1]

airy godmothers and demonic foes can appear in many guises.
They're so common, we often take their presence for granted.
Their roles are clear – they're there to either help or hinder heroes. But
what prompts their appearances? What needs are they responding
to? With an angel, or a fairy godmother figure, it's clear – they
appear when things hit rock bottom in a character's story line and
provide the necessary energy for the story to flow forward towards
a resolution when it's stuck somewhere. But what about monstrous,
demonic, or devilish fiends? What governs their appearances?
I believe there's a deep dynamic involved for both types of supernatural
beings – a dynamic we've touched on previously when we looked at
the connection between the Transformation structure and the Quest
structure. We saw previously how the 'negative' contains within it
the seed of the 'positive' and the 'positive' contains within it the seed
of the 'negative'. The diagram showing this is reproduced below for
convenience:[2]

Structures			Steps							
	1	**2**	**3**			**4**		**5**	**6**	
Transformation	⊐	⌐	←			→		⌐	⊐	
	1	**2**	**3**	**4**	**5**	**6**	**7**	**8**	**9**	**10**
Quest	⊐	⌐	←	→	←	→	←	→	⌐	⊐

To explore this connection, let's look at some examples. The
appearance of a *houri* (a celestial being in Islamic culture) to
Bahá'u'lláh, which resulted in him founding a religious movement,
happened when he was imprisoned in the Black Pit of Tehran,
which was considered the foulest place on earth at the time.[3]

A similar vision is recounted by Boethius in his *Consolation of Philosophy*, in which Philosophy appears to him as a female spirit with supernatural features when he's in prison, in the depths of despair, facing the prospect of death.[4] And, on the other hand, what brings Grendel out of his bog in the Anglo-Saxon epic of *Beowulf* but the extravagant sumptuousness of the mead hall described at the beginning of the earliest known extant version of the story?![5]

The dynamic connection is this:

Angels' and other benign supernatural beings' story lines typically emerge from a state of an *excess of evil*; monsters', devils', or demons' story lines typically emerge from a state of an *excess of good*.

As noted above, the expansion of each of the steps in the Transformation structure involves a triplicity: The single (⟵) step in the Transformation structure expands to a triple (⟵ ⟶ ⟵) sequence; the (⟶) step expands to a triple (⟶ ⟵ ⟶) sequence. There's a sense in which the return to step 4 in the Transformation structure becomes a simultaneous arrival and departure point – the same applies to the 'arrival' at the marked state (⌐).

Marie Louise von Franz—a student of Carl Jung and his intellectual successor—notes that

> in fairy tales there are often three steps and then a finale. You will always read that the number three plays a big role in fairy tales, but when I count it is generally four … [t]he three are always clear unities: 1, 2, 3, with certain repetition, which is why the fourth is so often ignored, for the fourth is not just another additional number unit; it is not another thing of the same kind, but something completely different. It is as if one counted, one, two, three – bang! The one, two and three lead up to the real *dénouement*, which is represented in the fourth and which is generally something static; there is no longer a leading-up, dynamic movement in it, but something comes to rest.[6]

Von Franz's 'one, two, three – bang!' sequence is elegantly minimal. It reminds me of the Latin saying *veni, vidi, vici* (I came, I saw, I conquered), attributed to Julius Caesar. Although the linguistic structure is formed of three elements, the dynamic quality of the events behind it fits von Franz's four-fold model exactly: Why did Julius Caesar 'set out' in the first place if not because of reports, hearsay, possibilities? *One.* His journey got him close enough to 'see' the enemy with his own eyes. *Two.* This allowed him to plan and execute his campaign—*three*—from which he emerged a victorious 'conqueror'. *Bang!*

Von Franz points to a crucial connection between the static and dynamic elements that coexist in a literary form. The methodology used here allows us to explore this subtle relationship between the static linear and the dynamic elements of story in a way that I don't think has ever been possible up to now. We've looked at how to scribe the former. Here, I'm proposing we use the following symbols for the latter: (⊔), (⊐), (⊐).

The Revelation structure is the first of two dynamic story structures described in this book. It's distinctive in that it traces a character's changing state of being in relation to how they perceive their environment. Thus, the symbols, which appear in the body of a story, depict that relationship, rather than a character themselves, or the 'forward' ('positive') or 'backward' ('negative') quality of their steps:

First of all, a state of doubt or uncertainty, imbalance – perhaps a rumour, niggling worry, or hope (⊔).

The source of that feeling is investigated – and its nature confirmed or refuted (⊐). The difference here is that this symbol appears on a separate line underneath the linear mapping and occurs in the middle of the story line, rather than framing it at either end of the linear mapping.

In order to deal with the realisation, a desire or wish is articulated, and a plan of action formulated. This requires either an assertion or denial, cancelling the initial uncertainty, which results in an unmarked state (⊐), and opening up a space for change. The result will inevitably produce a change in the environment (be it physical, mental, or both) as the action unfolds.

The doubt, confirmation/refutation, assertion/denial sequence is scribed as follows:

$$\square \quad \daleth \quad \daleth$$

Call this the Revelation structure.[7]

I've found the qualitative *veni, vidi, vici* sequence to be the most elegant way of referring to the three steps of the dynamic lead-up von Franz describes:

The Revelation structure

Steps	Symbols	Structure	Example (attr. Julius Caesar)
1	$\square$	Doubt	*veni* (I came)
2	$\daleth$	Verification: confirmation/ refutation	*vidi* (I saw)
3	$\daleth$	Assertion/denial (statement or action which cancels doubt)	*vici* (I conquered)

The Revelation structure, which emerges from and returns to a character-based mark ($\daleth$), is a key feature of the story of *Beowulf*.[8] At the beginning, we're told that King Hrothgar—whose name literally means 'Quick-Spear' or 'Joy-Spear' to whom 'success in warfare' was given, and 'honour in war'—wants to build a mead hall, but not just any mead hall – a hall 'which the sons of men should hear of forever', 'the best of royal halls' in which men know neither 'sorrow' nor the 'misery of men' (the tension rises). The hall, which he names Heorot, is towering, 'high and horn-gabled'. Hrothgar's men gather, eat, and sleep there. Things are good. Really good. So good that word of them reaches Grendel. Grendel is described as a 'ghastly demon' and 'fiend in hell', 'grim and greedy', 'savage and cruel'. Having sensed rumours of how wonderful Heorot is, he visits the mead hall at night, to see it with his own eyes. Before the night is over, he has left, 'proud in plunder' with a 'banquet of bodies', having made his attack and emerged with his spoils. When Hrothgar's men awake, there are thirty fewer of them than there had been the previous evening. No one can account for the men's disappearance. It's as if they've vanished into thin air. And there, you have the static reversal of fortune.

Grendel came. Grendel saw. Grendel conquered. And all because he sensed an *excess of good!* As we've noted, the relationship between the initial state of an *excess of good* and the appearance of a demon; and the initial state of an *excess of evil* and the appearance of an angel in the Revelation structure links to the Transformation structure, remarkable for linking natural and supernatural dimensions of being. As a reminder, the Transformation structure is rendered as follows:

$$□ ⌐ ← → ⌐ □$$

Either one of the steps in the Transformation structure can expand three times in a nested dynamic manner to generate a new compound structure: the Call and Response structure. The Call and Response structure comes in two variations, depending on which step in the Transformation structure is expanded: the first step (←) or the second one (→).

In Variation 1, the story starts off with a Transformation structure, in which a transgressive state of excess—either an excess of evil or an excess of good (step 3 below)—is resolved (step 4 below), but is resolved excessively. This launches a process of expansion. The second step (step 4 below) expands from (→) to (→ ← →) and we get the following:

1	2	3	4	5	(6)			
□	⌐	←	→				⌐	□

$$→ ← →$$

Applying this to *Beowulf,* the transgressive lack (step 3) that Hrothgar experiences as an excess of evil leads him to create the mead hall (step 4). His desire to create excessive goodness transgresses against the natural order (step 4). Grendel—disturbed by the nightly 'noise of revelry ... loud in the hall', the 'harmony of the harp' and the 'sweet song of the poet' who sings the song of all creation'—sets out to find out what is behind it all in a classic *veni* step:

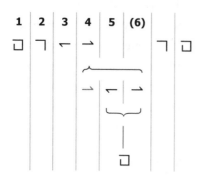

The expansion of Step 6 brings forth the *vidi* step:

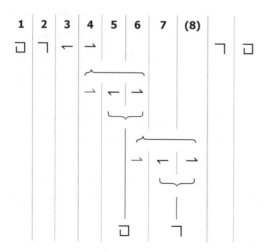

This is where Grendel comes face to face with the hall for the first time and his suspicions – if not his worst nightmares – are confirmed. The expansion of Step 8 brings forth the *vici* step, which is where he attacks:

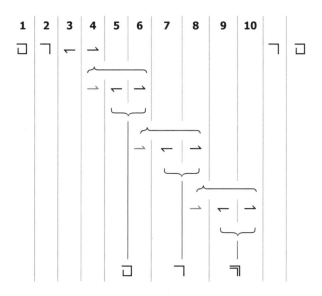

When a Transformation structure (Steps 3–4 above) generates a Revelation structure (Steps 4–10 above), the combined structure can be scribed as follows:

Steps

1	2	3	4	5	6	7	8	9	10	11	12
⊐	⊓	←	→	←	→	←	→	←	→	⊓	⊐
		(⊐	⊓)	⊐		⊓		⊐		(⊓	⊐)

Call this the Call and Response Variation 1 structure.

Steps 3–4 form the core steps of a Transformation structure; steps 5–10 show that there's a clear link between the Revelation and Quest structures in the Call and Response structure, but the way in which the Quest structure expands from the Transformation structure in the Call and Response structure is different to the way in which the Quest structure expands from it as a stand-alone structure. The difference is this: the Call and Response structure involves only one step of the Transformation structure expanding to 7 steps; the

Quest structure involves both steps in the Transformation structure expanding from 1 step to 3.[9]

There's another difference, as well. Just as the Revelation structure deals with the crossing over from one state of being to another – from a transcendent dimension of being to the immanent dimension in which we find ourselves (and potentially vice versa), so the expansion from Transformation to Quest in the Call and Response structure indicates a shift between these dimensions, often involving a related narrative shift from one character's story line to another's. The Quest structure, however, remains firmly fixed in the immanent dimension of being. Where it expands from Transformation to Quest, each story line links to a single character. Moreover, the Revelation structure, which underpins the Quest part of a Call and Response structure and governs its expansion out of the Transformation structure in the first place, starts with a rumour, or state of doubt. It's dynamic. Its main focus is a series of perceptual relationships. A Quest structure starts with a clear problem that a character is aware of. It's linear. Its main focus is an objective problem that can be solved.

Thus, both the Dynamic Revelation structure and the Linear Transformation structure can be seen as Threshold structures. They link physical and metaphysical dimensions of being. The Transformation structure, as previously noted, typically features divine intervention. The Revelation structure, similarly, involves threshold crossings (actual or implied) from the immanent to the transcendent dimensions of being.

All three structures (Transformation, Revelation, and Quest) are found in the Call and Response structure,[10] which typically links to elements with the following characteristics:

The Call and Response structure (Variation 1, with initial Transformation structure)

Steps	Symbols	Structure		
1	⊐	Opening		
2	⌐	Initial situation (set-up: who, when, where – character and setting)		
3	⟵	State of lack	⎱	**Transformation structure** (with resolution not achieved)
4	⟶	State of excess		
5	⟵	**Quest structure** Problem	⊐	**Revelation structure** Rumour/doubt (*veni* step)
6	⟶	Journey		
7	⟵	Meeting with ...	⌐	Verification: confirmation/ refutation (*vidi* step)
8	⟶	... friend/helper		
9	⟵	Meeting with ...	⌐|	Assertion/denial (*vici* step) (statement or action which cancels doubt)
10	⟶	... enemy/ hindrance		
11	⌐	Final situation (outcome/resolution)		
12	⊐	Closing		

The line between steps 4 and 5 indicates a shift from one character's story line to another character's story line which results in the emergence of a Revelation structure. In Variation 1 of the Call and Response structure, the Transformation structure comes first; the Revelation structure (underpinning what unfolds as a Quest structure) second. But there's an alternative version of the Call and Response structure which can emerge from the Transformation structure. The diagram below shows the linear representation of the Transformation structure again:

If the first step expands from (←) to (← → ←), we get the following:

1	2	3	4	5	(6)		
כ	ר	←			(→)	ר	כ

←	→	←

If we apply this to the complete story of the annunciation, as it unfolds in Luke 1:5–38 in the story line, in step 3, the elderly Zacharias and Elisabeth have an intense desire for a child (vv. 5–10). The angel Gabriel senses this and appears to Zacharias in the temple (v. 11) – a classic *veni* step:

1	2	3	4	5	(6)		
כ	ר	←			(→)	ר	כ

←	→	←

כ

The expansion of Step 5 brings forth the *vidi* step:

1	2	3	4	5	6	7	(8)		
כ	ר	←					(→)	ר	כ

←	→	←

כ

←	→	←

כ	ר

This is where Zacharias and the angel meet face to face. 'And when Zacharias saw him, he was troubled, and fear fell upon him' (v. 12). The angel tells Zacharias that his prayers have been answered, and prophesizes great things (vv. 13–17). The expansion of Step 7 brings forth the *vici* step. Zacharias says, 'Whereby shall I know this? for I am an old man, and my wife well stricken in years.' (v. 18).

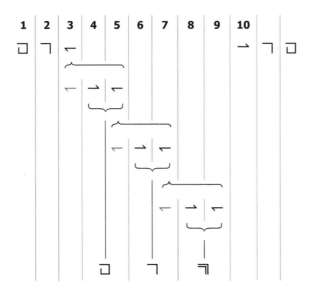

At this display of incredulity rather than faith, the angel, experiencing what appears to him as a flagrant transgression against the natural order, strikes Zacharias dumb (vv. 19–22) in a final Transformation structure.

In vv. 26–38, a similar Call and Response structure to the one just analysed unfolds. There's an implied need for a Saviour, the manifestation needing to unfold through space-time – as a revelation. The ensuing Revelation structure relates to the Saviour's appearance. In Mary's story line, the angel Gabriel appears (a veni step, vv. 26–28). She's troubled (v. 29); he tells her she'll conceive (vv. 30–33); Mary asks, 'How shall this be'? (v. 34). The angel explains that she'll conceive of the Holy Ghost (vv. 35–37) – a *vidi* step. In the final unfolding pair, Mary accepts the call (v. 38) – a *vici* step,

cancelling doubt, moving from potentiality to potency to actuality
– and the events which lead to the birth of Jesus continue to unfold.

The steps of this variation on the Call and Response structure
typically link to elements with the following characteristics:

The Call and Response structure
(Variation 2, with final Transformation structure)

Steps	Symbols	Structure		
1	⟥	Opening		
2	⟍	Initial situation (set-up: who, when, where – character and setting)		
3	⟵	**Quest structure** Problem	⟥	**Revelation structure** Rumour/doubt (*veni* step)
4	⟶	Journey		
5	⟵	Meeting with …	⟍	Verification: Confirmation/refutation (*vidi* step)
6	⟶	… friend/helper		
7	⟵	Meeting with …	⟍⟍	Assertion/denial (*vici* step) (statement or action which cancels doubt)
8	⟶	… enemy/hindrance		
9	⟵	State of lack		**Transformation structure**
10	⟶	State of excess		(with resolution not achieved)
11	⟍	Final situation (outcome/resolution)		
12	⟥	Closing		

The shift in the narrative from one character's story line to another
character's story line around steps 8 and 9 typically signals the
emergence of a Transformation structure. The combined structure
can be scribed as follows:

						Steps					
1	**2**	**3**	**4**	**5**	**6**	**7**	**8**	**9**	**10**	**11**	**12**
⟥	⟍	⟵	⟶	⟵	⟶	⟵	⟶	⟵	⟶	⟍	⟥
(⟥	⟍)	⟥		⟍		⟍⟍		⟵	⟶	(⟍	⟥)

Call this the Call and Response Variation 2 structure.

Stories that follow the Call and Response structure typically follow one of two patterns: either Variation 1:

A state of excess (negative or positive) from which an initial Transformation structure results. The resolution is, in turn, excessive.

A shift from one character's story line to another character's story line around steps 4 and 5 which results in the emergence of a Revelation structure,

or Variation 2:

A state of excess (negative or positive) from which an initial Revelation structure results. The resolution is, in turn, excessive.

A shift from one character's story line to another character's story line around steps 8 and 9 leads to a Transformation structure ending. Resolution isn't usually achieved.

Both of the shifts referred to above are typically accompanied by a 'gear change', 'phase shift', or 'switch of registers', from physical to metaphysical or vice versa.[11]

Just as in fractal forms, where small-scale elements are found repeated at larger scales, so it is with story. In the sequence of three Biblical stories (Zacharias and Elisabeth's; Mary and Joseph's; and the story of the Nativity), we have a *veni, vidi, vici* (I came, I saw, I conquered) sequence, followed by events which lead up to the story of the Massacre of the Innocents. Each of the individual stories follows the Call and Response structure, but they all combine to form a larger-scale sequence, which, in turn, follows an overarching Call and Response structure.

Some interesting symmetries can be observed in the Call and Response Variation 1 structure:

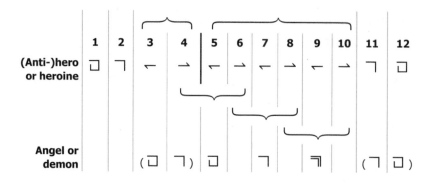

There are 8 steps which can form 4 pairs, as in the top division, grouped to show Transformation and Quest structures (3–4 and 5–10 respectively) and 3 triples, as in the bottom division, grouped to show the Revelation structure (4–6, 6–8, 8–10). An interesting fractal pattern appears here, where the 1:3 ratio in the pairs (3–4:5–10) of the top row (3–8) results from the single to triple expansion of the forward arrows (4–6, 6–8, 8–10) in a 1:2 ratio.

The arrangement for Variation 2 is shown below:

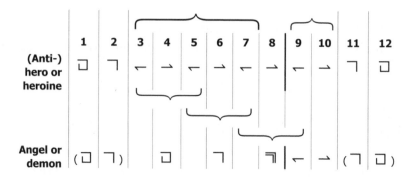

As previously noted, in this variation, where the Revelation structure shifts to the Transformation structure between steps 8 and 9, an important shift from one character's story line to another character's story line typically occurs, usually also marked by a 'shift of registers' that goes from physical to metaphysical or vice versa. It seems to be the energy of the unfolding process itself that makes this happen.

Beowulf opens with a Call and Response Variation 1 structure that culminates in Grendel's attack, committed because he seeks to neutralise the threat to his environment. This, in turn, sets off a rumour (Step 3) that travels over the seas (Step 4) and reaches Beowulf (Step 5). This marks a transition between the metaphysical realm of and the physical realm in which Beowulf lives.[12] Beowulf responds to the call (Step 6) – this completes his *veni* step. He encounters Grendel, drawing on his wit and strength to stay awake in order to face him (Steps 7, 8) – this completes his *vidi* step. He just manages to defeat Grendel (Steps 9, 10) by ripping Grendel's arm off – this completes his *vici* step, but an imbalance in the natural order remains, as Grendel's mother is rather unhappy about this. She decides she wants revenge. Her story line then unfolds through a Call and Response Variation 1 structure.

Here follows a deeper analysis of the complex story of Beowulf to demonstrate how these elements can work in practice. It shows an example of the Call and Response Variation 1 structure in steps 1–11, and an example of Variation 2 of that structure in steps 11–14, concluding at step 32. The structures which make up the story are indicated in the columns on the left.

Structures

C&R1	C&R2	C&R3	Quest	C&R4	C&R5	Quest	Steps	Symbols	Structure	Outline of content (Beowulf) (multiple characters' story lines)[13]
							1	⊓	Opening	Listen! (Hwæt) (1)
							2	⌐	Initial situation (set-up: who, when, where – character and setting)	A line of kings is introduced, leading to King Hrothgar. (1–63)
							3	←	Transgression against the natural order	Hrothgar wishes to build a hall 'which the sons of men should hear of forever.' (64–73)
							4	→	An (excessive) attempt to restore the natural order is made. A *veni* step is set up ...[14]	The hall (named Heorot) is built and becomes a site of feasting and merrymaking ... (74–83)

Structures

C&R1	C&R2	C&R3	Quest	C&R4	C&R5	Quest	Steps	Symbols	Structure	Outline of content (Beowulf) (multiple characters' story lines)[13]
							5	←	... extended ...	... which disturb Grendel ... (84–114)
							6	→	... and in reaching its completion, sets up a *vidi* step, which is ...	... who sets out to see what is causing the disturbance. (115–117)
							7	←	... extended ...	He arrives at the site ... (118–120)
							8	→	... and in reaching its completion, sets up a *vici* step, which is ...	... and when he comes across the excessive goodness of the hall readies himself ... (120–122)
							9	←	... extended ...	... enters the hall (implied) ...
							10	→	... and in reaching its completion, allows the completion of the Call and Response structure	... and makes a meal of Hrothgar's best warriors. (122–125)
							11	⌐	Outcome/resolution	
							12	← →	Transgression against the natural order; an attempt to restore the natural order is made. A *veni* step is set up ...	The thanes wake, discover that they have been attacked, seek out Grendel's tracks, and lament (Thanes' tragic *veni* step). (126–134)
							13	← →	... extended, and in reaching its completion, sets up a *vidi* step, which is ...	Grendel returns and feasts again (Thanes' tragic *vidi* step). (134–137)
							14	← →	... extended, and in reaching its completion, sets up a *vici* step, which is resolved at 32.	Powerless against him, the thanes flee (Thanes' tragic *vici* step). (138–146) Grendel continues to hound them (159–166) and occupies Heorot. (166–169)
							15	⌐	Outcome/resolution	The hall is left empty. Twelve winters pass. (126–149)

Structures

C&R1	C&R2	C&R3	Quest	C&R4	C&R5	Quest	Steps	Symbols	Structure	Outline of content (Beowulf) (multiple characters' story lines)[13]
							16	←	Transgression against the natural order	Hrothgar is at his wits' end. He can't figure out what to do about Grendel. His remaining thanes are desperate. (170–193)
							17	→	An attempt to restore the natural order is made. A *veni* step is set up ...[15]	The story travels across the sea ... (149–158)[16]
							18	←	... extended ...	... and is heard by ... (194)
							19	→	... and in reaching its completion, sets up a *vidi* step, which is ...	... Beowulf. (194–198) Beowulf sets out to help Hrothgar. (nested Quest) (198–228)
							20	←	... extended ...	Beowulf and his men are stopped and questioned by the coast guard (nested Trickster Variation)[17] (229–257), who leads them to Heorot (257–330) where they're addressed by a noble (331–337), by Wolfgar, the Wendels' leader (348–370), who introduces them to Hrothgar (nested Revelation) (371–498) who welcomes them (607–612). Beowulf is challenged by Unferth (nested Trickster) (499–606) but trumps the challenge. The queen calms the situation and prays God he prevail (Queen's *veni*). (612–628) Beowulf vows to defeat Grendel or die in the attempt (628–638) (Beowulf's *veni*; Grendel's *veni*). (702–709) (nested Quest)
							21	→	... and in reaching its completion, sets up a *vici* step, which is ...	The hosts retire. (639–668) Beowulf prepares to meet Grendel. He renounces his weapons, trusting in his own sense of truth, strength and courage. (669–702).

Structures

C&R1	C&R2	C&R3	Quest	C&R4	C&R5	Quest	Steps	Symbols	Structure	Outline of content (Beowulf) (multiple characters' story lines)[13]
							22	←	... extended ...	Beowulf and Grendel come face to face ... (Beowulf's *vidi*; Grendel's *vidi*) (710–817)
							23	→	... and in reaching its completion, allows the completion of the Call and Response structure.	... and Beowulf defeats Grendel. (818–836) (Beowulf's *vici*; Grendel's *vici*)
							24	⌐	Outcome/ resolution	Grendel's arm is hung from the ceiling for all to see. (Queen's *vidi*) (837–956) Beowulf and his men are rewarded. (957–1233)
							25	←	Problem	But Grendel's mother is on the warpath ...
							26	→	Journey	... and is heading towards Heorot.
							27	←	Meeting with ...	She arrives ...
							28	→	... friend/helper	... sees the arm and retrieves it ...
							29	←	Meeting with ...	... comes face to face with a hero ...
							30	→	... enemy/ hindrance	... and kills him, then withdraws. (1233–1309)
							31	⌐	Outcome/ resolution	Beowulf is summoned. (1310–1382) (Queen's *vici* thwarted)
							32	← →	Resolution of Call and Response structure which unfolds in steps 11–14	Beowulf defeats Grendel's mother (Queen's *vici* realised) (nested Quest) and is rewarded further. (1383–1887)
							33	⌐	Outcome/ resolution	Beowulf returns home safely, recounts his tale, and is respected as a ruler. (1888–2210)
							34	←	Transgression against the natural order	A thief steals from a dragon. (2211–2306)

Structures

C&R1	C&R2	C&R3	Quest	C&R4	C&R5	Quest	Steps	Symbols	Structure	Outline of content (Beowulf) (multiple characters' story lines)[13]
							35	→	an attempt to restore the natural order is made. The dragon's *veni* step is set up ...	The dragon sets out at night to find the culprit. (2306–2311)
							36	←	... extended ...	The dragon uses senses ...
							37	→	... and in reaching its completion, sets up a *vidi* step, which is ...	... and fire ...
							38	←	... extended, and in reaching its completion, sets up ...	... to wreak vengeance ...
							39	→	... a *vici* step ...	... on humans. (2300–2323)
							40	← →	(Nested Call and Response structure: Transgression against the natural order; an attempt to restore the natural order is made. Beowulf's *veni* step is set up ...	Beowulf, faced with this threat, decides to respond. (2324–2400)
							41	← →	... extended, and in reaching its completion, sets up a *vidi* step, which is ...	The thief confesses and leads a group of warriors to the dragon's barrow. (2401–2416)
							42	← →	... extended, and in reaching its completion, sets up a *vici* step, which is ...	Grendel forgives the thief and swears an oath (*veni* step). (2417–2537) He enters the cave bearing only protective armour (2538–2549) and is sensed by the dragon (*vidi* step); (2550–2568) they meet and fight (*vici* step). (2569–2601) Beowulf fares badly.

Structures

C&R1	C&R2	C&R3	Quest	C&R4	C&R5	Quest	Steps	Symbols	Structure	Outline of content (Beowulf) (multiple characters' story lines)[13]
							43	(← →)	(Nested Quest)	Wiglaf comes to Beowulf's aid. They defeat the dragon, but Beowulf has been dealt a mortal blow. (2602–2715)
							44	← →	… extended, and in reaching its completion, allows the completion of the nested and frame Call and Response structures.)	Sensing he's near death, Beowulf settles his affairs. (nested Quest) (2715–2820)
							45	⌐	Outcome/ resolution	The immediate threat to the kingdom is neutralised; physical and literary memorials to Beowulf's memory are constructed. (2821–3182)
							46	⊔	Closing	However, the Geats fear an attack by the Swedes … (2999–3003)

The Call and Response structure clearly appears to be linked to the appearance of supernatural or superlative beings and to the action of magic. In the most commonly known version of *Cinderella*, the fairy godmother's story line follows this pattern: she appears in response to a state of an excess of evil, facilitates Cinderella's transformation, which allows Cinderella to appear at the ball, then vanishes (she comes, she sees, she conquers, then disappears – as does Cinderella, who comes to the palace, is seen by all, including the prince, and conquers his heart). The Fairy Godmother's story line essentially follows a Call and Response Variation 1 structure, but being a supernatural being, each element in her story line is a mini Transformation structure. The dynamics are different between Cinderella and the Prince. The Prince's bachelorhood isn't an extreme state – in context, it's simply problematic. Even though Cinderella's appearance at the ball outshines her rivals', her appearance is neither excessively good nor excessively beautiful in context. It's comparatively better, not superlatively better. No monster appears as a result, although it could be argued that the injunction to leave by midnight lays the foundation for the slipper to be left behind, the deadline, for me, doesn't justify the unfolding of a Revelation structure. The events are problematic in context. They're not extreme. Cue a series of Quest structures rather than Revelation structures. The Revelation structure *does* unfold, however, if we consider an ideal love found, then lost. Then the Prince's story line can be seen to follow a Call and Response Variation 1 structure. It all depends on how the initial problem is defined.

In Basile's version of *Sleeping Beauty*, (*Sun, Moon, and Talia* from the *Pentamerone*, 1634), a king finds the sleeping Talia and takes advantage of her. His non-consensual and thus excessively evil act brings forth the appearance of 'kindly fairies' who 'attend the birth' of her twins, Sun and Moon, who are instrumental in awakening *Talia*.

Just as the king's story line unfolds through a Call and Response structure, so does the evil queen's story line in *Snow White*. The sequence is triggered, in her case, by the state of an excess of good (Snow White's extreme beauty) which develops from an earlier imbalance in the natural order, where a lack is perceived, and help is sought from a supernatural source to cancel the initial deficit (the mother's wish for a child with hair as black as ebony, skin as white as snow, and lips as red as blood).

Only when Snow White becomes 'the fairest of them all' (note the superlative) does the queen's evil witch-nature kick in. Although she only draws on her magic later, the magic is always there, lurking under the surface, waiting to cross over into the physical world from the metaphysical world. 'Mirror, mirror on the wall ...' There's a sense in which the strong desire that Snow White's mother has for a child 'with skin as white as snow, hair as black as ebony, and lips as red as blood' is the causal factor that results in Snow White's superlative beauty. The strength of the would-be mother's desire in the face of the extreme lack she feels brings forth an equally strong response – the excess of evil (the lack) bringing forth an equivalent but opposite excess of good. Structurally, the mother and the stepmother are linked via the Call and Response structures common to both of their story lines.

As in *Beowulf*, there seems to be a need to balance out the initial invocation of supernatural (or superlative) powers to bring things into balance once more. On the one hand, the evil spirit is evoked *as a result* of the appearance of an excess of good; on the other, the Saviour character appears *as a result* of the manifestation of an excess of evil. Each balances out the other. The Call and Response structures lend themselves extremely well to creating suspense. Is it any wonder, therefore, that they feature in so many ghost stories?

While the Call and Response variations are common, other composite structures which unfold in a similar double/triple (Transformation/Revelation) sequence. These often involve a Trickster Awe step (described in chapter 12) in the *vidi* section, as in *The Story of Sidi-Nouman* from *The Arabian Nights* analysed briefly in chapter 12 and in the story entitled *Go I Know Not Whither and Fetch I Know Not What*, as published by Afanas'ev, analysed in appendix 1.[18] In these complex stories, both of which contain multiple nested components, the Revelation/Quest or Revelation/Trickster or Revelation/Trickster Variation sections frequently appear in threes, each sequence being, in turn, part of a larger overarching Revelation structure. The key indicators to these are often the presence of magic or the supernatural, and the shift in narrative from one character's story line to another's.

This leads us to two key groups of questions:

Firstly, why is it, in stories, that an excess of good or evil brings forth demons, ghosts, or monsters ... and fairy godmothers, angels, or divinely inspired heroes? And what does this have to do with what many people call 'real life'? Our everyday '9-to-5, Monday-to-Friday, weekend-break, 4-weeks-of-holiday-a-year' life?

Secondly, if the Call and Response structure (typically combining Transformation, Revelation and Quest or Trickster or Trickster Variation structures) can be found in so many stories which involve interaction between physical and metaphysical dimensions of being, should we consider it a key structure, to which the other three are subservient—if not redundant— by comparison? Should we even consider it as a distinct story structure in its own right?

With regards to the first issue, (the stories of) the assassination of Julius Caesar and the regicide of Charles I and the (arguments leading to the) justifications of those acts could be seen to be 'real-life' examples of this structure at work, both acts arguably being examples of a Transformation structure preceded by a gradual unfolding of a Revelation structure. Caesar sets himself up as an emperor; Charles I sets himself above parliament. Did the protagonists deserve what they got? Did they transgress against the natural order? The excessive states of hubris are among the reasons put forward in the stories told to justify the respective murders. And the stories have stuck.

The links between story, life, and the Oneness-of-Being might even go deeper ...

Why does humour come through for us in tough times? Why does catharsis allow for personal growth? Why else if not that laughter and tears are the 'real life' equivalents that appear as a result of a Revelation structure operating within us?! And if so, then just as Comedy and Tragedy are naturally related to – and rely on – our embedded sense of categorical distinctions, and our instinctive recognition of category mistakes and category corrections, so the Revelation structure relies on and is naturally related to our embedded sense of universal values.

The relationship between what we know to be 'good, harmonious (or proportional) and true' and our efforts to realise that balance in our 'real lives' is clearly at the heart of the Revelation structure's dynamic. Without an absolute, non-relativist sense of what constitutes 'natural order', we would neither sense transgression against it, nor would we sense the need for the transcendental (or metaphysical) to bring the physical state of being into a better state of balance for the natural order to be restored between them and vice versa. The Revelation structure points to the invisible threshold between the world of ideals and the actual world – the transcendent and immanent dimensions of being, a threshold that manifests when there's an imbalance between either side of that boundary and that dissolves when things are in balance. It points to a unified structure that is, in some way, sentient, or self-aware. To realise a state of balance between internal and external in 'real life' is a constant challenge.[19]

It's as if the Revelation structure exists because we have a notion not only of what is good – what is truly good – but also of the transcendental ideals that have provided the foundation for the way we have chosen to organise our 'real lives' for the better from the very earliest times onward. Where there's harmony and balance, there's a sense of unity, of being one (and at one) with the universe; not stuck in a state of suspended animation, but being able both to be 'in the moment' and to flow dynamically and fluidly in a transcendence of the moment, like Zeno's arrow, simultaneously being always—and never—at rest. This paradoxical state – which acts like a benevolent trickster – sets up the possibility for us to experience the Oneness-of-Being. Often, this is triggered by a particular form of surprise which we turn to in the next chapter.

NOTES

1   Spencer-Brown, *Laws of Form*, 86.

2   The relationship is described more fully on pp. 81–83.

3   Bahá'u'lláh, "Súriy-i-Haykal," in *Bahá'í Reference Library: Writings of Bahá'u'lláh*, edited by Shoghi Effendi, 2019, paragraph 6, accessed 14 June, 2019, https://www.bahai.org/library/authoritative-texts/bahaullah/summons-lord-hosts/3#719232199.

4   Boethius, *Consolation of Philosophy*, translated by Joel C. Relihan (Indianapolis, IN: Hackett, 2001), book 1, prose passages 1 & 2, pages 2, 6.

5   "Beowulf", in *The Southwick Codex*, The British Library, Cotton MS Vitellius A XV, 132r–201v, https://www.bl.uk/collection-items/beowulf. The modern English version quoted here is that of Benjamin Slade, published on line at http://www.heorot.dk/beo-intro-rede.html.

6   Marie Louise von Franz, *An Introduction to the Psychology of Fairy Tales* (Irving, TX: Spring Publications, 1978), 64–65.

7   Framing opening/closing and initial/final character symbols are implied here, but the Dynamic structure is visualised more intuitively as a three-step structure underpinning a Quest structure, as will be shown, so for convenience, and to distinguish it from the Chinese Circular Structure, it's rendered thus.

8   All quotes are from Slade's "Beowulf".

9   The relationship can be seen to be analogous to the difference between (3 x 2) and (2 x 3).

10   The resonance of the 'one, two, three – bang!' effect is noteworthy. The form of the methodology makes the fractal quality of story more visible. It can be perceived both in a spatial (structural) unified sense and in a temporal linear distinct sense.

11   I return to these shifts towards the end of chapter 16, where I consider the relationship between the Call and Response, and Voyage and Return structures; and in chapter 21, where I discuss plot patterns.

12   There's also something of the supernaturally transcendent about Grendel and his demonic powers that demands an epic hero be called forth to deal with him.

13   The numbers cited are the line numbers used in the on-line edition. The story structure follows the unfolding of the story in chronological order. The plot pattern of the narrative, however, is not chronological. A number of subplots

which involve the stories of characters' past deeds are not charted fully, but will be found to follow nested Quest or Call and Response structures.

14 Unlike a Transformation structure story, the attempt at restoration here is carried out by a mortal. No divine being intervenes – no blessing, no invocation of or mention of the gods occurs. This points to the unfolding of a Call and Response structure.

15 As noted in the previous footnote, unlike a Transformation story structure, the attempt at restoration here is carried out by a mortal. There is no divine intervention – no blessing, no invocation of or mention of the gods. This clearly points to the unfolding of a Call and Response structure.

16 An implied Revelation structure can be traced here in the summoning of the song *(veni)*, its performance *(vidi)*, and its transmission *(vici)* which enables the story to travel to—and be heard by—Beowulf.

17 The Trickster Variation structure is described in chapter 12.

18 As noted previously, the Trickster Variation structure is described in chapter 12 and the distinctive quality of the Trickster Awe step it contains should be noted. A detailed analysis of *The Story of Sidi-Nouman*, in which it plays a key part, is forthcoming.

19 I've put the words 'real world' in inverted commas here to highlight my use of them in the general sense in which they are commonly used to indicate the physical aspect of being as, contrary to contemporary custom, I tend to use the phrase 'the actual world' for the physical dimension of being and the phrase 'the real world' for the metaphysical dimension.

12

FROM 'HUH?!' TO 'AH!'

THE TRICKSTER VARIATION STRUCTURE

Similes are metaphors in need of a ratio.

ARISTOTLE, TRANS. C. D. C. REEVE,
Rhetoric III.4.3 (1407a14)[1]

Related to the Trickster structure, but qualitatively different, the Trickster Variation structure (like the Revelation and Transformation structures) unfolds as a result of a perceived sense of imbalance in the natural order.

Previously, I defined Trickster steps as follows:

Where an enemy seems to be a friend but is actually an enemy; or a friend seems to be an enemy but is actually a friend, call this the Trickster step,

and I defined Comic steps, which are closely related to Trickster steps as follows:

Where an enemy's behaviour is like the behaviour of a friend; or a friend's behaviour is like the behaviour of an enemy, call this the Comic step.

In some stories, however, meetings between two characters on Conflicting Quests don't fit either one of these models. At times, an event related to a meeting is neither tricksterish nor comic but so surprising, awe-inspiring, horrifying, or shocking, it seems to stop the flow of story in its tracks, leaving a character in a state of awe, thinking, 'Huh?!' When this happens, call this the Trickster Awe step.

The Trickster Awe step sets up a cognitive dissonance within the body of a story, so I use the (⇌) symbol to denote it. A distinguishing feature of the Trickster Awe step is a shift from one character's story line to another.

Trickster steps are balanced by Transformational Twists; so is the Trickster Awe step, the unfolding of which resolves in an explanation for the unusual event.[2] When this happens, call this the Trickster Variation structure.

The Story of Sidi-Nouman, from *The Arabian Nights* is a story based on the Trickster Variation structure.[3] The story, which contains magic, invokes the Revelation structure which is mapped to the Caliph's story line in the 'bare bones' analysis below, but it also applies to Sidi-Nouman's.

Analysis of the Caliph's story line in *The Story of Sidi-Nouman*

Steps	Symbols	Structure	Outline of content	Revelation steps and structure
1	⊐	Opening	Once upon a time …	
2	⌐	Initial situation (set-up: who, when, where – two characters on different quests)	… Haroun Al-Raschid, Caliph of Baghdad …	
3	←	Problem	… wishes to find out whether laws are being enacted justly in Baghdad, …	
4	→	Journey	… so he and his vizier Giafar go out into the city in disguise. (*Nested Quest for the vizier, who acts as the caliph's friend/helper by accompanying him and arranging the disguise.*)	
5	←	Meeting between …	In the market square, they see a man treating a horse cruelly – apparently a daily occurrence.	⊐ (A state of doubt, or of oscillation arises, associated with an excess of evil)

Analysis of the Caliph's story line in *The Story of Sidi-Nouman*

Steps	Symbols	Structure	Outline of content	Revelation steps and structure
6	⇌	... the two characters which sets up a cognitive dissonance (Trickster Awe step)	They have no idea why he's treating the horse this way, so Giafar later issues an order for the man to present himself at the palace. *(Another nested Quest for the vizier as the caliph's friend/helper.)*	(The man is ordered to come to the palace.) (*veni* step)
7	⊢	Meeting between ...	The man arrives at the court and is brought into the presence of the caliph.	⌐ (The man arrives ...
8	⇌	... the two characters which resolves the cognitive dissonance (Transformational Twist)	He tells a story (complex nested structure) that provides an explanation for his behaviour. The caliph issues a just view on the man's conduct, ...	... and tells his story.) (*vidi* step) (*Nested Quest, ending with a Transformational Twist*) ⌐⌐ (The state of doubt or oscillation is eliminated.) (*vici* step)
9	⌐	Final situation (outcome/ resolution)	... which Sidi-Nouman agrees to abide by in future, ...	(A verdict is issued that resolves the problem(s).)
10	⊐	Closing	... and balance is restored as a result.	

To work out what state(s) of excess allow(s) the Revelation structure to unfold in the two characters' story lines referred to above, we need to unpack the story told at step 7 (shaded) and put the events in chronological order, for while a story can be told in almost any order, as long as it eventually makes sense, story unfolds in chronological order.

As Sidi-Nouman tells his story, we learn of two women who wanted to become magicians. One embraced white magic; the other, whose name was Amina, black magic. Through an arranged marriage, Amina ended up married to Sidi-Nouman. Sidi-Nouman had no idea she was a magician, but found it strange that although she'd join him for meals, she'd only eat a few grains of rice, lifting them up individually to her mouth on the point of a pin ... and that she'd never lose weight or lack energy. He couldn't explain it. His suspicions raised (*veni* step), he noticed she regularly left the house at night, so decided to follow her discreetly (*vidi* step), which is when he found that she went to a graveyard to feast on corpses with a female ghoul (*vici* step)! Back at home, he confronted her gently. Infuriated at having been found out, she turned him into a dog. After a long series of adventures, the white magician and her mother worked together to return Sidi-Nouman to human form and helped him get revenge. He returned home, surprised his wife, and, by means of a potion the white magician had given him, changed her into a horse (Transformation structure, ending a Call and Response Variation 2 structure). It was this horse that he brought to the market square and whipped to a frenzy every day to teach his wife a lesson. Having heard the story, the Caliph, wishing to restore some sense of balance and justice to the situation, turns to Sidi-Nouman and asks, 'Don't you think that being changed to an animal is punishment enough for her?' which leads to a final 'Ah!'-type resolution of the over-arching story.

In the story that Sidi-Nouman tells, there are four points at which major imbalances in the natural order can be detected. They all relate to instances where the metaphysical and the physical realms meet. The metaphysical elements here all relate to magic or the supernatural in some way:

- The midnight feast at the graveyard, where Amina and a ghoul meet and seek nourishment from the flesh of a freshly buried human corpse.

- Amina's use of magic to transform Sidi-Nouman into a dog and the attempt to kill him in that form.
- The white magician's use of magic to transform Sidi-Nouman back into a man.
- Sidi-Nouman's use of magic to transform Amina into a horse (and his ensuing inhumane behaviour towards her).

Each of these involves a Transformation structure from which a Dynamic Revelation structure unfolds, underpinning a Linear structure, typically Quest, Trickster, or Trickster Variation. The combinations produce Call and Response structures. It could be argued that Sidi-Nouman's behaviour towards Amina, in her horse form, unwittingly draws the attention of the Caliph and results in a restoration of a just balance by the end of the story. The over-arching frame story structure of the Caliph's story line is a classic Trickster Variation structure.

In the story of *The Washerman and His Ass* outlined in chapter 9, the Trickster Awe step is found at step 12. It results in a nested Quest for the qazi, who has a problem, sends for a member of the congregation (who acts as a friend/helper character) to find out why the couple are waving a halter and nosebag at him. Tasked by the qazi to fulfil a Quest, the messenger expects the couple to tell him; they choose not to (a Trickster step arising from Conflicting Quests). They're determined to see the qazi, and tell him that they will *only* explain their actions to the qazi in private (a Transformational Twist). The couple are brought into the qazi's presence, and explain that he's actually their donkey, magically transformed to a learned man of law through the action of the wise mullah—a story which, if made public, would seriously damage the qazi's reputation (for us, this is a Comic step arising from Conflicting Quests with no intention to dupe; for the qazi, it's a Trickster Awe step). He decides to go along with their story, on condition they're sworn to secrecy (a nested Trickster structure ending in a Transformational Twist). As a result, he – and not the mullah – benefits at the end of the story, while the couple succeed in their quest to have someone of their faith, whom they consider family, perform the last rights for them when they die.

In *The Story of Sidi-Nouman*, although the Caliph's judgement restores balance at the end of the story, he draws a line at interfering with the magical forces at play in his kingdom. Happy to let the white magician continue practising, he advises Sidi-Nouman to let Amina live out her days as a horse, thus limiting her ability to perform black magic. The parallel paths that Amina and the white magician follow at the beginning of the story act like a self-regulating mechanism. Amina's use of magic is counteracted and neutralised by the white magician. However, when the effects spill over, and Sidi-Nouman takes things too far in the story, the Trickster Variation structure, with its embedded Revelation structure (and the Caliph's related story line) restore order – not through magic, but through the application of wisdom, the basis of which are universal values of beauty, truth, goodness, uniting to contribute to the Oneness-of-Being. This is unusual in relation to the overarching Transformation structure which frames the entire story, as the Transformation structure always points to an interaction between the divine and mortal realms; between metaphysical and the physical dimensions of being. In fact, this question leads us to the very heart of the story: magic … is balanced by—and trumped by—wisdom.[4]

'The Oneness-of-Being' (articulated as *waḥdat al-wujūd*) is a Sufi term. Unsurprisingly, perhaps, there's a link here between this sense of 'The Oneness-of-Being' and the Revelation structure. Back in chapter 9, we looked at a story in which Goha got into a conversation with a man he met while searching for his donkey. The mapped-out version appears once again below, for convenience:

Analysis of Goha's story line in the story of *When Goha Lost His Donkey*

Steps	Symbols	Outline of content
1	⊐	Once upon a time …
2	⌐	… Goha …
3	⟵	… lost his donkey …
4	⟶	… so he went to look for it.
5	⟵	Meeting a man on the way, Goha asked the man whether he had seen it.
6	⇌	"I've seen the donkey officiating as a judge," came the reply.
7	⟵	Goha processed the response …
8	⇌	… and answered, "I knew he'd be a Cadi … when I taught him philosophy, I noticed his ears weren't sewed up."
9	⌐	[The story is left unresolved.]
10	⊐	[The ending is open-ended.]

Goha (aka Nasr-el-Din Hodja, or Mullah Nasr-el-Din) stories typically come from two distinct traditions: a Sufi tradition and a secular tradition. Stories from the Sufi tradition typically end on or involve cognitive dissonances. Stories from the secular tradition tend to follow more closed structures, as in the story of *Nasr-el-Din Hodja and the Walnut Tree* which featured earlier in this book, where it was used as an example of a Quest structure. We discussed how step 6 in the donkey story could be interpreted as a Conflicting Quest step, in that the man wasn't trying to help Goha find his donkey; he was just trying to lift his spirits. I also noted that this could be interpreted as a Comic step, based on the fact that the man (who appears to be a friend, or at least in no way an enemy) behaves *like* an enemy. And yet, there seems to be something else going on as well. If it were just a Comic step, the comic reaction would be simpler; more immediate – here, there's more than just an element of surprise. There's a sense of astonishment, of being taken slightly aback.

Both of the statements in the story have this quality. On the one hand, there's a social comment on the incompetence of judges implied in the first statement. On the other, Goha's answer is strange. The juxtaposition of animal/human in the acceptance that a donkey could be a judge, the use of stupid/stubborn stereotypes in association with incompetent judges' behaviour are obvious. As noted earlier, there's a niggling sense that something else is going on. That unresolved ending … why would Goha talk about anyone's ears being sewn up? It was this point that struck me most of all when I reflected on this story. It acted on me like a Trickster Awe step. I faced a dilemma which I strongly felt I needed to resolve.[5] The only way I could reconcile the cognitive dissonance – rightly or wrongly – was to think beyond the world of law courts and philosophy. If one's ears were sewn up, it would be much easier to attend to the 'wisdom of the heart'. What Goha could be saying is that the Cadi – in parallel to the popular saying, 'the law is an ass' – is a stereotypically unjust, stupid judge, selfishly open to bribery and corruption, and that had the ass had his ears sewn up, he would have been a more effective judge, as he would have been trained to follow the wisdom of the heart, and would have fostered a sense of natural law – more attuned to following the 'spirit' of the law than an unnatural legal code, in which injustice was enshrined in the 'letter' of the law, and thus less likely to engage in unjust practices. The natural law of common sense, of justice, and of truth provide the bases on which our legal systems are ideally founded, however imperfectly they might attain those ideals in practice – it's an ongoing work in progress which we engage with in and through story.

So far, we've looked at the stories of *Nasr-el-Din Hodja and the Walnut Tree* and of *When Goha Lost His Donkey* from different perspectives and traced the presence of several possible story structures in them – much depends, in both cases, on how we see the initial (⇌) step, and that's the point. Each possibility (Trickster step, Comic step, or Trickster Awe step) is a seed from which a different story structure unfolds. And story structures differ.

All we need to do is count the steps of the Quest, Rags to Riches, and Death and Rebirth structures and compare all of them both quantitatively and qualitatively to the steps of the Call and Response structure to clearly see that the story structures are separate and distinct. Of course, a story can be retold using another structure, but if you try and use two or more Linear structures *simultaneously* in relation to same character's story line, you may find it a challenge at best, maddening at worst. If the way in which we view an event influences the way in which an ensuing story structure unfolds, then why not use that information to inform and improve our decision-making processes? And if Tragedy and Comedy result from category mistakes and category corrections, might this not point to the importance of facing things head on and seeing them for what they are and not what they seem to be, or what we wish they were instead?

Yet again, we find story at the heart of all of this. Story is the ground of stories. Might there perhaps be a structure which could play a universal over-arching 'story of story' or 'story structure of story structures' role?

I believe there is. It's a story structure that points to a process of keeping the real and actual worlds in balance prophylactically as an ongoing process of living in harmony with nature; a story structure which can help us find a better balance between seeing things for what they are and dealing harmoniously with them; a story structure that has a long history, thousands of years old, of helping people keep things in balance; a structure which is culturally specific, but transcends cultural boundaries; an interesting and unique Dynamic story structure that can be seen to underpin all Linear structures universally. This story structure is the focus of the next chapter.

NOTES

1   εἰκόνες μεταφοραὶ λόγου δεόμεναι (*eikones metaphorai logou deomenai*), Aristotle, *Rhetoric*, 1407a14, 119.

2   The structure relates the Trickster and Revelation structures in a static:dynamic way.

3   *The Arabian Nights Entertainments*, edited by Andrew Lang (London, New York and Bombay: Longmans, Green & Co., 1898), 331–345, https://archive.org/details/arabiannightsen00fordgoog/page/n352/. The frame story starts on p 316. The sources in which the story is found are listed under the entry for story 351 in Ulrich Marzolph, and Richard van Leeuwen's *The Arabian Nights Encyclopedia*, 2 vols (Santa Barbara, CA: ABC-CLIO, 2004), Vol. 2, Appendix I, 769. A detailed analysis of *The Story of Sidi-Nouman* is forthcoming.

4   In the source, *The Story of Sidi-Nouman* is paired with *The Story of the Blind Beggar Baba Abdalla*, which follows a similar structure. The second story resolves through the Caliph dispensing mercy. Both stories thus balance each other masterfully – something that the methodology outlined here helps bring to the surface.

5   I return to this aspect of the story in chapter 14, where the story is discussed in relation to the Dilemma structure.

13

COMING FULL CIRCLE – THE GROUND OF STORY

THE CHINESE CIRCULAR STRUCTURE

... the world, when ever it appears as a physical universe*, must always seem to us, its representatives, to be playing a kind of hide-and-seek with itself.

* unus = one, vertere = turn. Any given (or captivated) universe is what is seen as the result of a making of one turn, and thus is the appearance of any first distinction, and only a minor aspect of all being, apparent and non-apparent.

Its particularity is the price we pay for its visibility.

GEORGE SPENCER-BROWN, *Laws of Form*[1]

What story structure does this text follow?

In ancient times when heaven and earth did not yet exist
There was only image without form
    dark obscure
    formless soundless
    unfathomable profound
No-one knows its gate.

Two spirits merged into life
To regulate heaven and organize earth
Vast!
No-one knows how far they reach
Boundless!
No-one knows where they will stop and rest

From this they divide into *yin yang*
Separate into eight poles
Hard and soft complete each other
And the ten thousand beings then take form

Coarse *qi* making insects
Subtle *qi* making humans

Therefore the vital spirits belong to heaven
And the bony frame belongs to earth
The vital spirits re-enter the gate
And the bony frame reverts to its root
How can 'I' continue to exist?

The opening lines of the extract set up a cognitive dissonance in relation to space-time. We're in ancient times. How ancient? It's impossible to tell. And as for an image that has depth, but lacks form ... how can that even exist?

So far so good. We have all the features of a typical story opening here.

But what about the protagonist? Is it life? Is it the 'two spirits'? Is it (the) 'image'? If so, then (the) image of what?[2]

The text quoted above is from a work known as *Jing Shen*, meaning 'vital spirits', chapter 7 of the *Huainanzi* (Master Huainan), a treatise with 21 chapters on cosmology, medicine, public speaking and much else, compiled in the 2nd Century BCE under the patronage of the nobleman Liu An (c.179–122 BCE).[3] Despite being a literary text, parts of it were specifically designed to be read aloud at court and much of the content would have been discussed orally, perhaps even derived from oral discussions.[4] But what story structure does the text follow?

When I first came across the text, I tried to analyse it using the structures we've covered so far – Quest, Transformation, Rags to Riches, Death and Rebirth, Trickster, Trickster Variation, Revelation, and Call and Response. Nothing seemed to work. I asked myself: Is there a problem? If so, what is it? Is there unimpeded flow? I thought that perhaps there might be. The story does seem to flow forward uninhibitedly,[5] and yet there seems to be something else going on below the surface. There's a sense that as soon as a meaning for one element is fixed, the meaning of the rest of the text shimmers and goes into hiding. There's definitely a 'static/dynamic' thing going on here. But I couldn't make the structures fit. I was stuck. And then I attended a lecture on Chinese Medicine and Culture in March 2015 at the Temenos Academy in London.

In it, the speaker, Sandra Hill, proposed that a cyclical structure based on five elements – Earth, Wood, Fire, Metal, Water – underpinned all aspects of traditional Chinese culture. If that was true, I thought, then it must underpin Chinese stories. In the intervening period between that lecture and the writing of this, I became increasingly convinced that she was right.

The diagram above is based on the originals found in Hill's book, *Chinese Medicine from the Classics.*[6]

Four of the five elements are arranged at cardinal points around the fifth (Earth), placed at the central hub. Starting from Earth at the centre, we travel around the circle clockwise from Wood (at '9 o'clock') to Water, then return to Earth, following the cycle of the seasons. In doing so, we also follow the life cycle of a fruit-bearing plant – with life **e-merging** symbolically from the seed in spring, thrusting upward. In summer, the structure clearly **divides** into a greater number of parts. The shoot breaks through the surface of the earth. Leaves, buds, flowers appear – divided, but unified:

a single organism, which involves development of the plant above ground and deep in the earth, a root system, invisible to the eye. In autumn, fruit develops and is harvested, **separating** from the tree. Leaves fall, seeds are sown, lying dormant in the earth through winter, **completing** a life cycle, returning to and rejoining the earth before life can take form again to germinate once more in spring. The cycle spans four main phases: emergence, division, separation, completion. The cycle starts and ends in the centre. In the return, we 'come full circle'. Life is born to die. Completion allows both a return and a regeneration – a dying to be reborn, in both senses of 'dying'.

I went back to the text … and it dawned on me … five key concepts appear regularly in it. They can be seen particularly clearly in the following lines. The words relating to these terms are highlighted in bold in the passage reproduced below:

Two spirits **merged** into life
To regulate heaven and organize earth
Vast!
No-one knows how far they reach
Boundless!
No-one knows where they will stop and rest

From this they **divide** into *yin yang*
Separate into eight poles
Hard and soft **complete** each other
And the ten thousand beings then **take form** (Lines 7–16)

Merge – Divide – Separate – Complete – Take form.

Not only do these key words match the five-element system Sandra Hill spoke about; they also mirror the model that she presented.

The centre point of the model can be seen to be both the point of origin and the point of return of the first cycle in the *Jing Shen*, which spans lines 1–6 for the origin, with the return at line 16.

In ancient times when heaven and earth did not yet exist
There was only image **without form**
    dark obscure
    formless soundless
    unfathomable profound
No-one knows its gate. (Lines 1–6)

… the ten thousand beings then **take form** (Line 16)[7]

The cycle Hill described fits more than just the cycle of seasons, and the growth cycle of plants. The five elements relate to cardinal points (North = Water), and to qualities (Earth = dampness, Wood = wind, Fire = heat, Metal = dryness, Water = cold) as outlined in the *Spring and Autumn Annals*, a classic Confucian text dating from the 5ᵗʰ Century BCE.[8]

The four stages of the cycle are usually described as generation, growth, harvest, storage, which have many different meanings, and relate to spring, summer, autumn, winter; wood, fire, metal, water. The earth at the centre allows the movement from one stage to the next. In the map of the year this is seen as four periods of two weeks which are based on the moon cycles and are called the four gates of the year – the gate of heaven, the gate of earth, the gate of humans, the gate of ghosts. We have just passed through the gate of heaven – two weeks of Chinese New Year celebrations – which herald the beginning of spring. The four gates correspond to the Celtic Imbolc, Lammas, Beltane, Samhain - the cross-quarter days.[9]

In the *Book of Documents*, the arrangement is described as the *Wu Xing* arrangement.[10] One can also think about it in terms of *yin* and *yang*, active and passive, masculine and feminine, cold and hot, wet and dry qualities originating in the mystery of the *dao*, from which all life stems, and which *yin* and *yang* keep in balance according to traditional Chinese philosophy, across a number of

belief systems.[11] The centre is where *yin* and *yang* are in perfect
balance (☯). Traditionally, the Chinese use a broken line to
symbolise *yin* energy [– –] and an unbroken line to symbolise *yang*
energy [—]. Following the cycle of the seasons round, the rising
of *yang* energy in spring is symbolised as ⚎, the flourishing of it
in summer as ⚌, the fall of *yang* and rise of *yin* energy in autumn
as ⚍ and the strongest phase of *yin* energy, in winter, as ⚏. The
unbroken *yang* line, traditionally associated with the masculine is,
in the form, equivalent to Spencer-Brown's mark; the broken *yin*
line, traditionally associated with the feminine, with his 'mark over
mark' symbol for the unmarked state.[12] The table below shows these
relationships. Spencer-Brown's symbols show the complementary
aspect of the Chinese symbols, the 'mark' being used for the 'rising'
phases; the 'mark over mark' for the 'flourishing' ones:

Associations linked to the Chinese Circular Structure

Steps	Symbols	Seasons	Elements	Cardinal points	Yin/ Yang	Structure
1	⊐	Balance	Earth	Centre	☯	Opening
2	⊐	Spring (rising *yang*)	Wood	East	– – ⸺	Initiation/ emergence
3	⊐	Summer (flourishing *yang*)	Fire	South	⸺ ⸺	Division
4	⊐	Autumn (rising *yin*)	Metal	West	⸺ – –	Separation
5	⊐	Winter (flourishing *yin*)	Water	North	– – – –	Completion
6	⊐	Balance	Earth	Centre	☯	Re-integration/ re-formation/ re-centring

There seems to be an oscillatory connection between each of the
outer points and the central hub ('Earth') that is linked to the
'gates' Hill mentioned.[13] The relationship creates a dynamic cycle
of change which moves continuously from one state to another. It's
a perfect, inherently balanced structure in which each of the five

points comprises both static and dynamic qualities, opening up a variety of interpretative approaches.

While this may be confusing, and it may seem difficult to allow a clear meaning to be deduced, clarity is achievable if interpretation is based on an intuitive appreciation of the flowing process which underpins every aspect of the model. I've found the process of engaging with it in this way rather like the process Philip Pullman has Lyra describe in *Northern Lights*, the first book in the trilogy entitled *His Dark Materials*, to explain how she engages with the alethiometer, a truth-measuring device, featuring multivalent symbols which she operates instinctively—using reason but guided by intuition. In the book, when Farder Coram asks her, "And how do you know where these meanings are?" she replies,

> "I kind of see 'em. Or feel 'em rather, like climbing down a ladder at night, you put your foot down and there's another rung. Well, I put my mind down and there's another meaning, and I kind of sense what it is. Then I put 'em all together. There's a trick in it like focusing your eyes."
>
> ...
>
> Farder Coram was a chess player, and he knew how chess players looked at a game in play. An expert player seemed to see lines of force and influence on the board, and looked along the important lines and ignored the weak ones; and Lyra's eyes moved the same way, according to some similar magnetic field that she could see and he couldn't.[14]

As the *Huangdi Neijing* or *Inner Classic of the Yellow Emperor*, an 8th Century CE compilation of documents that date back to the Warring States era (5th to 3rd Centuries BCE) puts it:

> The four seasons of *yin yang* are the end and the beginning of the ten thousand beings; the root of death and of life. Going against their succession destroys life. Going with their succession prevents illness. This is to obtain the way (*dao*).[15]

The short passage, itself, flows round the cycle, and is another example of a passage that can be seen to be based on the Chinese Circular Structure, which can be more easily followed with the addition of the following symbols which make it easier to follow the rising and flourishing aspects of the *yin* and *yang* (unmarked and marked) states as they travel around the circle:

Symbols	Description of symbols
	Used to indicate origination from Earth/Balance
	Used to indicate both a point (here Spring/Emergence) and a direction of flow
	Used to indicate return to the centre
	Used to indicate a 360° arc which launches a move in the opposite direction to the next point along the circumference
	Used to indicate the attainment (however temporary) of a state of Yin/Yang (Heaven and Earth) being in balance

Analysis of an extract from the *Huangdi Neijing*, Chapter 2, *The Way of Heaven*

	Steps		Structure	Text
1	Balance		Opening	The four seasons of *yin yang* are the end and the beginning of
2	Spring		Initiation/ emergence	the ten thousand beings;
3	Summer		Division	the root of death and of life.
4	Autumn		Separation	Going against their succession destroys life.
5	Winter		Completion	Going with their succession prevents illness.
6	Balance		Re-integration/ re-formation/ re-centring	This is to obtain the way.

As we travel round the cycle, we engage with the essence of each element, but also with its relationship to the whole. Moreover, while in most instances, points can be engaged with through confirmation, in others, points can be engaged with through opposition. As the *Jing Shen* indicates, ambiguity and bivalence lie at the heart of the system:

Therefore the sage responds to what is by means of what is not and so penetrates its inner principle. (Line 215, Trans. Hill)

An example of how this works can be found in a passage from the *Lingshu*, also from *The Inner Classic of the Yellow Emperor*. The text below is as per the source; the translations in square brackets are my own editorial insertions. In the source text, these are referenced either earlier in the body text or in notes. In the passage, a dialogue between the mythological emperor Huangdi and his doctor, Qi Bo is recounted, in which the emperor asks,

And what is the meaning of *de* (virtue), *qi* [(energy)], *sheng* (life), *jing* (essences), *shen* [(spirits)][16], *hun* [(mind/spirit)][17], *po* [(attributes)][18], *xin* (heart/mind), *yi* (intent), *zhi* (will), *si* (thought), *lü* (reflection), *zhi* (wisdom)?

Qi Bo replies: Heaven in me is virtue, earth in me is *qi*. Virtue flows, *qi* spreads out and there is life. When two essences embrace, that is called the spirits; that which faithfully follows the spirits in their coming and going is called the *hun*; that which associates with the essences in their entries and exits, is called the *po*. That which takes charge of the being is called the heart/mind (*xin*). When the heart/mind is applied, that is called intent (*yi*); when intent is permanent, that is called will (*zhi*). When will is maintained but also changes, that is called thought (*si*); when thought spreads far and powerfully that is called reflection (*lü*), when reflection is actualized, that is called wisdom (*zhi*). Wisdom is nothing other than the ability to nourish life (*yang sheng*).[19]

If we follow the text around the cycle, we'll find a repeated Chinese Circular Structure the passage both conceals and reveals:

Analysis of an extract from the *Lingshu* (Interpretation 1)

	Steps		Structure	Text
1	Balance		Opening	Heaven in me is virtue, earth in me is *qi*.
2	Spring		Initiation/ emergence	Virtue flows, *qi* spreads out and there is life.
3	Summer		Division	When two essences embrace, that is called the spirits;
4	Autumn		Separation	that which faithfully follows the spirits in their coming and going is called the *hun*;
5	Winter		Integration/ formation/ completion	that which associates with the essences in their entries and exits, is called the *po*.
6	Balance		Re-integration/ re-formation/ re-centring	That which takes charge of the being is called the heart/mind (*xin*).
7	Spring		Initiation/ emergence	When the heart/mind is applied, that is called intent (*yi*);
8	Summer		Division	when intent is permanent, that is called will (*zhi*).
9	Autumn		Separation	When will is maintained but also changes, that is called thought (*si*);
10	Winter		Integration/ formation/ completion	when thought spreads far and powerfully that is called reflection (*lü*),
11	Balance		Re-integration/ re-formation/ re-centring	when reflection is actualized, that is called wisdom (*zhi*).
12	(Compressed Cycle)		Confirmation/ closing (leading to potential re-intergration and emergence in the reader)	Wisdom is nothing other than the ability to nourish life (*yang sheng*).

Emergence	Wisdom is	Division	nothing other than
Separation	the ability to nourish	Completion	life

In steps 7–10 in this version, the energy is mapped flowing clockwise. Here the emphasis is on the naming – the intent named at (7) being the first emergence of 'That which takes charge of the being', the permanence leading to an internal division at (8), the relationship between the static and dynamic, the maintained and the changing here brings us to 'separation' at (9) and the spreading of thought far and wide further at (10) separating from the source from which it emerged at (6) and when the reflection of 'that which takes charge of the being [which] is called the heart/mind (*xin*)' is actualised at (11), we experience a return to balance in the form (12) and the compressed cycle emerges as a response.

I interpret the last sentence as the emergence of the subject, 'wisdom' (Spring). For something to be considered 'nothing other than' another thing, a principle of division is introduced (Summer). For 'nourishment' to occur there has to be a separation, a 'space between' two things (Autumn). With the appearance of the last word, 'life', the sense of the sentence is complete. We come full circle. We arrive at the fifth point (Winter) which allows a return to the centre, the point of origin of the sentence, now reached through our understanding of the meaning which generated the sentence in the first place. We've come 'full circle'.

However, another interpretation is possible—one that is perfectly complementary. In this interpretation, the text follows the cycle up to step 6. From there, rather than going around clockwise, we reverse the direction of travel, going anticlockwise from winter:

Analysis of an extract from the *Lingshu* (Interpretation 2)

	Steps		Structure	Text
1–6	Full cycle		Full cycle	Heaven in me is virtue, earth in me is *qi*. … That which takes charge of the being is called the heart/mind (*xin*).
7	Winter		Integration/ formation/ completion	When the heart/mind is applied, that is called intent (*yi*);
8	Autumn		Separation	when intent is permanent, that is called will (*zhi*).
9	Summer		Division	When will is maintained but also changes, that is called thought (*si*);

Analysis of an extract from the *Lingshu* (Interpretation 2)

	Steps		Structure	Text
10	Spring	⟳	Initiation/ emergence	when thought spreads far and powerfully that is called reflection (*lü*),
11	Balance	⊙ ⟳	Re-integration/ re-formation/ re-centring	when reflection is actualized, that is called wisdom (*zhi*).
12	(Compressed Cycle)		Confirmation/ closing (leading to potential re-intergration and emergence in the reader)	Wisdom is nothing other than the ability to nourish life (*yang sheng*).

Completion	Wisdom is	Separation	nothing other than
⟲		⟳	
Division	the ability to nourish	Emergence	life
⟲		⟳ ⊙	

In steps 7–10 in this version, the energy is mapped flowing anticlockwise. Here, the emphasis is on the application of heart/ mind at (7), the permanence leading to a separation of the static from the dynamic at (8), the duality of permanence being maintained yet also changing brings us to 'division' at (9) and the spreading of thought far and wide linking back to the source from which it emerges at (10).

In this interpretation, the subject of the last sentence isn't emergent wisdom, the kind that produces a response of, 'Hmmm … wisdom … now what does that mean exactly?' but rather, 'Ah! Wisdom! Yes, I know what that means … but what does it imply?' This brings the subject out at Winter, where the sense of understanding is complete. From there, in 'nothing other than' we have a sense of separation going towards division, which brings us swiftly to 'the ability to nourish', with the emphasis on nourishment and sustenance, with life energy flowing from one thing to another, sustaining it, leading to the emergent realisation that, in the form, they (wisdom, life, and the ability to nourish) are one-and-the-same. The realisation immediately brings us into balance with life, closer to the Oneness-of-Being in which we can find true purpose, balance, and fulfilment.

The idea of reversal isn't just supported by engagement with the textual content; it's also found in early sources—here, in reference to using the trigrams for evaluation and for divination:

The numbering of the past is flowing with the current.
The knowledge of the future is countercurrent.
This causes the Yi to count backwards.[20]

There's an interesting relationship between the quote above and the complementary readings of the last line of the extract from the *Lingshu* (Wisdom is nothing other than the ability to nourish life (*yang sheng*)). The emergent clockwise reading can be seen to be declarative, directed towards the past; the anticlockwise reading to be optative, directed towards the future. Holding both in balance and aligned in the present is to achieve 'the Way'. The same applies to the complementary interpretations of the second part (steps 7-11).[21]

As we have seen from the two interpretations of the above passage, the structure has a sense of flow, of binary opposition, but its oppositional elements are conjoined. They're one-and-the-same. The different points of view complement each other and combining them gives us a better understanding of the object we're contemplating. It's appropriate, therefore, to scribe this structure as an alternation between states. George Spencer-Brown's *Laws of Form* is prefaced by a quotation from the *Dao De Jing*: 'Conceived of as having no name, it is the Originator of heaven and earth.'[22] The Calculus of Indications outlined in the work is built on a single mark (⌐) which creates a distinction in the space in which it's conceived. The unmarked state is indicated as (⌐). The Chinese Circular Structure seems to oscillate continuously between the marked and unmarked states, which are equivalent to *yin* and *yang* – two aspects of a holistic, integrated whole, which Spencer-Brown calls 'the form'. As previously outlined, *yin* lines are traditionally dual; *yang* lines single, relating to Spencer-Brown's 'mark over mark' and 'mark' respectively, with the association also extending to the flourishing and rising phases of the change in energy around the circle.[23]

Scribe the Chinese Circular Structure as follows:

Call this the Chinese Circular Structure.

Adding the graphic depictions to the table presented earlier, we get the following:

The Chinese Circular Structure

Steps	Symbols	Seasons	Elements	Cardinal Points	Yin/yang	Structure	Symbols (clockwise cycle)
1	⊐	Balance	Earth	Centre	☯	Opening	◉
2	⌐	Spring (rising yang)	Wood	East	– – ——	Initiation/emergence	◯
3	⌐	Summer (flourishing yang)	Fire	South	—— ——	Division	◯
4	⌐	Autumn (rising yin)	Metal	West	—— – –	Separation	◯
5	⌐	Winter (flourishing yin)	Water	North	– – – –	Completion	◉
6	⊐	Balance	Earth	Centre	☯	Re-integration/re-formation/re-centring	◉

There's a story entitled *Hsün Chü-po Visits His Friend*, dating from a 5th Century CE edition of an earlier classic (now lost) – a collection of anecdotes entitled *Shih-shuo hsin-yü* (New Anecdotes of Social Talk).[24] The story, as translated by John Kwan-Terry, goes like this:

Hsün Chü-po[25] travelled a great distance to see his friend, who was stricken ill. It happened that at this time the prefecture came under attack by the Tartars.

"Death will soon claim me," his friend said to Chü-po. "Please leave while you may!"

"I've come a long way to see you," Chü-po replied, "and you ask me to leave? Is this proper conduct for Hsün Chü-po, to cast aside the principle of righteousness and run away, leaving his friend behind?"

Then the Tartars came, and they said to Chü-po, "Our great armies are here and the people have fled the land. What manner of man are you that dare to linger?"

"My friend lies ill, and I cannot endure the thought of leaving him," Chü-po answered. "Spare his life and take mine in its stead!"

At this, the Tartars marvelled. "Indeed, we are iniquitous men who have come to the land of the righteous." So they gathered their troops and departed, and the prefecture was saved from destruction.

The story fits the Chinese Circular Structure perfectly!

Analysis of *Hsün Chü-po Visits His Friend*

Steps		Structure and symbols		Elements/ seasons	Outline of content
⦿ 1 [Opening] ⊔		[Implied]			
◯ 2 Initiation ⌐		Hsün Chü-po travelled a great distance to see his friend, who was stricken ill. It happened that at this time the prefecture came under attack by the Tartars.			
	⦿ 1 [Opening] ⊔	[Implied]	⦿	Earth/ balance	[Implied]
	◯ 2 Initiation ⌐ [Implied]	Initiation	◔	Wood/ spring	Friend
		Division	◑	Fire/ summer	Becomes sick
		Separation	◕	Metal/ autumn	Wishes to see Hsün Chü-po
		Re-formation/ re-integration/ completion	◒	Water/ winter	Sends for Hsün Chü-po

Analysis of *Hsün Chü-po Visits His Friend*

Steps	Structure and symbols		Elements/ seasons	Outline of content
3 Division [Implied]	Initiation		Wood/ spring	The Tartars
	Division		Fire/ summer	decide to leave their country
	Separation		Metal/ autumn	to attack the prefecture
	Re-formation/ re-integration/ completion		Water/ winter	and include it under their rulership
4 Separation [Implied]	Initiation		Wood/ spring	The message reaches Hsün Chü-po
	Division		Fire/ summer	who leaves his own town
	Separation		Metal/ autumn	to travel a great distance
	Re-formation/ re-integration/ completion		Water/ winter	to see his sick friend.
5 Completion [Implied]	(☐ ㄱ) "Death will soon claim me," his friend said to Chü-po. ㄱ ㄱ "Please leave while you may!" ㄱ (☐) (A ⭘⭘⭘⭘ cycle is implied here.)			
6 Reintegration/ new opening ☐	(☐ ㄱ) "I've come a long way to see you ," Chü-po replied, "and you ask me to leave? ㄱ Is this proper conduct for Hsün Chü-po, to cast aside ㄱ the principle of righteousness and run away, leaving his friend behind?" ㄱ (☐) (A ⭘⭘⭘⭘ cycle is implied here.)			
3 Division ㄱ	Cycle	Then ☐ the Tartars ㄱ came, and they said to Chü-po, ㄱ "Our great armies are here and the people have fled the land. ㄱ What manner of man are you that dare to linger?" ㄱ (☐)		
4 Separation ㄱ	Cycle	(☐ ㄱ) "My friend lies ill, (ㄱ) and I cannot endure the thought of leaving him," (ㄱ) Chü-po answered. "Spare his life and take mine in its stead!" ㄱ (☐)		
5 Completion ㄱ	Cycle	(☐) At this, the Tartars ㄱ marvelled. ㄱ "Indeed, we are iniquitous men ㄱ who have come to the land of the righteous." ㄱ (☐)		

Analysis of *Hsün Chü-po Visits His Friend*

Steps	Structure and symbols	Elements/ seasons	Outline of content
● 6 Re-integration ⊐	Cycle	(⊐) So they ⌐ gathered their troops ⌐ and departed, ⌐ and the prefecture was saved from destruction. ⌐ (⊐)	
	[Closing]	[Implied]	Earth/ Balance [Implied]

I find the fractal quality of the Chinese Circular Structure awe-inspiring. Each part of the cycle can be broken down intuitively into a complete cycle of its own, as demonstrated in the first part of the story in the analysis above.

Couldn't we, however, interpret the story as a Trickster Variation structure story?

Analysis of *Hsün Chü-po Visits His Friend* using the Trickster Variation structure

Steps	Symbols	Structure	Story lines	
			Hsun Chü-po's	The Tartars'
1	⊐	Opening	[Implied]	[Implied]
2	⌐	Initial situation (set-up: who, when, where – two characters on different quests)	Hsun Chü-po	
3	↩	Problem	... had a friend who was ill.	[... wanting to expand their territory ...]
4	→	Journey	He travelled a great distance to see him. They converse. [Nested Quest (unsuccessful) for Hsun Chü-po's friend.]	... attacked the prefecture
5	↩	Meeting between ...	Hsun Chü-po and the Tartars meet	

Analysis of *Hsün Chü-po Visits His Friend* using the Trickster Variation structure

			Story lines	
6	⇌	... the two characters which sets up a cognitive dissonance (Trickster Awe step)	Hsun Chü-po tells the Tartars to spare his life and take his instead.	The Tartars order Hsun Chü-Po to leave.
7	⇋	Meeting between ...	[Implied]	
8	⇌	... the two characters which resolves the cognitive dissonance (Transformational Twist)		At this, the Tartars marvelled. "Indeed, we are iniquitous men who have come to the land of the righteous." So they gathered their troops and departed ...
9	⌐	Final situation (outcome/resolution)	... and the prefecture was saved from destruction.	
10	⊐	Closing	[Implied]	[Implied]

Obviously, the story can be interpreted both ways, but which approach is the most valid? The Linear Trickster Variation structure one, or the Dynamic Chinese Circular Structure one?

Why not both? The relationship between Linear and this Dynamic circular structure has many similarities to the relationship between western and Chinese medicine. Western medicine treats disease, isolates causes, alleviates symptoms. Chinese medicine seeks to keep a person healthy, in balance, and prescribes treatments which take into account seasonal variations in *yin yang* energies, seeing the human organism as an indissolubly linked part of the cosmos. If the systems are treated exclusively, they're limited. There's much benefit to be had from seeing them as complementary, with one informing the other in mutual understanding and appreciation.

Linear story structures lend themselves to rational exploration; Dynamic story structures like the Revelation structure and the Chinese Circular Structure allow a more intuitive approach to be used. There's so much more to be gained from seeing the two types of story structures not simply in an 'either/or' way but in a 'both/ and' way.

Using the Chinese Circular Structure to approach not just classic texts such as the *Huainanzi* or traditional Chinese stories, but stories in general, can shed new light on stories generally. The process can often provide revelatory insights, as we'll see in chapter 18.

The combination of linear and dynamic approaches points to the deep common ground of story itself, the very purpose behind story as a universal phenomenon, and a direct link between 'universal consciousness' and 'individual consciousness' and the importance of acknowledging 'universal consciousness' as the source of story. The 20th Century physicist Max Planck articulated the relationship this way: 'I regard consciousness as fundamental. I regard matter as derivative from consciousness.'

The Chinese Circular Structure probably brings us as close as we can get to the source of story as it forces us to work out for ourselves whether or not this is a manifestation of universal consciousness.

Spencer-Brown's view is this:

we cannot escape the fact that the world we know is constructed in order (and thus in such a way as to be able) to see itself....It seems hard to find an acceptable answer to the question of how or why the world conceives a desire, and discovers an ability, to see itself, and appears to suffer the process. That it does so is sometimes called the original mystery. Perhaps, in view of *the form* in which *we* presently *take* ourselves *to exist*, the mystery *arises from* our insistence on *framing* a question where there is, in reality, *nothing* to question.

But *in order* to do so, evidently it must first cut itself up into at least one state which sees, and at least one other state which is seen. In this severed and mutilated condition, whatever it sees is *only partially* itself. We may take it that the world undoubtedly is itself (i.e. is indistinct from itself), but, in any attempt to see itself as an object, it must, equally undoubtedly, act* so as to make itself distinct from, and therefore false to, itself.

In this condition it will always partially elude itself.
* Cf ἀγωνιστής = actor, antagonist. We may note the identity of action with agony.

This potentially enlightening passage goes right to the core of the relationship between being (as being) and being (as becoming). In the form, they're one-and-the-same. They are story. It's up to us to maintain these two static and dynamic aspects of being in balance. How we do so ... is through stories. We're stories that story 'story' and if we're successful in maintaining balance, we simultaneously become story storying 'story'. And this happens universally.

Apart from the Chinese Circular Structure, there are a number of culturally specific story structures that I've found to date. They form the subject of the next chapter, which will take us further along a road towards achieving a greater understanding of the role and purpose of story.

NOTES

1   Spencer-Brown, *Laws of Form*, 1979, 105–106. The passage in question is on pp. 85–86 in the 2011 edition. The text is essentially the same apart from the final footnote, which is more extensive in the 1979 edition.

2   Note the parallels here with Genesis 1:26–27 to do with image, unity, duality, and multiplicity (And God said, Let us make man in our image, after our likeness: and let them have dominion over the fish of the sea, and over the fowl of the air, and over the cattle, and over all the earth, and over every creeping thing that creepeth upon the earth. / So God created man in his own image, in the image of God created he him; male and female created he them.)

3   All citations are from Liu An, *Jing Shen: The Vital Spirits, A Translation of Huainanzi Chapter 7*, translated by Deena Freeman, Alan Hext, and Sandra Hill (London: Monkey Press, 2010).

4   Liu An, *The Huainanzi*, edited by John S. Major, Sarah A. Queen, Andrew Seth Meyer, Harold D. Roth, Michael Puett and Judson Murray (New York; Chichester: Columbia University Press, 2010), 4, 198, 225/6; David Schaberg, "Remonstrance in Eastern Zhou Historiography," *Early China* 22 (1997): 133–179.

5   This points to a Creation Myth structure, which is presented in chapter 17, but does this text really follow this structure? Is there the same sense of uninterrupted flow as in Genesis 1?

6   Sandra Hill, *Chinese Medicine from the Classics: A Beginner's Guide* (London, UK: Monkey Press, 2014), 16, 18, 20, 31.

7   A further cycle can be traced in the lines which follow (17–23). The entire chapter is 300 lines long. It's composed of four over-arching cycles of 75 lines which go through each aspect of the five-part cycle, the first starting in the centre; the last returning to it. Furthermore, each set of 75 lines goes through the cycle. In addition, within each of these sections, smaller alternative sub-cycles can be identified, and further cycles related to key terms, such as 'heaven and earth', 'sun and moon', 'blood and *qi*' can also be traced through the work.

8   Sandra Hill, *Chinese Medicine*, 14.

9   Email communication from Sandra Hill, Friday 6 March 2015.

10 Summarised in *Yi Jing*, translated by Wu Jing-Nuan (Washington, DC: The Taoist Center, 1991), x–xi. The full text translated into English is found

in *The Sacred Books of China: The Texts of Confucianism*, 2nd ed., edited by Max Müller, translated by James Legge, Vol. 3 (Oxford: Clarendon, 1899), https://archive.org/details/sacredbooksofchi12conf/page/n9. See Legge's notes on 'Ti' in his preface to *Sacred Books*, xxii–xxix and further references to the five elements on pages 47, 140–141. Legge sees no connection between the Yi Jing (or I Ching) and the 5-Element system. Alfred Huang corrects Legge on this in his book, *The Numerology of the I Ching* (Rochester, VT: Inner Traditions International, 2000), 25–52. The five-element system is clearly a foundational framework from which the Yi Jing trigrams can be seen to derive dynamically. See also the reference to the 'six treasuries' and 'five elements' in Bernhard Karlgren, "The Book of Documents," *The Museum of Far Eastern Antiquities Stockholm* 22 (1950): 1–82, at 17, 30.

11   Sandra Hill, *Chinese Medicine*, 2–21.

12   The gender associations of the parts of the form are explored in James Keys [George Spencer-Brown], *Only Two Can Play This Game* (Bath: Cat Books, 1971), 45, 104–105, and especially 111. For Spencer-Brown, they were co-extensive and dynamically linked, as he shows in chapter 11 of *Laws of Form*, in which he introduces oscillation – a dynamic oscillation so fast it gives rise to the illusion of material fixity (⊡).

13   The model can be expanded in this way to fit the eight trigrams of the I Ching around the central hub.

14   Philip Pullman, *His Dark Materials* (London: Scholastic, 2001), 130.

15   *Neijing Suwen*, chapter 2, *The Way of Heaven*, Monkey Press, 1999, 137, quoted in (Hill S., 2014, 11).

16   See Liu An, *Jing Shen*, 51.

17   Liu An, *Jing Shen*, 101.

18   Liu An, *Jing Shen*, 93, 101.

19   Quoted in Sandra Hill, *Chinese Medicine*, 147. Chinese characters not reproduced here.

20   Shuo Gua, *Discussion of the Trigrams*, chapter 3, in *Yi Jing*, trans. Jing-Nuan, 282.

21   This links to the Greek concept of grasping *kairos* – the fleeting moment of opportunity – and manifesting its potential in a balanced way across chronos, or the extensive flow of time. On this, see Debra Hawhee and Sharon Crowley, *Ancient Rhetorics for Contemporary Students* (New York: Pearson Longman, 2004), 36–52; Debra Hawhee, *Bodily Arts: Rhetoric and Athletics in Ancient Greece* (Austin, TX: University of Texas Press, 2004),

65–85. The declarative starts with a static flourishing marked state (⌐); the optative with a dynamic rising unmarked state (⌐|).

22 The Chinese characters for verse 3 of the *Dao De Jing* are used as an epigraph on page xxxii of Spencer-Brown's *Laws of Form* (無名天地之始). The English is from James Legge's translation at https://ctext.org/dictionary. pl?if=en&id=11592. The source text continues '(conceived of as) having a name, it is the Mother of all things. / Always without desire we must be found, / If its deep mystery we would sound; / But if desire always within us be, / Its outer fringe is all that we shall see. / Under these two aspects, / it is really the same; but as development takes place, it receives the different names. / Together we call them the Mystery. / Where the Mystery is the deepest / is the gate of all that is subtle and wonderful.'

23 See the opening passage and definition of Form in Spencer-Brown, *Laws of Form*, 1,3.

24 Y. W. Ma and Joseph S. M. Lau, *Traditional Chinese Stories: Themes and Variations* (New York: Columbia University Press, 1978), 3.

25 He was a native of Ying-ch'uan (central and southern portion of the present Honan Province) and lived in the period of Emperor Huan (r. 147–167) of the Eastern Han Dynasty.

26 Max Planck, "Interviews with Great Scientists VI: Max Planck," *The Observer*, January 25, 1931, https://www.newspapers.com/search/#l-nd=1&query=Interviews+with+Great+Scientists+VI%3A+Max-+Planck&t=1000.

27 Spencer-Brown, *Laws of Form*, 85.

14

THREE FURTHER CULTURALLY SPECIFIC STRUCTURES

DILEMMA TALES, KI-SHŌ-TEN-KETSU

STORIES, AND KOANS

A monk asked, Where is the true meaning of Buddhism?
The master held up his fly whisk.
The monk gave a shout and the master hit him.

SOLALA TOWLER, *The Spirit of Zen*[1]

The story structures outlined in this chapter all link to particular cultures and introduce three aspects of story we have yet to explore: the introduction of open-ended story structures; the role (or roles) that story seekers (people interested in engaging with stories) play with regard to how stories develop; and the role (or roles) these story structures play in the communities and cultures in which they're traditionally found.

We start with a story from West Africa:

Analysis of characters' and story seekers' story lines in a Dilemma structure story

Steps	Characters' story line symbols	Story seekers' story line symbols	Structure	Outline of an African Dyola story[2]
1	⊐	⊐	Opening	[Implied]
2	⌐	⌐	Initial situation (set-up: who, when, where – character and setting)	Two hunters in the forest …
3	⟵	(⟵	Problem	… suddenly become thirsty.
4	⟶	⟶	Journey	One said, "I'll dig a well. You find a bucket."
5	⟵	⟵)	Crossroads/ paradox	In the same instant he broke open the ground with a mighty kick, and pure fresh water gushed forth. Immediately the second hunter produced a bucket, and they quenched their thirst.

Analysis of characters' and story seekers' story lines in a Dilemma structure story

Steps	Characters' story line symbols	Story seekers' story line symbols	Structure	Outline of an African Dyola story[2]
6	⇌	⇌	The story seeker(s) is/are presented with a dilemma, which becomes ...	Which man was the most worthy?
7		↜	... their problem. (↜ → ↜ implied)[3]	
8		→	The discussion they have involves individual and collective powers of reasoning which help them reach an outcome or resolution, ...	
9	↜	↜	... which they turn to the story spinner to present, leading to ...	
10	⇌	⇌	... the eventual resolution of the dilemma, which links to ...	
11	⌐	⌐	... a new state of balance in the social order.	
12	⌐	⌐	[Closing]	[Implied]

The story structure can be mapped horizontally thus:

A							⌒					
	1	2	3	4	5	6	7	8	9	10	11	12
Characters	⌐	⌐	↜	→	↜	⇌		↜	⇌	⌐	⌐	
Story seekers	⌐	⌐	(↜	→	↜)	⇌	↜	→	↜	⇌	⌐	⌐

Steps 7 and 8 – the first step being where the story seekers take over from the story spinner, who leaves the story open-ended – expand to a nested Quest structure, in which the story seekers, faced with a problem of needing to find a solution to the dilemma (←) go on a journey (→), drawing on and using their collective ideas, thoughts, and experience that act as their friends and helpers (← →) to come up with an answer which they find satisfactory, and present to the story spinner. If accepted, this defeats their lack of a solution to the dilemma (← ⇌) (steps 9, 10), and while potential further discussion can ensue, this brings this story to a close.[4]

The bracket above the horizontal sequence in steps 7–9 shows how the sequence of steps can be reduced to the minimal number that enables the story structure to be mapped, reducing ← → ← to ← (A), resulting in the following outline:

Story spinner	⊔ ⌐ ← → ← ⇌ ← ⇌ ⌐ ⊔
Story seeker	⊔ ⌐ ← → ← ⇌ ← ⇌ ⌐ ⊔

And it can be reduced to a single line as follows:

$$\text{⊔ ⌐ ← → ← ⇌ } \boxed{\text{← ⇌}} \text{ ⌐ ⊔}$$

Call this the Dilemma structure.

When the story spinner leaves the story unresolved, a story seeker or seekers need to bring the Open-Ended story to its conclusion. The grey shading marks the qualitative difference between the Open-Ended Dilemma structure and the Closed Trickster or Trickster Variation structures. The initial and final situations in stories that follow a Trickster Variation structure are given by the story spinner. Compare *The Story of Sidi-Nouman* (chapter 12) and the dilemma tale outlined above, which illustrate the difference clearly.[5] *The Story of Sidi-Nouman* is opened and closed by a story spinner without the listeners needing to be engaged in deciding how the story ends. This isn't the case with a Dilemma structure story.

Should the structures be mapped differently on a structural level, rather than simply colour-coding them? After all, the Dilemma structure could be mapped in three further ways:

A - Dilemma structure with the last three steps compressed:

◻ ⌐ ↩ → ↩ ⇌ ⌐ ◻

B - Dilemma structure with the first three steps compressed:

◻ ⌐ ↩ ⇌ ↩ ⇌ ⌐ ◻

C - Dilemma structure with the first and last three steps compressed:

◻ ⌐ ↩ ⇌ ⌐ ◻

While all three interpretations are possible, they seem to me to be too compressed. As versions A and C leave out the audience participation, without which a Dilemma structure story can't fulfil its purpose, these two versions don't fit. Although version B might seem as if it could work, I feel the first step is too compressed. Ideally, we need to feel the characters in the story experience the problem (↩) which takes them on the journey (→) that brings them to a crossroads (↩), which results in the posing of a dilemma (⇌). The sequence of the first three steps can be compressed in the story seekers' story line, though – they just encounter a story. And yet, the structure suggests there may well be a reason for them doing so – whether or not they're aware of this.

The 10-step Dilemma structure outlined above seems to be the most elegant way of describing its distinctiveness. It has all of the essential parts on which the Dilemma structure depends, in minimal form, which is an important part of identifying key elements of story structures.

The Dilemma structure is perfectly matched to its function. In its West African cultural context, it helps people enter into a discussion to seek consensus on moral standards within their social structures.[6] Through considered discussion, it encourages them to cultivate wisdom and reinvigorate present culture in a tradition that links new answers to an oral tradition of past answers, held mainly by the story spinners and community elders.

Seen in this wider cultural context, a story which follows a Dilemma structure could be seen to be nested within a story which follows a Call and Response Variation 1 structure, where there's an inciting transgression against the natural order in the community which results in an impasse. The excess of evil brings forth the balancing force for good in the form of the story spinner (a *veni* step), who tells a Dilemma tale (a *vidi* step), which is designed to bring about a shift in awareness (a *vici* step), resulting in a more harmonious state of being in the community, or at least a realisation of what needs to be done in order to move towards it.

A similar tradition can be found in Far Eastern cultures, in the oral traditions in which the Ki-Shō-Ten-Ketsu structure is said to have originated.

The Ki-Shō-Ten-Ketsu structure is a story structure widely used in Japan, found also in China and Korea. In Chinese, it's known as *Chi-Chen-Juan-He*; in Korean, as *Ki-Sung-Chon-Kyul*.[7] Commonly found in Japanese poetry, Japanese writers nowadays often use it when writing Manga stories.[8] It's characterised by a doubly reinforced opening (*ki, shō*) to introduce the topic, followed by a 'twist' (the *ten* section) in which a new character or theme in stark contrast with the previous sections is introduced 'out of the blue' which builds up tension, a unique feature of the structure. The tension is then resolved in the final *ketsu* section.[9]

A classic example of a story which follows the Ki-Shō-Ten-Ketsu structure is a poem by the Japanese polymath, Rai San'yō:

Analysis of a Ki-Shō-Ten-Ketsu structure story: example 1

Steps	Symbols	Structure	Example (Rai San'yō, trans. Conrad)[10]
1	⊐	[Opening]	[Implied]
2	⌐	Introduction (*ki*) 'to rise/start'	Let me tell you about the two daughters of Itoya, who live in Osaka.
3	→	Development (*shō*) 'to continue'	The elder one's sixteen; the younger one's fifteen.
4	⇌	Twist (*ten*) 'to turn/change'	Generals, throughout history, have killed their enemies with bows and arrows.
5	⌐	Synthesis (*ketsu*) 'to unite/join'	The two daughters of Itoya kill their suitors with their eyes.
6	⊐	[Closing: New state of oscillation from which a new structure can emerge.]	[Implied]

The Ki-Shō-Ten-Ketsu structure isn't limited to Japanese texts. There are many passages in the Chinese *Huainanzi* (which we looked at earlier) which follow a Ki-Shō-Ten-Ketsu story structure, for example:

Analysis of a Ki-Shō-Ten-Ketsu structure story: example 2

Steps	Symbols	Structure	Example (*Huainanzi*, 10.23)[11]
1	⊐	[Opening]	[Implied]
2	⌐	Introduction (*ki*) 'to rise/start'	To dress in brocades and embroidery and ascend the ancestral temple is to value [outer] refinement. To hold gui and zhang tablets in front of yourself is to esteem [inner] substance.
3	→	Development (*shō*) 'to continue'	If your [outer] refinement does not overwhelm your [inner] substance, you may be called a Superior Man.
4	⇌	Twist (*ten*) 'to turn/change'	Therefore, it takes a year to build a chariot, but if it lacks a three-inch long linchpin, you cannot gallop off in it.

Analysis of a Ki-Shō-Ten-Ketsu structure story: example 2

Steps	Symbols	Structure	Example (*Huainanzi*, 10.23)[11]
			It takes a carpenter to frame up a door, but without a foot-long door latch, you cannot close it securely.
5	⌐	Synthesis (*ketsu*) 'to unite/join'	Therefore when the Superior Man acts, he thinks about the results.
6	⊔	[Closing: new state of oscillation from which a new structure can emerge.]	[Implied]

When presented in this (closed) form, scribe the Ki-Shō-Ten-Ketsu structure horizontally thus:

Call this the Ki-Shō-Ten-Ketsu structure.

Scholars are rightly arguing that oral discourse and orally held traditions played a far more important role in the formation of classic Chinese texts in the Han Dynasty (the 'golden age' of Chinese culture) than people previously thought.[12] It's easy to imagine a story spinner breaking off a Ki-Shō-Ten-Ketsu structure story at the *ten* section, opening the content out for debate, and inviting audience members to share their own ideas on how the initial *ki/ shō* and subsequent *ten* sections could potentially be reconciled in a final *ketsu* section.

The text of the *Huainanzi* was compiled under the patronage of the then ruler of Huainan, Liu An and if, as Liu An's biographer, Ban Gu (32–92 CE), wrote

[m]any of the empire's masters of esoteric techniques journeyed [to Huainan] and made their home [at Liu An's court]. Subsequently [Liu An], with the following eight men, Su Fei, Li Shang, Zuo Wu, Tian You, Lei Bei, Mao Bei, Wu Bei, and

Jin Chang, and various Confucians [*ru*] who were disciples
of the Greater and Lesser Mountain [traditions], together
discoursed upon the Way and its Potency and synthesized and
unified Humaneness and Rightness to compose this work[13]

and these 'masters' were, according to Ban Gu, part of 'several
thousand guests and visitors' summoned by Liu An to his court,
then even allowing for exaggeration, it's not hard to imagine
discourse outweighing reading, with orality contributing—in a
major way—to the work, which was presented orally and designed
to stimulate debate.[14] The theory is clearly plausible – particularly
so if structures such as the Ki-Shō-Ten-Ketsu and Chinese Circular
Structure were used as models. Open debate of this kind builds
cultural capital and consensus.

Where the structure is Open-Ended, the structure involves the
active participation of a story seeker for it to reach its conclusion, so
two columns are shown below to distinguish this. The structure(s)
involved in the story seeker's story line typically match the structures
already outlined earlier in the chapter in relation to the Dilemma
structure.

The Open-Ended Ki-Shō-Ten-Ketsu structure

Steps	Story spinner (symbols)	Story seeker (symbols)	Structure
1	⊐	⊐	[Opening]
2	⌐	⌐	Introduction (*ki*) 'to rise/start'
3	→		Development (*shō*) 'to continue'
4	⇌	⇌	Twist (*ten*) 'to turn/change' (a contrast is presented to an audience for debate so a harmonious means of reconciling the resulting clash of ideas might be debated, with an expandable nested (⇌ ← ⇌) sequence implied)
5	⌐	⌐	Synthesis (*ketsu*) 'to unite/join' (a means of reconciliation is arrived at collectively through discussion)
6	⊐	⊐	[Closing: new state of oscillation from which a new structure can emerge.]

The structure can be mapped horizontally thus:

Story spinner   □ ┐ → ⇌ ┐ □
Story seeker   □ ┐ → ⇌ ┐ □

It can be reduced to a single line as follows:

□ ┐ → ⇌ ┐ □

Call this the Open-Ended Ki-Shō-Ten-Ketsu structure.

Finally, another culturally specific structure from this region: the koan. While stories which follow a Ki-Shō-Ten-Ketsu structure pose strongly contrasting topics and invite an audience to reconcile them, a koan poses a more paradoxical problem for an individual story seeker to solve by themselves. A koan is designed to provoke a crossing from an unenlightened state to an enlightened one.[15]

Unsurprisingly, the Koan structure demands the introduction of empty space, which is one of Spencer-Brown's simple expressions involving marks:[16]

The empty space is the closest we can get within the form to the 'nothing', the 'mystery', the void from—and in—which form emerges as the first distinction.[17] It's a perfect way of denoting the enlightened state of 'no-thought' which koans aim to induce. As Zen author, Osho, notes,

'Koan' means an absurd question which cannot be answered, any way you try. It is unanswerable. And one has to meditate on that unanswerable question: 'What is the sound of one hand clapping?' Now, one hand cannot clap. So the answer is, from the very beginning, impossible. But one has to think about it. And Hui-neng [the sixth patriarch of Zen, to whom Osho ascribes the invention of the koan,] says when you think about that which cannot be thought, by and by, slowly,

> thinking becomes impossible. One day, suddenly the whole structure of thinking falls to the ground, shattered. Suddenly you are in a state of no-thought. That's what meditation is.[18]

As James Austin writes, in *Zen and the Brain*, 'only the flash of profound insight' allows a koan to be 'realized, not solved.'[19]

As for where insight and/or realisation emerge from, we enter into the realm of what Keats described as 'negative capability', and George Spencer-Brown, as the 'absence of form'.[20]

The following table describes how the Koan structure works:

A Koan structure example

Steps	Story spinner (symbols)	Story seeker (symbols)	Structure	Example (Hakuin Ekaku)
1	⊔	⊔	[Paradoxical opening which is actually a closing]	[Implied]
2	⏋	⏋	Koan presented	You know the sound of two hands clapping.
3	⇌	⇌	Paradox which sets up a cognitive dissonance	What is the sound of one hand clapping?
4	╗		Resolution of paradox leading to enlightenment	
5	⊔	⊔	[Paradoxical closing which is actually an opening]	[Implied]

The structure can be mapped horizontally thus:

Story spinner ⊔ ⏋ ⇌ ╗ ⊔
Story seeker ⊔ ⏋ ⇌   ⊔

And it can be reduced to a single line as follows:

⊔ ⏋ ⇌   ⊔

Call this the Koan structure.

For the story spinner, the enlightened state is one they revisit, hence it's marked in the story structure as (⊐). It's as if they hold the dynamic aspect of the structure so the story seeker can follow a linear story line. For the story seeker, enlightenment is revealed, which is why it's scribed as the absence of a mark (   ). In Spencer-Brown's work, they both represent the unmarked state in the form. With koans, the story seeker's quest is mainly internal but can involve interaction between story spinner (the master) and story seeker (the disciple seeking enlightenment). This can take the form of a conversation, or a non-verbal interaction, as the quote at the start of this chapter illustrates. Where this happens, the conversation often takes the form of a Trickster and/or Trickster Variation structure.[21]

Open-Ended stories that follow a Dilemma structure, an Open-Ended Ki-Shō-Ten-Ketsu structure, or a Koan structure can only be resolved when one or more story seekers engage with the story individually or collectively. The impetus to seek a resolution, in all cases, comes from the Trickster Awe step which the story spinner leaves the story seekers with at the end of the story. These Open-Ended consensus-seeking story structures act in a similar way to maieutic (Socratic) questioning, or sophistic debate, where a cognitive dissonance is often deliberately set up to lead a person to doubt and question, guiding them to the realisation of a deep truth. Plato's dialogues and allegories, Zeno's paradoxes (e.g., 'the arrow in flight is always still'), and dialectic debate (in its best sense) in which a proposition is presented and two opposing positions argued in order for a shared consensus to be reached are all designed to do this.[22] For it to work, both parties need to be both fully engaged with their respective positions, believing it to be true; and both parties need to be prepared to change their point of view, their common aim being to reach a shared position they both can agree is true – at least within reasonable doubt. Story depends as much on story seekers as it does on story spinners – and the Open-Ended structures outlined here are key to opening ourselves collectively to the power of story and bringing it to life within us – as individuals and as members of our communities. The stories we tell shape us as communities. Where stories differ, it's vital to engage in open-ended debate in order to reach consensus. The debate can be difficult, challenging, even painful – but it has the potential to be cathartic.

The koan is designed to provide a gateway to enlightenment, the second birth that all humans are called to go through, but the road isn't without challenges. Kant once wrote:

> Enlightenment is man's emergence from his self–imposed nonage.[23] Nonage is the inability to use one's own understanding without another's guidance. This nonage is self–imposed if its cause lies not in lack of understanding but in indecision and lack of courage to use one's own mind without another's guidance. *Sapere aude!* "Have the courage to use your own understanding", is therefore the motto of the enlightenment.[24]

There's a Zen parable about a young novice who wanted to be enlightened. He worked for nine long years in a monastery – cooking, cleaning, listening to the master expound on Zen wisdom, tried to solve koan after koan – all to no effect. One morning, the master called the young novice to him and said, "You've been here for a long time and I've nothing more to teach you. If you truly seek enlightenment, leave the monastery, turn your face to the dawn, and head up the mountain. My predecessor lives a day's journey up the path. Seek him out. He may be able to help you." The novice thanked the master, said goodbye to his colleagues, and set out. He climbed for the rest of the day, rested under the stars that night, and continued up the path the next morning. As he journeyed, he met an old man coming down the path carrying an axe and a bucket. The young man asked him if he knew where he could find the monk who used to be head of the monastery at the foot of the mountain.

The man said, "I am that man. Why are you looking for him?" "Please, master – I seek enlightenment. Will you teach me? What do I need to do? What is it like to be enlightened?" The man laughed and said, "Before enlightenment, chop wood carry water; after enlightenment, chop wood carry water." At that moment, the young novice became enlightened.

The story structures presented in this chapter – the Open-Ended Dilemma, Ki-Shō-Ten-Ketsu and Koan structures, and the Closed Ki-Shō-Ten-Ketsu structure – are all closely linked to specific cultural contexts. There's another, much more universal open-ended story structure that demands the involvement of a story seeker for the story to unfold. That structure is the focus of the next chapter.

NOTES

1   Solala Towler, *The Spirit of Zen: Teaching Stories on the Way to Enlightenment* (London: Watkins, 2017), introduction.

2   William Bascom, *African Dilemma Tales* (The Hague: Mouton, 1975), 29–30.

3   Equivalent to the initial three (← → ←) steps in a Quest structure: Problem, Journey, Meeting. If, in the next step, their powers of reasoning render an incorrect answer, then the structure becomes a Trickster structure, and the sequence loops back to the Problem step (step 7) until the flow follows a Quest-type structure, which is resolved in the final (⇌) step, where the story seekers 'turn the tables' on the story spinner who presented them with the paradox that set them on their journey in the first place, bringing both story lines to a resolution.

4   For a discussion of the use of dilemma tales to facilitate problem solving, train critical thinking, and resolve conflict in communities, see William Bascom, *African Folktales in the New World* (Bloomington, IN: Indiana University Press 1992), 2, 13–14; and Kwadwo Opoku-Agyemang and Rogers Asempasah, "Theorising the ambiguous space: The narrative architecture of the dilemma tale as an interpretive frame for reading Morrison's B," *Asemka* (2006): 164–178, at 171. https://www.scm.uni-halle.de/gsscm/online_ papers/online_papers_2006/morrisons_beloved/?lang=en.

5   A detailed analysis of *The Story of Sidi-Nouman* is forthcoming.

6   In addition to noting the use of dilemma tales to resolve issues within local communities, Bascom presents the view of dilemma tales being used for training in political and legislative oratory – both of these being practised in formal, institutional social frameworks designed (when functioning at their best) to help societies achieve and maintain balance. Bascom, *African Dilemma Tales*, 1, 2, 14.

7   Jai Hee Cho, "A Study of Contrastive Rhetoric between East Asian and North American Cultures as Demonstrated through Student Expository Essays from Korea and the United States," PhD diss., Bowling Green State University, 1999, http://faculty.fullerton.edu/jcho/dissertation.htm, 12.

8   See David Cahill, "The Myth of the "Turn" in Contrastive Rhetoric." *Written Comunication* 20, no. 2 (2003): 170–194. Cahill's view that the structure is more flexible and not as generic as some might consider it to be does not invalidate the distinctiveness of the structure, nor does it invalidate the argument presented here.

9   The treatment of opposition in the The Ki-Shō-Ten-Ketsu structure has more in common with Blakean metaphysics than with Hegelian dialectic. The Ki-Shō-Ten-Ketsu structure reconciles opposition; Hegelian dialectic resolves it. In Blakean metaphysics, contraries fuel progression, which is the dynamic aspect of the static moment of realisation fuelled by the Ki-Shō-Ten-Ketsu structure.

10 For alternative translations, see Senko K. Maynard, *Japanese Communication: Language and Thought in Context* (Honolulu, HI: University of Hawaii Press, 1997), 159–162; and T. E. Waters, "On Narrative Structure: Kishōtenketsu and Obokuri-Eeumi," 29 January, 2013. http://blog.tewaters.com/2013/01/on-narrative-structure-kishotenketsu.html.

11 Liu An, *The Huainanzi,* edited by John S. Major, Sarah A. Queen, Andrew Seth Meyer, Harold D. Roth, Michael Puett and Judson Murray (New York; Chichester: Columbia University Press, 2010).

12 Scholars such as John Major, while acknowledging the role of orality, privilege written sources, but in face of more recent studies, in particular by David Schaberg (e.g., "Remonstrance in Eastern Zhou Historiography," *Early China* 22 (1997): 133–179; *A Patterned Past: Form and Thought in Early Chinese Historiography,* (Cambridge, MA: Harvard University Press, 2002), and other works), Martin Kern ("Creating a Book and Performing It: The 'Yao lüe' Chapter of the 'Huainanzi' as a Western Han 'Fu'," in *The 'Huainanzi' and Textual Production in Early China,* edited by Sarah A. Queen and Michael Puett, 124–150 (Leiden: E. J. Brill, 2014), https://doi.org/10.1163/9789004265325_006) and Michael Nylan ("Translating Texts in Chinese History and Philosophy," in *Translating China for Western Readers: Reflective, Critical, and Practical Essays,* edited by Ming Dong Gu and Rainer Schulte, 119–148 (Albany, NY: SUNY Press, 2014), 120–122, 140; and other works), this position seems more and more in need of revision. For a similar hypothesis relating to the tradition of *The Arabian Nights,* see Ulrich Marzolph and Richard van Leeuwen, *The Arabian Nights Encyclopedia,* 2 Vols. (Santa Barbara, CA: ABC-CLIO, 2004), 10–11.

13 Liu An, *The Huainanzi,* 8.

14 See comments in note 4 on orality, and the references in note 12, above.

15 The principle of crossing is key to Spencer-Brown's work. It also features symbolically in Schwaller de Lubicz's symbolist analysis of the meaning of a pharaoh's crossed arms in death, holding sceptres which can, in turn, be double-crossed. See René Adolph Schwaller de Lubicz, *The Temple of Man,* translated by Deborah Lawlor and Robert Lawlor (Rochester,

VT: Inner Traditions International, 1998), 476–478, 79–80. The links to the intertwining of the serpentine tails of FuXi and Nüwa to Hermes' *Kerykeion* (Mercury's *Caduceus*) and the theme of 'Redemption' outlined in Jules Cashford's *From Thoth to Mercurius* (Ilford, Somerset: Kingfisher Art Productions, 2017), 1–2, 31, 49, 74, 78 are worth contemplating. Walter J. Friedlander's arguments about the prehistory of the caduceus are superseded by the above authors', however his links between boundary-crossing, trade, and crossroads in relation to the symbolism of Hermes are noteworthy. See *The Golden Wand of Medicine: A History of the Caduceus Symbol in Medicine*, Vol. 35 of Contributions in Medical Studies (Westport, CT: Greenwood, 1992), 32–33, 129.

16   Spencer-Brown, *Laws of Form*, 5.

17   Spencer-Brown, *Laws of Form*, 4–5.

18   Osho, "Zen: The Path of Paradox, Vol. 2," 107, *Internet Archive*, n.d., accessed 23 January, 2018. https://archive.org/details/zen-the-path-of-paradox-volume-2/page/106/.

19   James H. Austin, *Zen and the Brain: Toward an Understanding of Meditation and Consciousness* (Cambridge, MA and London, UK: MIT Press, 1999), 112, 117.

20   Spencer-Brown, *Laws of Form*, 4–5.

21   For example, the story spinner's story line might follow a Trickster structure; the story seeker's, a Trickster Variation structure.

22   For this reason, I believe the *Dissoi Logoi* to be an initiatic text.

23   Nonage: The period of a person's immaturity or youth, before they have 'come of age'. Origin: Late Middle English: from Old French *nonage*, from *non-* 'non-' + *age* 'age' (OED).

24   Immanuel Kant, "What Is Enlightenment?" translated by Mary C. Smith, http://www.columbia.edu/acis/ets/CCREAD/etscc/kant.html. People who know me well know that I have a tendency to rant against an uncritical reception of Kant's work and the general view that the history of philosophy shows a trajectory of progress. The grounds of my rant against Kant's work lie mainly in his reformulation of Aristotle's Categories of Being, a reformulation which serves no practical purpose that I can see. I find his stance inconsistent, and troubled. The split between the noumenal and the phenomenal which never troubled Goethe as much as it did Kant taints Kant's work with inconsistency and I stand with Salomon Maimon and J. M. Robertson, the latter having evaluated Kant's position thus: 'So far, on the other hand, is Kant's moral fanaticism from safeguarding the moral

sense that we actually find him, the absolutist, the professed ascetic of veracity, grossly transgressing his own law where there is hardly a shadow of excuse for it.' (Rt Hon John Mackinnon Robertson, *Letters on Reasoning*, 2nd ed., Rev. with additions (London: Watts, 1905), 191). In terms of approaches to knowledge, there's much to be said for the more integrative injunction which originates with the seven sages of Greece Γνῶθι σαυτὸν (*gnothi seauton*) 'know thyself') (Pausanias. *Phocis, Ozolian Locri*, 10.24.1, from Pausanias: Description of Greece in Four Volumes, Vol. 3, translated by William Henry Samuel Jones (Cambridge, MA: Harvard University Press; London: W. Heinemann, 1965). http://www.perseus.tufts.edu/hopper/text?doc=Paus.+10.24), as well as for the wisdom of Zen, and the power of story.

15

RIDDLES

THE RIDDLE STRUCTURE

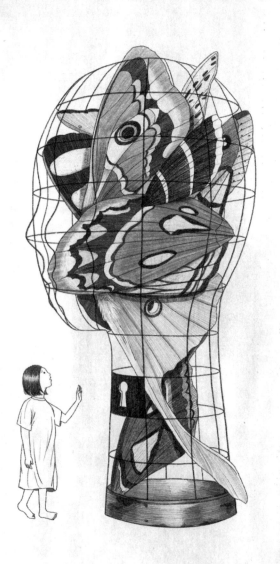

'Since,' [Ammonius] went on to say, 'inquiry is the beginning of philosophy, and wonder and uncertainty the beginning of inquiry, it seems only natural that the greater part of what concerns [Apollo] should be concealed in riddles, and should call for some account of the wherefore and an explanation of its cause.'

PLUTARCH, TRANS. BABBITT,
On the E at Delphi (De E apud Delphos), 2[1]

The solution of the riddle of life in space and time lies outside space and time.
When the answer cannot be put into words, neither can the question be put into words.
The riddle *does not exist.*

WITTGENSTEIN, TRANS. PEARS AND MCGUINESS,
Tractatus Logico–Philosophicus, 6.4312, 6.5[2]

We solve puzzles; we resolve dilemmas; we answer riddles.[3] Puzzles follow the Quest structure. Dilemmas, the Dilemma structure. Riddles follow the Riddle structure. For the purposes of this work, riddles are considered a type of story (another example of why the approach outlined in this book points to the need to redefine the word 'story').

A riddle is based around a question we know the answer to but are not immediately aware what is it. As soon as we've worked it out, we've found the answer to the riddle.

In chapter 9, I described Comedy as being structure neutral and based on Aristotelian category mistakes. In chapter 10, I described Tragedy as being structure neutral and based on category corrections. Riddles are based on category confusions. The category confusions seem to be consistently related to the category of substance. Take this riddle, for instance:

I saw close to the houses of men
A strange creature that feeds cattle.
By tooth-hoard and nose-haul
(A useful slave), it scruffs the ground,
Scratches at plants, dogs walls
Or drags fields for plunder—seeks
A crop-catch and carries it home.
Its prey bent stalk and weak root;
Its gift is firm grain and full flower
On a glittering plain—growing, blooming.
[What might it be?]

(Riddle from the Exeter Book, K-D 34)[4]

Riddles appear in many forms. Most of the riddles below are drawn from the Exeter Book, but the one on pages 242–243 is in the form of a Dosukhna, a form which presents the story seeker with the challenge of finding a single word or phrase that provides a common answer to a pair of seemingly unrelated questions based on strong contrasts.

The beginning of a Riddle structure story: an example

Steps	Symbols	Structure	Example (Old English Riddle from the Exeter Book, K-D 34)[5]
1	⊐	[Opening]	[Implied]
2	⌐	Substance alluded to but not stated	I saw close to the houses of men A strange creature ...
3	⇌	Attributes listed, creating a cognitive dissonance	... that feeds cattle. By tooth-hoard and nose-haul (A useful slave), it scruffs the ground, Scratches at plants, dogs walls Or drags fields for plunder—seeks A crop-catch and carries it home. Its prey bent stalk and weak root; Its gift is firm grain and full flower On a glittering plain—growing, blooming. [What might it be?]

What happens next depends on the structure the story seeker follows and the role the story spinner plays. Three common options I've come across are the Quest, the Trickster and the Trickster Variation structures. Where the story seeker's journey follows a Quest structure, the full Riddle structure can be mapped thus. :

Analysis of story lines in a Riddle structure with a Quest structure ending

Steps	Story spinner (symbols)	Story seeker (symbols)	Structure	Example (Old English Riddle from the Exeter Book, K-D 30)[6]
1	⊐	⊐	[Opening]	[Implied]
2	⌐	⌐	Substance alluded to but not stated	I am …
3	⇌	⇌	Attributes listed, creating a cognitive dissonance	… sun-struck, rapt with flame, Flush with glory, flirt with the wind— I am clutched by storm and touched by fire, Ripe for the road, blood-wood or blaze. My path through the hall is from hand to hand As friends raise me, proud men and women Clutch and kiss me, praise my power And bow before me. To many I bring A ripe bliss, a rich blossoming. [What am I?]
4		←	Seeker, presented with problem …	
5		→	… goes on an internal journey …	
6		←	… and meets	
7		→	… a friend or helper; then goes …	(Here, rational enquiry, experience, existing knowledge, memory, and logic all act as friends or helpers.)

Analysis of story lines in a Riddle structure with a Quest structure ending

Steps	Story spinner (symbols)	Story seeker (symbols)	Structure	Example (Old English Riddle from the Exeter Book, K-D 30)[6]
8	⟵	⟵	... and meets the story spinner ...	
9	⇌	⟶	... to get their answer confirmed or refuted	
10	⟵	⟵	The answer is considered ...	
11	⇌	⇌	... and a response given	(If the answer is refuted, the seeker loops back to step 4; if the answer is confirmed, the doubt is removed, the riddle is solved and the cognitive dissonance resolved.)
12	⌐	⌐	The substance is confirmed	[Holy cross or wassail cup.]
13	⊔	⊔	[Closing]	[Implied]

Alternatively, if the seeker's journey matches a Trickster structure, the overarching Riddle structure can be mapped as follows:

Analysis of story lines in a Riddle structure with a Trickster structure ending

Steps	Story spinner (symbols)	Story seeker (symbols)	Structure	Example (Old English Riddle from the Exeter Book, K-D 13)[7]
1	⊔	⊔	[Opening]	[Implied]
2	⌐	⌐	Substance alluded to but not stated	I saw six creatures scratch the ground, Their four lively sisters strutting round;

Analysis of story lines in a Riddle structure with a Trickster structure ending

Steps	Story spinner (symbols)	Story seeker (symbols)	Structure	Example (Old English Riddle from the Exeter Book, K-D 13)[7]
3	⇌	⇌	Attributes listed, creating a cognitive dissonance	The house of each pale skin on shell, A fine, filament robe hung on a wall, Well-seen. Though each had been stripped Of a gossamer skin, none was nude Or raw with pain; but quickened, covered, And brought to grass and grain by God— They pecked,, strutted, and stripped sod. [What were they?]
4		←	Seeker, presented with problem ...	
5		→	... goes on an external journey ...	
6	←	←	... and meets ...	
7	⇌	⇌	... a Trickster step from the story spinner ...	(Here, when the story spinner is asked for a clue, they deliberately seek to send the story seeker off in the wrong direction, on a wild goose chase. The seeker loops back to (4) and follows either a Quest (if the Trickster step (7) is spotted), Trickster, or Trickster Variation structure.)
8	←	←	... then approaches the story spinner ...	
9	⇌	⇌	... to get their answer confirmed or refuted	(Step (9) becomes the balancing Transformational Twist that cancels out step (7).)
10	←	←	The answer is considered ...	

Analysis of story lines in a Riddle structure with a Trickster structure ending

Steps	Story spinner (symbols)	Story seeker (symbols)	Structure	Example (Old English Riddle from the Exeter Book, K-D 13)[7]
11	⇌	⇌	... and a response given	(When the answer is confirmed, the doubt removed, the riddle solved, the cognitive dissonance is resolved. Step (11) becomes the balancing Transformational Twist that cancels out Trickster Awe step (3). Otherwise, the seeker loops back to (4) again, as in step (7).)
12	⌐	⌐		[Ten chickens.]
13	⌑	⌑	[Closing]	[Implied]

If the seeker's journey matches a Trickster Variation structure, the overarching Riddle structure can be mapped as follows:

Analysis of story lines in a Riddle structure with a Trickster Variation structure ending

Steps	Story spinner (symbols)	Story seeker (symbols)	Structure	Example (Original)
1	⌑	⌑	[Opening]	[Implied]
2	⌐	⌐	Substance alluded to but not stated	What ...
3	⇌	⇌	Attributes listed, creating a cognitive dissonance	... makes the timidest infantryman confident? [What] makes the bravest waterfowl hesitant?
4		↼	Seeker, presented with problem ...	
5		⇀	... goes on an internal journey ...	
6		↼	... and meets ...	
7		⇌	... a revelatory 'Aha!' moment ...	
8	↼	↼	... then approaches the story spinner ...	

Analysis of story lines in a Riddle structure with a Trickster Variation structure ending

Steps	Story spinner (symbols)	Story seeker (symbols)	Structure	Example (Original)
9	⇌	→	... to present what they think is the answer ...	
10	↼	↼	... the answer is considered ...	
11	⇌	⇌	... and a response given	(If the answer is refuted, the seeker loops back to step 4 and follows either a Quest or Trickster Variation structure; if the answer is confirmed, the doubt is removed, the riddle is solved, and the cognitive dissonance resolved.)
12	¬	¬		[A pike.]
13	⊐	⊐	[Closing]	[Implied]

The three structural mappings outlined above can be represented thus:

Riddle with Quest ending

	1	2	3	4	5	6	7	8	9	10	11	12	13
Story spinner	⊐	¬	⇌					↼	⇌	↼	⇌	¬	⊐
Story seeker	⊐	¬	⇌	↼	→	↼	→	↼	→	↼	⇌	¬	⊐

Riddle with Trickster ending

	1	2	3	4	5	6	7	8	9	10	11	12	13
Story spinner	⊐	¬	⇌			↼	⇌	↼	⇌	↼	⇌	¬	⊐
Story seeker	⊐	¬	⇌	↼	→	↼	⇌	↼	⇌	↼	⇌	¬	⊐

Riddle with Trickster Variation ending

	1	2	3	4	5	6	7	8	9	10	11	12	13
Story spinner	⊐	⌐	⇌					←	⇌	←	⇌	⌐	⊐
Story seeker	⊐	⌐	⇌	←	→	←	⇌	←	→	←	⇌	⌐	⊐

The three versions detailed above can be reduced to a common form, following consecutive reduction steps shown at levels A, B, and C in the tables below.

Riddle with Quest ending

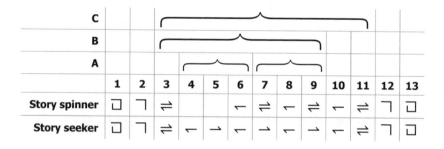

	1	2	3	4	5	6	7	8	9	10	11	12	13
Story spinner	⊐	⌐	⇌			←	⇌	←	⇌	←	⇌	⌐	⊐
Story seeker	⊐	⌐	⇌	←	→	←	→	←	→	←	⇌	⌐	⊐

Riddle with Trickster ending

	1	2	3	4	5	6	7	8	9	10	11	12	13
Story spinner	⊐	⌐	⇌			←	⇌	←	⇌	←	⇌	⌐	⊐
Story seeker	⊐	⌐	⇌	←	→	←	⇌	←	⇌	←	⇌	⌐	⊐

Riddle with Trickster Variation ending

	1	2	3	4	5	6	7	8	9	10	11	12	13
C			⌐‾‾‾‾‾‾‾‾‾‾‾‾⌐										
B		⌐‾‾‾‾‾‾⌐											
A			⌐‾‾⌐		⌐‾‾⌐								
Story spinner	□	⊓	⇌					←	⇌	←	⇌	⊓	□
Story seeker	□	⊓	⇌	←	→	←	⇌	←	→	←	⇌	⊓	□

This justifies mapping the Riddle structure as outlined above:

$$\square\ \sqcap\ \rightleftharpoons\ \sqcap\ \square$$

Call this the Riddle structure.

As noted at the beginning of this chapter, riddles come in different forms, just as there can be many narrative forms or telling of a particular story. The different forms will always be recognisable as riddles and while there are exceptions to every rule, as a general rule, riddles follow a Riddle structure.

Parables can also follow a Riddle structure:

Example of a Riddle structure parable

Steps	Symbols	Structure	Example: 'The Blind Leading the Blind' (Matthew 15:11, 14–20)
1	□	[Opening]	[Implied]
2	⊓	Character and setting	[The Pharisees] are blind leaders of the blind.
3	⇌	Point presented as an extended analogy, linking (and separating) source and target domains	And if the blind lead the blind, both will fall into the ditch.

Example of a Riddle structure parable

Steps	Symbols	Structure	Example: 'The Blind Leading the Blind' (Matthew 15:11, 14–20)
4	٦	Resolution which emerges from separating (and reuniting) source and target domains	Not that which goeth into the mouth defileth a man; but that which cometh out of the mouth, this defileth a man … whatsoever entereth in at the mouth goeth into the belly, and is cast out into the draught … those things which proceed out of the mouth come forth from the heart; and they defile the man … … to eat with unwashen hands defileth not a man. [despite the Pharisees thinking that it does].
5	◻	[Closing]	[Implied]

Comic riddles, such as the bawdy ones in the Exeter Book, achieve their effect by creating a substantial category mistake (pun intended) behind which is the category confusion of the riddle.[8] We're given a general term: 'a being' (e.g., Old Exeter Riddle Book riddle number K-D 29), 'a thing' (K-D 34), 'me/my/I' (K-D 15, 40), etc., to create the category confusion with regard to the substance of the thing being described. A list of attributes follows to help people guess the riddle. In bawdy riddles, the object to be guessed is usually innocuous, but the attributes describing it are selected for their salaciousness and connection to intimate bodily parts or functions. Part of what makes the joke funny is that this is a riddle, and what is supposed to be guessed at, or made obscure, is being made obvious; what should be confusing is being made plain—not to mention the comic effect of breaking taboos in the telling, which creates a category mistake in the quality of the social situation. It's one of the things that gives bawdy riddles their comic potential. Substance, in the Aristotelian sense, relates not to the physicality of an object but to the non-physical element that distinguishes a living person from a corpse.[9] The Riddle structure's function seems to be to help point us to the true meaning of substance.

A story spinner who poses a riddle isn't deliberately trying to trick us. Their intention isn't an intention to dupe. They'll give us the answer—eventually. The riddles they pose are gifts – gifts that have the potential to unlock memories and knowledge, to forge connections deep within us, and support holism.

People have been asking, 'What's the meaning of life?' for millennia. The question remains unsolved. In the passage which opened this chapter, Wittgenstein sees this as a riddle. He never formulates 'the riddle of life' – on the one hand, he doesn't need to; on the other, he can't. The solution, if it appears, is something that can't be put into words; something ineffable. Not only does that riddle transform into a koan, but the transformation has the potential to help us find our own answer to the riddle. It can feel as if we've travelled beyond the known to the unknown and come back transformed, which brings us to what Christopher Booker calls the 'Voyage and Return' plot – if it even exists. Whether it does or doesn't is a question we'll be exploring in the next chapter.

NOTES

1   Plutarch, *Moralia*, translated by Frank Cole Babbitt. Vol. 5 (Cambridge, MA; London: Harvard University Press, 1936), 2.385c, 202–203. http://www.perseus.tufts.edu/hopper/text?doc=Perseus:text:2008.01.0243:section=2.

2   Ludwig Wittgenstein, *Tractatus Logico-Philosophicus*, translated by D. F. Pears and B. F. McGuinness (London and New York: Routledge Classics, 2001), 87–88.

3   The distinction is made by Bascom, *African Dilemma Tales*, 12.

4   Riddle 32 in *A Feast of Creatures: Anglo-Saxon Riddle Songs*, edited and translated by Craig Williamson (Philadelphia, PA: University of Pennsylvania Press, 2011), 92. The commonly accepted answer is 'a rake'.

5   Riddle 32 in Williamson, *A Feast of Creatures*, 92.

6   Riddle 28 in Williamson, *A Feast of Creatures*, 88.

7   Riddle 11 in Williamson, *A Feast of Creatures*, 71.

8   The reference is to the first of Aristotle's 10 Categories of Being: Substance, as referenced in chapter 9.

9   'Substance (*Ousia*), in the truest and strictest, the primary sense of that term, is that which is neither asserted of nor can be found in a subject. We take as examples of this a particular man or a horse.' Aristotle, *Categories*, 2a11, 19; 'we then should speak falsely … calling a dead man a man', *De interpretatione* 21a20, 155; 'the *essence* (*to ti ēn einai*), whose formula is the definition, is also called the substance of each particular thing', *Metaphysics* 5.1017b, 241. In the Greek, '*essence*' literally stands for a thing's 'being'. Other definitions in the Liddell, Scott, Jones *Greek-English Lexicon* include: the 'thing-in-itself', and 'the what it was to be'.

16

MOVING BETWEEN WORLDS

THE VOYAGE AND RETURN STRUCTURE

Well, here we go, dear Reader, together for one last trip. First we must take off into space. Inner space, outer space, it is all the same this time. Wherever you go in outer space, your image goes in inner space, so you can look at it from either side as you please.

So then, are we all ready? Fasten your seat-belts, Ladies and Gentlemen! If anybody has cold feet, now's the time to own up. Unfasten your seat-belt, and get out while you still can. What, Madam, you get travel-sick? Then please don't come! And you, Sir, I see that your ego is your only means of support. You had please better stay at home.

...

Now Ladies and Gentlemen, no more questions please, is everybody ready for the re-entry? All drunk your sedatives? Good. All in a hurry to get back, sure we understand. People down there waiting for you, wondering where you are. Naturally. Of course. Miss Terylene will be passing round Customs Declarations Forms which you are to fill in stating your desired destination and nature of business. Mr. Calculus will be calling base and making the necessary bookings. It depends to some extent on vacancies. Vacancies where, did I hear you say, Madam, Sir? Where? In the maternity wards of course!

GEORGE SPENCER-BROWN, WRITING AS JAMES KEYS,
Goodbye Trip in *Only Two Can Play This Game*[1]

According to Christopher Booker, the stories of *Goldilocks and the Three Bears*, *Brideshead Revisited*, and *The Tale of Peter Rabbit* follow a 'Voyage and Return plot' because all of these stories involve characters either travelling to a mysterious realm beyond the boundaries of the known world, or to an unfamiliar part of the world they inhabit.[2] After an initial state of excitement, events in the stories gradually take darker and darker turns, with the character(s) emerging from the experience transformed in some way. At first, Booker's definition is wide enough to include the stories mentioned above. Later, however, he writes that 'The whole point of Voyage and Return stories is that their central figures' sudden, disconcerting plunge into a strange, unfamiliar world happens to them *without their wishing it.*'[3] I agree. However, this doesn't apply to Goldilocks, or to Charles Ryder, or to Peter Rabbit. They all cross the thresholds that separate the familiar from the unfamiliar, but they do so willingly, fully aware of what they're doing.

For me, if a protagonist crosses over a threshold willingly, or with the aid of a friend or helper character (as Virgil helps Dante), their story line will follow a Quest, Rags to Riches, or Death and Rebirth structure.

What's more, many—if not most—of the stories that follow this trope seem to be literary stories, so perhaps the Voyage and Return structure is primarily a literary (narrative) structure (or plot pattern). Given the strength of the available evidence, one has to ask whether the Voyage and Return structure should be considered a *bona fide* story structure at all.

For example, the story of Orpheus and Euridyce, is one Booker claims follows a 'Voyage and Return plot' on the basis that Orpheus takes a return trip to the underworld in it.[4] Yet despite Orpheus not being at all happy about the idea of visiting Hades to try to get Euridyce back, he decides to cross the threshold himself. His story line at that point follows a Quest structure. In Ovid's account, the story, as translated by A. S. Kline, starts with Orpheus and Euridyce's wedding:

> Hymen ... was present at Orpheus's marriage, true, but he did not speak the usual words, display a joyful expression, or bring good luck. The torch, too, that he held, sputtered continually, with tear-provoking fumes, and no amount of shaking contrived to light it properly. The result was worse than any omens. While the newly wedded bride, Eurydice, was walking through the grass, with a crowd of naiads as her companions, she was killed, by a bite on her ankle, from a snake, sheltering there.[5]

It's a classic Revelation structure opening.[6] Euridyce's death is tragic, but it doesn't translate Orpheus directly into the underworld.

Her death presents Orpheus with a problem which he sets out to solve himself and a Quest structure unfolds. There's no barrier to Orpheus' descent to the underworld. Although he'd rather not have had to go on the journey, he isn't transported there against his will. His quest ends tragically. He returns to the 'world of the living' without his wife and shuns all women. One might see this show of undying loyalty as a good thing; the 'Ciconian women' don't. They berate him for scorning their love and go on a quest to solve their problem. In a highly compressed *dénouement* which combines a Quest structure,[7] two Transformation structures,[8] and a Revelation structure,[9] the women enter a state of Bacchic frenzy, tear Orpheus apart, and separate his spirit from his body. His spirit is then able to seek out his lost love in the underworld wandering through 'the fields of the Blessed'. Having found her, he can then spend eternity sometimes walking 'side by side, or he would follow when she chose to lead, or at another time he walked in front, looking back, safely,—at Eurydice.'

The story lines that Odysseus' and Aeneas' stories follow with respect to their journeys to the underworld follow Quest structures. However reluctant they may be to enter the underworld, neither one of them is transported there against his will.[10]

So, is there a Voyage and Return structure? I think there is. For me, Voyage and Return structure stories involve characters *with problems in their own dimension of being* who are transported to a different dimension of being through the intervention of an external agency – usually against their will. They're then faced with a new problem: how to return to the dimension from which they came. A nested Quest structure typically unfolds, at the end of which, the characters typically find their way back to the familiar dimension of being where they started out, armed with a solution that helps them solve their original problem.

Although it contains many nested stories which follow different story structures within it, the children's joint overarching story line in C. S. Lewis's *The Lion, the Witch and the Wardrobe* can be seen to follow a Voyage and Return structure:

An example of a Voyage and Return structure story

Stages	**Symbols**	**Structure**	**Example (The four children's joint story line from the story of *The Lion, the Witch and the Wardrobe*, C. S. Lewis – Bare Bones)**
1	□	Opening	Once upon a time ...
2	┐	Initial situation (set-up: who, when, where – character and setting)	... four siblings ...
3	↼	Problem	... are evacuated during WWII. Stuck inside due to bad weather, they decide to expand their perspectives and explore the spacious old house they're in.
4	⇀	Translation to a different dimension of being	They enter a magical land through a wardrobe in a series of visits.
5	↼	Problem (of return to origins)	Edmund is captured. They can't return without him and are enlisted to defeat the White Witch.
6	⇀	Solution to both problems (3, 5) usually via nested Quest and/or other structures	They defeat the White Witch, free Edmund, become Kings and Queens of Narnia, and find new perspectives on life.
7	↼	Return to origin	They're magically returned to their previous lives in an altered state of consciousness.
8	⇀	Resolution of initial problem	They come to terms with their experiences and apply what they have learned to their 'normal' lives, re-evaluating the meaning of reality and illusion; truth, lies, and falsehood.
9	┐	Final situation (outcome/resolution)	They achieve closure.

An example of a Voyage and Return structure story

Stages	Symbols	Structure	Example (The four children's joint story line from the story of *The Lion, the Witch and the Wardrobe*, C. S. Lewis – Bare Bones)
10	□	Closing	'And that is the very end of the adventure of the wardrobe. But if the Professor was right it was only the beginning of the adventures of Narnia.'

Scribe the structure as follows:

Call this the Voyage and Return structure.

But what powers the force that takes the children off to Narnia in the first place? In *The Lion, The Witch, and The Wardrobe*, winter has taken hold permanently. There's an excess of evil. The state of excess is somehow felt through the wood of the apple tree that grew from a seed brought from Narnia from which the wardrobe is made.[11] This opens up a portal to Narnia, through which the children step, and their story unfolds from there. It's a classic Call and Response structure which contains within it a nested Voyage and Return structure story.

But what—if anything—does this force have to do with the forces that take Sinbad or Gulliver off course when they set out on their journeys? *The Seven Voyages of Sinbad* is a cycle of stories nested within the larger frame story of *The Thousand and One Nights* (*The Arabian Nights*). Although it was a later addition to the written corpus, it was the cycle that spurred Galland in the late 17th Century to collect and translate all the stories from the tradition that he could find.[12] In the story,[13] Sinbad sets out because he's almost reached rock bottom – his fair-weather friends have left him, his parents have died, and he learns that money is useful, but it doesn't last forever … he needs to earn it. The voyages, which are trade quests, aren't the features that make Sinbad's story fit a Voyage and Return structure. The shipwrecks, storms, and other events that throw him off course or leave him stranded in an unfamiliar place are the important translation points. They're acts of nature. That he survives them is as much to do with his faith as his wit, his cunning, and his common sense. At the end of the day, what most satisfies Sinbad is the opportunity to retell his adventures – a chance comment by a namesake of his, Sinbad the Porter, provides Sinbad with an excuse to do so. At the start of the story, while Sinbad the Porter accepts the comfort and wealth in which Sinbad the Sailor lives as the will of Allah, he nevertheless berates it. Sinbad the Sailor overhears the comment (a poetic *cri de coeur*) and is so moved by it that he invites Sinbad the Porter into his house. He shares his wealth, his hospitality, and *his story* with his namesake; and by the end of the week or so, the two develop a firm friendship which lasts to the end of their days. It's through that bond of friendship that Sinbad the Sailor finally finds the true friendship he was missing when he first decided to set out on his trading journeys.

Like Sinbad the Sailor, when Gulliver sets out to trade, in *Gulliver's Travels*, he's hard up and willing to take a risk in order to make his fortune. He's shipwrecked, taken hostage, helps two warring empires populated by diminutive hominids settle their disputes, finds a boat and makes his way back to England with enough Lilliputian livestock to set himself up in business (after his first voyage) showing, breeding, and finally selling the creatures, making his fortune from the proceeds, but it's not long before he's gone on three further voyages, and published stories about them, lamenting that the stories he's told seem to have done nothing to change the despicable behaviour of the 'Yahoos' in English society.

There seems to be no purpose behind the storms that throw both Sinbad and Gulliver off course – they're examples of a convenient literary topos that has allowed authors to use a cyclone to translate a young girl and her dog to a land of Munchkins, witches and wizards;[14] to use storms at sea to translate a young man called Robinson to an island he names 'The Island of Despair';[15] a Swiss family to a remote island they call 'New Switzerland'[16] (written ostensibly 'for the instruction and amusement of my children, but it's very possible that it may be useful to other young people …'); not to mention using an asteroid storm to translate a modern space-travelling family Robinson way off course to roam uncharted parts of space on Space Station One while trying to find their way back to earth;[17] and finally, to use an energy wave to strand the USS Voyager in the Delta Quadrant.[18] What really governs their translations to a different dimension of being?

Stories start out from, and return to, a state of oscillation (⊐). These opening and closing states—openings which take us into the world of story and closings which bring us back, transformed— justify calling stories 'journeys'. To story[19] is to journey, to travel, to explore a different dimension of being and return changed by the experience. To voyage, to return, and to be transformed as a result of the experience is … to story. George Spencer-Brown refers to this process in the epigraph to this chapter; the same process can be seen at work in the way in which dilemma tales can function in West African culture – where, as a result of a problem in a particular community, a story is told that sets up a cognitive dissonance. The resolution of that dissonance (as it relates to the story world) serves to resolve the original problem in the community which was the reason for the story to be told in the first place. Every story has this quality. Perhaps this is a clue to why the most effective Voyage and Return stories have to do with telling stories – the Narnia stories are a religious allegory. *The Tale of the Shipwrecked Sailor* from ancient Egypt is about the importance of eloquence and story to finding balance in life by being 'brave and control[ling] your heart': 'How happy is he who tells what he has tasted, when the calamity has passed.'[20] Baum's story was developed from a book devised solely for entertainment into a cinematic version which privileges character development through self-reflection on the experience, through a process of retelling, which becomes the whole point of the story. Defoe wrote *Robinson Crusoe* to retell a real story[21] in a way that highlighted religious and social topics relevant to his age.

The Space Family Robinson (in most narratives) are still stuck in space (forever?),[22] although in Irwin Allen's series for 20th Century Fox Television, *Lost in Space*; *The Epilogue* featured a Dorothy-like transformative self-realisation for Dr Smith, the saboteur responsible for launching the family – and, unwittingly, himself – on a journey of no return, while in *Endgame*, the series finale of *Star Trek: Voyager*,[23] one iteration of the story is changed through hindsight gained from a timeline re-entry, which changes the flow of the story through a melding of two timelines, innovatively transforming the relationship between space and time across story structure and plot pattern levels when timelines meld, and distinct spaces overlap and co-exist through time. Acting inversely on one another, one advancing as the other retreats, the retelling of the story is incorporated into the telling, and order is eventually restored.

Both the story of *Tackety Boots*[24] and the story of *The Blinding of Tiresias*[25] involve magical transformations which happen through an external agency against the character's will and are eventually reversed. The reversals are why I classify these stories as following Voyage and Return rather than Transformation or Call and Response structures). Arguably at the heart of the most successful of all of these stories is the deep need to tell stories – for isn't every story a manifestation of a Voyage and Return structure that The Unknown Storyteller's story line follows in the telling of that story?

There's a sense of ebb and flow connected to the Voyage and Return structure that connects different dimensions of being and provides a driving force behind a rarely encountered story structure, the first of two we'll look at in the next chapter, neither of which has a clear closing.

NOTES

1   James Keys [George Spencer-Brown], *Only Two Can Play This Game*, 117, 121, 125–126.

2   Christopher Booker, *The Seven Basic Plots: Why We Tell Stories* (London and New York: Continuum, 2005), 87–106, 250–252, 393–396.

3   Booker, *Seven Basic Plots*, 585 (italics mine).

4   Booker, *Seven Basic Plots*, 103.

5   Ovid, *Metamorphoses*, 10.1—11.84, 263–289, at 263.

6   The Revelation structure unfolds as follows: the lack of happy omen is ominous – it presents a rumour (a *veni* step) related to the wedding which has not yet been solemnised. When it's solemnised and Euridyce walks out as a new bride (a *vidi* step), she receives a fatal snake bite (a tragic *vici* step).

7   The Bacchantes' problem is that Orpheus is unresponsive to their advances; their weapons are their friends and helpers, but these are defeated by Orpheus' music. The structure loops back and this problem is addressed through the aid of their Bacchic frenzy, which leads to them killing Orpheus.

8   Orpheus' rejection of the women's advances is seen as a transgression against the natural order, for just as in the case of Narcissus, love should flow freely, not be stopped. The transformation, for Orpheus, is his death. However, the Bacchantes' action is extreme and, in itself a transgression against the natural order, as a result of which they are transformed into oak trees by Bacchus.

9   The Revelation structure here balances out the initial framing Revelation structure which involves Hymen's premonition of evil. The tension of the intensity of unfulfilled and unconsummated love that Orpheus maintains with his loyalty summons forth the wrath of the Bacchantes, who challenge him, their challenge succeeds in defeating him and releasing his spirit and his spirit is then able to join Euridyce's in the afterlife. The Revelation pair forms an overarching frame that echoes a Transformation structure, which is common to most, if not all, the stories in Ovid's *Metamorphoses*. Within Transformation structure frames, other structures do occur, and add variety and interest to the collection, for example with the story of Orpheus and Euridyce, analysed earlier.

10 The death event could be seen as a Trickster Awe step, following which the nested Quest unfolds.

11 See the end of C. S. Lewis' *The Magician's Nephew*.

12 Ulrich Marzolph and Richard van Leeuwen, *The Arabian Nights Encyclopedia*, 558.

13 *The Arabian Nights: Tale of 1001 Nights*, translated by Malcom C. Lyons and Ursula Lyons, 453–518.

14 L. Frank Baum, *The Wonderful Wizard of Oz* (Chicago, IL and New York: George M. Hill, 1900).

15 Daniel Defoe, *The Life and Strange Surprizing Adventures of Robinson Crusoe, of York, Mariner*, 3rd ed. (London: W. Taylor, 1719).

16 Johann David Wyss, *The Swiss Family Robinson*, 1812; (Salt Lake City, UT: Pink Tree Press, 2000); Project Gutenberg, 2000. http://www.gutenberg.org/cache/epub/3836/pg3836-images.html.

17 Del Connell and Dan Spiegle, *Space Family Robinson* (New York: Gold Key Comics, 1962–1982).

18 *Star Trek: Voyager.* 1995–2001. https://www.imdb.com/title/tt0112178/?ref_=fn_al_tt_1.

19 The phrase is used as a verb here.

20 Miriam Lichtheim, *The Old and Middle Kingdoms*, Vol. 1, Ancient Egyptian Literature: A Book of Readings. (Berkeley, CA: University of California Press, 2006), 211–215.

21 Bruce Selcraig, "The Real Robinson Crusoe," *Smithsonian Magazine* on Smithsonian.com, July 2005, https://www.smithsonianmag.com/history/the-real-robinson-crusoe-74877644/.

22 Kevin Burns, director, *Lost in Space Forever* (Los Angeles: Emmett Street Films et al, 1998), https://www.imdb.com/title/tt0244630/.

23 Allan Kroeker, director, *Star Trek: Voyager, Endgame*, (New York: Paramount Network Televison, 2011), https://www.imdb.com/title/tt0394911.

24 Phil McDermott, *Transformations: Stories to Tell in the Classroom* (Alresford: Liberalis Books, 2015), 16–24.

25 Ovid, *Metamorphoses*, 3.316–338, 89–90.

17

THE EBB AND FLOW OF STORY

THE PERPETUAL MOTION AND CREATION MYTH STRUCTURES

Ebb, ocean of life, (the flow will return,)

WALT WHITMAN, *As I Ebb'd with the Ocean of Life*[1]

There's a rarely encountered story structure which I've found in only a few stories, mostly relating to the movements of the planets, that exemplifies a to-and-fro/ebb-and-flow movement particularly well:

Example of a Perpetual Motion structure story

Stages	Symbols	Structure	Example (The Moon's story line in the story of *The Moon and His Two Wives*, a version transmitted orally by a London-based story spinner, identity unknown)
1	☐	[Opening]	[Implied]
2	⌐	Initial situation (set-up: who, when, where – character and setting)	The moon waxes and wanes because he has two wives. One is a fantastic story spinner but a terrible cook; the other, a fantastic cook but very bad-tempered.
3	←	Problem	When the moon is with his story spinner wife, he grows thin and hungry, ...
4	→	Journey	... so he rolls over to the other side of the sky, to visit his other wife.
5	←	Problem	She feeds him until he's fit to burst and can't eat any more.
6	→	Journey	When he's had enough of her food and moods, he rolls over to the other side of the sky to visit his other wife, who makes him laugh.
...	←	Problem[2]	As a result, he grows thin and hungry. [The cycle loops perpetually from step 3 to step 6]

This version features waxing and waning of the moon and its movement across the sky. Another features the relationship between the Moon and Venus (as the Morning and Evening Star).[3] Both versions, however, link to the same underlying structure, in a sequence which can be scribed as follows:

◻ ◗ ← → ← → ...

Call this the Perpetual Motion structure.

Julien d'Huy, a French academic interested in the archaic roots of modern culture, cites two further Perpetual Motion structure stories. In this case, they're nested within Riddle structures.[4] He notes that

> a tale from Gascony mirrors the story of Oedipus and the Sphinx, but the Gascon monster asks many riddles. One of them ("The brother is white, the sister is black. Every morning, the brother kills the sister. Every evening, the sister kills the brother. Nevertheless, the brother and the sister never die") is an inverted copy of a fragment from an Oedipus attributed to the fourth-century tragedian Theodectes ("There are two sisters. One gives birth to the other, then that one gives birth to the first"; the answer is 'Night and Day'). Both words— ἡμέρα [*hemera*] and νύξ [*nyx*], respectively—are feminine in Ancient Greek.[5]

A further version, which also features the relationship between day/night and sun/moon is a Bushman tale in which 'the moon is a man who has angered the sun. Every month the moon reaches round prosperity, but the sun's knife then cuts away pieces until finally only a tiny piece is left, which the moon pleads should be left for his children. It's from this piece that the moon gradually grows again to become full.'[6] In this narrative, the continual recurrence of the cycle is assumed, as it is in Brown's account of the Malawian version of the story. And finally, the song *There's a Hole in my Bucket* follows an extended Perpetual Motion structure,[7] as do *Where Have all the Flowers Gone?*, *Found a Peanut*, *Yon Yonson*, *Michael Finnegan*, and others.[8]

There's only one other structure I've located (so far) in which no closing occurs. I call it the Creation Myth structure. It's the structure which the first chapter of the Book of Genesis follows, when mapped as a Linear structure.⁹ Creation just flows. When that happens, a forward step unfolds, perpetually – at least up to a point:

Call this the Creation Myth structure.

Its essential components are:

The Creation Myth structure

Stages	Symbols	Structure
1	☐	Opening
2	⌐	Character(s) emerge(s)
3	→	An unfolding proceeds
...	...	[and continues to unfold in perpetuo ...]

The Creation Myth structure unfolds unproblematically ... up to a point, and that point is the point at which the unfolding becomes problematic. But it doesn't have to be a problem. It only becomes a problem if one views conflict as the main driver for story. This lack of conflict makes the Creation Myth structure distinct from all of the other structures previously outlined.

Janet Burroway cites dramatist Claudia Johnson as saying, 'Whereas the hierarchical or "vertical" nature of narrative, the power struggle, has long been acknowledged, there also appears in all narrative a "horizontal" pattern of connection and disconnection between characters which is the main source of its emotional effect. In discussing human behaviour, psychologists speak of "tower" and "network" patterns, the need to climb (which implies conflict) and the need for community, the need to win out over others and the need to belong to others; and these two forces also drive fiction.'¹⁰ The argument makes sense. It indicates a positive force that drives story that exists before conflict comes in – and that positive force is the need for union. But the argument only makes sense up to a point. Why should 'the need to climb' automatically imply conflict and not a yearning for balance? 'Vertical' and 'horizontal' aren't mutually exclusive. They're both required to achieve balance. One needs both to realise the perfectly balanced sphere, the centre of which is everywhere; the boundary nowhere.

While not all stories need to involve conflict, they do depend on characters and on purposeful sequences of events relating to them.[11] The Perpetual Motion and Creation Myth structures are both driven forward by the Dynamic structures.

With the Perpetual Motion structure, the Revelation structure comes in to play because each iteration of a Quest structure is based on a state of excess. Thinking back to the Malawian tale, we have the moon at its fullest, fit to bursting. There's a clear state of (relative) excess which could be seen to lead to doubt ('Will I burst? Can I eat any more?' – a *veni* step), observation and acknowledgement ('I am full and round! I need to lose weight!' – a *vidi* step), and action ('I'll roll across the sky and visit Chekechani' (the name of the story spinner wife in this narrative version) – the arrival completes a *vici* step). At the same time, the 'I came, I saw, I conquered' Revelation sequence can apply to an interpretation based on a state of (relative) lack, where the moon misses the conditions he knows exist at Chekechani's. A set of moves ensues, starting with the thoughts and memories of her, his missing her (a *veni* step, based on abstract entities), his arrival at her house (a *vidi* step, involving concrete interaction), and his resultant obliteration of the problem of his weight gain with his decision to stay at her house (a *vici* step, involving a solution to the problem). This continues until a state of excessive loss of weight is reached, which starts the cycle off once more.

The Linear Creation Myth structure also has a sense of unfolding, linked to the Dynamic Revelation and/or Chinese Circular structures. As previously pointed out, linear/static and circular/dynamic ways of analysing stories structurally are complementary, not mutually exclusive and with the Creation Myth structure, there's a sense of further potential opening up with every step that drives the flow of story forward, rather than the sense of there being a problem to solve or a lack of some kind to deal with. The dynamic quality of the Revelation structure perfectly complements the linear flow of the Creation Myth structure. The potential is sensed, the process of realising it started, and, when complete, the foundation for the next cycle of generation appears. Its iterations are underpinned by the Chinese Circular Structure.

The Perpetual Motion structure has an embedded oscillatory quality which operates within a framework which remains constant. The Creation Myth structure, however, has an embedded static quality. It moves in the same way, in a forward trajectory, remaining the same in essence, but always dynamically developing. In this sense, they can be seen as complementary aspects of a triplicitous unity which echoes Spencer-Brown's Form, the Daoist *yin/yang* symbol, and Sakyamuni's 'links of conditioned coproduction', where an element of the static is contained within the dynamic and vice versa (☯).[12]

The two story structures presented in this chapter are the last in the group of 18 structures I've identified to date, excluding Comedy and Tragedy, both of which I see as being structure neutral. A description of the characteristics of each step in each of these story structures can be found in appendix 4. Having explored the structures individually, in the next 3 chapters, I'd like to take a wider view and examine the group as a whole, looking at commonalities between the structures, and ways of classifying them, but first, I'd like to look at the energy which drives story – and how it helps fashion each of the 18 story structures outlined so far.

NOTES

1   Walt Whitman, *Complete Poetry and Collected Prose* (New York: Library of America, 1982), 396.

2   Steps 3,4 and 5,6 can be expanded to two Quest structures.

3   Dayle L. Brown, *Skylore from Planet Earth: Stories from Around the World – The Moon* (Bloomington, IN: AuthorHouse, 2012), 13; see also Patrizia Monzani and Beate Kunath, directors, *The Moon and his two Wives*, 2002; Chemnitz: Chemnitzer FIlmwerkstatt e.V., YouTube: 7EHKZdUphGQ.

4   Julien d'Huy, "L'Aquitaine Sur La Route d'Oedipe? La Sphinge Comme Motif Prehistorique," *Société d'études et de recherches préhistoriques des Eyzies* 61 (2012): 15–21, at 15.

5   d'Huy's source for the Gascon tale is Jean-François Bladé, *Contes Populaires de la Gascogne*, Vol. 1 (Paris: Maisonneuve Frères et Ch. Leclerc, 1886), 9.

6   Dave Laney, *African Starlore*, 2006, http://sirius-c.ncat.edu/EthiopianEnochSociety/Africa-Star/.

7   In the version by Harry Belafonte and Odetta, the vamp (mainly a V-I progression of dominant-tonic chords forming an oscillating perfect cadence) provides a perfect musical accompaniment to complement the structure. YouTube: AthT8kw7CIo.

8   Interestingly, the form seems to lend itself to the introduction and confirmation of substance (*Yon Yonson*) the cycle of life and death (*Where Have all the Flowers Gone?*) or the futility of experiencing a cycle of living death (*There's a Hole in my Bucket*; *Michael Finnegan*).

9   An analysis of the text of Genesis I as it maps to the Chinese Circular Story Structure is forthcoming. The linear forward flow should be self-evident. For a mapping of Genesis 1:1–2, 4a to the creative principles outlined in *Laws of Form*, see Josef Freystetter, "Zeit in Form: Ein Strukturvergleich von Laws of Form und Genesis 1,1 - 2,4a." PhD diss., Universität Witten/Herdecke GmbH, 2020.

10 The term 'power struggle' is attributed to novelist Michael Shaara by Janet Burroway, *Writing Fiction: A Guide to Narrative Craft*, 4th ed. (New York: HarperCollins, 1996), 34–35.

11 Prot-*agon*-ists – see note by George Spencer Brown, appended to the quote on pages 205–206.

12 The three are one-and-the-same. Spencer-Brown makes a direct link between Sakyamuni's links of conditioned coproduction and his own Calculus of Indications. See Spencer-Brown, *Laws of Form*, viii.

18

FINDING HARMONY IN STORY

LINEAR AND DYNAMIC STORY STRUCTURES

Before sorrow, anger,
longing, or fear have arisen,
you are in the center.
When these emotions appear
and you know how to see through them,
you are in harmony.
That center is the root of the universe;
that harmony is the Tao,
which reaches out to all things

Once you find the center
and achieve harmony,
heaven and earth take their proper places
and all things are fully nourished.

STEPHEN MITCHELL, TRANS.,
The Second Book of the Dao, CHAPTER 2[1]

Throughout the history of ideas, there's been a quest to find harmony in and through story. We see this in the composition of genealogical narratives, or narratives which trace the lineage of monarchs to justify a claim to legitimacy. We see it in the narratives which tell of national callings, of chosen peoples, of countless New Jerusalems. We see it in the Renaissance attempts to create 'theatres of the world'.[2] We see it in the sacred architect's quest to 'unite heaven and earth' in the design of places of worship;[3] in the quest to 'reach the centre' which is a metaphorical goal of both voyages of exploration and of scientific discovery; in the mythic quest to 'find the holy grail'; and in the quest to find the 'monomyth' that represents 'story's story'. This work is one of many such examples. Since Campbell's 'monomyth' structure was later associated with the structure of George Lucas' initial *Star Wars* film,[4] the 'monomyth' has gradually become a (rather restrictive) standard for judging the merits of Hollywood film scripts and Broadway musicals.[5]

As noted in chapter 3, Campbell defines 'monomyth' stories as ones in which 'a hero ventures forth from the world of common day into a region of supernatural wonder: fabulous forces are there encountered, and a decisive victory is won: the hero comes back from this mysterious adventure with the power to bestow boons on his fellow man.' These three phases, which he describes as Separation, Initiation, Return, fit the Call and Response Variation 2 structure (outlined in chapter 11) perfectly:

Campbell	Outline	Stages	Structure
Separation	A hero ventures forth from the world of common day ...		Revelation/Quest Rumour/doubt (*veni* step)
Initiation	... into a region of supernatural wonder: fabulous forces are there encountered ...		Verification: confirmation/ refutation (*vidi* step) (nested structures with ⇌ steps implied)
Return	... and a decisive victory is won.		Assertion/denial (statement or action which cancels doubt) (*vici* step)
	The hero comes back from this mysterious adventure with the power to bestow boons on his fellow man.		Transformation (The transgressive lack or excess in the natural order that launches the hero on their path at the start of the story is addressed, although the redress may result in a different state of imbalance)

Campbell further subdivides the three main parts of his 'monomyth' structure into a further 17 components, in sections of 5, 6, and 6 parts respectively:

Separation
The Call to Adventure
Refusal of the Call
Supernatural Aid
The Crossing of the First Threshold
The Belly of the Whale

Initiation
The Road of Trials
The Meeting with the Goddess
Woman as the Temptress
Atonement with the Father
Apotheosis
The Ultimate Boon

Return
Refusal of the Return
The Magic Flight
Rescue from Without
The Crossing of the Return Threshold
Master of the Two Worlds
Freedom to Live

While the 'monomyth' structure works for 'hero's journey' epics, try fitting the story of *The Three Little Pigs* to the 'monomyth' structure – in either its 3-part, or its 17-part forms, and you'll probably struggle. This is because the 'monomyth' follows an overarching Call and Response Variation 2 structure, in which other story structures can be nested; *The Three Little Pigs* follows a Quest structure.

The Chinese Circular Structure, however, can very easily be charted through the unfolding of the story of *The Three Little Pigs*! The pigs **emerge** as characters; they're **divided** from their home. Their goal is to look after themselves and learn how to live independent lives. Their paths **separate** and they **complete** the building of three houses – but will their attempt to achieve their goal succeed? (One cycle). The wolf **emerges, divided** from his goal of finding food, tries to feed on the pigs, remains **separated** from them, and is roundly trounced when the pigs unite forces and work together to defeat the wolf, achieving their goal of becoming self-sufficient little piggies when they end up living together, with the wolf's death restoring order, balance and harmony, bringing all of their story lines to **completion** (another cycle).

This realisation made me look at other story structures I'd identified and when I did, I noticed that the Chinese Circular Structure doesn't just fit the Quest structure, as outlined in the example above; it can be traced through every single one of the Linear structures covered in this work.

To trace how the Chinese Circular Structure underpins Linear structures, I've applied the following rules:

1. Map symbols using a 1:1 correspondence, so that each element in a Linear structure maps to a specific element in the Chinese Circular Structure.

2. Map symbols using a 1:3 correspondence, so that each element in a Linear structure can map to three elements in the Chinese Circular Structure. This relates to the expansion of: (←) to (← → ←); (→) to (→ ← →); and (⇌) to (⇌ ← ⇌). This links a rising element to its complementary rising element, or a flourishing element to its complementary flourishing element in the Chinese Circular Structure; it also links to an expansion of (← →) to (← → ← → ← →) (Transformation to Quest) which results in each of the two Linear story structures having the same starting and ending points in the Chinese Circular Structure.

3. Map symbols using a 1:4 correspondence, so that each element in a Linear structure can map to a full cycle around the Chinese Circular Structure.

4. The (⇌) step can result in a change in direction of flow around the Chinese Circular Structure. This is in line with Chinese traditions.

5. Combining points (1) and (3), the (⇌) step can be mapped to a reverse full cycle and a single step in the original direction of travel, effectively rendering 1 step and 5 steps as equivalent.

6. Maintain the integrity of a full cycle of the Chinese Circular Structure.

7. Map the story structures in relation to individual characters' story lines.

The Chinese Circular Structure can be traced through Genesis I by mapping the recurring elements in the text as follows: character to **emergence**, pronouncement to **division**, appearance to **separation**, and naming to **completion**. An alternative mapping of the Creation Myth structure would treat each element as a complete Chinese Circular Structure cycle.[6] Once it starts, the Perpetual Motion structure sets off a sequence of paired cycles starting one step or season further along in the Chinese Circular Structure cycle with each repeated Quest structure which it contains nested within it.

In the Rags to Riches structure, as shown in the table below, the complete cycle which spans steps 1–3 brings the positive state of affairs to completion. From there, four triple moves spanning steps 4–7 take the character forward while the initial points take them backward around a complete cycle. The Saviour character follows an implied nested Quest structure of their own (1–2, 8–11). The cycles which span 8–10 can be seen to trace the Saviour character's story line from the main character's point of view. These join to bring the story to a close at 11. The balance between the four triple cycles, with their backward-flowing starting positions, and the three quadruple cycles, in which the main character is static, is notable, as is the quality of a Revelation structure in the way in which it builds.

Comparison of Rags to Riches and Chinese Circular structures

1	2	3	4	5	6	7	8	9	10	11

The Chinese Circular Structure can also be found underpinning the Transformation structure, where each element of the Linear structure is in a 1:1 correspondence with the elements of the Chinese Circular Structure.

Comparison of Transformation and Chinese Circular structures

1	2	3	4	5	6
□	ㄱ	↼	⇀	ㄱ	□

The Chinese Circular Structure can also be traced in the Death and Rebirth structure:

Comparison of Death and Rebirth and Chinese Circular structures (Full)

Death and Rebirth structure			**Chinese Circular Structure**	
Stages	**Symbols**	**Structure**	**Steps**	**Symbols**
1	□	Opening	1 – Origin	□
2	ㄱ	**Establishment** of characters	2 – Emergence	ㄱ
3	↼	A **division** between a character's desire and the realisation of desire creates a problem	3 – Division	╗
4	⇀	which is resolved, but results in a **separation** from the desired goal, as ...	4 – Separation	ㄱ
5	↼	... there's a price to pay. Until it is paid, there's **a lack of completion**	5 – Completion	╗
6	⇀	An attempt to avoid paying the price **emerges**	6 – Emergence	ㄱ
7	↼	The attempts fail. There's a ***submersion***. The main characters remain **divided** from the realisation of their desire. The Saviour character goes on a journey ...	7 – Division (at first step of nested Quest)	╗
8	⇀	... and resolves the **separation** (nested structure)	8 – Separation (at last step of nested Quest)	ㄱ

Comparison of Death and Rebirth and Chinese Circular structures (Full)

Death and Rebirth structure			Chinese Circular Structure	
Stages	Symbols	Structure	Steps	Symbols
9	⌐	This allows **completion** which leads to ...	9 – Completion	⌐|
10	⌐⌐	... a closing	10 – Return to origin	⌐⌐

In the symbolic mapping which follows, the Saviour character's Quest structure spans steps 7–8. When these are mapped in a 1:1 correspondence in relation to the main character's story line, then the same point in the Chinese Circular Structure is reached at step 9, allowing the story to progress to its closing.

Comparison of Death and Rebirth and Chinese Circular structures (Symbols)

1	2	3	4	5	6	7	8	9	10
⌐⌐	⌐	←	→	←	→	←	→	⌐	⌐⌐

If the Riddle structure (covered in chapter 14) is seen as a binary structure, which defines, divides, separates, and reunites source and target domains, then the Chinese Circular Structure corresponds to that structure as well. Similarly, the story seeker's experience when confronted with a koan could also be said to follow the Chinese Circular Structure. The same applies to the unfolding and resolution of both Dilemma and Ki-Shō-Ten-Ketsu stories (covered in chapters 14 and 15).

Each step in the central (← →) pair in the Voyage and Return structure can be mapped in a 1:3 ratio to the Chinese Circular Structure as the sequence represents a nested Quest structure in the main character's story line. The (←) step maps to the rising phases; the (→) to the flourishing phases in both structures. The middle steps in each sequence balance each other out in the process.

Comparison of Voyage and Return and Chinese Circular structures

1	2	3	4	5	6	7	8	9	10
⌐	┐	←	→	←	→	←	→	┐	⌐
◑	◯	◯	◯	◯	◯	◯	◯	◯	◉

One group of Linear structures had me puzzled, though: Trickster, Trickster Variation, Call and Response (in both its variations). The key to understanding how the Chinese Circular Structure linked to these came when I analysed another Chinese story, *The Biography of Yü Jang*. The story, in William H Nienhauser, Jr's translation, illustrates this close correspondence between Linear and Dynamic structures particularly well.[7] It comes from *Shih-chi*, the earliest known history of China, composed by court historian Ssu-ma Ch'ien (145–86 BCE), which he finished in 91 BCE. It provides a useful introduction to how the Chinese Circular Structure works with the remaining Linear structures listed above, by focusing first on the Trickster structure.

The brief structural analysis of the story which follows shows how it maps to both Linear (Quest, Trickster) and Dynamic (Chinese Circular) structures. The key thing to note here is that the Chinese Circular Structure cycle sometimes flows in reverse.

Analysis of the narrative of *The Biography of Yü Jang*

Text	Structural analysis
Yü Jang was a man of the state of Chin.[8] Formerly he had served the heads of the Fan and Chung-hang clans, but found no means of gaining recognition. He left them and served the earl of Chih, who truly honoured and favoured him. When the earl made war on Lord Hsiang of Chao, Lord Hsiang conspired with the states of Han and Wei[9] to annihilate the earl. After eliminating him, they divided his lands into three parts. Lord Hsiang felt such great enmity for the earl of Chih that he lacquered the latter's skull and made it into a drinking cup.	Three cycles (Each cycle follows a Quest structure) (Note the parallelism of the sympathetic link between skull/person here and clothes/person at the end of the story.)

Analysis of the narrative of *The Biography of Yü Jang*

Text	Structural analysis
Yü Jang fled to the mountains and said with a sigh: "For a man to die for one who understood him is like a woman making herself pretty for one who loves her. Since the earl of Chih understood me, I should sacrifice my life to avenge him. If I can repay him in this way, my soul need not be ashamed." Then changing his name and taking on the guise of a criminal,[10] he entered the palace as a criminal sentenced to hard labour so that he could work at repairing the privy. With a dagger hidden under his clothes, he hoped to stab Lord Hsiang.	Two cycles (Start of main Quest structure) (Start of Trickster structure 1)
When Lord Hsiang went to the privy, he became suspicious and questioned the criminal working there. Yü Jang was found to be concealing a weapon. "I wanted to avenge the earl of Chih," Yü declared.	Cycle
The lord's attendants wanted to execute him, but Lord Hsiang said, "He's a righteous man. Out of respect I can only avoid him. The earl of Chih died with no heir, and yet this subordinate of his wanted to avenge him. He is truly one of the world's worthy men." Finally, he had Yü released.	Reverse cycle (End of Trickster structure 1)
After a short time, Yü Jang smeared his body with lacquer to make it appear leprous, swallowed charcoal to make his voice harsh, made his outward appearance unrecognisable, and came begging in the marketplace. Even his wife failed to recognise him. He met a friend who did know him and said, "Aren't you Yü Jang?" "Yes, I am."	Cycle (Start of Trickster structure 2)
In tears, his friend said, "With your talents, if you offered your service to Lord Hsiang, you'd surely be admitted as a close aide. Once you're so accepted, you could do what you've been desiring. Wouldn't that be a lot easier? Would this not be a simpler way to avenge yourself on Lord Hsiang than causing hurt to your person and making yourself suffer?"	Cycle
"If I were to present myself as his servant," Yü Jang replied, "and yet seek to kill him, I'd be harbouring two minds in serving one lord. What I am doing now calls for great sacrifice. But the very reason I'm doing it is to bring shame to those later subordinates who serve their lords with two minds." Then he left.	Reverse cycle (End of Trickster structure 2)

Analysis of the narrative of *The Biography of Yü Jang*

Text	Structural analysis
Some time later, soon after Lord Hsiang left his residence, Yü Jang hid under a bridge over which Lord Hsiang was to pass. When the lord reached the bridge, his horse shied, and he said, "Yü Jang must be here!" He sent men to investigate and, indeed, it was Yü Jang. Thereupon Lord Hsiang reprimanded him: "Did you not formerly serve the houses of Fan and Chung-hang? The earl of Chih destroyed them, and yet you sought no revenge but offered your service to him. Now that the earl is dead, why in this instance alone do you feel such a pressing need for revenge?"	Two cycles (Start of Trickster structure 3)
"When I served Fan and Chung-hang, they both treated me like a common fellow, and I therefore repaid them as an ordinary fellow might. But the earl treated me like a man of national eminence, and I thus must requite him as a man of national eminence should."	Reverse cycle (End of Trickster structure 3 – loop 1)
Lord Hsiang sighed deeply and in tears said, "Alas for you, Yü Jang! What you did for the earl of Chih won you a great name. I pardoned you once and that was the limit of what I could do for you. You should have known it, for now I cannot release you again." He then ordered his soldiers to surround Yü Jang.	Reverse cycle (End of Trickster structure 3 – loop 2)
"I've heard that an enlightened sovereign does not conceal the merits of a man," Yü Jang said, "and a loyal servant has the duty to die for his name. Formerly, my lord, you pardoned me and there was no one in the empire who did not praise your magnanimity. For what I've done today, I'll certainly suffer death, but I beseech you to let me strike at your robes as a gesture of revenge so that I can thereby die without regret. I don't dare to hope for your consent, but am merely taking the liberty of disclosing what is in my heart."	Cycle (Start of nested Quest) (The last sentence is a compressed reverse cycle)
Then Lord Hsiang, feeling that there was nothing more righteous to do, ordered a servant to take his robes to Yü Jang. Yü Jang drew his sword, leaped three times,[11] and struck them, calling out, "Now I will be able to face the earl of Chih down below!" Then he fell on his sword and died. On that day all those men of a kindred spirit in Chao shed tears for him.	Simultaneous double cycle (Reverse for Lord Hsiang;[12] Standard for Yü Jang) (End of main and nested Quest structures; a final Transformation structure underpinned by a reverse cycle is implied)

The Trickster structure features two characters on Conflicting Quests whose story lines intersect. In the final scene of the story analysed above, the Conflicting Quests suggest the story lines be mapped to flow in opposite directions. As a result, one character emerges at Spring, starts out travelling forward, experiences a reversal, adjusts, and re-enters at Winter; the other emerges at Winter, travels backward, reverses, adjusts, and then re-enters at spring. As a result, each character ends up where the other character started out.

Comparison of Trickster and Chinese Circular structures (Symbols)

1	2	3	4	5	6	7	8	9	10

A similar pattern can be found in the Trickster Variation structure.

Previously in this chapter, the Transformation, Revelation/Quest, and Call and Response structures were shown to be linked. By isolating the structures that combine to make the composite whole, the Chinese Circular Structure can be traced through both variations as well. While there's a flow forward in both characters' story lines in the mapping below, both could flow backward, or in opposition.

Comparison of Call and Response Variation 1 and Chinese Circular structures

1	2	3	4	5	6	7	8	9	10	11	12

The Call and Response Variation 2 structure can be mapped in a similar way. It is interesting to consider the quality of the state of excess which initiates the Transformation structure, or leads up to it – does this relate to the direction of flow around the Chinese Circular Structure? Or is a binary reading always possible? The process of exploring these possibilities has the potential to shed further light on the form and function of this structure.

In this chapter, the ways in which the Chinese Circular Structure can be mapped to the 16 Linear structures identified to date have been demonstrated. The rules governing the mapping allow flexibility while also preserving consistency and rigour. Applying them to the analysis of a narrative or a story structure will reveal subtleties regarding the potential for expansion and contraction which other approaches (some of which are outlined in appendix 3) cannot provide. The stable dynamism of the Chinese Circular Structure, its inherent balance, and its acknowledgment of the ineffable are just some of its awe-inspiring qualities. It's ideally qualified—both functionally and visually—to represent what Campbell sees as the 'navel of the world', the ubiquitous source and generator of life. Its circularity clearly links to the flow of Linear structures. What's more, as a structure, it has far more validity in terms of being thought of as a monomyth than Campbell's model of 'the hero's journey'. It's far more universally applicable. The benefit of realising this is that it can shed new light on stories which follow Linear story structures – not just Chinese stories, but stories, universally. Although Linear story structures can all be seen to be underpinned in some way by the Chinese Circular Structure, they're also interrelated in their own right. We saw previously how the Quest structure expands from the Transformation structure. In the next couple of chapters, we'll look at how story structures can be classified; we'll explore how story structures which have the same initial step can be seen to be related, what role threshold crossings play, and what purpose story structures might serve.

The underlying 'static-dynamic'/*yin-yang* complementarity in the relationship between Linear and Dynamic story structures goes back to ancient China and the legendary duo, FuXi and Nüwa.

FuXi's tomb has been in existence in Huaiyang county, in the Henan province in Central China for around 3,000 years. Accounts consistently associate Nüwa, the female figure, with the circle and FuXi, the male figure, with lines and squares. As legend has it, it was through FuXi that the 8 trigrams which form the basis of the *I Ching* developed; some of the earliest myths which accord Nüwa primacy of place as creator goddess describe her as creating humans by dipping a rope in mud and swinging it round her – the drops of mud that were dispersed as a result creating the human race. Depictions dating from between the 3rd Century BCE to the 7th Century CE show them as a male-female pair with serpentine tails intertwined. Nüwa carries a compass; FuXi, a set square. The symbols are universally linked to heaven and earth; metaphysical and physical; eternal and temporal; infinite and finite; or, in Spencer-Brown's terms, unmarked and marked states. They're manifested in the shape of the round coins with square holes at their centres, used uninterruptedly in China from around the 3rd Century BCE to 1911.[13] They underpin the design of sacred buildings universally.[14] They underpin the perennial challenge of how to 'square a circle'.[15] Both coexist in, emerge from, and are a manifestation of the unnameable *dao*. They underpin the entire approach outlined here – an approach to analysing story structure which, as this chapter shows, offers a deep and truly universal way of appreciating the same-different wonder that is 'consciousness', revealed in, as, and through story.

NOTES

1   Stephen Mitchell, *The Second Book of the Dao* (New York: Penguin, 2009), 4.

2   Frances A. Yates, *Theatre of the World* (London: Routledge & Kegan Paul, 1969).

3   Adrian Snodgrass, *Architecture, Time and Eternity: Studies in the Stellar and Temporal Symbolism of Traditional Buildings*, 2 Vols. (Delhi: P. K. Goel for Aditya Prakashan, 1990); Richard Foster, *Patterns in Thought: The Hidden Meaning of the Great Pavement of Westminster Abbey* (London: Jonathan Cape, 1992).

4   Michael Kaminski, *The Secret History of Star Wars: The Art of Storytelling and the Making of a Modern Epic* (Kingston, Ontario: Legacy Books Press, 2008), 104.

5   Tristan Bancks, "Beyond the Hero's Journey: 'Joseph [Campbell] is my Yoda (1).'—George Lucas," *Australian Screen Education* 33 (Spring 2003): 32–34, https://go.galegroup.com/ps/anonymous?id=GALE%7CA112130487; Peter J. Casey, *What Hollywood's Addiction to The Hero's Journey is Doing to the Broadway Musical* (Parts 1, 2), 10 April, 2015. https://majortominor.wordpress.com/2015/04/10/what-hollywoods-addiction-to-the-heros-journey-is-doing-to-the-broadway-musical/#comments.

6   An analysis of the text of Genesis I as it maps to the Chinese Circular Structure will be forthcoming. For a mapping of Genesis 1:1–2, 4a to the creative principles outlined in *Laws of Form*, see Josef Freystetter, "Zeit in Form: Ein Strukturvergleich von Laws of Form und Genesis 1,1 - 2,4a." PhD diss., Universität Witten/Herdecke GmbH, 2020.

7   Y. W. Ma and Joseph S. M. Lau, *Traditional Chinese Stories*, 41–42.

8   Chin was one of the major states toward the end of the Spring and Autumn period; its territory covered the land between the southern part of the present Shansi Province and the southern part of Hopei Province.

9   Chao, Han, and Wei were three of the seven major states in the Warring States period. Chao encompassed the southern part of the present Hopei Province, the eastern part of Shansi Province, and the land to the north of the Yellow River in Honan Province. Han included the eastern part of Shensi Province and the north western part of Honan. Wei spanned the northern part of modern Honan and the southwestern part of Shansi Province. These lands were built primarily on the former territory of Chin.

10   Or, perhaps, mutilating himself to gain the appearance of a criminal (various mutilations such as tattooing or amputation were used as punishments then).

11   Leaping was a ritual means for expressing extreme grief.

12   Lord Hsiang's reverse cycle is governed by the direct specific threat of assassination, which is nullified with the death of Yü Jang. Lord Hsiang's honour and safety are assured.

13   A pictorial account of these, with evidence of cast 'coin trees' of this type from tombs predating the official introduction of this form of coinage can be found at http://primaltrek.com/chinesecoins.html and http://primaltrek.com/moneytree.html.

14   Adrian Snodgrass, *Architecture, Time and Eternity*.

15   The problem of squaring the circle involves finding out how a square (or sometimes a rectangle) with the same area as a given circle can be derived from it using compass and set square. See Jay Kappraff, *Beyond Measure: A Guided Tour through Nature, Myth, and Number* (Singapore: World Scientific, 2002), 172–176; Adam Tetlow, *The Diagram: Harmonic Geometry* (Glastonbury, Somerset: Wooden Books, 2021), 22–23.

19

THE UNFOLDING OF STORY

FROM 5 POTENTIAL STEPS (⅃), (⅂), (→), (←), (⇌), 18 STORY STRUCTURES

In ... the ontopoietic unfolding of life, the soul plays ... a "counting"
role, but this "counting" is understood as introducing the distinctiveness
of the phases of temporal progress: it involves an organizing,
articulating, and dynamically operating function, a living function.

ANNA-TERESA TYMIENIECKA, *Life's Primogenital Timing*[1]

The 18 story structures outlined in this book are all interconnected. Not only are the 16 Linear structures all linked to the Chinese Circular Structure, but they can all be shown to emerge from a limited set of initial conditions and develop in the same unfolding way from these, each in its own manner, in response to the nature of the problem that calls them into being. In this chapter, we'll be looking at how this works so that in the next chapter, we can explore the links between Linear structures. This will allow us to explore story's laws far more deeply than we have been able to up to now.

We start with a state of infinite potential – the opening of a story which deliberately confounds our notions of time and space (e.g., 'Once upon a time'):

⊐

from which emerges a distinction[2] – a mark in space-time (e.g., 'There was ...') which typically distinguishes a character and setting:

⊓;

from here, given that another mark simply restates the existing one, we can eliminate it, leaving two possibilities for the next event, which will either be related to marks or steps:

firstly, the marked state can either be followed by a mark of recursion or cancellation:

(I.A) ⊐ ⌐ ⊏

(I.B) ⊐ ⌐ ⫪

and secondly, by a step forward, a step backward, or an oscillation:

(II.A) ⊐ ⌐ ⇀

(II.B) ⊐ ⌐ ↽

(II.C) ⊐ ⌐ ⇌

From these, all 18 story structures identified to date unfold.

The appearance of the mark of recursion strictly speaking returns us to the origin without a story having unfolded at all, so from this point of view, (I.A) is discounted.

Two structures identified to date flow from (I.B):

I.B.1 The Revelation structure

(i) ⊐ ⌐ ⫪

I.B.2 The Chinese Circular Structure

(ii) ⊐ ⌐ ⫪ ⌐ ⫪ ⊏

The former is separate from the initial opening and 'who, when, where' mark; the latter includes these. Both structures are classified as Dynamic story structures and can be found to underpin the Linear story structures outlined below.

A further 16 story structures emerge from the three possible initial steps (II.A–C).

In these, a character whose story starts with a forward step (II.A) allows the following four story structures to unfold:

II.A.1 The Creation Myth structure

(iii) □ ⌐ → → → → ...

II.A.2 The Ki-Shō-Ten-Ketsu structure

(iv) □ ⌐ → ⇌ ⌐ □

II.A.3 The Open-Ended Ki-Shō-Ten-Ketsu structure (the structure depends on the story seeker's involvement for closure)

(v) □ ⌐ → ⇌ ⌐ □

II.A.4 The Rags to Riches structure (the grey shaded pair of marks expands to a nested Quest structure)

(vi) □ ⌐ → ← → ← → ← → ⌐ □

A character whose story starts with a backward step (II.B) allows the following ten story structures to unfold:

II.B.1 The Transformation structure

(vii) □ ⌐ ← → ⌐ □

II.B.2 The Quest structure

(viii) □ ⌐ ← → ← → ← → ⌐ □

II.B.3 The Trickster structure

(ix) □ ⌐ ← → ← ⇌ ← ⇌ ⌐ □

II.B.4 **The Trickster Variation structure** (the grey shaded mark indicates a nested Quest structure in one character's story line, resolving the 'Huh?!' to an 'Ah!' for the other character)

(x) ☐ ⅂ ← → ← ⇌ ⇌ ⇌ ⅂ ☐

II.B.5 **The Dilemma structure** (an Open-Ended structure which depends on the story seeker's involvement for closure)

(xi) ☐ ⅂ ← → ← ⇌ ⇌ ⇌ ⅂ ☐

II.B.6,7 **The Call and Response structure (Variations 1 and 2)** (the grey shaded pairs of marks denote a Transformation structure; the non-shaded marks, Revelation/Quest structures)

(xii) ☐ ⅂ ← → ← → ← → ← → ⅂ ☐

(xiii) ☐ ⅂ ← → ← → ← → ← → ⅂ ☐

II.B.8 **The Death and Rebirth structure** (the grey shaded pair of marks expands to a nested Quest structure)

(xiv) ☐ ⅂ ← → ← → ← → ⅂ ☐

II.B.9 **The Voyage and Return structure** (the grey shaded pair of marks expands to a nested Quest structure)

(xv) ☐ ⅂ ← → ← → ← → ⅂ ☐

II.B.10 **The Perpetual Motion structure** (the structure repeats *in perpetuo*)

(xvi) ☐ ⅂ ← → ← → ...

A character whose story starts with an oscillatory step (II.C) allows the following two story structures to unfold:

II.C.1 The Riddle structure

(xvii) ⊔ ⌐ ⇌ ⌐ ⊔

II.C.2 The Koan structure

(xviii) ⊔ ⌐ ⇌   ⊔

The forms of (xix) **Comedy** and (xx) **Tragedy** are structure neutral, and depend on Aristotelian category mistakes and category corrections respectively to achieve their effects.

Note that no Dynamic story structure ends with a marked state (this applies to the Revelation and Chinese Circular structures); the Linear story structures vary in their starting points, but no Linear story structure ends with a backward step. This points to a key insight into an intrinsic drive that story … has … to move … forward.

Falsification

The notation allows experimentation, to investigate whether there are *laws of story* which govern how a story unfolds, based on one or more of the story structures outlined in this work. While a full discussion of this is beyond the scope of this book, I'd like to point out here that, as Propp demonstrated in terms of functions, steps in a story structure can't be placed in any old sequence in a plot pattern or narrative telling. There are patterns which work and patterns which don't. For example, if we take the Quest structure in its standard form (Quest 1 in the table below) and reorder the steps so the three backward steps in the structure are grouped together in sequence, followed by the forward steps, can we successfully tell a story based on a Quest structure with the steps in the rearranged order (Quest 2)?

Functional comparison of standard and altered Quest structure sequences

Structure/option	Steps									
Quest/1 (standard form) ✓	1	2	3	4	5	6	7	8	9	10
	⊐	⌐	←	→	←	→	←	→	⌐	⊐
Quest/2 (altered form) ×	1	2	3	5	7	4	6	8	9	10
	⊐	⌐	←	←	←	→	→	→	⌐	⊐

To prove the point, an example of a story which follows the Quest structure told in the order shown as Quest 2 above follows, without any links to adjoining steps in Quest 1. It's based on the pigs' story lines in the story of *The Three Little Pigs*:

> Once upon a time, three pigs lived together with their mother who thought it was time they established themselves and set out to seek their fortune. The pigs saw the advantages of this, meeting people with various materials, meeting the big bad wolf, setting off on their individual journeys, building houses from different materials, two of which were destroyed, allowing the pigs (or just one pig in some versions) to defeat the wolf and survive (either alone or together) to live on happily ever after.

Obviously this can't be considered an effective conventional narrative. The only way in which the narrative reordering can be made to work is by reference to the functional links between the steps outlined in Option 1, thus:

> Once upon a time, three pigs lived together with their mother who thought it was time they established themselves and set out to seek their fortune. The pigs saw the advantages of this. Little did they know that her plan would result in two key meetings for each of them: a meeting with people carrying materials, and a meeting with a big bad hungry wolf. They set off on their individual journeys, and having duly met people who gave them materials to build houses from, two of which were destroyed by the big bad wolf, one house proved a match for him, allowing

the pigs (or just one pig in some versions) to defeat the wolf and survive (either alone or together) to live on happily ever after.

While 'clunky', the narrative version preserves the links between the steps. The methodology provides a visually intuitive link to working *with* the 'flow' of story rather than going against it. 'Little did they know', for instance, foreshadows the meetings in a way which highlights tension (←) and 'having duly met' links the chronology of the story structure to the plot pattern of the narrative. Without the verbal signposts, the narrative becomes inconsistent, hard to follow, and extremely perplexing. This shows how important the backward/forward pairings are, and that if we keep these pairs together, then there's scope to vary the order and change the plot pattern.

This key insight will be of interest to you as a writer, as it will help you to map out a character's story line in chronological order and work out the story structure(s) their story line follows. Where you treat your characters' stories non-chronologically in terms of plot pattern, your maps of the characters' story lines will allow you to identify important elements you need to include very easily. They'll also help you identify – and more importantly, avoid – plot holes in your characters' story lines.

There clearly are *laws of story* on which a well-told story depends. This insight has useful implications for writers. It also shows that the methodology can open up exciting avenues of research into which patterns work and which don't and why. It provides literary analysts with a new tool to complement existing ones – a tool which has the potential to provide far deeper insights into the workings of story underlying a narrative than other methods currently available, which is what we'll be exploring briefly in the next chapter.

NOTES

1   Anna-Teresa Tymieniecka, "Life's Primogenital Timing: Time Projected by the Dynamic Articulation of the Onto-Genesis," in *Life: Phenomenology of Life as the Starting Point of Philosophy*, edited by Anna-Teresa Tymieniecka, 25th anniversary publication, Book 3 (Dordrecht: Kluwer Academic Publishers, 1997), 7–8.

2   In Spencer-Brown's Calculus of Indications (CoI), on which this work is based, and from where the primary symbols used here derive, all acts which mark a distinction are taken to be tokens of the first distinction.

20

THE EMBRYOLOGY OF STORY STRUCTURE

THRESHOLD AND NON-THRESHOLD STRUCTURES, CLOSED AND OPEN-ENDED STRUCTURES

Mnemosyne ... was the Greek Goddess of Memory ...
a more comprehensive idea than our Memory. To start with, she is
a Goddess, suggesting that she is imagined as an active agent with
a mind and powers of her own. Here the Cosmos itself is imagined
as a Living Being having memory, and this memory could not be
otherwise than a memory of the whole. This suggests, in turn, that the
archetype of human memory is the memory of our origins, the sacred
memory of the source – what Yeats calls the Great Memory. The figure
of Mnemosyne also combines two things often later distinguished:
firstly, what we might now in general terms think of as the human
faculty of memory, which stores and restores the past and so structures
categories of perception and thought – 'holding all things together in
the mind and soul' as the [Orphic Hymn to her, written between 300
BC to 300AD] has it; and secondly, she generates the Muses, whom we
might more usually associate with Imagination. The mythic image of
Mnemosyne asks us to consider this relationship.

JULES CASHFORD, *Mnemosune: The Great Memory*[1]

Story, as it manifests in human awareness, is a form of story
manifesting universally. One of the features of story is that it
clearly follows the form of distinct story structures, as outlined
in this book. As humans, we're uniquely able to reflect on this.

In this chapter, we'll explore answers to two questions related
specifically to story structures: 'How do different story structures
relate?' and 'What purpose might they serve?'

'How do different story structures relate?'

In chapter 19, I outlined how story structures can be classified
according to how they start. While all of the story structures start

from the same point – the oscillation that sets up a cognitive dissonance in relation to space and time, – each of the story structures then unfolds in a different way. We know which story structures have common starting points; so ... what – if anything – do the story structures in each group we defined in the previous chapter have in common?

I've already described how the Transformation structure expands and generates the Quest structure, so it stands to reason that similar relationships can be traced in other Linear story structures. In fact, two basic Linear structures can be seen to generate most other Linear structures.

The two basic Linear story structures are:
   • The Transformation structure,
   • and the Creation Myth structure.

The Transformation structure

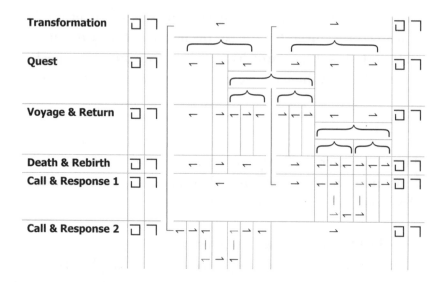

From the Transformation structure to the Quest structure

I've described how the Transformation structure expands into the Quest structure in chapter 7. Furthermore, each of the pairs in the Quest structure can potentially expand in its turn.

The expansion of the Quest structure

The first pair of the Quest structure (problem-journey) doesn't seem to expand – it seems to generate the forward movement of the structure.

The Quest structure always relates to a problem that's within our power to solve. Of course, we sometimes need a little help from our friends, but the friend or helper role in Quest structure stories is clear: it's secondary and supportive. The responsibility for reaching a solution lies with us. The friends or helpers aren't always external. They're often internal qualities – our faith, our intelligence, our faculties of reason and of perception, our memories, our emotions, and our gut instincts. The Quest structure shows us that as far as these kinds of problems go, we *can* prevail. We have all the tools we need to do so – if we choose to use them. If we're clear about the problems we face and can trust we have the right friends or helpers to assist us, then the Quest structure is the ideal one to follow.

From the Quest structure to the Voyage and Return structure

The second pair of steps in the Quest structure (meeting with friend/helper) expands to give the Voyage and Return structure. Although the translation to another dimension of being happens against the character's wishes, the dynamic of the journey is ultimately friendly – rather than the character meeting a friend or helper, the character is forced to make a journey and become their own friend or helper. This expansion has a sympathetic resonance with the expansion of Quest from Transformation outlined earlier. In the latter part, the character is, in the language of story, taken out of their comfort zone and forced to make sense of unfamiliar experiences so they can come back renewed and tell their story.

From the Quest structure to the Death and Rebirth structure

An interesting relationship links the expansion of the third pair of steps in the Quest structure (meeting with enemy/hindrance) to the Death and Rebirth structure. The pair expands in the Death and Rebirth structure to include both the 'main' character's *submersion* phase while simultaneously giving rise to the Saviour character's nested Quest structure. This simultaneous pairing of the negative *submersion* and the positive Saviour Quest links, yet again, to the manner in which the Transformation structure expands to the Quest structure – where the seed of the positive is contained in the negative, and the seed of the negative contained in the positive. The juxtaposition of both ultimately restores flow.

From the Transformation structure to the Call and Response structures

The expansion of a single Transformation structure step dynamically (from 1 step to 7) gives rise to the Revelation structure, which is balanced by the other step in the Transformation structure, resulting in one of two possible variations on the Call and Response structure. If the second step expands (in response to the transgression against the natural order), then a Call and Response Variation 1 structure unfolds. If the first step expands, leading to the final dénouement (whereby balance is restored, but things are never the same as they were), we get a Call and Response Variation 2 structure.

The links to the Transformation structure here serve to point out the strength of the energetic pulse which either generates flow in a Variation 1 structure or a build-up and release of tension in a Variation 2 structure, a factor which is of particular usefulness to writers as it's a key story structure which keeps readers hooked when engaging with the plot pattern or narrative structure of a story. In poetic terms, both variations can be interpreted in an iambic (weak-strong) or in a trochaic (strong-weak) pattern. In musical terms, Variation 1 naturally diminuendos; Variation 2 naturally crescendos.[2]

From the Transformation structure to the Perpetual Motion structure

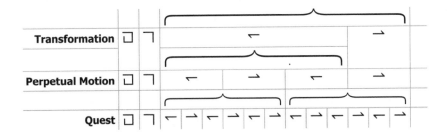

From the above table, it can be seen that the Perpetual Motion structure also unfolds from the Transformation structure. If the second step in the Transformation structure is expanded in the same way as its counterpart, we see an oscillation build:

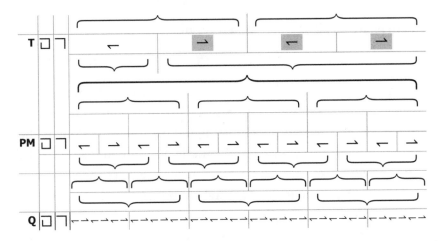

This double/triple pattern of oscillation unfolds perpetually, driving the structure forward. It would seem that this links to the fundamental existence of duple and triple time signatures, the duple and triple subdivisions of beats, and the 2:3 ratio that produces the interval of a perfect fifth in music. If there's a connection—and I see no reason why there shouldn't be—then story structure goes very deep. It extends past narrative to rhythm, harmony, and unfolds in melody. But to what purpose?

The Creation Myth structure

In my view, the structure that story seeks to realise for itself is the Creation Myth structure. It just flows. The initial step is a forward step ($\rightarrow$) which simply flows forward:

$$\Box \; \daleth \; \rightarrow \; \rightarrow \; \rightarrow \; \rightarrow \; \ldots$$

The structure seems to have a perfection that mirrors the perfection of both figure and mood that Sister Miriam Joseph ascribes to the AAA-1 syllogistic form, known as *Barbara* in what she calls 'perennial' or classical syllogistic logic.

The perfection of figure has to do with the arrangement of the shared middle term which joins the two propositions (the premises) and acts catalytically to join the unlike terms, conclusively:

All *a*s are *b*s; all *b*s are *c*s; therefore, all *a*s are *c*s.

The arrangement, in which the *b*s are placed consecutively, is an arrangement called 'Figure 1'. Sister Miriam Joseph explains that 'Figure [1] is … called the perfect figure because in it alone is the middle term really in the natural, middle position; in it alone is the natural synthesis of the terms given in the premises themselves. It represents the spontaneous, natural movement of thought in the process of reasoning.'

The perfection of mood has to do with the type of statements that are used – these are all universal affirmative statements, of the type 'All *a*s are *b*s'. The premises cover all of the *a* term, and all of the *b* term respectively, and—as far as what's being considered is concerned—leave nothing out.[3]

The Creation Myth structure has this flowing, perfect quality, which is why I believe it's the one we should be following—or seeking to return to—as the ideal structure for our lives to follow, while the other structures help us deal with problems which arise on the way. But none of us is alone – we're all in this together, and when two characters' story lines cross, and those characters' intentions align with universal values, there's potential for one of the story structures in the Open-Ended group to unfold as an alternative to both story lines joining and following a Creation Myth structure.[4]

If we're lucky, we'll reach a point where story 'stories' us – individually and collectively. This is what the Creation Myth structure is all about. It's perhaps one of the most moving functions of the Greek chorus voicing their thoughts as one, in and of story. While a musical composition (the musical equivalent of a story) can potentially follow any story structure, the manifestation of perfect music (the musical equivalent of story) arguably follows a Creation Myth structure—it just flows. Experience a piece of music performed with an exquisite sense of musical line, with the illusion of it having no downbeats at all, and you'll get what I mean.

When story 'stories', it goes on a voyage. When we listen to—or tell—stories, we voyage, but story returns. When we story with story, story gets to know itself. And in doing so, it re-members … us, and itself. What's interesting to note here is that when the opening of the Creation Myth expands, the Rags to Riches structure emerges:

	1	2	3	4	5	6	7	8	9	10	11
Creation Myth	⊐	⌐	→	...	⌐‾	⌐‾‾	⌐				
			⌐‾	‾‾	‾⌐		⌐‾	‾‾⌐			
Rags to Riches	⊐	⌐	→	←	→	←	→	←	→	⌐	⊐

As shown in the table above, the first forward step (step 3) in the Creation Myth structure (→) expands to produce the Rags to Riches structure: step 3 expands to give steps 3–5 of the Rags to Riches structure; step 5 expands to produce steps 5–7; step 7 expands to produce steps 7–9. The last pair of steps (Steps 8–9, shown in grey in the table above) becomes a hinge. It opens up to produce a mirrored expansion (9–13 in the table below balancing out steps 3–7). The hinge step (step 8, marked in grey in the table below) results in the unfolding of the nested Quest for the Saviour character:

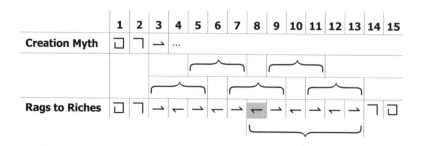

	1	2	3	4	5	6	7	8	9	10	11	12	13	14	15
Creation Myth															
Rags to Riches															

The close connection between the two structures highlights the inherent message of hope within the Rags to Riches structure. Step 8 is where the 'Cinderella' character experiences a return to the state of *subversion* in an altered state of consciousness. At the same point, the Saviour character sets out on their quest to restore order and balance. The Rags to Riches structure can be reduced to (→ ↼ →) which can be reduced further to (→). If this expands according to the Creation Myth structure, and the story just flows forward, then (→) expands to (→ →) and life flows forward along with story. One of the insights that arises from this comparison is the importance, if stuck in a (←) step in a Rags to Riches story, of looking backward to a prior (→) step in order to go forward. It's through connecting to the positive seed from which the story structures unfold that we can find resolution and a restoration of balance. The applications to therapy, self-development, and education are ripe for exploration.

So far, we've seen how story structures unfold from the Transformation and Creation Myth structures, but the following Linear structures still remain unaccounted for:

Trickster
Trickster Variation
Dilemma

Ki-Shō-Ten-Ketsu
Open-Ended Ki-Shō-Ten-Ketsu
Koan
Riddle

All of these have (⇌) steps. The Trickster, Trickster Variation, and Ki-Shō-Ten-Ketsu structures are Closed structures. The (⇌) steps in all of these involve two characters' story lines crossing, typically on Conflicting Quests.

Whether or not a Quest structure flips over to a Trickster structure depends partly on the quality of the link between our powers of sensation and our powers of reasoning, and partly on how we relate to our internal faculties. Faulty reasoning, mistaken assumptions, and unsound logic all manifest as internal tricksters. Sometimes our fears, our insecurities, our emotions, our lack of faith, our inadequate reasoning, our mistaken tendency to value rational thought over contemplative thought (and vice versa) can act in that way too. Using the faculties we have can sometimes be tricky, but it's all part of the rich tapestry of life. We just need to make sure we avoid falling into their traps – which is where recognising the difference between Trickster and Quest structures can really help. As soon as we recognise a trickster character as such, we flip out of the Trickster structure and into a Quest structure, and we can find our way to flow.

Being able to compare all three of these closed structures based on the quality of the Trickster step they have in common reveals that they're all powered by the need to achieve balance – not just on an individual level, where the individual characters' story lines follow Quest structures, but collectively. Unless these characters achieve this, they remain stuck in a Trickster loop. The Trickster Variation structure points to a way out, but it remains for the story seeker to explore that path for themselves. In the case of the Ki-Shō-Ten-Ketsu structure, two contrasting themes are juxtaposed, with the link as yet unrevealed. The cognitive dissonance that this sets up demands resolution. That resolution results in a new level of understanding and appreciation of common features and meaningful connections between things previously thought to be unconnected, achieving balance through understanding.

> The drive for balance inspires and informs the *laws of story* and, as a consequence, how understanding and appreciating balance – individually and collectively – can help us seek and find fulfilment and find meaning in our lives.

The other four structures—the Open-Ended Ki-Shō-Ten-Ketsu, Dilemma, Riddle, and Koan structures—are all open-ended. In all of these, the (⇌) steps are points at which a story spinner's and a story seeker's story lines cross. The cognitive dissonance associated with the (⇌) step is based on an action which connects to the natural order.

All four of these Open-Ended structures depend on a story spinner setting up a cognitive dissonance for a story seeker, opening up new potential avenues of thought. We often lack clarity: we know something is wrong, but we're not quite sure what. We find it hard to put our finger on it. In these situations, we need the wisdom of those who have travelled the path before us and can act as guides. The interactions, in the first three (koans being excluded here), remain firmly rooted in the practical world. This is, I believe, one of the important functions that troubadours, minstrels, jesters used to perform in society (and that the best clowns still do) to bring healing, harmony, and balance to situations in which people were stuck in unproductive loops.

The Koan structure is particularly effective for this. If we've experienced this 'double crossing',[5] it's particularly important for us to tell the stories of our experiences clearly – whether privately to ourselves, or publicly to others, by *living* the *telling*.[6] The telling of *any* story – and that includes the living-out of our life story – follows a process that maps onto the Voyage and Return structure.

Whether or not it unfolds as a tragic process is largely related to our individual and collective relationship with story.

The Dynamic story structures

Only the two Dynamic structures (the Revelation structure and the Chinese Circular Structure) are left to analyse. Both involve alternations between the marked and unmarked states. In the case of the Revelation structure, these relate to clearly differentiated qualitative states: doubt (⊐), confirmation or denial (⊓), and affirmation or refutation, cancelling doubt (⊐). In the case of the Chinese Circular Structure, these relate to different qualitative states of balance associated with *yin/yang* energy, indicating successive rising and flourishing *yin* or *yang* qualities.

The Revelation structure powers the expansion of the extended part of the Call and Response structures. As outlined briefly in chapter 13, the Chinese Circular Structure can be found to underpin all of the Linear structures described in this work, the driver behind this being a tendency towards balance.

If a system is to maintain balance, the dynamic quality of the Chinese Circular Structure needs to come into play. There's power in acknowledging the central balanced *yin/yang* hub where the 'Earth' element facilitates the moves and shifts that take us through the cycle. If we're feeling lost, the Chinese Circular Structure provides a powerful tool that can help us analyse where we happen to be in a particular story structure. It can provide us with a different perspective on matters. If we're stuck, and we analyse our position with respect to the Chinese Circular Structure, there's a good chance we'll find that it will provide the insight we need to integrate marked and unmarked aspects of form in a one-and-the-same balance, and allow a state of *flooooow* to come into being and get us flowing again.

'What purpose might story structures serve?'

Story structures arise within us in response to different kinds of problems; each problem bringing forth the perfect story structure we need to follow in order to solve each one. The tragedy is that we've not generally been aware of it – or rather, we haven't been *until now*. There's much we can learn from story, and much it can do to transform us and shape our own stories.

Story's laws are embodied in us as deeply as story is, and we can learn much – individually and collectively – by following these laws. The laws underpin both story and the storying of story. Story seeks to realise itself in balance in our realisation of our calling, our vocation, when we find our purpose in life. And story structures can help us find that. Following the map, understanding why different story structures exist, how they relate, and ultimately realising they serve a purpose can help us achieve balance in our lives, through story. We can help ourselves achieve that goal much more effectively by drawing on story's laws than if we had no awareness of how or why story structures exist. The beauty of the methodology outlined here is that it offers us a way to explore the form of story structure on its own terms – and while it's open to content, and allows for individual interpretation, it presents clear frameworks and story structures that have been tried and tested over millennia and proved to be the most effective means of problem-solving we have available.[7]

While debates among story spinners and classifiers of stories persist as to what constitutes myth, wonder tale, or folk tale, at the end of the day, they're stories (as, I argue, are essays, riddles, jokes, parables, and other forms). If we look at story structures, we can clearly see a common dynamic driving them all forward: a common search for balance. As we've seen in many story structures, there's a clear presence of the metaphysical, which has led me to see a clear distinction between 'Threshold structures' and 'Non-Threshold structures'. The former provide a threshold which allows a passage within story to and from the transcendent dimension of being; the latter operate chiefly in the immanent dimension of being. The Creation Myth structure straddles both. The story structures outlined can be classified on this basis as follows:

Classification of Threshold and Non-Threshold structures

Threshold Structures	Non-Threshold Structures
Transformation	Quest
Trickster Variation	Trickster
Death and Rebirth	Perpetual Motion
Rags to Riches	Voyage and Return
Call and Response (2 Variations)	Ki-Shō-Ten-Ketsu
Revelation	Open-Ended Ki-Shō-Ten-Ketsu
Chinese Circular Structure	Dilemma
Koan	Riddle

Creation Myth

We readily embrace the emotional, the rational, the metaphysical, the magical in stories – these are key elements of the Threshold structures listed above, and we'd be well-served by actively engaging with them and exploring their potential in our everyday lives. In doing so, we embrace the muses – the daughters of Mnemosyne, who were born 'all of one mind'[8] – the muses that help us remember who and what we are. They all help us flow.

It may be strange to see the Voyage and Return structure classified as a Non-Threshold structure, but I don't see the Voyage and Return structure as a Threshold structure. For me, it provides an 'uncoupling' of a normally 'coupled' state of being, in which the transcendental and immanent are inter-connected and simultaneously mutually aware. The uncoupling seems to allow us to experience both of the paired elements separately in order to appreciate their interconnectedness more fully. Where there's a threshold crossing, it generally points to a Threshold structure.

The Transformation structure (the primary Threshold structure) generates the Non-Threshold Quest, Trickster, Perpetual Motion, and Voyage and Return structures. The other Non-Threshold structures are Open-Ended, and a separate classification based on endings is outlined below:

Classification of Linear story structures by endings

Closed	Open-Ended	No Clear Ending
Quest	Dilemma	Perpetual Motion
Transformation	Open-Ended Ki-Shō-Ten-Ketsu	Creation Myth
Rags to Riches	Koan	
Death and Rebirth	Riddle	
Trickster		
Trickster Variation		
Call and Response (2 Variations)		
Ki-Shō-Ten-Ketsu		
Voyage and Return		

The two Dynamic structures are the Revelation structure and the Chinese Circular Structure; Comedy and Tragedy are structure neutral.

In principle, the 18 structures I've identified in this work are distinct and identifiable, but it's more interesting and rewarding to see them as flexible organic building blocks, capable of being varied – particularly when used in combination in complex stories involving a number of characters' intersecting story lines, as can be seen in the analysis presented in appendix 1.

I don't presume to reach beyond the domain of the gods, to reach past them to the other side of the creation of this world, but story demands we acknowledge the presence of the metaphysical powers which govern certain story structures. We can ignore them, although I wouldn't advise it; we can deny them, although we do so at our peril. They act as friends and helpers, but eventually, we need to leave them behind, along with the stories they appear in, if we're to become one with the common source from which they – and we – originate. Perhaps it's only then that we can experience the 'double crossing' that involves the Voyage and Return trip we need to make in order to tell story's story while simultaneously engaging in our own Creation Myth story.

The Creation Myth structure involves transcending the ebb/flow duality in order to simply flow-er into *flooooow* and in doing so, reaching beyond the indefinite boundary of the known to touch – the infinite known ... and beyond that, who knows? The infinite unknown ...???

> *Who really knows? Who shall here proclaim it?—*
> *from where was it born, from where this creation?*
> *The gods are on this side of the creation of this (world).*
> *So then who does know from where it came to be?*
> *This creation—from where it came to be, if it was produced or if not—*
> *[s/]he who is the overseer of this (world) in the furthest heaven,*
> *[s/]he surely knows. Or if [s/]he does not know . . . ?*[9]

Ultimately, we have to balance the 'actual' and the 'real'; the knowable and the unknowable, and maintain the delicate harmony between them as we move through our lives. Having expanded our horizons, and the importance of story and telling stories, it's now time we focused on the art of storytelling (both written and oral), which is what we'll be exploring briefly in the next chapter.

NOTES

1   Jules Cashford, *Mnemosune: The Great Memory* ([Ilford, Somerset:] Kingfisher Art Productions, 2013), 1–2.

2   Writers will find it an interesting exercise to play with these inherent qualities – use a contrasting dynamic here and see what happens – particularly when wanting to use comedy or bathos, for instance.

3   Sister Miriam Joseph, *The Trivium* (Philadelphia: Paul Dry Books, 2002), 158. In Joseph's text, the figures are indicated with Roman numerals (e.g., Figure I). As the citation has been quoted in isolation, the Roman numeral has been replaced here by the Arabic numeral '1' for consistency, and to minimise any potential confusion.

4   The work of Mihaly Csikszentmihalyi on flow is relevant here. In his February 2004 TED talk, *Flow, the Secret to Happiness*, he notes, importantly, that 'you can't be creating anything with less than 10 years of technical knowledge immersion in a particular field ... it takes that long to be able to ... begin to change something in a way that it's better than what was there before.' https://www.ted.com/talks/mihaly_csikszentmihalyi_flow_the_secret_to_happiness, 10:14–10:46.

5   My use of 'double crossing' here is informed both by the common use of the phrase to indicate duplicity and by Schwaller de Lubicz's insightful comments about the symbolic meaning of double crossing as a *function*: 'Each *neter* [or aspect of the ineffable] is ... a trinity that includes a masculine aspect, a feminine aspect, and the product: Amun-Mut-Khonsu. This is the esoteric sense of the Chinese *yin* and *yang*, exoterically represented by an emptiness and a fullness, which is misleading because the container does not have its masculine aspect within the contained, this latter being merely the complement given by *a thing* that is itself the consequence of an action and its own reaction. Reaction is the reversal of the direction of the action, provoked by the resistance immanent in the nature of the activity, or "action in function." ... This is expressed by the double crossing; an example is the double crossing of the sceptres of the dead king. The sceptres are the hekat, represented by a hook symbolizing the action, the seed, the ferment; and the nekhakha, which Egyptologists translate as "whip" or "flagellum," represented by a staff from which issues a triple flow: the effect of the resistance immanent in action, substance in its triple measure. Physically expressed, it is energy acting on substance in order to fix it, or that which acts and that which undergoes action. The hekat is held in the left hand, the receiving side, the

north, the above; the nekhakha is held in the right hand, the returning, giving, and doing side, the south, the below. The living king is the active and reactive (mystical) power that creates Nature. The king will be dead when this power has produced body, quantity, determined form; this is the first crossing. But when the complementation of this appearance is realized in its turn—the second crossing of the sceptres—then the appearance ceases and the creative power is liberated again after having known form; each sceptre is back in its place, the hekat on the left, the nekhakha on the right.' He also notes the 'in all harmonic proportions the inverse of the mean is equal to the half-sum of the inverse of the extremes; thus 2/35 = 1/30 + 1/42. We discover here the application of the double inversion or double crossing of functions that corresponds to true pharaonic thinking and to its symbolism, which our mathematicians have tried to resolve in a numerical fashion.' René Adolph Schwaller de Lubicz, *The Temple of Man*, translated by Deborah Lawlor and Robert Lawlor (Rochester, VT: Inner Traditions International, 1998), 78–80, 178/9.

6   See the quote by Anna-Teresa Tymieniecka which appears as the epigraph to chapter 19.

7   For a detailed exploration of arguments and scientific studies supporting the case for viewing stories as the most efficient ways of retaining and transmitting information, problem-solving, and community-building, see Kendall Haven, *Story Proof: The Science Behind the Startling Power of Story* (Westport, CT: Libraries Unlimited, 2007).

8   Gk. ὁμόφρονας (*homophronas*). Hesiod, *Theogony*, translated by Martin Litchfield West (Oxford and New York: Oxford University Press, 1988), 53, page 4.

9   The 'Nasadiya Sukta' or 'Hymn of Creation' from *The Rigveda*, translated by Stephanie Jamison and Joel Brereton (New York: Oxford University Press, 2014), Vol. 3, 10:129, 1607–1609. Text in square brackets adapted by Leon Conrad.

21

PLOT PATTERNS: THE PATTERNING OF STORY

SCENES, SEQUENCES, NESTING, AND LATTICING

You have to make the first mark somewhere.

PHILIP PULLMAN, *Let's Write it in Red* [1]

While events in stories unfold chronologically, events in narratives needn't be arranged in chronological order. Narratives don't necessarily have to start and end with the same events as the stories on which they're based, but they do need to start and end. The success of what happens in the middle depends on the story spinner's art.

There are many ways of telling a story well. Great story spinners – whether they work in print or in speech – are masters at developing tension, excitement, and engagement. They can build suspense slowly, sending tingles of expectation up our spines; delight us with plot twists; leave us in suspense with cliff-hanger endings; surprise us by confronting us with the sudden, the unusual, the unexpected. They can make us follow a story with eyes wide, hearts pounding, muscles tense, focused completely on what's happening: fearing the worst; hoping for the best, then letting us down slowly as one sequence reaches its climax, resolves it, and melts into the start of another. What is this magic they wield? Where does their power to hypnotise us come from?

Partly, I think, their power derives from their ability to integrate story structures and plot patterns. Great story spinners integrate these aspects of story brilliantly. The two elements can be viewed as counterparts to narratologist Mieke Bal's description of the difference between actor and actant respectively:

The term "actor" has the abstract meaning of "the agent that acts." "Actant" has a functional meaning, "the one who makes the action move forward." [2]

Plot pattern covers how a story is told in language – it's the actor of the story. In technical terms, it's equivalent to *sjuzhet, récit, discourse*.

The actant, however, the thing that gives it direction, and dictates its flow, is story structure, equivalent to *fabula, histoire*. Story, as I've defined it, depends on both.[3] The story seeker makes sense of both. The story spinner balances both. Story depends on a story spinner to be told. The relationship can be portrayed as follows:

Story			
Story spinner			
Plot pattern		Story structure	
Space	Time	Space	**Time**
Narrative			

The actor is mainly fixed in space, but flexible in terms of time; the actant is mainly fixed in time, but flexible in terms of space. If I lift a mug of coffee, I'm an actor. The lifting is an action. The action takes place through time, but the main focus is on me, a physical being, and a translation of an object (the mug of coffee) from one position in space to another. The description will be based on perceived changes in physical form. The actant is the motivation, the dynamism, the emotional force behind the action – the metaphysical stuff that unfolds through time, but is hard to pinpoint precisely in terms of location in space.[4] Plot patterns focus on the actor and privilege space; story structures focus on the actant and privilege time. To tell stories, we need both. To tell stories well, we need both aspects to be well-balanced.

We're far more Mercurial when it comes to thinking than we are when it comes to moving. Our thoughts can flit all over the place – the mind imposes far fewer limits on us than our physical form does. Our physical movements are limited by the physical frame of our body and our levels of flexibility and agility. It's why we find sleight-of-hand, and other art forms based on heightened control of the body (Bharatanatyam dance, trapeze art, contemporary shadow theatre performance, etc.) so appealing. They derive much of their performance magic from their ability to create the illusion that they can transcend the physical limitations of the body and allow it to become an instrument of the imagination, rather than the other way round. The artistry comes from the imagination, is realised through the bodies of performer and spectator, the transparency of the artistry allowing the performer's imagination to connect directly to the viewer's.

The story spinner's camera lens is far more flexible and versatile than its cinematic equivalent. It's one of the advantages that animation and CGI storyboarders have over live-action storyboarders. Story spinners have the potential to be even more flexible; they have an ability that's truly magical.

Space and time can't be separated. They're interconnected. You can't have one without the other. Nevertheless, it's sometimes useful to focus on them separately. In what follows, I'd like to look at four specific elements of plot patterns: scenes, sequences, nesting, and latticing.

Scenes

In scenes, space is privileged. In narrative terms, actors are represented grammatically by substantives, or 'substance words', i.e., nouns, pronouns, or noun phrases. These point to entities which can be conceived of as occupying physical (concrete) or metaphysical (abstract) space. A character, by definition, has to take up space (or at least be treated by an author as if they do – the personification of an abstract concept is a case in point). Whenever a character appears in a story, they'll manifest – literally or figuratively – in a particular point in space (and time, but I'm isolating the spatial aspect for discussion here – I'll get to the temporal aspect in a while). When introducing or describing a character or setting, story spinners will typically use plot patterning techniques which show movement mainly in relation to space:

- A description of a character or setting that travels from inside to outside
- A description of a character or setting that travels from outside to inside

- Direct assertion (a literal 'pointing to' to show something to the reader or listener; a mark 'somewhere' in space which distinguishes something)[5]
- Indirect implication (a creation of a metaphorical frame for a reader or listener to fill in for themselves; a mark in abstract terms, referring to a relationship of some kind).

Whilst all of the techniques described above privilege space, references to time (historical period, season, time of day, a person's age, etc.) will inevitably come in, but the focus, in terms of plot patterning, is primarily on space. Story spinners use different characters' points of view to illustrate different aspects of the story they're spinning. The characters can shift position, and the story spinner can spin the story from different perspectives, based on characters' locations and orientations in space – from any point, from the opening of a story onwards.[6]

How do story spinners privilege time in scenes? As we've established, story structure unfolds through time. Moreover, one of the rules we've established for analysing story structure is that all relevant events need to be arranged in chronological order, but stories are often told differently.

Story spinners can arrange events in a variety of ways:

- Forward (in story structure order)
- Backward (in reverse chronological order)
- Non-sequentially (rarely encountered as a plot pattern where events are placed in random, strictly non-consecutive order)
- In mixed order (two or more of the above, e.g., reconstructions, detective novels, flashbacks)

Of course, where different characters are involved, story spinners can apply different treatments different plot patterns to characters' story lines to distinguish between characters or add variety to their spinning.

In scenes, story spinners can treat time in relation to plot patterns using:

- Pace (speed: fast/slow)
- Pause (timing: stop/go)

Another tool that story spinners have in their tool kit when it comes to the plot patterning of scenes is based on space and time coming together. Whether within a single scene, or in transitions between scenes, story spinners can play with pace – the unfolding can be long and slow – Proust's long sentences are a good example: they give readers a chance to dive deep. Alternatively, story spinners can sketch a scene in quick brush strokes – using few words and minimalistic imagery, just enough to create a vivid image before moving on to the next scene.

Sequences

Using sequences, story spinners can take us across vast distances in space or vast stretches of time in an instant; they can take us from moment to adjoining moment, leading us through a landscape while describing its changing features in minute detail. The moves, themselves, can be gradual unfoldings, like slow cinematic cross-fades (a plot pattern which unfolds along the lines of an extended Revelation structure works well here), or they can be quick, sudden, surprising, unexpected, dramatic! Philip Pullman instinctively points to how two things work in relation to surprise and suspense: (a) the link between space and time, with specific reference to (b) the relationship between known and unknown (from the story seeker's perspective):

Surprise is *when* something happens that you don't expect: suspense is *when* something doesn't happen that you do expect. Surprise is *when* you open a cupboard and a body falls out. Suspense is *when* you know there's a body in the cupboard – but not which cupboard. So you open the first door and... no, not that one. And up goes the suspense a notch.[7]

Surprise and suspense both depend on contrast. Surprise takes the story seeker on a Trickster Variation journey; suspense is linked to the Revelation structure.

Moving up a level, beyond the ways in which scenes are ordered, transitioned to and from, and treated in terms of perspective, larger-scale sequences of scenes and their treatments can also be analysed in terms of space and time. A story can unfold across different locations, but also different worlds. Myths embody this quality perfectly. The Voyage and Return structure, for instance, demands a shift from one place to another and back, a move which happens primarily through space. Time-travel novels achieve a similar effect, but they do so primarily through temporal organisation. The transitions are effected in just the same way as those between scenes. Although the treatment, in terms of plot pattern, obviously differs, the differences relate to space, as the transitions happen chronologically.

At the next level up, we find nesting.

Nesting

Nesting can happen at the larger sequence level, or at the smaller scenic level. *The Arabian (or 1,001) Nights* is a good example of the former. It's a classic nested story, in which the story of King Shahriar's cuckolding (which maps to a Trickster structure)[8] results in the butchering of new wives (Call and Response structures)[9] until Scheherezade comes into his life (Trickster Variation structure).

It's at the Trickster Awe step in this structure that nested stories typically start to unfold, often going five or six layers deep.

At the level of an individual scene, G can tell H that E told F that D told them that A told D that B met C—a nested structure which is easier to map out visually than verbally:

Events	Descriptions					
5	G tells H that	(s)he (G) heard	E tell F that	D told them (E) that	A told D that	B met C
4		G hears	E tell F that	D told them (E) that	A told D that	B met C
3				D tells E that	A told them (D) that	B met C
2					A tells D that	B met C
1					A sees	B meet C

However many nested levels you have, they all boil down to one mark in the form.[10] Having said that, nesting can't happen unless the events featured in them occur in linear form first, in chronological sequence. In the example above, the sequence starts in the bottom right cell and proceeds upwards, row by row. By the time we get to the top, we've squished time and nested separate events in a single spatially framed scene.

Scenes are combined in different ways over time in plot patterns to create sequences. Time and space often coincide – sometimes even clash – at threshold crossings, which often introduce mystical moments, revelations, interjections – the creative interjections (or *logoi*) which bring life to life in and through story.[11]

Latticing

Most people stop at nesting. At the extreme end of the gamut that spatial patterning allows, stretching out to the very limits of the potentially indefinite realisable limits of human spatial awareness, we find latticing. This is the domain of mythopoeia.

In researching one of the topics for this book when it was in the early stages of the writing process, I followed a series of links on the Internet which serendipitously led me to a notice about a lecture hosted by the Folklore Society at the Warburg Institute, part of the University of London, in September 2014. Little did I know how important that lecture would be.

Half the lecture turned out to be about the history of a little-known Jewish storytelling tradition – that of the Drut'syla. The other half was a demonstration, although a much better way of describing it, is that it was a manifestation of story. Story, on that autumnal evening in London, took the form of a diminutive, bright-eyed, smiling woman called Shonaleigh Cumbers who stood at the front of the 1950s lecture room, transforming it and those within it with her presence and the stories she brought out of the depths of her being, in an interactive storytelling performance, by the last—as far as we know—of her kind. Shonaleigh was trained by her grandmother, Edith Marks (d. 1988), an Auschwitz survivor, who'd learned the stories from *her* grandmother, in a tradition that had been handed down from in their family from grandmother to granddaughter for generations. The community of which the Drut'sylas were a part would gather during Jewish festivals, some of which went on for days, and the Drut'syla would start telling stories. Many of these would be known to the community. They'd often choose what they wanted to hear, or where/when in the story they wanted the Drut'syla to start.

The telling was interactive. As Simon Heywood, who's researched the tradition,[12] and Shonaleigh herself demonstrated, the Drut'syla would start with a story, and inevitably come to a motif which linked to another story – for a Drut'syla's repertoire is formed of 12 interlinked cycles of stories, each containing 8–12 subcycles, each subcycle containing around 30–50 nested, interlinked stories.[13] The discipline of learning them took years, a process which resulted in them being deeply embodied, but also involved learning the Midrash (interpretative meanings) which went with them. As a link was voiced, Shonaleigh explained, a ritual – well-known and expected in the community – unfolded. The Drut'syla would say, "But that's another story ..." and if someone in the audience wanted to hear it, they'd respond, "... which I'd like to hear," or words to that effect. And if not, they'd say, "... for another time," and the Drut'syla would continue telling the story she'd been telling.

To claim to embody well-nigh 4,000 stories is quite a feat. While some remain incredulous and sceptical, I have no doubt that Shonaleigh represents a rare unbroken oral tradition—not just of an enormous, mythopoeic lattice of stories, embodied in the memory of one person, but of the discipline and exercises that are part of the tradition which allow one person to contain several worlds, stories from which are recallable at will, and which, at certain points, connect subcycle to subcycle, with some nodes allowing transitions from one cycle to another. In engaging with the tradition, it's not difficult to imagine Greek myths or myths from other cultures being held in similar ways. One example is that of the Haida mythtellers, a fraction of whose corpus of stories have been written down, and a fraction of those translated into English by Robert Bringshurst in his *Masterworks of the Classical Haida Mythtellers* trilogy. The seeming enormity of the task appears daunting, and yet it's definitely humanly possible.[14] The lattice is part of an oral tradition that's held in trust by one person, with the stories within it and the dynamic connections between them being kept alive collectively by a community. The lattice doesn't live in the story spinner in isolation, nor is it dispersed among story spinners; it manifests in a unique collective space which binds a community together. As to whether you see it as *extra*ordinary or ordinary depends simply on your awareness. We either phase-shift, or ... we don't. But sometimes, just sometimes, story can shift us *despite* ourselves. Whatever way it happens, it's pure poetry.

As I note in my introduction, some of the best story spinners are poets. Their words frame this work and as we near the end of this work, it's time to look at poetry and reveal unrealised connections between story structure and the musicality of regular poetic forms by applying the simple methodology outlined in this work. I've found that the approach taken here can reveal deep insights about form, function, and the meaning of poems that follow regular poetic forms, which we'll be looking at in the next chapter – the penultimate in this book.

NOTES

1   Philip Pullman, "Let's Write it in Red," in *Dæmon Voices: Essays on Storytelling*, 141–168 (Oxford: David Fickling, 2017), at 145.

2   Mieke Bal, *On Storytelling: Essays in Narratology* (Sonoma, CA: Polebridge, 1991), 86. See also Roland Barthes, "An Introduction to the Structural Analysis of Narrative," in *New Literary History: On Narrative and Narratives* 6, no. 2 (Winter 1975): 237–272, at 243, https://doi.org/10.2307/468419.

3   Skinner summarises the difference as follows: plot is 'the time of the telling'; story is 'the time of the thing told'. Richard Skinner, *Writing a Novel: Bring Your Ideas to Life the Faber Academy Way* (London: Faber & Faber, 2018), 95. See also the glossary entries for these terms in H. Porter Abbott, *The Cambridge Introduction to Narrative*.

4   The injunction, 'Show, don't tell' is related to this. A particularly good analysis of how to achieve this elusive result can be found in Robert Olen Butler, *From Where You Dream: The Process of Writing Fiction* (New York: Grove, 2005), 15.

5   'If a content is of value, a name can be taken to indicate this value. Thus the calling of the name can be identified with the value of the content.' '… if the content is of value, a motive or an intention or instruction to cross the boundary into the content can be taken to indicate this value. Thus, also, the crossing of the boundary can be identified with the value of the content.' Spencer-Brown, *Laws of Form*, 1–2.

6   For a discussion of the role of the narrator and its relation to focalisation, see Mieke Bal, *On Storytelling*, 102–107 and Philip Pullman, "The Classical Tone: Narrative Tact and Other Classical Virtues," in *Dæmon Voices: Essays on Storytelling*, 239–258 (Oxford: David Fickling, 2017).

7   Philip Pullman, "Let's Write it in Red," 158, italics mine.

8   This applies to the intersection of his story line with that of his first wife.

9   The part of the king's story line which covers his initial marriage, and the discovery of the wife's infidelity follows a Call and Response Variation 1 structure; the part which covers his subsequent marriages and execution of new wives follows a Call and Response Variation 2 structure. There's a structural shift from the king acting within the mortal dimension of being – getting married, producing offspring, ensuring the temporal line of succession (Quest/Revelation) to the king acting as divinely ordained monarch whose word is final, issuing a non-negotiable death sentence (Transformation).

10   See Leon Conrad, "Laws of Form – Laws of Narrative – Laws of Story," in *Laws of Form: A Fiftieth Anniversary* 72 (Series On Knots & Everything), edited by Louis H. Kauffman, Fred Cummins, Randolph Dible, Leon Conrad, Graham Ellsbury, Andrew Crompton, and Florian Grote, 785–806 Singapore: World Scientific, 2022, Section 1: 'Clarke's Application of the CoI', at 788–793.

11   There are many ways in which the word *logos* was used in ancient Greece. Two key things to note in this context are the use of *logos* to denote a complete utterance: a combination of *onoma* and *rhema* (noun + verb = sentence). This is the sense of *logos* as 'The Word' at the beginning of St John's Gospel. Secondly, a similar distinction between static and volatile aspects of *logos* identified by stoic philosophers, who saw a similar triune structure they described as *logos spermatikos* with its two aspects: the *logos endiathetos* and the *logos porphorikos*. 'The former is immanent in man as the Latin 'ratio,' while the latter (upon his lips) is expressed as 'oratio.'" Duane Williams, *The Linguistic Christ – Understanding Christ as the Logos of Language: The Metaphysical Etymology of Heideggerian Linguistics* (Lewiston, NY: Edwin Mellen Press, 2011), 19. See also Mieke Bal, *On Storytelling*, 77–79.

12   Simon Heywood and Shonaleigh Cumbers, "War and the Ruby Tree: The Motif of the Unborn Generations in Jewish Women's Story-Telling," in *War, Myths, and Fairy Tales*, edited by Sara Buttsworth and Maartje Abbenhuis, 219–237 (Singapore: Palgrave Macmillan, 2017), https://doi.org/10.1007/978-981-10-2684-3_10 and Simon Heywood, "Silver Threads of Fear: Restoring the agency of female protagonists in Jewish women's storytelling traditions," in *Strategies of Silence: Reflections on the Practice and Pedagogy of Creative Writing*, edited by Moy McCrory and Simon Heywood, 34–42 (London: Routledge, 2021).

13   Estimated figures communicated by Simon Heywood, in an on-line conversation, on 16 October, 2018, as at that date, based on recordings of performances of a single cycle made up to that date. The process of archiving the entire corpus is ongoing at the time of writing.

14   See the work of Lynne Kelly (http://www.lynnekelly.com.au), particularly her *Knowledge and Power in Prehistoric Societies* (Cambridge: Cambridge University Press, 2015) and *The Memory Code: Unlocking the Secrets of the Lives of the Ancients and the Power of the Human Mind* (London: Atlantic, 2017).

22

DANCE DYNAMICS: THE PATTERNING OF POETRY

POETRY AND STORY—THE STORY STRUCTURES OF POETIC FORMS: LIMERICKS, SONNETS, GHAZALS, LANDAYS, AND HAIKUS

*... music begins to atrophy when it departs too far from the dance; ...
poetry begins to atrophy when it gets too far from music; but this must not
be taken as implying that all good music is dance music or all poetry lyric.*

EZRA POUND, *ABC of Reading*[1]

Any traditional story spinner worth their salt typically has a gamut of tools up their sleeves which they use to engage audiences. They have tools to wake up audience members that have gone to sleep; tools to bring stragglers, wanderers, and daydreamers back to join other listeners in the shared story world; tools to entertain fidgety children; and tools to work magic. The most magical of these tools relate to music and poetry. Music and poetry have long been linked to story. At a live storytelling performance, when the story spinner calls out, 'Crick!' to invite us to join in some warm-up games, or to regain our attention, the expected audience response ('Crack!') should mirror the pitch, speed, and volume of the story spinner's original. It's with reference to this practice that one of the major promoters of modern performance storytelling in the UK is called 'The Crick Crack Club'.

These storytelling tools and the purposes they serve can still be found in literary texts. There's a reason why poetry permeates literary works based on oral storytelling traditions and cycles of traditional stories. The Arabic text of *The 1,001 (or Arabian) Nights* is one example. It contains a number of poems, which, in the oral tradition from which they derive, are designed to weave a web of magic, to draw listeners in, to win them over, and attune them to the story.

One of the main printed versions starts out with a formulaic beginning invoking the name of the Almighty and the prophet (pbuh), following which the story is introduced with an introductory passage, rich with sound patterns, which flows forward with a jaunty rhythm to set up the story, after which the story spinner launches into a more prosaic style. The introduction is as follows:

Transcription of Arabic text[2]	Rhyme scheme	Poetic translation
ḥukiya wāllahu a'lam	A	As God is my witness, I swear,
ānnahu kāna fī mā maḍá		as has been told many times
min qadīm al-zamān	B	in prose and in rhyme,
wa sālifi al-'aṣri wal-awān	B	That once upon a time
malikun min muluki sāsān	B	In a place – not yours and not mine
bi-jazā'iri al-hindi wal-ṣīn	C	A Sassanian King ruled beyond the waves
ṣāhibu jundin	D	Over a land – west of India, west of China.
wa-a'wānin	C	He owned a thrave of slaves;
wa-khadamin	C	Commanded an army of braves;
wa-hasham	A	No king had finer wives or courtiers anywhere;
lahu waladān	B	And he had two sons sublime:
ahaduhumā kabīr	E	One older,
wal-ākhir ṣaghīr,	E	One younger,
wa-kānā fārisayni	F	Both warriors brave,
wa-batalain	(F)	Who sent many an enemy to an early grave.
wa-kāna al-kabīru	G	The older was more skilful than the younger;
afrasu min al-ṣaghīr	(G)	The younger sought to match the skill of his brother.
wa-qad malaka al-bilāda	H	They served their father, who held the land
wa-ḥakama bil-'adli bayn	(H)	in thrall, dispensing justice and goodness
al-'ibād		amongst all.

A similar device is used, as David Pinault points out, at the beginning of the story of *Maryam the Christian*:[3]

Transcription of Arabic text	Rhyme scheme	Poetic translation
wa-qad kāna li-khurūj tilka al-jāriyah min madīnat abīhā	A	And as for the story of how that young maiden left her father's city ...
hadīth gharīb	B	and her strange plight ...
wa-amr 'ajīb	B	now that's a story that'll incite
nasūquhu 'alā al-tartīb	B	wonder which I'll tell you tonight
ḥattā yaṭraba al-sāmi' wa-yaṭīb	B	to lift your spirits and bring you delight.

Both of the translations are mine. They're designed to match the rhyme schemes of the originals as closely as possible and give a sense of how the poetry serves to heighten anticipation and encourage focus and attention. Rudyard Kipling uses a similar approach in the opening of *The Butterfly That Stamped*, which he wrote to be read aloud—and what an opening it is![4] It's redolent with patterns – not just in sounds and letters, but in sentences, in emotions, in connotations, in ideas:

THIS, O my Best Beloved, is a story—a new and a wonderful story—a story quite different from the other stories—a story about The Most Wise Sovereign Suleiman-bin-Daoud— Solomon the Son of David.

There are three hundred and fifty-five stories about Suleiman-bin-Daoud; but this is not one of them. It is not the story of the Lapwing who found the Water; or the Hoopoe who shaded Suleiman-bin-Daoud from the heat. It is not the story of the Glass Pavement, or the Ruby with the Crooked Hole, or the Gold Bars of Balkis. It is the story of the Butterfly that Stamped.

Now attend all over again and listen![5]

It's no wonder that story spinners draw on poetry (a compressed art of space-time patterning). At every level—sounds, letters, syllables, words, phrases, clauses, sentences, ideas, emotions—poets form and fashion living words to act as conduit for an act of poetic expression framed by a cry; a sigh. When we're born, we cry; when we die, we sigh. The cry, an expression of the pain of separation, necessary for self-recognition; the sigh, an expression of relief at the re-crossing of the distinguishing threshold, transcending it, so it no longer separates or divides. The space between contains poetry. How we form it and fill it is up to us, as poets, engaging in an ongoing process of cosmic autopoiesis – the great poem of creation.

Sonnets, haikus, rubaiyyat, villanelles, and other regular forms of poetry put constraints upon poets which liberate, rather than limit poetic expression. They have the potential to link us to a poetic way of life, a way of living harmoniously in the moment … if, that is, we realise they can perform this role.

My exploration of the links between regular poetic forms and story structure turned up many surprising connections that add a considerable amount to the appreciation of formal poems and their connection to living life po(i)etically. While the subject demands fuller treatment in a separate work, I'd like to share with you, in a preliminary way, some of the insights I've had to date.

I'll only be looking at the link between story structure and regular forms of poetry here: specifically, limericks, sonnets, ghazals, landays and haikus. The approach is just one of many possible ways of analysing such poems and complements conventional ways of analysing them.

In exploring the link between story structures and regular forms of poetry, I found I had to apply some basic rules, based on the generic nature and quality of poetic forms. The rules feature three simple but important elements: metre, rhythm, and rhyme. Each of these three elements involves a playful engagement with pattern, based on setting up an anticipated sequence and confirming or defeating the anticipated outcome.

Let's take metre first. Metre works by repeating a regular pattern of beats – in pairs or triads. In musical terms, these are the equivalents of time signatures – in duple time ($\frac{2}{4}$, $\frac{4}{4}$, etc. – resulting in repeated 'dum-di, dum-di'; or 'dum-di-da-di, dum-di-da-di' patterns) or in triple time ($\frac{3}{4}$, etc.– resulting in repeated 'dum-di-di, dum-di-di' patterns).

Each beat can be subdivided into groups of two (simple duple, or simple triple) or three (compound duple, or compound triple – ($\frac{6}{8}$, $\frac{9}{8}$, etc.)). The process applies to every level of division fractally.

As soon as a particular type of metre is set up, so is an expectation of a repeat pattern. And usually, the expectation is for a two-bar, or (most commonly) a four-bar phrase, with three-bar phrases providing variety in places.[6]

If I were to tap out the following rhythm, and ask you to respond, keeping the response to only one tap per beat, what would your rhythmic response be?

'Dum-di, dum-di ...'

'   '?

Perhaps it was, '... *dum*-di, dum-di!' or something very close.

What if I'd said, '*dum*-di-da-di, *dum*-di-da-di ...'?

I wouldn't be surprised if you responded, ' ... *dum*-di-da-di, *dum*-di-da-di!'

Metre sets up an expectation for the fractal repetition and expansion of a pattern at one tap per beat. If it weren't for rhythm, which adds more interest to the mix, we'd soon be bored. Rhythm adds more interest to the mix.

Take two basic bars of $\frac{4}{4}$ time – a regular repeated '*Dum*-di-da-di, *dum*-di-da-di', like this:

$\frac{4}{4}$ ♩ ♩ ♩ ♩ | ♩ ♩ ♩ ♩ :]

Tap out that metre with your fingers – on your leg or on a nearby surface; whatever works for you. Keep it going. Now feel the following words fit over the metre:

> Supercalifragilisticexpialidocious ...
> Um-diddle-iddle-iddle
> Um-diddle-ay ...
> Um-diddle-iddle-iddle
> Um-diddle-ay ...

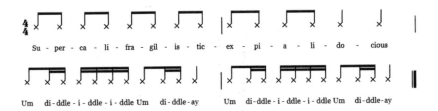

Su - per - ca - li - fra - gil - is - tic - ex - pi - a - li - do - cious

Um   di - ddle - i - ddle - i - ddle Um   di - ddle - ay   Um   di - ddle - i - ddle - i - ddle Um   di - ddle - ay

The metre that underpins the sequence stays constant, but the rhythm that flows over the top of it changes, adding variety and interest.

Here's another example:

How would you bring this incomplete nonsense sequence to a satisfying close?
Ma-la pa-la saa-fa-li taa
Ma-la pa-la[7] ...

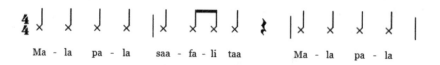

Ma - la   pa - la   saa - fa - li taa   Ma - la   pa - la

When I first tried, I felt it demanded to be rendered as a four-bar phrase, extended as in the following examples:

Version 1:

Ma - la   pa - la   saa - fa - li taa   Ma - la   pa - la!

Version 2:

Ma - la   pa - la   saa - fa - li taa   Ma - la   pa - la   saa - fa - li taa.

or through silence, as in this example:

Version 3:

This engagement with the instinct to respond to the patterns that are set up in poetry, through metre and rhythm, will be our key to analysing the story structure of regular forms of poetry. The openings and closings of poems are implied (☐), and a poem's title and form are the 'initial situation' (ㄱ). From there, my analysis of poetic form follows the patterns of fulfilled or unfulfilled expectation set up by the form, starting with metre first and foremost, rather than the content (which can be analysed separately using the methodology outlined in the book so far).

To analyse the story structures of regular metrical forms of poetry, I've applied these rules:

- **The opening and closing of a poem (☐) are implied.**
- **The 'character' of a poem (ㄱ) is its form.**
- **The backward step (↽) indicates *anticipation* of expected outcome which is set up through metre, rhythm, and/or rhyme.**
- **The forward step (⇀) indicates *fulfilment* of that expectation through the completion of a metrical, rhythmic, and/or rhyming pattern.[8]**
- **An oscillatory step (⇌) indicates a state of defeated expectation which typically evokes a Trickster Variation, Open-Ended Ki-Shō-Ten-Ketsu, Koan, Dilemma or Riddle structure. All of these are Threshold structures and indicate a phase shift in levels in the reader's awareness.**

This is different to the analysis of story structure, where each character is indicated by a mark (⌐) and the subsequent steps relate to whether something (a) supports the solution of a problem or moves forward, (b) thwarts it or moves backward, or (c) sets up a cognitive dissonance of some kind. Here, we're dealing purely with patterns of anticipation and expectation.

It's a new way of looking at poetic forms. Nobody, up to now, as far as I'm aware, has looked at poetry in this way. No one, as far as I'm aware, has linked specific story structures to regular poetic forms. Nobody, as far as I'm aware, has been able to qualitatively link poetry to the particular functions of these story structures and outline a consistent theory, across a variety of literary forms, in relation to how story 'stories'. To explore this further, let's start simply:

Limericks

To demonstrate how this works, step by step, we'll use a simple Limerick – the example below is by Salman Rushdie:

The marriage of poor Kim Kardashian
Was krushed like a kar in a krashian.
Her Kris kried, "Not fair!
Why kan't I keep my share?"
But Kardashian fell klean outa fashian.[9]

The first thing we do is note the first two structure steps:

Analysing the story structure of a limerick by Salman Rushdie

Story structure steps	Line numbers	Poetic form	Story structure symbols
1		Opening (implied)	⌐
2		Limerick in AABBA rhyme scheme	⌐

The focus for now will simply be on metre and rhythm. We'll come to rhyme and content later. The first line of this limerick sets up a rhythmic sequence. Presented in the notation used to mark the metrical and rhythmic units of poetry, where ⌣ stands for a weak stress and / stands for a strong one, the rhythmic pattern, which starts with a weak stress followed by three strong-weak-weak sequences is notated as follows:

Analysing the story structure of a limerick by Salman Rushdie

Story structure steps	Line numbers	Poetic form	Story structure symbols
1		Opening (implied)	⊐
2		Limerick in AABBA rhyme scheme	⌐
3	1	⌣ / ⌣ ⌣ / ⌣ ⌣ / ⌣ ⌣	

The rhythm clearly spans a four-bar phrase. In simple triple time ($\frac{3}{4}$), it would be notated like this:

$\frac{3}{4}$ 𝄾 𝄾 ♩ |♩ ♩ ♩ |♩ ♩ ♩ |♩ ♩ ♩ |

It sets up a pattern of expectation and anticipation for a balancing phrase. This is notated as a backward step (⟵) in the table below:

Analysing the story structure of a limerick by Salman Rushdie

Story structure steps	Line numbers	Poetic form	Story structure symbols
1		Opening (implied)	⊐
2		Limerick in AABBA rhyme scheme	⌐
3	1	⌣ / ⌣ ⌣ / ⌣ ⌣ / ⌣ ⌣	⟵

Imagine a pause (⌒) after the end of the fourth bar … imagine you don't know what comes next. Let the anticipation build – get a feel for the metre. To me, it feels as if another four-bar phrase should follow. The simplest option would be a repeat of the first:

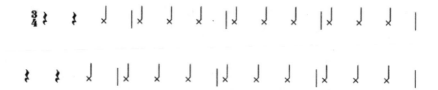

This is, in fact, what happens in the poem, and the second line confirms the expectation. This is shown as a forward step (→) in the table below:

Analysing the story structure of a limerick by Salman Rushdie

Story structure steps	Line numbers	Poetic form	Story structure symbols
1		Opening (implied)	⊐
2		Limerick in AABBA rhyme scheme	¬
3	1	⌣ / ⌣⌣ / ⌣⌣ / ⌣⌣	←
4	2	⌣ / ⌣⌣ / ⌣⌣ / ⌣⌣	→

But there's also a sense, in the form, that while line 2 fulfils the expectation set up in line 1, it also sets up a new expectation. When I pause here (⌒), I get the feeling there should be another four-bar phrase to come – perhaps even a pair to balance out the first pair. The new expectation is noted as a backward step (←) in the table below:

Analysing the story structure of a limerick by Salman Rushdie

Story structure steps	Line numbers	Poetic form	Story structure symbols
1		Opening (implied)	⊐
2		Limerick in AABBA rhyme scheme	¬
3	1	⌣ / ⌣⌣ / ⌣⌣ / ⌣⌣	←
4	2	⌣ / ⌣⌣ / ⌣⌣ / ⌣⌣	→ ←

The third line of the poem follows, but it's a short line – the expectation set up in line 2 of the poem isn't fully met, and the expectation builds. This is shown as a backward step (←) in the following table:

Analysing the story structure of a limerick by Salman Rushdie

Story structure steps	Line numbers	Poetic form	Story structure symbols
1		Opening (implied)	⊐
2		Limerick in AABBA rhyme scheme	⌐
3	1	‿ / ‿‿ / ‿‿ / ‿‿	←
4	2	‿ / ‿‿ / ‿‿ / ‿‿	→ ←
5	3	‿ / ‿‿ /	←

There's a sense that a balancing two-bar phrase is needed to complete the unit. When it appears, one element of anticipation is met – the element relating to the need for a balancing line to line 3; but there's another element of anticipation which has yet to be met – the element relating to the need for a fourth balancing four-bar phrase:

Analysing the story structure of a limerick by Salman Rushdie

Story structure steps	Line numbers	Poetic form	Story structure symbols
1		Opening (implied)	⊐
2		Limerick in AABBA rhyme scheme	⌐
3	1	‿ / ‿‿ / ‿‿ / ‿‿	←
4	2	‿ / ‿‿ / ‿‿ / ‿‿	→ ←
5	3	‿ / ‿‿ /	←
6	4	‿ / ‿‿ /	→ ←

In the tables, I've notated the pulse of the metre and the metre generally runs in a 1:1 correspondence with the number of syllables. However, this can vary and it adds rhythmic variety. Some weak beats, for instance, like the first weak beat in line 4, can have two syllables.

If I take the poem from the top metrically and rhythmically and pause here, I experience the strongest sense of anticipation yet – there's definitely a build-up of tension here. In musical notation, this is what I hear:

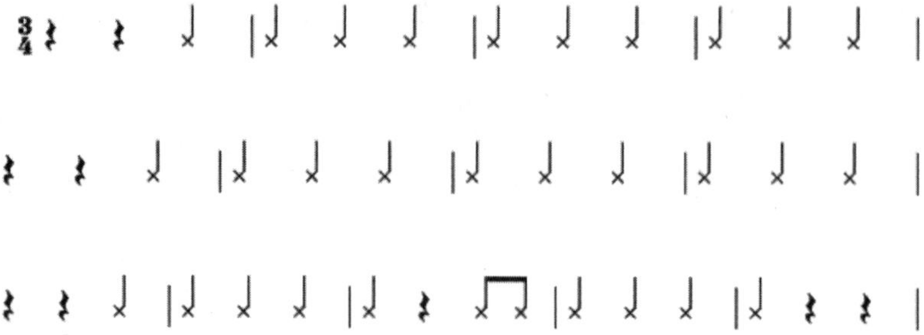

I get a definite sense that the sequence cries out for a fourth four-bar phrase to complete the set – a rhythmic 'problem' (↼), if you like, that cries out for a 'resolution' (⇀).

When the final line begins to unfold, I feel a sense of expectant relief starts to build, and when it's complete, I feel a sense of satisfaction at the fulfilment of the expectation, which is notated as a forward step (⇀) in the following table:

Analysing the story structure of a limerick by Salman Rushdie

Story structure steps	Line numbers	Poetic form	Story structure symbols
1		Opening (implied)	❏
2		Limerick in AABBA rhyme scheme	⏋
3	1	⌣ / ⌣ ⌣ / ⌣ ⌣ / ⌣ ⌣	↼
4	2	⌣ / ⌣ ⌣ / ⌣ ⌣ / ⌣ ⌣	⇀ ↼
5	3	⌣ / ⌣ ⌣ /	↼
6	4	⌣ / ⌣ ⌣ /	⇀ ↼
7	5	⌣ ⌣ / ⌣⌣⌣ / ⌣ ⌣ / ⌣ ⌣	⇀

The response pattern here is purely linked to the rhythm. Take away words, take away rhymes, take away the story. With these gone, we're simply left with a rhythmic pattern. And the pattern of fulfilled and defeated anticipation that this particular rhythmic pattern gives rise to ... tells a story. The rhyme scheme sets up a similar sequence:

An analysis of the story structure of the rhyme scheme of a typical limerick

Story structure steps	Poetic form	Rhyme scheme	Analysis	Story structure symbols
1	Opening (implied)			⌐
2	Limerick in AABBA rhyme scheme			⌐
3	⌣ / ⌣⌣ / ⌣⌣ / *dí*	A	By the end of the line, an expectation of a repeat of the metre, rhythm, and rhyme pattern is set up.	←
4	⌣ / ⌣⌣ / ⌣⌣ / *dí*	A	By the end of the line, the expectation set up in the first line is fulfilled. A new expectation is set up for a balancing pattern to follow.	→ ←
5	⌣ / ⌣⌣ *dá*	B	The first line of a pair of contrasting lines is given, setting up a new set of expectations.	←
6	⌣ / ⌣⌣ *dá*	B	The second line of the contrasting pair is given. The expectations are met. A new expectation is set up for a completion of the rhythmic pattern.	→ ←
7	⌣ / ⌣⌣ / ⌣⌣ / *dí*	A	By the end of the line, the expectation of a pattern that will balance out the first two lines is fulfilled, providing closure.	→

An analysis of the story structure of the rhyme scheme of a typical limerick

Story structure steps	Poetic form	Rhyme scheme	Analysis	Story structure symbols
8	Outcome or resolution		The potential realised by the poet in the poem for the merging of form and content to be realised in the reader or listener is released.	⌐
9	Closing (implied)			⌐

In experiencing the poem both through the patterns in rhythm and metre and through the patterns in the rhyme scheme, I'm able not only to appreciate the poem as a whole, but to reflect on the effect it's had on me:

Analysing the story structure of a limerick by Salman Rushdie

Story structure steps	Line numbers	Poetic form		Story structure symbols
1		Opening (implied)		⌐
2		Limerick in AABBA rhyme scheme		⌐
3	1	⏑ / ⏑ ⏑ / ⏑ ⏑ / ⏑ ⏑	A	←
4	2	⏑ / ⏑ ⏑ / ⏑ ⏑ / ⏑ ⏑	A	→ ←
5	3	⏑ / ⏑ ⏑ /	B	←
6	4	⏑ / ⏑ ⏑ /	B	→ ←
7	5	⏑ ⏑ / ⏑ ⏑ ⏑ / ⏑ ⏑ / ⏑ ⏑	A	→
8		Outcome or resolution (The potential realised by the poet in the poem for the merging of form and content to be realised in the reader or listener is released.)		⌐
9		Closing (implied)		⌐

If we condense the (↤ ↤) steps that go across lines 2 and 3 of the poem to (↤), we end up with the following familiar story structure:

At first glance, I thought limericks followed a Linear Quest structure, but then I considered the qualities of the story structures in more depth. At the end of a successful poem, there's a sense that we've crossed a threshold. Either we're transported to a metaphysical realm, or (in the case of bawdy poems and limericks, as Gershon Legman argues) we experience some kind of transgression.[10] My hypothesis is that it's reasonable, therefore, to see the story structures which poems follow as being Threshold structures. The Quest structure is a Non-Threshold structure while the Call and Response and Revelation structures are Threshold structures. If we rule out the Quest structure, we're left with the Revelation structure. This, with its three *veni, vidi, vici* steps and single-step expansion pattern, is a far more appropriate choice.[11] However, the Revelation structure, which has three expansions of the (↤) step, would mean that the structure would end on a (↤) step rather than a (↦) step.

In terms of content, the poem is a wry comment on the 2011 marriage of Kim Kardashian and Kris Humphries. Their relationship and wedding were the subject of intense media interest. The marriage lasted 72 days. The divorce announcement caused a marked rise in activity amongst Kardashian detractors. While the characters' story lines seem to follow a Trickster structure, the compressed elements presented in the Limerick (Kar krash; "Not fair!") suggesting a backward step (↤) and the outcome (not a resolution) suggests a forward step (↦). The problem it alludes to is a far bigger one, potentially to do with transgression against love, and a critical view of media focus on notoriety and celebrity rather than on worthwhile human achievement. The content clearly points to an overarching Transformation structure. Put the findings from the analysis of structure and content together (the former following a Revelation structure, the latter a Transformation structure) and we can see how a seemingly superficial poem serves as a powerful piece of social commentary, highlighting the transgression against love on the one hand (revealed by the Transformation structure element of the content) and the gradual revelation of this to the reader, bringing a deeper appreciation of Rushdie's achievement to light, through the way in which, structurally, the Limerick facilitates the unfolding of a Revelation structure as the reader proceeds through the poem. Where the poem evokes a reaction in the reader, they may well have been following a Call and Response Variation 2 structure, and a reflection on the inherent qualities of the structure, which is a Threshold structure, with a shift in character story lines between steps 8 and 9, and the inherent lack of resolution which is associated with this structure adds much to the appreciation of the poem and its context. Whether or not there's a Quest structure that could unfold – internally or externally – as a result of engaging with the poem is up to the reader.

The content of a specific limerick will follow its own story structure, although the form lends itself to Transformation structure content. In writing a limerick, the poet follows a Call and Response Variation 1 structure. The limerick form itself follows the Revelation structure. The reader experiences it as a Call and Response Variation 2 structure. But why do some forms appear in some cultures and not in others? What do they say about us as human beings? A couple of examples follow, showing the potential of this approach to bring something new and exciting to the process of literary criticism and cultural analysis.

Sonnets

In an English sonnet in iambic pentameter, with an ABBA ABBA ABBA CC rhyme scheme, the following patterns can be seen:

An analysis of the story structure of an English sonnet

Story structure steps	Poetic form	Rhyme scheme	Story structure symbols	Analysis
1	Opening (implied)		⊐	
2	Sonnet in iambic pentameter in ABBA ABBA ABBA CC rhyme scheme		⌐	
3	$\smile$ / $\smile$ / $\smile$ / $\smile$ / $\smile$ _dí_	A	↤	By the end of the line, an expectation of a repeat of the rhythm and the introduction of a new rhyme syllable is set up.[12]
	$\smile$ / $\smile$ / $\smile$ / $\smile$ / $\smile$ _dá_	B		By the end of the line, an expectation of a repeat of the rhyme and rhythm of the couplet is set up.
	$\smile$ / $\smile$ / $\smile$ / $\smile$ / $\smile$ _dá_	B		The first line of the second couplet is given.
4	$\smile$ / $\smile$ / $\smile$ / $\smile$ / $\smile$ _dí_	A	↦	The second line of the second couplet is given. The expectations for the first quatrain are met. There's a sense of doubt here, which requires verification (a _veni_ step)
5	$\smile$ / $\smile$ / $\smile$ / $\smile$ / $\smile$ _dí_	A	↤	An expectation of a second quatrain is set up. The expectation is met. There's a sense of verification here (a _vidi_ step).
	$\smile$ / $\smile$ / $\smile$ / $\smile$ / $\smile$ _dá_	B		
	$\smile$ / $\smile$ / $\smile$ / $\smile$ / $\smile$ _dá_	B		
6	$\smile$ / $\smile$ / $\smile$ / $\smile$ / $\smile$ _dí_	A	↦	
7	$\smile$ / $\smile$ / $\smile$ / $\smile$ / $\smile$ _dí_	A	↤	An expectation of a third quatrain is set up. The expectation is met. There's a sense of confirmation/finality here (a _vici_ step)
	$\smile$ / $\smile$ / $\smile$ / $\smile$ / $\smile$ _dá_	B		
	$\smile$ / $\smile$ / $\smile$ / $\smile$ / $\smile$ _dá_	B		
8	$\smile$ / $\smile$ / $\smile$ / $\smile$ / $\smile$ _dí_	A	↦	

An analysis of the story structure of an English sonnet

Story structure steps	Poetic form	Rhyme scheme	Story structure symbols	Analysis
9	$\smile$ / $\smile$ / $\smile$ / $\smile$ / $\smile$ *dú*	C	↶	The expectations for a new rhyme scheme are set up. There's a sense in which there's a need for the 'excessive' balance of the thrice repeated structure to be counterbalanced by a new structure.
10	$\smile$ / $\smile$ / $\smile$ / $\smile$ / $\smile$ *dú*	C	→	The expectations for a new rhyme scheme are met, but is the couplet sufficient to restore balance?
11	Outcome or resolution		⌐	The potential realised by the poet in the poem for the merging of form and content to be realised in the reader or listener is released.
12	Closing (implied)		⌑	

Looking solely at the level of the responses generated by the rhythmic patterns and rhyme schemes of English sonnets which have an ABBA ABBA ABBA CC rhyme scheme (or similar), the four distinct sections clearly map to a Call and Response Variation 2 structure:

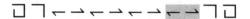

The approach, when applied to Shakespeare's sonnets, gave considerable support to Clare Asquith's theory that Shakespeare could well have been a Recusant (a staunch Catholic in an era of religious repression against Catholics) and that his writings reflect this in a hidden way.[13] Sonnet 65, one of my favourites, is one of several of his sonnets which have clues that point to this:

Since brass, nor stone, nor earth, nor boundless sea,
But sad mortality o'er-sways their power,
How with this rage shall beauty hold a plea,
Whose action is no stronger than a flower?

O, how shall summer's honey breath hold out
Against the wreckful siege of battering days,
When rocks impregnable are not so stout,
Nor gates of steel so strong, but Time decays?

O fearful meditation! where, alack,
Shall Time's best jewel from Time's chest lie hid?
Or what strong hand can hold his swift foot back?
Or who his spoil of beauty can forbid?

    O, none, unless this miracle have might,
    That in black ink my love may still shine bright.

While the form follows a Call and Response Variation 2 structure, as shown above, the story structure relating to the content can be interpreted as follows:

Analysis of story structure of content of Shakespeare's Sonnet 65

Story structure steps	Story structure symbols	Structure	Outline of content
	Underlying story structure		
1	⊐	Opening	[Implied]
2	⌐	Initial situation (set-up: who, when, where – character and setting)	Materials which appear solid are defeated by mortality, time. They all eventually decay.
3	⇌	Paradox which sets up a cognitive dissonance	What chance do beauty or youth have against this all-powerful fiend? How can we ever defeat the advancing onslaught of time?

Analysis of story structure of content of Shakespeare's Sonnet 65

Underlying story structure			
4		Resolution of paradox leading to enlightenment	We can't, unless we cultivate inner beauty and find the perfect form for it to be revealed in a way which transcends the limitations of time, to take us beyond the boundaries of time, to touch the eternal.
5	⛶	[Paradoxical closing which is actually an opening]	The reader or listener is invited to resolve the paradox and find meaningful dynamic connections in the poem to their own situation.

The content follows a Koan structure. While the interpretation is personal, and others are possible, the argument remains sound. The way in which the story structure of the form (Call and Response Variation 2) and the story structure of the content (Koan) interact reveals an almost desperate underlying urge to transcend a deeply felt injustice, to be liberated from it, and to soar far above and beyond it. The urge is clearly there in the Call and Response structure, and the Koan structure confirms and adds to the urgency. Taken together, both analyses shed light on the poem in context, and provide deep justification for interpreting the sonnet in line with the theory which Asquith presents.

Moreover, clues to the underlying drivers can be found in the choice of words Shakespeare uses: the word 'rage' in line 3, for instance, the militaristic 'siege' and 'battering' in line 6; the love (of a Catholic towards God?) shining through the (Protestant?) blackness of his words in print, and the rage he clearly feels against some kind of deeply felt transgression are obvious in the pounding rhythm of the last line, in which weak beats seem to demand that the reader stress them: 'That *in* **black** *ink* **my** *love* **may** *still* **shine** *bright*.' If this isn't a Recusant's viewpoint, then perhaps it's the inner rage of an unwilling outwardly conformist Anglican seeking redemption by a mysterious 'miracle' of grace (line 13) – grounded in the same remarkable mystery which gives us the awe-inspiring ability to link story structure both to poetic form and to content in order to appreciate a poem's subtle depth, complementing other ways of analysing poetry. The poem could (also), of course, be read as a lament to the fleeting quality of youth, and beauty. Personally, I find the spiritual interpretation far more convincing.

I've found Italian sonnets, which have an ABBA ABBA CDCDCD rhyme scheme in three distinct sections, follow a Revelation structure. Each quatrain sets up an expectation which is fulfilled based on a same/different pair. The poem opens (⊐ ⊐). At the end of the first quatrain, we know a pattern has been set up, but we're not quite sure what that pattern is yet. The first couplet's (← → ←) sequence has the quality of the first step in the Revelation structure (the *veni* step: ⊐). By the end of the second quatrain, the pattern is confirmed. The (← →) pair here has the quality of the second step in the Revelation structure (the *vidi* step: ⊐). The final sestet has a nested (← → ← → ← → ←) sequence which condenses to (←) and qualitatively provides the third step in the Revelation structure (the *vici* step: ⊐).The Revelation structure is nested, and unfolds through each section, as well as being the structure of the overarching form. Like its English counterpart, it provokes a Call and Response Variation 2 structure in the story seeker, which provides the final transformational step which brings closure (← →). Again, this insight provides food for reflection on how the qualities of the story structure that the rhythmic and rhyming patterns follow interact with those of the story structure of the content, offering an exciting way to bridge the subjective and objective realms of poetic composition, appreciation, and analysis through the text.

Rhyme schemes, forms, and metres build expectancy in us as readers or listeners. The sense of expectancy is linked to our exposure to the patterns, our responses being proportional to our familiarity with them. Overfamiliarity breeds contempt; lack of familiarity underwhelms. The fun comes in terms of 'breaking the rules' once a 'golden mean' of familiarity has been achieved. The more experienced we are as story seekers, the greater appreciation we'll have of what is going on. When a poem follows a set structure, expectation is fulfilled. When a story seeker realises that a rule is broken, or the poet has deviated from the norm in some way, a

Trickster Variation structure is set in motion within them through a Trickster Awe step. Great works reveal hidden depths the deeper we allow ourselves to engage with them. The appeal of shallow works simply wears off, leading us to seek more sophisticated examples which reveal these depths through engagement – both analytical and emotional.

This methodology has further potential for provoking new insights into poetry, which can be seen particularly in the following analyses of ghazal, landay, and haiku forms.

Ghazals

It was Urdu ghazals that gave me my first insight into the link between metrical form and story structure. The ghazal is a poetic form based on a series of couplets in which a rhyme scheme is set up in the first couplet, and returned to in the second line of each ensuing couplet as a refrain in an AA BA CA DA EA ... sequence. The lines are of equal length.

Ghazals often deal with the theme of love, and it's traditional for the poet to include their name as a signature in the last couplet of the ghazal. As ghazals run between 5 and 25 couplets traditionally, and there's no fixed number of couplets that make up a ghazal, this feature is important in the context of oral performance. When listeners hear the name of the poet who composed the ghazal in the first place, they know the poem should come to an end soon. The ghazal, one of the most widespread forms of Urdu poetry, makes up around 75% of all poems in that language.[14] Given its popularity, I was astonished to find that the ghazal follows the rarest of all the story structures I've found: the Perpetual Motion structure![15]

As I see it, the story structure relates to the strong sense of similarity and difference present in the constraints of the poetic form of the ghazal. The natural undulating regularity of the ghazal perfectly matches the quality of the Perpetual Motion structure. Once a line length has been set up, it usually stays constant. Once a rhyme scheme is established, it sets up a strong expectation of its return. Until the initial line length is established, we have a 'problem'. Until the rhyme scheme is established, the fulfilment of expectation we're anticipating as listeners remains, as yet, unrealised. The poem embodies this play of expectation – of anticipation – in its form. It's there for the poet as much as for the listener. In this sense, the first line of each couplet sets up a backward step (←) and the second a forward step (→). Here's one example:

Example of an Urdu ghazal by Wali Mohammed Wali (1667–1707)[16]

Urdu transcription	Translation
Dekhna har subah tujh rukhsaar ka, Hai mutaala matlai-anwaar ka.	To see your face every morn, Is to see the glorious flush of dawn.
Bulbul-o-parwana karna dil ke tain, Kaam hai tujh chehra-e-gulnaar ka.	To turn my heart to a Philomel or moth, This is the task of your fire-bloom face.
Subah tera daras paaya tha sanam, Shauq-e-dil muhtaaj hai takraar ka.	I saw you just this morning, Love, Lo, my heart yearns again.
Mah ke sine upar ai shama roo, Dagh hai tujh husn ki jhalkaar ka.	Your beauteous glimmer, O flaming face, Has caused the blemish in the moon's breast.
Dil ko deta hai hamaare pech-o-taab, Pech tere turrah-i-tarraar ka.	The folds in your spiralling crest, Make my heart twist and turn.
Jo sunia tere dehn son yak bachan, Bhed paaya nuskha-i-israr ka.	To hear one word from your lips, Is to pluck the mystery's heart.
Chaahta hai is jahan mein gar bahisht, Ja tamaasha dekh us rukhsaar ka.	If thou seekest heaven on earth, Go, behold that beauteous face.
Ai Wali kyon sun sake naseh ki baat, Jo diwana hai pari rukhsaar ka.	What cares he for the counsellor wise, He who is charmed by a fairy face?

If we analyse the ghazal using the rules outlined above, the opening (⊔) is implied, and we acknowledge that the 'character' of a poem (⊓) is its form.

The poem starts, and we follow the rhythmic pattern of the Urdu, which is a 'variation on a theme' (here based around a pentameter). This is the backward step (←) which indicates an *anticipation* of an expected outcome which is set up through 'rhythm' but achieved through 'verse'. We strongly expect a similar rhythmic pattern to follow. There's an expectation which is almost as strong, but not quite, that a rhyme pattern will be set up. When the second line is complete, the anticipation is fulfilled. This is indicated by a forward step (→). At the same time, because we know it's a ghazal, the completion of the couplet brings an anticipation of another couplet to follow (←). When the second couplet is complete, the anticipation is fulfilled (→). At the same time, because we know it's a ghazal, the completion of the couplet brings an anticipation of another couplet to follow (←) ... and so the pattern continues, precisely following a Perpetual Motion structure until the appearance of the poet's name (here, Wali) signals the final couplet of the ghazal and the poem is realised, complete (⌐). The poet is immortalised. Content and form unite. In that unity, we're brought closer to the mystery of the ineffable (☐).

Shakespeare's Sonnet 126 is notable for its irregularity. It's written in iambic pentameter in rhyming couplets with an AA BB CC DD EE FF rhyme scheme with two final lines left blank and follows the same Perpetual Motion structure as the ghazal. This realisation adds so much to the appreciation of this poem, particularly when interpreted as a spiritual 'call to account'.

Landays

Landays are two-line poems which form an important part of Afghan culture, particularly among women. There are nine syllables in the first line; thirteen syllables in the second, which typically ends with the sound 'ma' or 'na' – not all landays rhyme. The form unfolds as follows: the opening (☐) is implied. The introduction of the form (⌐) sets up the expectation for the two-line pattern to emerge. The first line sets up an expectation (←) which is fulfilled with the completion of the second line (→). The poem, and the story structure of the poetic form come to a close (⌐) with the ending implied (☐). The poetic form thus follows a Transformation structure. While most landays have content that also links to a Transformation structure, a surprising amount link to an Open-Ended Ki-Shō-Ten-Ketsu structure, as the following examples from Eliza Griswold's moving selection published on the

Poetry Foundation website show:[17]

Two story structures relating to landay content

Transformation	Open-Ended Ki-Shō-Ten-Ketsu
The drones have come to the Afghan sky. The mouths of our rockets will sound in reply.	When sisters sit together, they always praise their brothers. When brothers sit together, they sell their sisters to others.
In Policharki Prison, I've nothing of my own, except my heart's heart lives in its walls of stone.	My love gave his life for our homeland. I'll sew his shroud with one strand of my hair.
I dream I am the president. When I awake, I am the beggar of the world.	In battle, there should be two brothers: one to be martyred, one to wind the shroud of the other.

While the landay form follows a Threshold structure (the Transformation structure), I found that the content of landays I analysed was split between Threshold (Transformation) and Non-Threshold (Open-Ended Ki-Shō-Ten-Ketsu) structures. The link to Non-Threshold structures ran counter to the general rule that the other regular forms of poetry I analysed followed. I felt that something exciting was about to reveal itself. What I found was not only new to me, it took my breath away.

In the examples based on a Transformation structure given above (a Threshold structure *par excellence* in which physical and metaphysical worlds are closely linked), I typically found that the setting and action were clearly based in the physical world, and what was foregrounded was human action, not divine action. While the Transformation structure is clearly suited to stories like those of Ovid's *Metamorphoses*, there were no swift-acting gods in these landays – at all.

In the examples based on an Open-Ended Ki-Shō-Ten-Ketsu structure (a Non-Threshold structure, grounded in the physical world), I felt a clear sense of there being a 'cry to heaven' intimated, a clear invocation of divine justice; divine retribution. Where normally an exchange between story spinner and story seeker would lead to a resolution of a cognitive dissonance, in these landays, the solution seemed to be sought in the metaphysical realm.

The realisation added considerably to my appreciation and experience of the poetry and the cultural context in which it emerged. This is by no means the only possible interpretation. There may be landays with content that follows other story structures; you may have a different view of how to classify and/or interpret these landays. Personally, I found the insights resulting from these findings, which led me to a deeper understanding and appreciation of the poems and the culture in which they spontaneously arise, inspirational, revelatory, and surprisingly rewarding. It certainly increased my respect for the poets who found a way to express the almost inexpressible in the wake of extreme emotional and physical hardship and increased my respect for the spontaneous ways in which the voice of The Unknown Storyteller can be traced at work through different cultural and social situations.

Haikus

Haikus are short poems with no set rhyme scheme (although sound-based patterns such as consonance, alliteration, and assonance feature strongly). Traditionally associated with Japanese culture, they typically have three lines, of 5, 7, and 5 syllables respectively. Furthermore, classic haikus have a key 'season word' (*kigo*) which relates them to a particular season.[18]

Content-wise, I assumed they'd tend either towards Koan or Dilemma structures because of their inherent paradoxical quality, but what I found surprised me. Take these examples, for instance:

> In this world
> we walk on the roof of hell,
> gazing at flowers. *Issa*

> Not yet become a Buddha,
> this ancient pine tree,
> dreaming. *Issa*

>They end their flight
one by one—
>crows at dusk. *Buson*

To a prospective student:

>Don't imitate me;
it's as boring
>as the two halves of a melon. *Bashō*[19]

For me, these—and other haikus—follow an Open-Ended Ki-Shō-Ten-Ketsu structure, which closely follows the elemental cycle of the Chinese Circular Structure. As this is a Dynamic structure, the interpretation of the opening differs slightly from the way I've treated openings when analysing poetic forms up to now. The haiku's opening is implied (Earth/Balance: ⊐). It reaches us and is presented as a form (Earth/Balance: ⊐). This dual interpretation of the opening of a haiku reflects the important *yin/yang* balance central to both the haiku and the Chinese Circular Structure. In a haiku, there are typically two related images. The relation is often oppositional, but unlike the images typically presented in a koan, rarely paradoxical. The first image initiates the sequence (Wood/Spring: ⊓). The second replaces it, but sets up a question, or feeling of doubt – 'What's the relation here?' (Fire/Summer: ⊓) The reader is encouraged, first, to find a way of acknowledging the separation in the opposition (Metal/Autumn: ⊓), then reconcile it (Water/Winter: ⊓), and lastly, to reflect on the insight and how it relates to universal harmony (Earth/Balance: ⊐).

There's a definite sense of an ascent or expansion from the concrete content of the haiku to a sense of universal balance afforded by an interaction with the poem, not through paradox (as in a koan), but through the 'sigh' effect, like an 'Ahhh!' – a confirmation of something intuitively known, revealed to us again through the poet's vision. It's as if a veil is lifted, and I see directly the *extra*ordinary as ordinary. When that happens, I feel I've 'come home'.

Dr. Tadao Ichiki, an expert teacher of haiku composition and a translator of haiku to and from Japanese and English, describes the essence of haiku as 'suggestive brevity', with a characteristic 'pause or gap' which 'may perhaps be likened to (+) and (–) in electricity, separated by a gap' which compels the reader or listener to bridge the gap. 'The "spark" jumps the gap between two apparently different or unrelated ideas, and makes a connection. The mind must make a leap.'[20] The leap is not the end point, though. When the experience is framed by the Chinese Circular structure, a much greater sense of engagement with the poet's initial experience – the insight that gave rise to the haiku – becomes possible.

My appreciation of Bashō's haikus increased exponentially when I linked his season words to the dynamic qualities of each season as outlined in the Chinese Circular Structure.[21] In every Bashō haiku I looked at, I always found a link that illuminated its meaning.[22]

> A crow
> has settled on a bare branch—
> autumn evening. *Bashō*[23]

Opening (Earth/Balance: ☐) [Implied]
Formation (Earth/Balance: ☐) The haiku is presented as a form.
Step 1 (Spring/Wood/Emergence: ㄱ) Image 1: A crow has settled on a bare branch—
Step 2 (Summer/Fire/Division: ㄱ) Image 2: autumn evening.
Step 3 (Autumn/Metal/Separation: ㄱ) 'What's the relation here?': The season word here is 'autumn', relating to 'separation': of day and night; of life and death.
Step 4 (Winter/Water/Re-integration: ㄱ) How can I recognise and reconcile the opposition? The separate phases are stages of a perpetual cycle that comes from and returns to a common source.
Step 5 (Earth/Balance: ☐) The haiku enables us to see similarity in difference, continuity in disparity. To quote Blake – 'To see a world in a grain of sand / And a Heaven in a wild flower, / Hold Infinity in the palm of your hand / And Eternity in an hour.'[24]

Formation (Earth/Balance: ⊡): The haiku comes alive within the reader.
Closing (Earth/Balance: ⊡) [Implied]

> The old pond—
>   a frog jumps in,
>   sound of water. *Bashō*

Opening (Earth/Balance: ⊡) [Implied]
Formation (Earth/Balance: ⊡) The haiku is presented as a form.
Step 1 (Spring/Wood/Emergence: ⊐) Image 1: The old pond—a frog jumps in,
Step 2 (Summer/Fire/Division: ⊒) Image 2: sound of water.
Step 3 (Autumn/Metal/Separation: ⊐) 'What's the relation here?':
The season word, 'frog' here, links to 'spring' (emergence). Ichiki, citing the American Imagist, J. G. Fletcher, comments: 'Bashō omitted the explanations of the temple, the ancient pond, the sound of a frog's leap, and stillness. ... This haiku may be considered the epitome of haiku!'[25] At first, the haiku could seem to be about disturbance, separation, both linked to 'autumn' in the Chinese Circular Structure; the 'spring' association indicates that the emotional quality is more hopeful, energetic, vital, however.
Step 4 (Winter/Water: ⊒) How can I recognise and reconcile the opposition? On reflection, a realisation emerges that the change has served to draw our attention to the unchanging. I recognise in me something already vitally known, but perhaps forgotten, or not paid enough attention to. Fletcher notably mentions the associations he feels Bashō implies: an ancient temple; the still, sacred atmosphere of the surroundings; the full picture coming to life in us – emerging in us, even – as a result of a disturbance of the stillness.
Step 5 (Earth/Balance: ⊡) The haiku is a means of recognising the ever-present sense of the eternal: imperceptible, unless through distinction. For how, without there being a distinction between marked and unmarked states can the unity of both, in the form, be known? Realising how they interconnect allows a deep sense of harmony and balance to emerge.

Formation (Earth/Balance: ☐) The haiku comes alive within the reader.

Closing (Earth/Balance: ☐) [Implied]

Whereas Bashō draws on the season words to illuminate deep meaning in his haiku, Buson takes a different approach:

> Every night
> Has come to dawn
> From the white plum-tree. *Buson*[26]

Opening (Earth/Balance: ☐) [Implied]

Formation (Earth/Balance: ☐) The haiku is presented as a form.

Step 1 (Spring/Wood/Emergence: ⌐): Image 1: Every night has come to dawn

Step 2 (Summer/Fire/Division: ⌐) Image 2: From the white plum-tree.

Step 3 (Autumn/Metal/Separation: ⌐) 'What's the relation here?': The season words, 'white plum-tree' here, link to 'spring' (emergence). The first thing Ichiki notes about this haiku is that it's 'said to have been Buson's death-verse—his swan song—composed during his final illness.'[27] From darkness, in which the white plum-tree is indistinguishable from its surroundings, it emerges, with the dawn.

Step 4 (Winter/Water/Re-integration: ⌐) How can I recognise and reconcile the opposition? How can the emergence of light be reconciled with the impending threat of death?

Step 5 (Earth/Balance: ☐) Ichiku uses the word 'separated' rather than 'emergence' in his commentary, : 'The poet had separated himself from the work-a-day world and ceased to worry about it — he had come to lead a life in which every dawn was centred around the white plum-tree. Long under the spell of the mood described here, by setting it down he became certain of its preservation.' 'Separation', associated with 'autumn', is opposite 'spring' in the Chinese Circular Structure diagram. The key to the haiku, for me, is the irony of the need to reconcile the opposition, not separate it, in order for a new realisation to emerge. Perhaps this is what Buson achieved in his haiku – and in his life. For me, there's a cognitive dissonance that stems from trying to reconcile the cyclic emergence of day from night with the momentary flash of enlightenment linked to the singular momentary appearance of dawn. While the cycle repeats *in perpetuo*, and the single moment is a part of it, the single moment is over almost as soon as it's realised. However hard I try, I fail to reconcile the two ideas. The cognitive dissonance remains, unresolved. Buson's use of paradox doesn't really work for me. The dissonance isn't great enough to justify invoking a Koan structure and it falls short of the artistry Bashō displays in his use of season words. I can only resolve the dissonance through an appreciation of the haiku as an expression of irreconcilable personal suffering.

Formation (Earth/Balance: ☐) The haiku comes alive within the reader.
Closing (Earth/Balance: ☐) [Implied]

A summer shower!
… Clutching at grass-blades
A flock of sparrows. *Buson*[28]

Opening (Earth/Balance: ☐) [Implied]
Formation (Earth/Balance: ☐) The haiku is presented as a form.
Step 1 (Spring/Wood/Emergence: ⌐) Image 1: A summer shower!
Step 2 (Summer/Fire/Division: ⌐) Image 2: … Clutching at grass-blades / A flock of sparrows.
Step 3 (Autumn/Metal/Separation: ⌐) 'What's the relation here?': The season words in this particular haiku are 'a summer shower', which links to 'summer'. 'Summer' relates to 'division'.

Ichiki comments: 'A sudden summer shower is accompanied by a strong wind. Some sparrows that had been scampering about on the ground clutch at grass-blades to keep from being blown away. As the heavy shower continues, it eventually drives even the sparrows that had been in the trees to join their companions on the ground where, out of breath, they too cling tightly to the blades of grass'.[29] This, for me, has all the elements of a stalled 'winter' stage of the Chinese Circular Structure: a failed attempt to 'return' to stability, to

balance. There's definitely a powerful struggle going on here, though.
Step 4 (Winter/Water/Re-integration: 刌) How can I recognise
and reconcile the opposition? There's clearly tension here. Ichiki
continues: 'The expression "clutch at grass-blades" has the effect
of indicating that the rain was actually a heavy shower. Also, it
brings to mind the English expression "clutching at straws" which
describes what people are to do in desperation.'
Step 5 (Earth/Balance: 口) On the one hand, the haiku shows that
the strength of the grass roots and the birds' beaks can withstand
the force of the downpour and the wind. On the other, how reliable
is a blade of grass? There's a sense of desperation, of futility that
pervades the poem. Unlike Bashō's haikus, which provide a key that
links to the 'Earth/Balance' element, Buson's haiku presents a closed
door. The key to unlocking it – if it exists at all – lies solely within
the reader. Donald Keene, an American expert on Japanese culture,
notes that Buson's later years were marked by a remarkable series
of natural disasters and that he deliberately cultivated emotional
distance in his haiku as a result.[30] It certainly shows in the way in
which the content of his haiku seem to work against the flow of
the Chinese Circular Structure which underpins their form and,
again, the only way I can resolve the dissonance is to accept and
appreciate the emotional pain behind Buson's composition.
Formation (Earth/Balance: 口) The haiku comes alive within the reader.
Closing (Earth/Balance: 口) [Implied]
The insight provided through using the analytical method outlined
above enabled me to articulate for the first time why I'd previously
instinctively preferred Bashō's work to Buson's without knowing
why, while adding to my appreciation of Bashō's artistry and the
pain that drove Buson to write his haikus.[31]

   Whatever one's interpretation of a haiku, there's ideally a sense
of a return to origin (Earth/Balance: 口), and with that sense
of return, the haiku, as a dynamic form, comes full circle. If you
pause at the end of a haiku and listen closely, you may well hear
an echo of something—perhaps the silent voice of The Unknown
Storyteller—chuckling softly in the distance ...

NOTES

1   Ezra Pound, *ABC of Reading* (London: Faber and Faber, 1991), 14.

2   *Kitāb Alf Laylah Wa-Laylah* (version al-Ṭabʿah 1). Cairo: al-Maṭbaʿah al-ʿĀmirah al-ʿUthmānīyah, 1885, page 6. https://archive.org/details/McGillLibrary-rbsc_isl_arabian-nights_kitab-alf-laylah-wa-laylah_PJ7711A521885_v1-2-15548.

3   David Pinault, *Story-Telling Techniques in the Arabian Nights* (Leiden: E. J. Brill, 1992), 14.

4   'There is no line of my verse or prose which has not been mouthed till the tongue has made all smooth, and memory, after many recitals, has mechanically skipped the grosser superfluities.' Rudyard Kipling, *Something of Myself* (New York: Doubleday, Doran & Company, 1937), 223.

5   Rudyard Kipling, "Just So Stories," 1912; Project Gutenberg, 23 May 2010, 225–226, http://www.gutenberg.org/files/32488/32488-h/32488-h.htm#Page_225.

6   The use of three-bar phrases is one factor which distinguishes Haydn's approach to composition from Mozart's.

7   There are a number of possible rhythmic interpretations, but the sequence was conceived on the same rhythmical pattern at the start of the nursery rhyme, *Humpty Dumpty*: 'Humpty Dumpty sat on a wall / Humpty Dumpty ….'.

8   Meditating on it, a distinctive Necker Cube quality to this pairing may reveal itself. Fulfilment brings with it anticipation; anticipation cries out for fulfilment.

9   Michael R. Burch, *The Best Limericks of All Time: A Brief History of the Limerick, with Definitions and Examples*, n.d. Accessed 5 May, 2021, http://www.thehypertexts.com/The Best Limericks of All Time.htm.

10 As evidenced by Gershon Legman's collection *The Limerick* (New York: Random House, 1988), the Limerick's *raison d'être* is to provide a social valve to enable people to let off steam transgressively, through humour.

11 I discovered Legman's work only after having come to the conclusion that Limericks follow a Revelation structure, without really understanding why, but trusting the methodology, which provides a powerful tool to use to engage with the deep function of literary forms – both in prose and in poetry. The different ways in which the Revelation and Quest structures unfold from the Transformation structure are covered in chapter 11 of this work.

12   Clearly steps 3–5 can feature a (← → ←) sequence which can be reduced
     to (←).

13   Clare Asquith, *Shadowplay: The Hidden Beliefs and Coded Politics of William
     Shakespeare* (New York: PublicAffairs, 2005). While Asquith's argument
     has provoked controversy (see, for example, the exchanges between her
     and David Womersley following his negative review of the book (David
     Womersley, "The 'Da Vinci Code' of Shakespeare Scholarship," Review of
     Shadowplay: The Hidden Beliefs and Coded Politics of William Shakespeare,
     by Clare Asquith, *The Social Affairs Unit*, 5 December, 2005. https://web.
     archive.org/web/20170315013411/http://www.socialaffairsunit.org.uk/
     blog/archives/000685.php)), there is support for her views, however, in the
     material culture of embroidered bookbindings. For this, see Leon Conrad, "A
     Veil of Mystery: English 16th and 17th Century Woven and Embroidered
     Textile Bookbindings," Academia.edu, April 2005, https://independent.
     academia.edu/LeonConrad/Thesis-Chapters, 97–120.

14   K. C. Kanda, *Masterpieces of Urdu Ghazal From 17th to 20th Century* (New
     Delhi: Sterling Paperbacks, 1995), 1.

15   Questions about why this might be and what it signifies are beyond the
     scope of this work, but I hope they will be explored in future works.

16   K. C. Kanda, *Masterpieces of Urdu Ghazal*, 23. The English translation is by
     K. C. Kanda.

17   Eliza Griswold and Seamus Murphy, "Landays," *Poetry Foundation*, accessed
     30 October, 2018, https://static.poetryfoundation.org/o/media/landays.
     html.

18   For a brief commentary on season words (*kigo*) with annotated examples in
     haiku by Bashō and Buson, see Tadao Ichiki, *Suggestive Brevity: Haiku into
     the World* (Kyoto: Biseisha, 1985), 25–35; 101–103.

19   These examples are drawn from Bashō, Buson, and Issa, *The Essential Haiku:
     Versions of Bashō, Buson, & Issa*, edited and translated by Robert Hass
     (Hopewell, NJ: The Ecco Press, 1994), 158, 170, 89, 47.

20   Quoted in Harold G. Henderson, *Haiku in English*, (Rutland, VT and
     Tokyo, Japan: Charles E. Tuttle Company, 1997), 65.

21   Tadao Ichiki, *Suggestive Brevity*, 101–102.

22   A selection, detailing the season words in each can be found in Tadao Ichiki,
     Suggestive Brevity, 10–24. Ichiki lists a few specific 'season books' in Japanese
     by Ameyama, Hirai, Inahata, and Ōno in his bibliography. For a reference
     book in English, see William J. Higginson, *The Haiku Seasons: Poetry of the
     Natural World* (Tokyo, New York and London: Kodansha International,

1996). Lists in English can also be found on line. See, for instance, the World Kigo Database, *WKD ... Welcome!* n.d. Accessed 16 February, 2019. https://worldkigodatabase.blogspot.com/.

23   Bashō, Buson, and Issa, *The Essential Haiku*, 13, 18.

24   William Blake, "Auguries of Innocence," 1–4, *Blake: Complete Writings*, edited by Geoffrey Keynes (London: Oxford University Press, 1969), 431.

25   Tadao Ichiki, *Suggestive Brevity*, 12–13.

26   Tadao Ichiki, *Suggestive Brevity*, 27.

27   Tadao Ichiki, *Suggestive Brevity*, 28.

28   Tadao Ichiki, *Suggestive Brevity*, 30.

29   Tadao Ichiki, *Suggestive Brevity*, 12–13.

30   Donald Keene, *World Within Walls: Japanese Literature of the Pre-Modern Era, 1600–1867* (New York: Grove, 1978), 337–352.

31   For a view of the two poets and their works which contrasts with the view set out here, see Donald Keene, *The Winter Sun Shines In: A Life of Masaoka Shiki*, (Columbia, MA: Columbia University Press, 2013), 100–102.

EPILOGUE

WHAT MAKES STORY 'STORY'?

And I too cease: I have described the Way –
Now you must act – there is no more to say.

ʿATTÂR, TRANS. AFKHAM DARBANDI AND DICK DAVIS,
Canticle of the Birds[1]

NOTE

1   The last lines of the poem (lines 4482–4483) from 'Attâr, Farîd-od-Dîn, *The Canticle of the Birds*, edited by Diane de Selliers, translated by Dick Davis and Afkham Darbandi, commentary by Michael Barry (Paris: Diane de Selliers, 2013), 379.

APPENDIX 1

APPLYING THE METHODOLOGY TO A COMPLEX FOLK TALE

Analysis of *Go I Know Not Whither and Fetch I Know Not What*, a complex nested Russian folk tale in the narrative version by Aleksandr Afanas'yev, illustrations by Alexander Alexeieff[1]

1. Select a story to analyse.
The narrative version of this story is taken from Afanas'yev's collection of Russian folk tales in English translation.

2. Note the source version, where relevant.
Afanas'yev's narrative version is a literary version of an orally transmitted folk tale; the storyteller isn't known.

3. Summarise the story in 'bare bones' form.
The story follows a complex nested series of structures. Fedot, an able hunter, works for and is loved by the king. One day, when out hunting, he captures a bird that speaks to him and begs him not to kill it. He takes the bird home where it transforms into a beautiful woman who announces that he's her chosen husband, and she's his God-given wife. After they marry, she sets out to help him improve his position. With the aid of magical helpers, she weaves a beautiful carpet which the king's steward sees on sale at the market, buys, and sells to the king at a profit. Wanting to commission one for himself, the steward visits Fedot, sees Fedot's bird-wife and falls desperately in love with the unattainable woman. The king, noticing how desperate his steward is, asks him what's wrong. Learning of the stunning beauty, he decides to see her with his own eyes. When he sees her, he also falls in love with her. The king tells his steward that he'll have him hanged unless he arranges for Fedot to be sent on an impossible quest from which he'll never return so that he (the

king) can marry Fedot's widow. The steward consults with Baba Yaga and presents such a plan to the king. Planning to sabotage his ship, the king orders Fedot to sail to a distant country and bring back a stag with golden horns. Fedot's wife thwarts the king's plan, and Fedot returns swiftly, having fulfilled the task. The king reluctantly rewards him. Once again, he threatens the steward with death unless he comes up with a plan that works. The steward once again consults with Baba Yaga who advises him to tell the king to order Fedot to 'go I know not whither and fetch I know not what', which the king does. Fedot's wife gives him a ball of string which he follows to the door of a magical castle, as well as an embroidered handkerchief which she instructs him to use exclusively to dry his face and hands with. At the castle, when he uses this, the women who have given him hospitality recognise the embroidery as their sister's and take him to meet his mother-in-law. Having agreed to help him, she asks the creatures of land, sea, and air for help. An aged frog agrees to act as Fedot's guide. He leads Fedot to a robber's cave where Fedot meets a magical spirit named Shmat Razum (Smashed Sense) who agrees to serve him. Meanwhile, the king tries to win over Fedot's wife. To escape from him, she turns herself into a bird and flies away. Fedot returns with Shmat Razum, having (with his aid) obtained a magical garden, a magical army, and a magical navy as a result of them tricking three merchants. Back in his homeland, he asks Shmat Razum to build him a palace in front of the king's. His wife returns to him and transforms from bird to woman again. When the affronted king declares war on him, Fedot unleashes his magical troops, is victorious in battle, and ends up defeating and killing the king. When the people, having lost their ruler, ask Fedot to rule over them, he accepts, becoming the new king. His bird-wife becomes queen. One assumes that everyone lives 'happily ever after'.

4. Note the story opening and closing, stated or implied.
Two illustrations frame this narrative version of the story. The first is a series of unmanned canons shooting cannonballs; the second is

of two rows of archers in formation, bows at the ready. The archers'
arrows and bow strings are implied. There's a reversal here in that
the cannons which feature in the opening illustration are referred
to at the end of the story ('the guns from the ships kept firing at
the capital'), and the 'whole company of archers' that appears in the
final illustration is first introduced at the beginning of the story.
Thus, the illustrations perfectly serve a cognitive dissonance function,
with ouroboros-like features (*en ma fin git mon commencement*),
although this is not immediately apparent. It reveals itself after
engaging with the story, and studying the illustrations and their role
more closely.

The framed presentation of the narrative is, in turn, framed
within the form of a book (in physical or digital format) which acts
as a threshold into the world of the story.

**5. Identify the main characters and their initial situation (who,
when, where, and in what condition).**
At the opening and closing of the tale, the king and Fedot feature
strongly. The king is introduced as being 'unmarried'. Fedot isn't
described as having a problem until after he's married, when he's
'quite weary of … hunting', and his wife observes that they're
'none the better for it'. The steward has a number of problems: his
main one emerges when he falls in love with Fedot's wife, which
embroils him in two kinds of conflict: firstly, the conflict between
the moral respect he has towards their marriage and the feelings
he's developed for Fedot's wife; secondly, when the king asks him to
broker a situation that's intended to result in the king's taking her to
wife, a conflict between his own feelings, his sense of morality, and
the duty of obedience and allegiance he feels he owes the king. The
latter conflict is left unresolved – which is why I find his story line
particularly poignant. Fedot's wife, rather than having problems,
seems to be a driver of events, although in structural terms, she
acts mainly as Fedot's friend/helper. There's a sense that her story
line unfolds on a magical dynamic level which underpins the other
characters' linear story lines.

Fedot's wife is assisted by two spirit weavers; the steward, by Baba Yaga; Fedot, by his wife and the magical objects she creates or gives him, his mother- and sisters-in-law, the frog guide, Shmat Razum, and the merchants' magical objects. Other minor characters are involved, whose story lines are secondary to the story.

The presence of magic points to the probable presence of one or more Threshold structures, the Threshold structures being the Transformation, Trickster Variation, Death and Rebirth, Rags to Riches, Revelation, Call and Response (2 variations), Koan, and Chinese Circular structures.

6. Identify the problem(s) or *agon(es)* which caused the story to emerge for each of these characters – these are typically resolved (but sometimes left unresolved) at the end of the story.

When the emergence of an inciting problem in a narrative is unclear, it's often worthwhile going to the end of the story and seeing how things resolve. In this story, we meet the people of the realm as characters for the first time. Most immediately, one could argue, they've lost a king and need someone to provide them with stability and order; if we trace their story line back to the beginning of the story, however, is there an implied problem for them in the way the king rules? Is there a problem about the way in which he treats his subjects in general, and the other characters in the story specifically? Is the fact that he's unmarried a problem for the kingdom? Is there a problem about the way in which he treats the resources to which he has access? Either way, we're faced with questions in relation to the monarch. The main question being: What makes a king a true king? Moreover, there's a sense that there's a deeply felt need for balance in the natural order as manifested in the relationships between three things: the relationship between male and female qualities (symbolised by the king's lack of a wife on the one hand, contrasted strongly with Fedot's wife being his ideal partner); the relationship between the land and its inhabitants (symbolised by the king's attitude to hunting which could be seen as excessive); and finally, the relationship between the king and his subjects (symbolised by the king's attitude to the people who work for him and depend on him for their livelihood – while he's willing to pay the steward an excessive sum for a rare item, he doesn't pay Fedot enough for him to live on). This need for balance in the relationships between king and people, land, and personal and universal eudaimonia is one of the main drivers of the story, if not its main driver.

7. Identify the main structural parts of the story (beginning, middle, end, and any sub-sections).
The structure of the story follows the arcs of the various main characters' story lines.

The king
The king's story line frames the story – he rules, but unjustly (we find out as the narrative unfolds). While he gains material goods (the carpet), he fails in his attempt to usurp Fedot's bird-wife, ending up defeated and killed by Fedot.

Fedot
Fedot's providential meeting with his eventual bird-wife launches him on a series of quests which seem either unfortunate, or hopeless, or both, yet result in him gaining the highest rank in the realm, aided by magical forces. Fedot's story line involves a 'try, try, try again' quest to gain money through the sale of the carpet his wife produces. A Trickster structure subplot follows, in which the king sends him to get the stag with the golden horns, then another 'try, try, try again' quest that ends in him finding Shmat Razum. Another Trickster structure subplot involves Fedot and Shmat Razum tricking the merchants. Finally, Fedot ends up challenging, defeating, killing, and replacing the king, restoring harmony in the process.

The steward
The steward's story line provides the inciting incidents which propel both the king and Fedot on their individual quests. His wish to commission a carpet for himself leads him to fall desperately

in love, which makes the king ask what the matter is with him. The king, wanting to see the fabled beauty with his own eyes, does so, and falls in love himself. When he orders the steward to get rid of Fedot not once, but twice, the steward obeys out of loyalty, self-control, and a wish to survive. He turns to Baba Yaga for help, losing his chance of personal happiness, relegating himself to a destiny of unrequited love, his tragic story line petering out in the narrative, leaving the rest of his story line open to conjecture.

8. Arrange the events related to each character's story line in chronological order.

Events in the narrative generally appear in chronological order. While the king waits no longer than a month before he summons Fedot's wife to the palace and asks her to marry him, exactly how much time passes for Fedot before he reaches the magical castle is never stated. According to the narrative, he gets there 'after a long time or a short time—for speedily a tale is spun, with much less speed a deed is done'. The implication is that it takes much longer than a month, for the bird-wife estimates that the journey there and back will take 18 years. These events can thus be seen to follow on chronologically and can easily be laid out in the order in which they appear in the narrative. The only exceptions to this are the magical characters' back stories – we know nothing of the bird-wife's origins, or of the potential connection between Baba Yaga, and the bird-wife and her family. Shmat Razum mentions he's been serving 'these two old men in truth and faith' for 'nearly thirty years', but we never learn anything more about the circumstances that brought the latter three together. This points to the story potentially being part of a larger latticed oral corpus, something which we will come back to later on. The only sequence which needs unpacking comes at the end of the 'magical island' section, where Shmat Razum leaves the merchants, responds to Fedot, then carries him off, and dematerialises the island, following which the merchants awake and realise (a) they've been abandoned and (b) the island has vanished.

9. Within these story lines, look for pairs of 'unfortunate'/'fortunate' steps which relate to the ebb and flow of the story structure. The terms 'unfortunate' and 'fortunate' are relative to the solution of the character's initial problem (*agon*). Ask yourself, 'Where does the tide of the story's flow change?' 'Which elements of the story flow forward and help the character on their journey towards solving their problem?' 'Which elements of the story relate to a reversal of the flow, that delay or distract a character on their journey?' Are there any outliers? Are there any single steps that don't fit into a pair? Note these. Analyse them. What do they point to?

This process helps us identify noteworthy points in the main characters' story lines.

The king

At the outset, the king's 'unmarried' state seems to be the driver for his story line. He values his hunters, but there seems to be no scarcity of game, nor a lack of skill amongst his hunters. Although he knows nothing about her at that stage, his first encounter with Fedot's wife is through the magical carpet she's created. He wants the carpet. The steward sells it to him and gets paid handsomely for his trouble (nested Quest). The king's second encounter with her is when he first hears of her superlative beauty from his steward. He wants to meet her. The king arrives at Fedot's door (nested Quest). He sees Fedot's wife with his own eyes and falls in love. His story line then unfolds in a mirrored structure which spans from him sending Fedot on a quest to fetch the stag with the golden horns, which Fedot succeeds in doing, despite the king's plan to sabotage his efforts (nested Trickster); sending Fedot on his second quest (nested tragic Trickster) and attempting to marry Fedot's wife while he's absent (nested Trickster loop) but being thwarted. Finally, he's confronted by Fedot's return, and defeated by him (Transformational Twist). It's worth noting that at every key point, the king's story line features either magic or love, pointing to the strong likelihood of it being linked to one or more Threshold structures.

Fedot

Fedot's story line also features encounters with magic at key points, pointing to the likelihood of it following one or more Threshold structures. His meeting with the talking bird has the hallmark of a Trickster Awe step, which resolves in his marriage. Overworked and underpaid, he obtains money and silk at his wife's request, which she has made into a carpet which he takes to market and sells (nested Quests). He's tricked by the king, but Fedot turns the tables on him with the help of his wife, tricking his sailors in order to do this (nested Trickster structures). From this point, his story line falls into two sections: in the first, he sets out on a quest to 'go I know not whither and fetch I know not what', aided by his wife's gifts, her relatives, and the frog; in the second, he finds Shmat Razum who agrees to serve him (nested Quest completed, although Fedot still has to return with Shmat Razum). On the way back, they trick three merchants, and Fedot ends up having to fend off an attack by the king rather than being welcomed back by him. This results in Fedot defeating the king in battle. He ascends to the throne in his place, demonstrating, perhaps, the ideals of true kingship – the story at least puts this issue forward as a point for discussion.

Fedot's wife

Fedot's wife's story line hinges on her (chance?) meeting with Fedot as a bird, her transformation into human form, and their marriage. She helps him directly and indirectly through a variety of means. Although we never get beyond a rather two-dimensional character portrayal, there are hints in the narrative that point to hidden depths in her personality. Although she acts as friend/ helper to Fedot, her beauty is both the cause of his happiness and his being 'beset' by a series of 'misfortunes'. Her beauty is also the cause of both the steward and the king being thrown 'off kilter'. With her help, Fedot, despite having to undergo a long and tiring voyage, manages to return 'older and wiser'. Their reunion happens in the build-up to the final showdown between the king and

Fedot, in which the king is defeated and she becomes queen as a result of Fedot accepting the people's request that he 'rule the whole kingdom'. On the surface, her character portrayal could be read as a dated, misogynistic approach to the treatment of women; on the other hand, as an impersonal idealised feminine muse. A closer reading shows that Fedot's wife arguably has more of Blake's Jerusalem than she does Dante's Beatrice about her: she's the one who proposes; she's the one who calls the shots – she has Baba Yaga in awe of her, and it's the combination of both her vision and magical powers (which vicariously extend to Shmat Razum) and of Fedot's hard work that enables them both to ascend the throne as joint rulers rather than both ending up being 'put to a cruel death' at the king's command. Both characters show strengths and weaknesses. Both ultimately balance and support each other, and both rule together at the end – he as king; she as queen.

The steward

The steward's story line intersects with Fedot's, the king's, Fedot's wife's, and Baba Yaga's. In the first instance, it's unclear why he appears at the market. Whether he's on an errand for the king, or he's just passing by, his attention is drawn to the crowd that's gathered around Fedot to appraise his carpet, which could point to a Trickster Awe step. He performs the function of a friend/helper in the king's quest to obtain the carpet. Wanting to commission a 'better' carpet for himself, his quest is unresolved. He falls in love but has to cede to the king's desire and position. He ends up capitulating to the king's threats and helping the king in his attempts to wed Fedot's wife, to the detriment of his own unfulfilled love for her, aided by Baba Yaga (tragic Quests). His story line peters out disappointingly in the narrative.

Shmat Razum

Shmat Razum first appears in the narrative when Fedot discovers him in the cave. He's already been serving the 'old men' for 'nearly thirty years', but his back story isn't revealed. He agrees to serve

Fedot when Fedot extends an act of kindness to him, something the 'old men' have never done. He tags along with Fedot on the first part of his return journey. He provides the frog with his reward when asked to do so. When Fedot declares he's tired on the next leg of his return journey, Shmat Razum offers to carry him. He carries him through the air so fast that Fedot loses his cap, a key moment in the story. From this point, Fedot and Shmat Razum work as a team. Shmat Razum creates an island and seems to know what events will unfold as a result. He also tells Fedot exactly what to do in order to 'acquire a fortune'. His plan involves them tricking a band of merchants who carry three magical objects. Having helped Fedot acquire all three objects, he carries Fedot back to his homeland, leaving the merchants with nothing. He then builds a castle at Fedot's request. From that point, he disappears from the narrative, and his role in the story remains open to conjecture.

The merchants

The merchants' story line follows a tripartite structure. In the first section, intrigued by the 'marvel' of the island that's appeared as if out of nowhere, the captains of three merchant ships travelling together land and start to investigate. When entertained by Fedot, they're amazed at Shmat Razum's ability to materialise food out of thin air. In the second section, they offer to trade any one of the three magical objects they carry between them for Shmat Razum. They show all three to Fedot who says he'll only exchange Shmat Razum for all three. Considering his offer, they decide it's worth it and agree to the exchange. After asking Shmat Razum whether he'll serve them 'in faith and in truth', they take his equivocal response to be unequivocal and return to their ships with him. In the final section, he fulfils their initial request to '[treat] their crews to food and drink'. As a result, all three ships' crews get drunk and fall asleep. They wake from their satiated stupor to find Shmat Razum has abandoned them and that they've been tricked. With the island gone, they realise they've no recourse to any restitution. Their story line ends tragically: they grieve, hoist their sails and sail away.

10. Identify the quality of each element using the appropriate symbol:

Opening, Closing: Oscillatory step (⊐)

Character: Mark (⌐)

Forward step: Forward barb (⇀)

Backward step: Backward barb (↼). Meetings are always interpreted as backward steps in this approach to the analysis of story structure, as they stop the character in their tracks and delay or distract the character from continuing on their journey.

Trickster, Dupe, Comic, Transformational Twist, Trickster Awe steps: Double barb (⇌). These steps signify an interaction between two characters which involves a defeated expectation or cognitive dissonance of some kind.

Part	King	Fedot	Wife	Steward	Shmat Razum	Merchants	Outline
1	□	□	□	□	□	□	[Opening]
2	⌐						A king, who
3	∟						was unmarried
4	(↲↑)						had archers who provided him with game. *Ongoing nested Quests for the archers, scribed as a Transformation structure in the king's story line.*
5		⌐					Fedot was (i) one of these archers, (ii) good at his job, (iii) loved by the king.
6		[(↲↑)					One morning, Fedot went out very early to hunt for the king. *This appears to be the first part of a Quest structure for Fedot 'problem/journey'. Here, Fedot is acting as 'friend/helper' in the king's 'hunt' quest.*
7		(↙)	⌐				He saw a dove. *This initiates the second part 'meeting with friend/helper' of his unfolding Quest. The sequence which unfolds from 6–17 in his story line has an underlying Revelation or veni, vidi, vici structure on several levels: (6, 7–16,17), (7–11, 12–15, 16), (12–13, 14–15, 16).*
8		↑					He aimed at the dove and fired.
9		∟	[↲]				The shot injured her wing. *This initiates an initial Transformation structure, from which a Call and Response Variation 1 structure unfolds in the bird-wife's story line.*
10		↑	↑				She fell. *This concludes the initial Transformation structure in the bird-wife's story line.*
11		(↲↑)	((↲↑)				Fedot picked her up and prepared to wring her neck. *This concludes the second 'meeting with friend/helper' part of Fedot's unfolding Quest and initiates the first part of the bird-wife's.*

Part	King	Fedot	Wife	Steward	Shmat Razum	Merchants	Outline
12		↳	(↳				She told him to take her home, to put her on his windowsill, and that when she started to fall asleep he should beat her, and that he would be rewarded. *This initiates a ternary medial 'meeting with friend/helper' vidi structure in the bird-wife's unfolding Quest structure which follows an underlying Revelation structure, this section being the veni subsection. Step 12 loops back to step 7 in Fedot's story line.*
13		⇅					Fedot was surprised. *Fedot's story line shifts from Quest to Trickster Variation here in relation to the bird – she takes him by surprise. The structure could potentially be seen as a looping series of 'Huh?!'s, with the first 'Huh?!' relating to him realising that the bird talks; the next to him being surprised by the strangeness of her request and a third to him wondering what the mysterious result might be.*
14		(↓↑	↳				He did as she asked. *This pair of steps expands to a nested Quest with respect to Fedot as the bird's friend/helper. It's potentially a Trickster step with respect to the king if Fedot doesn't present the bird to the king, but this is neither expressed as an explicit transgression nor an intention to dupe in the narrative, so it isn't scribed this way here. While the king might not have been presented with this bird, Fedot continues to supply him with game, which completes his ongoing Quest [See 4; 18]. It initiates the vidi subsection in this section of the unfolding structure in the bird-wife's story line.*
15		⇅)↳	1				When he hit her lightly, she fell to the floor and turned into a woman of superlative beauty. *The superlatives imply that she once more surprises him – in a second (vidi) section of a looping Trickster Variation structure underpinned by a Revelation structure in his story line. This completes the vidi subsection in the medial 'friend/helper' vidi part of the unfolding Quest structure in the bird-wife's story line.*

Part	King	Fedot	Wife	Steward	Shmat Razum	Merchants	Outline
16							She told Fedot that he'd be her chosen husband and that she'd be his God-given wife. Fedot goes from bachelor to husband; moreover, magic is involved. Although Fedot agrees, it's unclear from the narrative how he reacts. It would make sense for (13) to be a veni step; (15), a vidi step, and this to be a complementary vici step in a composite Revelation and Trickster Variation structure. If so, the analysis suggests that the bird-wife is likely to have appeared as a result of an implied state of excess – probably related in some way to the relationship between the king and Fedot (see 4; 18). Other options might be a Quest structure (which doesn't work, as Fedot isn't on a quest to find a wife), or a Trickster structure (which doesn't work either, as Fedot—as far as we can tell—has no intention of deliberately duping the king). The quality of Fedot's story line in this section might at first seem to be a Call and Response-type Variation 1 structure, but where's the initial Transformation structure? Here, a Quest structure (7–11) initiates the sequence and effects a threshold crossing, but it isn't a Transformation structure in his story line. The triple sequence of 12–13, 14–15, and 16 features Trickster Awe steps in a veni, vidi, vici Revelation structure sequence. This sequence is followed by a clear Transformation structure (the marriage at 17) making this a Call and Response-type Variation 2 structure for him. The vidi section of the wife's story line concludes here.
17							They got married (nested Quest) and he carried on hunting as usual. There's a nested veni, vidi, vici sequence implied here with the idea of marriage proposed, agreed to, the ceremony arranged, and the marriage solemnised. In its compressed form, however, it forms a concluding Transformation structure which brings to a close a Call and Response Variation 2 structure in Fedot's story line and a Call and Response Variation 1 structure in his wife's. These mark the end of this section of the story and the beginning of a new section.
18							He found hunting tiring. The implication here is that he either shared this insight with his wife or she intuited it herself. Either way, the two steps scribed here relate to a nested 'problem/journey' pair leading to a 'meeting (with friend/helper)' step which comes up next and points to an unfolding nested Quest structure for both characters, each acting as the other's friend/helper.

Part	King	Fedot	Wife	Steward	Shmat Razum	Merchants	Outline
19		↑↓	≪↓				His wife told him that if he brought her 100–200 roubles, she'd transform their fortunes. *The central 'meeting with friend/helper' section of the characters' structures unfolds in 19–27 for the wife and in 19–31 for Fedot. Within this, there's a series of nested Quests for Fedot at 19–28, and a Quest and a Call and Response Variation 1 structure for the wife at 19–24 and 24–27 respectively.*
20		(↑↓	↑				Fedot raised the money by borrowing from people and brought her the sum. *Nested veni Quest.*
21		↑↓	↓				She told him to buy silks with the money.
22		(↑↓	↑				He returned with silks. *Nested vidi Quest for Fedot.*
23		(↑↓	↓				She told him to go to pray then go to sleep, which he did.
24			↑≫ ≪↓				She went out on the porch and opened her magic book. Two spirits appeared instantaneously (⊤). *Nested subsection which opens with a Transformation structure, part of an unfolding Call and Response Variation 1 structure here in the bird-wife's story line. Note the shift in dimensions typical of this threshold structure. The quality of the Transformation structure links to the implied extreme nature of the state of lack, and the instantaneous appearance of the spirits.*
25			↑↓ ↓				She ordered them to make a carpet. *Although in a latticed story, the magical helpers could have very rich individual story lines, in this self-contained narrative version, they act purely as friends/helpers to the bird-wife. As secondary characters in this instance, their story lines aren't scribed here.*
26			↑				In 10 minutes, they'd created a marvellous carpet.

Part	King	Fedot	Wife	Steward	Shmat Razum	Merchants	Outline
27			↲↱)))				They gave it to her and vanished. *In response to an excessive state, the spirits come (veni), they see (the lack of a carpet) (vidi); they conquer the state of shortfall, and produce the carpet (vici).*
28		(↲↱))	↲				When Fedot woke up, she told him to take it to the market, not to set a price, but accept what he was offered for it. *This concludes the 'meeting with friend/helper' section in Fedot's unfolding Quest structure and initiates the 'meeting with enemy/hindrance' section in his wife's.*
29		↲↲					He took it to the market, became the talk of the town. No one could decide the price. *This initiates an unfolding looping Trickster Variation structure in Fedot's story line which is nested as a substructure in a 'meeting with enemy/hindrance'-type sequence in the overarching Quest unfolding in his story line. Within this, both the merchants and the steward act as Fedot's friends/helpers. Their story lines follow either Quest or Trickster Variation structures, depending on whether the question of pricing the carpet is seen as a problem or as a 'dilemma' which sets up a cognitive dissonance for them. Either way, the structures are completed by the appearance of the steward and his subsequent resolution of the problem of setting a price on the carpet.*
30		↓↑↲		⌐(↲↓↱) ↓↑↲			The royal steward passed by, enquired about what was going on, and evaluated the carpet's worth. *The reason for the steward's passing by is implied but not stated. He sees the commotion, approaches to find out what's caused it and is told by the merchants that they cannot determine a price for a particular carpet. He sees the carpet and marvels at it. This indicates the unfolding of a looping Trickster Variation structure for him. The nested interaction which follows between him and Fedot is underpinned by a Revelation structure. It comprises three steps: (i) He asks where Fedot got the carpet; (ii) He asks how much Fedot will accept for it; (iii) He offers Fedot 10,000 rubles for it, which Fedot accepts. This exchange is not scribed in full here, as it reduces to a single (–) step, scribed at 31 for both characters. Fedot's not knowing what price to ask links to a 'Huh?!' state; the setting of the price links to the 'Ah!' state in his looping Trickster Variation structure.*

Part	King	Fedot	Wife	Steward	Shmat Razum	Merchants	Outline
31		(diagram)	(diagram)	(diagram)			They agreed to the exchange. Fedot got the roubles. The steward got the carpet. *The first pair of steps here completes the Trickster Variation structure which unfolds in Fedot's story line (29–31).* *As a result of Fedot's success, both his fortunes and his wife's improve. With Fedot's return with the proceeds of the sale of the carpet (nested Quest implied), their initial problem is solved and the overarching Quest structures which span parts 18–31 in their story lines reach a positive conclusion.* *It's interesting to note, in relation to how story structures nest and evolve in complex stories, that in this section, the bird-wife's story line features a number of Call and Response-type Variation 1 structures; Fedot's, a series of Call and Response-type Variation 2 structures (12–17, 18–28, 29–31); and the steward's, a Trickster Variation-type structure with the resolution coming out of a nested Call and Response-type Variation 2 structure underpinned by a Revelation structure, potentially followed by a Transformation structure (not scribed here) relating to his acquisition of the carpet, a magical object which brings both structures to a close and links this sequence to the next in his unfolding story line.*
32	(diagram)			(diagram)			The steward and the king met. *This pair of steps indicates an implied opening 'problem/journey' pair in both characters' story lines. What the ensuing structure turns out to be (i.e., whether a Quest, a Trickster, or a Trickster Variation structure) remains to be seen.*
33	(diagram)			1			The steward showed the king the carpet. *The king is amazed (Trickster Variation).*
34	(diagram)			(diagram)			The king wanted the carpet. *The king's declaration that he 'shall not give this carpet back' to the steward can be interpreted as a Trickster structure now nested within the unfolding Trickster Variation structure.*

Part	King	Fedot	Wife	Steward	Shmat Razum	Merchants	Outline
35	⌐⇑⟩⟩]			⌐⇑⟩⟩]			The king gave the steward 25,000 roubles for it, and the steward decided he'd order a 'better one'. *The Transformational Twist comes when the steward accepts the king's 25,000 roubles, pockets a handsome 15,000-rouble profit, and resolves to get 'a better one' for himself. Here, two possibilities present themselves in terms of how the ending is interpreted: Trickster, or Trickster Variation in the Steward's story line. I've gone with the former, seeing a Trickster structure, rather than a Quest structure resolving the king's Trickster Variation structure for him.*
36				[(⌐⟨—⟩)			He went to Fedot's house.
37			[(⌐⟨—⟩) ⥮	⥮			He came face to face with Fedot's wife, fell madly in love with her and left without saying a word. 'From that moment on he was not himself'. *This, in common with the previous instances in which a character is amazed, has the quality of a Trickster Awe step for the steward, although significantly there's no clear resolution to it to be found in the narrative in his story line. In the long span of the bird-wife's story line, this is an initial veni step which links her to the king's story line – it's as a result of this visit that he ends up hearing of her beauty in the first place. I see it as the opening of a Trickster Variation structure for her.*
38	[(⌐⟨			⟨			The king noticed something was wrong with the steward. *A nested veni step is initiated in both characters' story lines here.*
39	1			1			The steward told him he'd fallen in love with Fedot's wife, who was of incomparable beauty. *The nested veni Quest structure is completed in both characters' story lines here.*
40	⥮			⥮			The king wanted to see her for himself. *This vidi sequence marks the unfolding of a Trickster structure in both characters' story lines, with the king as the trickster and the steward as the dupe. The king's story line also intersects with Fedot's here, but as the sequence compresses to a Trickster structure which maps to the opening in part 49 for Fedot, it's not mapped here in his story line.*

Part	King	Fedot	Wife	Steward	Shmat Razum	Merchants	Outline
41	↷		↷				He went to Fedot's house, saw Fedot's wife and fell madly in love with her. *This initiates a nested vici sequence which marks the point at which the king, rather than conquering, is conquered. For the bird-wife, it marks the point at which the king first sees her, and is a vidi sequence in her unfolding story line. It forms a Trickster Variation structure in relation to the way in which the king's story line and Fedot's wife's intersect.*
42				↷			He decided to make her his queen. *This sequence completes the Trickster structure that was initiated in parts 38–40 in the steward's story line, a tragic Trickster structure for him.*
43	⌐↴			⌐↴			The king ordered his steward to get rid of Fedot so he could marry Fedot's wife. *Final Transformation structure for the steward, which reveals that the structure which unfolds through his story line from part 30 to here is a triple composite formed of three Trickster-type structures (Trickster Variation 30–31, Trickster 32–35 and tragic Trickster 38–42), followed by a Transformation structure here. As noted previously, the Trickster Variation structure which develops between the steward and Fedot's wife (36–37) is left unresolved.*
44	↳			↳			The steward left, 'more grieved than before,' but couldn't devise a way of getting rid of Fedot. *When the steward accepts the king's ultimatum, a nested Quest structure unfolds for him. He thus acts—albeit under duress—as a friend/helper in relation to the king's Quest structure.*
45				1			He walked through 'waste places and dark alleys'.
46				1			He met Baba Yaga, who told him how to set a trap for Fedot involving a cunning plan, and the steward rewarded her with gold. *Baba Yaga appears as the steward's friend/helper – and he, along with the sum of money that he pays her, act as friends/helpers for her.*
47	1 ⌐↴			1			The steward went to the king and told him about the cunning plan. *This solves the king's problem of finding a plan to get rid of Fedot, and the steward's problem of providing the king with one.*

Part	King	Fedot	Wife	Steward	Shmat Razum	Merchants	Outline
48	[(←↑]						The king ordered that preparations be made. *A nested Quest structure is implied here in which the unsuitable ship and crew are prepared by the king's navy, who act as the king's friends/ helpers – for the sailors, there's an implied nested Trickster structure here – unbeknownst to them, they're knowingly being sent to their deaths by the king. This section may be interpreted as a 'hinge' Transformation structure, which is how it's scribed here. It provides a final sequence in the king's unfolding story line, but it also gives rise to an opening 'problem/journey' section – a veni sequence in a Trickster structure that unfolds between the king and Fedot (shaded in white symbols on black below). The sailors' story line isn't scribed here, but it follows a tragicomic Trickster structure. They unintentionally turn the tables on the king, and get 'rewarded' by being furloghed, thus deprived of their ability to work as sailors. The Transformation structure 'hinge' is a noteworthy feature of this complex story.*
49	[(↓ 1 ↓ ⇅⇅↓	[↓ 1 ↓ ⇅⇅↓					When the preparations were complete, the king called for Fedot and ordered him to set sail in the unseaworthy vessel with its unsuitable crew to capture the stag with the golden horns alive and bring it back or face death. *In the king's story line, this initiates a Trickster structure; in Fedot's story line, I see this as an unfolding Trickster Variation structure. Their intertwining story line intersections are shaded in white symbols on black, with this being their veni section.*
50		(↓ 1 ↓					Fedot left the palace, troubled, and returned home to his wife. *This initiates a nested Quest for Fedot.*
51		↓	[↓ 1 ↓]				Seeing that he looked troubled, she asked him what the matter was with him and he told her what the king had asked. She told him not to worry. *Fedot's wife acts as the friend/helper in his unfolding Quest structure.*
52			↓ 1 ↓				She summoned her spirits and ordered them to bring back the stag. They did as she commanded. *This provides the potential solution to the problem of providing the king with the stag. The spirits' nested Transformation structure is implied but not scribed here.*

Part	King	Fedot	Wife	Steward	Shmat Razum	Merchants	Outline
53		1	1				She roused Fedot and instructed him to place the stag in a box, take it to sea, sail out for days and turn back on the 6th day. *This provides the potential solution to the nested Quest for Fedot which relates to his problem of surviving the journey in the unseaworthy vessel the king has prepared. It's the first in the triple series of structures. He has a plan mapped out. Now he just has to put it into action and bring it successfully to completion. In Revelation structure terms, he's completed a veni section and is about to embark on the vidi section.*
54		⟨symbol⟩					When questioned by the sailors, he deflected their enquiries. *Here, Fedot's story line follows a nested Trickster structure which forms part of the unfolding vici section in the overarching structure which spans (49, 50–53, 54–59). For the sailors, it's a Trickster Variation structure. In the intertwining sequence between Fedot and the sailors (shaded in light grey), it forms a veni sequence in the structure which spans (54, 56, 57) and culminates at 59 for them.*
55	⟨symbol⟩	⟨symbol⟩					A crowd came to see them off and the king appointed Fedot captain. *This second Trickster step in the king's story line alerts us to the fact that there's probably a Revelation structure underpinning a series of Trickster steps in both his story line and Fedot's (shown in white symbols on black), with this being the vidi sequence for them.*
56		⟨symbol⟩					On the 6th day, Fedot offered the sailors wine to get them drunk. When they were incapacitated, Fedot turned the ship round and set course for shore. *This second Trickster structure in the intertwining sequence between Fedot's story line and the sailors' (shaded in light grey) forms the vidi sequence for them. Ironically, it leaves them blindsided.*
57	1	⟨symbols⟩					Arriving safe and sound, he raised flags and fired a salute to signal their arrival, which the king heard. *In Fedot's and the sailors' intersecting pair of story lines (shaded in light grey), the arrival signals a successful solution to the task of surviving the journey in the unseaworthy vessel, and is the vici section for them; the raising of the flags and the firing of the salute initiates a veni section, the first of three subdivisions in the final vici sequence of the king's and Fedot's intersecting story lines (shown in white symbols on black).*

Part	King	Fedot	Wife	Steward	Shmat Razum	Merchants	Outline
58	⇵						The king made his way down to the port to see what was making the noise and saw that Fedot had returned. *Here, we have the vidi sequence of the final vici section in the king's and Fedot's intertwining story lines – the king has come down to the port to see for himself what the fuss is about and finds out that Fedot has returned.*
59		⇵)))					The king was furious, but when he realised Fedot had completed the task successfully, he couldn't punish Fedot, and had to release the sailors on furlough. *This completes the triple structure which was launched in parts 48/49. Fedot has managed to complete the king's 'impossible' quest and solved two problems: (i) surviving, and (ii) securing the stag for the king. By completing the first, Fedot has returned safe and sound to his wife; by completing the second, he's turned the tables on the king. For those interested in exploring the potential of the methodology to reveal deeper aspects of stories, it would be worth mapping out the story structures which unfold in the sailors' story line.*
60				[1]			The next day, the king summoned his steward, threatened him with death and charged him with finding a solution. *The order from the king forms another Transformation structure 'hinge' moment, which is similar to that in part 43, where the king gives orders for a plan to get rid of Fedot to be found. This is interesting as it shows the link between divine and temporal power residing in the monarch.*
61	↓			↓			The steward, threatened by the king, ... *Once more, a nested Quest unfolds in 61–64 for the steward which mirrors the similar sequence in parts 44–47.*
62				1			... set off ...
63				1			... and met Baba Yaga again. Baba Yaga instructed the steward on what to tell the king.

Part	King	Fedot	Wife	Steward	Shmat Razum	Merchants	Outline
64	⌐↑↓⌐			⌐↑↓			He told the king of her second cunning plan. *Again, this solves the problem of the steward needing to provide the king with a plan. In the king's story line, this completes an initial Quest structure, forming a veni sequence in a larger unfolding structure relating to Fedot and to his new mission. The single square bracket at the steward's story line shows an uncertainty about how his story pans out. Parts 60–64 could be an unfolding Call and Response Variation 1 structure, or a Quest-type structure. As his story line is left incomplete in the narrative, this is open to conjecture.*
65	((((↑↓⌐ ↓⌐	[(↑↓ ↓⌐					The king summoned Fedot and told him to 'go I know not whither, bring me back I know not what' and face execution if he should fail. *Following on from the veni sequence at 60–64 for the king, this sequence of steps provides a vidi sequence in his unfolding story line. It follows a Trickster structure. The final vici sequence unfolds for him at 154–164. In Fedot's story line, we see a looping series of Trickster-type steps start to unfold, underpinned by a Revelation structure in relation to how his story line and the king's intersect, with the sequence at 65 forming the veni section; the building of the castle at 149–151 the vidi section (see the note at 150); and that at 159–164, the vici section. The last two are nested within the more extended vici section of the story relating to the second mission that the king sends Fedot on, mapped out at 72, which extends from 72 to 164.*
66		(↑↓	(↑↓)				Fedot left the palace. Troubled, he returned home to his wife. *This initiates a nested structure for Fedot. The structures in his story line and in his wife's run in canon.*
67		↓	↓				Seeing that he looked troubled, she asked him what the matter was with him.
68		1↓	1↓				He told her what the king had asked, blamed his misfortunes on her beauty, and asked, "... what can we do?" *I see this as a Trickster Awe step for both characters. This step shifts the narrative from Fedot's story line to his bird-wife's.*
69			(↑↓)				She told him not to worry. *This pair of steps launches the first in a series of three nested looping Quest substructures underpinned by a Revelation structure within an overarching Trickster Variation structure for Fedot's bird-wife, this being a veni sequence.*

Part	King	Fedot	Wife	Steward	Shmat Razum	Merchants	Outline
70			1↓				She opened her book, summoned her spirits and asked them whether they knew how to 'go I know not whither, bring me back I know not what.' *This is a 'meeting with friend/helper' section for her. A vidi sequence unfolds.*
71			(1↓)				They said they didn't know, so she closed the book. *A tragic vici sequence is completed. The bird-wife's story line loops back to the 'problem' step in the Quest structure currently unfolding in her story line.*
72		[↓ 1	↓				She roused Fedot the next morning. *This initiates the second looping Quest substructure in the bird-wife's story line. It also, more importantly, initiates the long, nested Quest sequence which Fedot undertakes to fulfil the king's request which is divided into 3 main parts (I–III), each containing 3 subsections (A–C), each of which is subdivided into a further 3 sub-subsections (1–3). All of the triple structures conform to an unfolding veni, vidi, vici pattern. An overview of the structure of the top two levels is indicated directly below; the sections that make up the third level are indicated in the commentary to the relevant parts below. I (veni): (I.A. 72, 74–75), (I.B. 83–101), (I.C. 102–107) from Fedot's preparations for his journey to his arrival at his destination. II (vidi): (II.A. 108–113), (II.B. 114–119), (II.C. 120–123, 141–148) from Fedot's first direct interaction with Shmat Razum to his return to his homeland. Note the break here – it breaks when Fedot loses his cap; it starts again when he searches for Shmat Razum – in that 'break' in the 'vidi' sequence, Fedot can ironically and significantly sense neither his cap nor Shmat Razum. III (vici): (III.A. 149–153), (III.B. 159), (III.C. 160–164) from Fedot suggesting to Shmat Razum that he build 'a new castle on the seashore' to his defeat of the king in battle. A final Transformation structure (165–167) makes this an extended Call and Response-type Variation 2 structure. This pair of steps forms section I.A.1 for Fedot. While the king has tasked him with fulfilling an 'impossible' quest, Fedot's own task is to fulfil the quest and return safely to his wife. The conclusion to the sequence relating to the king's quest unfolds in parts 154 onwards for the king; the conclusion to the sequence relating to Fedot's safe return to his wife unfolds in parts 152–153.*

Part	King	Fedot	Wife	Steward	Shmat Razum	Merchants	Outline
73	(↱)⟩	(↱)	↑				She told him to go to the king, ask him for money for the journey, then come and bid her farewell. *In this nested Quest, Fedot acts as his wife's friend/helper. Within Fedot's Quest, the king becomes Fedot's friend/helper. The king's story line also implies a nested Quest in fulfilling this role. The vidi sequence in the Quest substructure ends in the wife's story line.*
74		↑	(↱)⟩⟩				She then gave him a ball of string to guide him, a handkerchief to wash his face with, and instructions on how to use them. *This is section I.A.2 for Fedot. It comprises the third looping vici Quest substructure in the bird-wife's story line. In all three, the bird-wife acts as Fedot's friend/helper (The source of the magical gifts is unclear in the narrative).*
75		↑					He bowed low to all four sides and set off. *Here, in section I.A.3 of Fedot's unfolding structure, he seems to have come to the end of a nested Quest (spanning 72, 74–75) but he's just setting out on his quest to 'go I know not where and find I know not what' for the king. This points to a tripartite structure which links to an unfolding Revelation sequence underpinning an unfolding series of story structures for Fedot, the first of which is the I.A Quest structure which appears here, nested in the series of Trickster-type structures which started at part 65. We pick up his story line again at part 83.*
76	[(↱)]			↑			The king waited a month, then summoned his steward. *Both story lines show an opening 'problem/journey' sequence in an unfolding Quest structure.*
77	↑			↓			He instructed the steward to go and fetch Fedot's wife to the palace. *The Quest structure continues to unfold in both characters' story lines. The steward's is arguably tragic, as he comes face to face with Fedot's wife for the first time since part 37. It would seem that he's given up any hope he may have been nurturing of seeing his unrequited love fulfilled.*

Part	King	Fedot	Wife	Steward	Shmat Razum	Merchants	Outline
78	(symbol)		(symbol)	(symbol)			The steward brought her to the king. The steward's story line follows a nested Quest here in which he acts as a friend/helper to the king in what turns out to be a Quest structure for the king. The steward's story line peters out rather abruptly here; he makes no further appearances in the narrative. For Fedot's wife, this pair of steps consists of a 'problem/journey' sequence in her unfolding structure.
79	(symbol)		(symbol)				The king proposed marriage. A new structure unfolds here for the king, his problem being to get the bird-wife to marry him. A Trickster Variation structure unfolds in her story line.
80	(symbol)		(symbol)				She refused. The king's story line features a Trickster structure here, the 'intention to dupe' relating to the fact that he wants to marry a woman whom he knows is already married. A Trickster Variation structure concludes in the bird-wife's story line, with the king's proposal clearly going against her principles. Both story lines feature a completed veni step in an unfolding sequence here.
81	(symbol) (symbol)		(symbol)				The king threatened her. The king's story line follows a looping Trickster structure; in the bird-wife's, another Trickster Variation structure unfolds. Both are vidi sequences in an unfolding triple sequence for each character.
82	(symbol) (symbol)		(symbol) (symbol) (symbol)				She turned into a blue dove and flew away. The Transformational Twist completes the bird-wife's Trickster Variation structure; the preceding steps in her story line here symbolise a nested Quest-type substructure, in which the striking of the floor and her magical powers of transformation are her friends/helpers. Note the Revelation structure underpinning the sequence which comprises her smile, her striking of the floor, and her physical transformation. This vici sequence in both story lines provides a tragic ending to the king's unfolding looping Trickster structure. A final Transformation structure is implied but not scribed here.
83		(symbol)					The ball led Fedot over rivers as a bridge, softening the ground when he needed a bed, then rolled up to the door of a grand palace and vanished. This initiates a (1.B.1) veni sequence in the extended structure unfolding through Fedot's story line.

Part	King	Fedot	Wife	Steward	Shmat Razum	Merchants	Outline
84		↳					Fedot entered and reached and met three beautiful maidens. *Parts 84–100 contain nested structures which eventually compress down to a (I.B.2) vidi 'friend/helper' sequence in Fedot's unfolding nested Quest structure.*
85							They questioned him, but he asked for food, water, and a place to rest first.
86							They offered him food, drink, and a bed to rest in.
87							When he woke up, they brought him a basin and a towel
88							He washed but refused to use the towel, saying he would use the handkerchief his wife had given him.
89							They saw the handkerchief which identified him as their brother-in-law.
90							He told them of his quest.
91							The mother called the beasts of the forests and the birds of the air and asked them whether they knew how to 'go I know not whither, bring me back I know not what.' *The mother's story line is a nested Quest which loops until it resolves, acting in the capacity of a friend/helper in Fedot's ongoing Quest structure.*
92							Both groups said they didn't know.
93							She went to her room and consulted her magic book, summoning two giants.
94							She asked them to take Fedot and her to the ocean, stopping 'right above the bottomless depth'.
95							She called for the creatures of the sea and asked them.
96							They said they didn't know.
97							A frog appeared and said he did know. *This is the third sequence in a triple 'try, try, try again' looping structure, under which a series of nested Revelation structures can be traced.*

Part	King	Fedot	Wife	Steward	Shmat Razum	Merchants	Outline
98							She lifted him up and ordered the giants to take them all back to the palace.
99							Back at the palace, she asked the frog how Fedot could find the way.
100		1					The frog said he'd guide him but was too old to walk. *This concludes the overarching (I.B.2) vidi sequence in the extended structure unfolding through Fedot's story line.*
101		↑↓					The mother found a jar of milk for the frog to ride in and told Fedot to carry the frog in it. *This (I.B.3) vici sequence completes the central (I.B.) meeting with friend/ helper' vidi sequence in the overarching Quest substructure currently unfolding in Fedot's story line which started for him in part 72 in response to the king's request in part 65.*
102		↓					They came to a river of fire. *This initiates a (I.C.1) veni Quest sequence in the extended structure unfolding through Fedot's story line.*
103							The frog helped Fedot to cross it. *The Frog acts as Fedot's friend/helper, completing the first of three subsections – here the frog guides him towards his intended destination. This concludes the (I.C.1) sequence in Fedot's story line.*
104		1					They came to a door in the side of a mountain. *This initiates a nested (I.C.2) vidi Quest in which they arrive at their destination.*
105		1					The frog told Fedot to go through the door, enter a cave, and hide there, then watch out for two men, observe what they do, then after they had left, to speak and do as they had done. *The Frog acts as Fedot's friend/helper, setting out a plan which follows a clear 'veni, vidi, vici' sequence. This concludes the nested (I.C.2) vidi Quest.*
106		↓			⌐		Fedot went through the door and entered the cave. It was dark. He found a cupboard to hide in. *This initiates a nested (I.C.3) veni Quest for Fedot, in which the cupboard acts as his friend/helper.*

Part	King	Fedot	Wife	Steward	Shmat Razum	Merchants	Outline
107		↗⌉			⌊↓↑⌋ (↓↑)		Fedot observed two men enter. They ordered Shmat Razum to bring them food and drink. They ate and drank. They ordered Shmat Razum to clear up. They left. *Nested Quest for the men, in which Shmat Razum acts as their friend/helper, involving two nested Transformation structures in his story line, begging a question regarding the associated state of excess, probably linked to his gifts being abused by the merchants. This concludes the nested (I.C.3) veni Quest for Fedot. Here, Fedot's percepts, concepts, and powers of reasoning and judgment act as further friends/helpers, revealing a triple nested set behind which an underlying Revelation structure can be traced.*
108		⌊((↓↗↑			(↓↑)		Fedot emerged and ordered Shmat Razum to bring him food and drink. *This forms a nested (II.A.1) veni Quest for Fedot, with Shmat Razum as his friend/helper, involving a third Transformation structure in Shmat Razum's story line, under which a Revelation structure can be traced.*
109		(↓			↓		He invited Shmat Razum to eat and drink with him, as he didn't like to eat alone. *I see this as initiating a (II.A.2.a) vici sequence in Fedot's overarching story line. For Shmat Razum, it initiates a pair of Trickster Awe steps through which Fedot surprises Shmat Razum and Shmat Razum resolves the cognitive dissonance at 112 by choosing to serve Fedot, thus, in terms of the theme of the underlying story structure, completing a Call and Response-type structure, restoring a state of balance in the natural order.*
110			1		↑↓		Shmat Razum was very thankful and agreed. *For Fedot, this concludes the nested (II.A.2.a) Quest underpinned by a Revelation structure which was initiated in part 109. For Shmat Razum, it provides the initial 'Huh?' exchange which elicits his response of thanks in his unfolding Trickster Variation substructure here. A nested Quest is implied for Shmat Razum in which he partakes of the food and drink, not scribed here.*
111		↓			↓		Fedot asked Shmat Razum whether he wanted to become his servant. *This initiates a nested (II.A.2.b) vici Quest for Fedot.*

Part	King	Fedot	Wife	Steward	Shmat Razum	Merchants	Outline
112		↑			⇈		Shmat Razum agreed to his proposal. This completes Shmat Razum's unfolding Trickster Variation-type structure. From 107–112, Shmat Razum's story line can be seen to follow a Call and Response-type structure, where the unappreciated and unthanked state we find him in can be seen as a state of an excess of evil, and Fedot's offer providing a release for him and a potential restoration of balance.
113		↑↓ ↑			[((•)))		Fedot ordered Shmat Razum to clear up and follow him, then left the cave. Fedot's first command to Shmat Razum as master/servant forms the concluding (II.A.2.c) vici sequence in his structure. Having found Shmat Razum, he now has to return with him. His departure from the cave forms the level 3 (II.A.3) vici section of Fedot's unfolding story line. I see the tasks Shmat Razum is given (of clearing up and of following Fedot) as forming the start of a new section for him as they're the first tasks he's given after he enters Fedot's service. It's unclear from the narrative whether he actually completes the first of these two tasks or not – but I'm assuming he does. If he doesn't, and leaves the food and furnishings for the merchants to find, then it initiates an unfinished Trickster structure which unfolds beyond the boundaries of this narrative. His acceptance of the summons is scribed here as a veni section of an unfolding series of Quests underpinned by a Revelation structure. It could be seen to act as a 'hinge' structure.
114		))					Outside, Fedot couldn't see Shmat Razum, and called for him. This initiates a nested (II.B.1) veni Quest for Fedot.
115		↑			↑↓		Shmat Razum assured him he was there and that he wouldn't desert him. This completes the nested (II.B.1) veni Quest for Fedot. Shmat Razum has a nested Quest here, but is acting as Fedot's friend/helper by reassuring him of his presence and his loyalty. It's ironic that in the vidi section, which has to do with sight, Shmat Razum assures Fedot that he's there, although he's invisible. Note here that the two characters' Revelation structures run together in canon and not in unison.
116		↓					Fedot sat on the frog. This initiates a nested (II.B.2) vidi Quest for Fedot in which the frog acts as his friend/helper.

Part	King	Fedot	Wife	Steward	Shmat Razum	Merchants	Outline
117		↑			(↓↑)		The frog carried Fedot across the river of fire. *This completes the nested (II.B.2) vidi Quest for Fedot. It's implied that Shmat Razum accompanies them, the arrival forming the vici section of the unfolding sequence for him. Nevertheless, the sequence has a Transformation structure quality to it.*
118		↓			↓		Fedot returned to the palace, and introduced the women to Shmat Razum and his powers. Shmat Razum entertained them. *This initiates a nested (II.B.3) vici Quest for Fedot. It's the first instance since the cave that we see Fedot use or show off Shmat Razum's powers and the first time that he uses his mastery over them in the service of others. A nested Quest unfolds here for Shmat Razum (which, again, is probably better interpreted as a Transformation structure).*
119		↑))			↑⌐		The mother was delighted and ordered the frog be rewarded. *This completes the nested (II.B.3) vici Quest for Fedot. From 113–119, Shmat Razum's story line can be seen to follow a Call and Response-type Variation 2 structure, through which Shmat Razum's powers are increasingly appreciated and the link between Fedot and Shmat Razum develops a more concrete quality.*
120		↓)))					Fedot left and became tired. *This initiates a nested (II.C.1) veni Quest for Fedot.*
121		↑			[↓]		He complained to Shmat Razum who said he would have carried Fedot had Fedot asked him to. *This concludes the nested (II.C.1) veni Quest for Fedot. A nested Quest for Shmat Razum as Fedot's friend/helper starts.*
122		↓					A wind carried Fedot off so fast that he lost his cap. *The experience of being carried initiates the nested (II.C.2) vidi sequence in this section of Fedot's unfolding story line. I see it as an unfolding Trickster Variation structure for him.*

Part	King	Fedot	Wife	Steward	Shmat Razum	Merchants	Outline
123		1			1		Noticing the loss of his cap, he called to Shmat Razum to stop. Shmat Razum said it was too late – it was already 5,000 versts behind them. *This concludes the nested (II.C.2) vidi sequence in this section of Fedot's unfolding story line. Interestingly, it maps to the loss of Fedot's hat, significant symbolically, as Shmat Razum literally means 'the destruction of rationality' ('Smashed Sense'). We pick up on the next (II.C.3) vici sequence in this unfolding structure in Fedot's story line at part 141 of this analysis. Depending on Fedot's reaction to the loss of his hat, it's possible to see this as an unfolding Trickster Variation sequence which contains the nested sequence which unfolds from part 124 and concludes with Fedot's acquisition of the magical objects in part 134. As this isn't clear from the narrative, it remains an open question. This step appears to be a 'journey' step in Shmat Razum's unfolding Quest structure. However, it'll turn out to be part of an initial Transformation structure in an unfolding Call and Response-type Variation 1 structure for him, which is significant in terms of shedding light on the interpretative problem highlighted above. In this interpretation, for Shmat Razum, the pattern this section follows is:* Transformation: 121–123 in which Shmat Razum sweeps Fedot away and Fedot loses his cap. Veni sequence: 124–125 in which Shmat Razum suggests a plan to Fedot that will help him acquire a fortune, in which a Trickster structure is initiated, with the merchants as the target for the dupes. Vidi sequence: 126–136 in which the merchants arrive and three magical gifts they carry are exchanged with Fedot for Shmat Razum, involving two Quest structures and a Trickster structure. Vici sequence: 137–142 in which Shmat Razum, as part of the ruse in which Fedot is complicit, goes with the merchants with no intention of staying with them, as a result of which Fedot gains the three magical gifts, Shmat Razum continues in his service, and the merchants are left to grieve their losses. *Both Trickster structures resolve at this point.*

Part	King	Fedot	Wife	Steward	Shmat Razum	Merchants	Outline
124		⌐↓			((↑↓) ↑↓		Shmat Razum asked whether Fedot would like him to create an arbour for him to rest in and acquire a fortune. *In Fedot's story line, parts 124–140 form a separate sequence which is nested within the overarching structure we're following, as they relate to a new problem for him. Part 65 in Fedot's story line initiated the sequence which links to the king's quest to send Fedot 'I know not whither' to get 'I know not what'. That thread is resumed at 141.* *Here, Shmat Razum takes the initiative and presents Fedot with an offer which he accepts. However, it has nothing to do with the quest Fedot is on for the king. This is the start of the first of three structures in an unfolding veni sequence for Shmat Razum. In relation to the merchants, they're Trickster structures which follow a clear looping Revelation sequence. In relation to Fedot, they're Quest structures, which condense to a 'friend/ helper' sequence in this section of his unfolding story line.*
125		↑))			↑↓		Fedot agreed; Shmat Razum created a magical island with a golden arbour. *By expanding the (→) step in the (→) sequence in Fedot's story line in parts 122–123 from 1 step to 7, a Quest underpinned by a Revelation structure will be seen to unfold, with the sequence at 124–125 providing a final Transformation structure which completes a Call and Response Variation 2 structure for him, with the creation of the arbour. This provides interesting insights into Fedot's character development. It shows how the loss of his cap is thematically linked to the appearance of the island, and it's from this point onwards that Fedot's agency increases and that he takes increasing charge of events using powers he's always had but is only now 'growing into'. This is one example of how this methodology can provide deep insights into the subtleties of the underlying story structure underpinning a given narrative and how it can be used to add richness to story spinning.* *This is the continuation of the veni structure in Shmat Razum's story line. He's creating the lure which will attract the merchants' attention. This is a Trickster step in his story line.*

Part	King	Fedot	Wife	Steward	Shmat Razum	Merchants	Outline
126		(((↑↓			(((↑↓	⌐	Shmat Razum told him 3 merchant ships would stop at the island, to trade him for their marvels, and that he would return to Fedot. *In this extended 'meeting with friend/helper' sequence in the unfolding veni Quest structure in Shmat Razum's story line (126–136), he acts both as instigator and as friend/helper to Fedot by revealing the plan that will enable Fedot to gain the fortune in which they will need to act as a 'trickster team'. The plan which Shmat Razum outlines in this sequence (like the frog's in part 104) follows a clear veni, vidi, vici structure, with each of the 3 sections being further subdivided into its own veni, vidi, vici structure. For Fedot, this sets up a Quest structure in which Shmat Razum once more acts as his friend/helper. Part 126 can be seen as section 1.a of this structure in Fedot's story line. (The different numbering style used here distinguishes between the structure of this nested sequence and the structure of the sequence which was suspended at 123 and resumes at 141.) The sequence from 124–140 is like a plaited braid, in which the characters' story lines interweave to form a complex whole. 126 forms the start of the vidi Trickster structure in this section of Shmat Razum's story line, in which Shmat Razum shows the merchants what he can do, with the intention of securing the trade for Fedot from them.*
127						[(((↑↓↓ ⇊	The ships passed and the merchants, surprised, decided to cast anchor and explore. *This is the start of an unfolding Trickster Variation structure for the merchants and forms section 1.a in their story line.*
128		(↓				(↓	Fedot invited them to rest. *The interaction with the merchants forms section 1.b in this section of Fedot's story line. The merchants' story line follows a Trickster Variation structure here and this initiates section 1.b in their story line.*
129					↓		He summoned Shmat Razum and ordered him to bring them food and drink. *This initiates the central sequence in this vidi section of Shmat Razum's unfolding story line.*

Part	King	Fedot	Wife	Steward	Shmat Razum	Merchants	Outline
130		↑			↑↓	↑	Shmat Razum fulfilled the request. *In Fedot's story line, this concludes section 1.b. In Shmat Razum's, this continues the vidi section of the three unfolding looping Trickster structures in this sequence. He continues to act as friend/helper to Fedot here.*
131		(↑↓))				↑↓	The merchants, amazed, offered an exchange. *This forms section 1.c in this section of Fedot's story line and completes section 1.b in the merchants'. The three sections from 1.a to 1.c in this section of Fedot's story line can be condensed to a pair of initial 'problem/journey' steps in a Quest/Trickster structure.*
132		(↑↓)				(↑↓)	Each merchant revealed a wonder: a box that summoned a garden, an axe that summoned a navy, a horn that summoned an army. *This forms section 2.a in Fedot's story line, which has the characteristics of a Trickster Awe step pair for him. Nested Quest for the merchants, with the goods as the merchants' friends/helpers which initiates section 1.c in their story line.*
133		↑↓				↑↓	Fedot offered to trade Shmat Razum for all three rather than just one as the merchants had originally proposed. *This forms section 2.b in Fedot's story line, which has the characteristics of Trickster pair for him as this is the first instance in which Fedot himself (rather than Shmat Razum) deliberately sets out to try to trick the merchants. It completes section 1.c in the merchants' story line. This concludes a veni section spanning 1.a–1.c (127–133) for them in an unfolding Call and Response-type structure based on a series of Trickster-type structures.*
134		↑↓))				((↑↓)	The merchants deliberated and agreed to the exchange. *Fedot and Shmat Razum intend to dupe the merchants; the merchants' gullibility allows them to be tricked. Thus, this forms section 2.c in Fedot's story line and forms a third Trickster step pair for him. It also forms section 2.a in the merchants' story line, where it appears as the start of a nested Trickster structure within the unfolding Call and Response-type structure based on a series of Trickster-type structures in their story line.*

Part	King	Fedot	Wife	Steward	Shmat Razum	Merchants	Outline
135					(symbol)	(symbol)	They asked Shmat Razum whether he would serve them 'in faith and in truth'. This forms section 2.b in the merchants' story line, which follows a Trickster step, as they're again duped by their own gullibility and their blind trust in the soundness of their unsound reasoning. In Shmat Razum's story line, it initiates an extended 'meeting with enemy/hindrance' sequence which concludes the central vidi Revelation structure, and forms part of a Trickster structure. There's a shift from Fedot's story line to Shmat Razum's in the sequence in which they operate jointly as tricksters towards the merchants here. This initiates the vici part of Shmat Razum's unfolding triple Trickster structure, in which the merchants agree to the trade and he tricks them into believing he'll stay with them.
136					(symbol)	(symbol)	Shmat Razum replied, "Why not?" and said, "It is all the same to me with whom I live." This forms section 2.c in the merchants' story line, which is a vidi section for them. In Shmat Razum's story line, we have the continuation of an unfolding vici Trickster structure which ends at part 142.
137					(symbol)	(symbol)	The merchants returned to their ships with Shmat Razum. This nested Quest for the merchants forms section 3.a in their story line, initiating a vici sequence. It's also a nested Quest/Transformation structure for Shmat Razum who merely accompanies them, the first in a nested Revelation sequence of three such structures for him.
138						(symbol)	The merchants ordered Shmat Razum to 'treat their crews to food and drink'. This initiates a nested Quest for the merchants which forms section 3.b in their story line.
139					(symbol)		Shmat Razum obeyed their orders. Second of three nested Quest structures, perhaps more appropriately interpreted as Transformation structures for Shmat Razum who simply acts as the merchants' friend/helper here.
140						(symbol)	The merchants' crews 'got drunk and fell asleep'. This completes the nested Quest for the merchants which forms section 3.b in their story line.

Part	King	Fedot	Wife	Steward	Shmat Razum	Merchants	Outline
141		↗					Fedot wondered out loud where Shmat Razum was. *This forms a nested (II.C.3.i) veni Quest for Fedot, the initial part of return segment of the second quest he's been on for the king.*
142		↓			↑ ↑ ↓		Shmat Razum replied, having left the merchants and returned to Fedot. *This initiates a nested (II.C.3.ii) vidi Quest for Fedot. Shmat Razum's deserting the merchants and returning to Fedot form a vici pair of Quest/ Transformation structures followed by the Transformational Twist that (a) nullifies the trade agreement struck between Fedot and the merchants; (b) marks the merchants' loss of both him and the magical objects they traded in exchange for him and (c) marks his dematerialisation of the island. Shmat Razum's actions link to section 3.c of the merchants' story line which unfolds from 145–147, although the merchants don't yet realise they've been tricked.*
143		↑					Fedot, pleased, asked him whether it wasn't time for them to go home. *This concludes the nested (II.C.3.ii) vidi Quest for Fedot whose story line resumes in part 148.*
144					↓		Shmat Razum lifted him up, and bore him away. *In relation to Fedot, Shmat Razum is a friend/helper here. The disappearance of the island probably occurs after this, but the step relating to this is scribed at 142 for ease of reference, as it connects Shmat Razum's story line to the merchants' rather than to Fedot's.*
145						↑↓	The merchants woke up and called for Shmat Razum to serve them with food and drink. *Nested Quest for the merchants which initiates section 3.c in their story line.*
146						↓	No answer came.

Part	King	Fedot	Wife	Steward	Shmat Razum	Merchants	Outline
147						⇑ ⇑⌐	They realised they'd been tricked, and had no way of finding the island again, so they went on their way. With the disappearance of the island which clinches the merchants' defeat, we reach the final 3.c vici sequence of the unfolding structure in their story line. For them, it's not only Shmat Razum's disappearance, and the realisation of their own folly, but his elimination of the island which robs them of any recourse to restitution that provide the double whammy which forces them to grieve and grieve before they continue on their way.
148		(←→)))			↑⌐		Fedot and Shmat Razum arrived on the coast of his homeland. This is a nested (II.C.3.iii) vici Quest for Fedot which completes the vidi (II) section in the unfolding story structure we're following in his story line. It forms a final Transformation structure which completes a Call and Response Variation 2 type structure, where three Trickster structures are underpinned by a Revelation structure as we've seen – with the Trickster elements played out against the merchants.
149		[((←→)					Fedot asked Shmat Razum to build a castle there. In the final (III) vici sequence in the overarching top-level story structure, this nested Quest for Fedot constitutes the (III.A.1) veni sequence in his unfolding story structure.
150					[(←↑)		Shmat Razum fulfilled his order, building a castle 'twice as good as the royal palace'. This initiates a (III.A.2) vidi Quest sequence in Fedot's unfolding story structure. It's unclear whether the palace turning out to be 'twice as good as the royal palace' is intentional or not, and if so, whether it's on the part of Fedot himself, or just a result of Shmat Razum's initiative. Fedot's tacit acceptance, however, and his next move would indicate either a challenge or an act of bravado. At this point, there is no clear intent on the part of Fedot to dupe or trick the king stated in the narrative. I've therefore interpreted this as an unfolding nested Quest structure for him. Whether Shmat Razum's sequence here is a Quest structure or a Transformation structure is open to interpretation – I've gone for a Quest structure for consistency. Either way it has the quality of a final sequence in an unfolding Call and Response-type Variation 2 structure spanning 121–150. It's unclear from the narrative how Shmat Razum's story line unfolds after this point.

Part	King	Fedot	Wife	Steward	Shmat Razum	Merchants	Outline
151		*(notation)*					Fedot opened the box and a garden surrounded the palace. *This concludes the (III.A.2) vidi Quest sequence in Fedot's story line. The appearance of the garden can be seen as a friend/helper in his return quest, in which he's (i) (one assumes) expecting to be reunited with his wife and (ii) heralding both his successful return and the completion of his task for the king. It's after his creation of the garden that his wife appears.*
152		*(notation)*	*(notation)*				While Fedot was 'feasting his eyes upon his garden', a blue dove flew in through a window, landed on the floor, and transformed into his wife. *This initiates a (III.A.3) vici sequence in Fedot's personal quest to be reunited safely with his wife. In his wife's story line, a nested structure is implied – possibly a Quest in relation to her desire to be reunited with Fedot.*
153		*(notation)*	*(notation)*				They exchanged stories. She told him that she'd been 'flying in forests and groves as a blue dove' since he'd left home. *This concludes the (III.A.3) vidi sequence in Fedot's personal quest to be reunited safely with his wife. His wife's back-dating of the time of her transformation to the time of Fedot's departure rather than her later meeting with the king makes this potentially into a Trickster structure for her – whether it is or not depends on whether or not her intention is to dupe Fedot. The inconsistency needs to be explained one way or another, and the narrative doesn't make this clear. Marking this step in grey highlights this ambiguity. It is, however, a Transformational Twist which resolves the dynamic in the wife/king's story line, which is why the step is marked as a double barb.*
154	*(notation)*						The next day, the king awoke and noticed the castle. *This initiates an initial Trickster Awe opening which forms a veni sequence in the king's unfolding story line which is part of a larger unfolding composite Call and Response Variation 2 structure which spans part 154–164 in his story line.*
155	*(notation)*						He enquired as to 'what insolent man had dared to build [it]'. *This initiates a medial Trickster Variation structure which forms a vidi sequence in the king's unfolding story line. A nested Quest is implied for his friends/helpers here.*

Part	King	Fedot	Wife	Steward	Shmat Razum	Merchants	Outline
156	⇅↓						He was told that it was Fedot, who was living there with his wife.
157	(↓						The king was enraged and summoned his armies. *This initiates a final, more extended vici Trickster structure section nested within the larger Trickster Variation structure unfolding in the king's story line.*
158	↑						He ordered the destruction of the garden, the palace, and the couple. *In the king's unfolding nested Trickster structure, the pair of moves which spans parts 157–158 can be seen as a 'problem/journey' pair.*
159	↓	(↓					Fedot saw he was being attacked. *This constitutes the (III.B.2) vidi section of the Trickster sequence unfolding in this part of the composite structure of Fedot's story line. In the king's story line, it initiates the central Trickster/Dupe section of his unfolding nested Trickster structure.*
160		↓					He took up the axe and horn and created a navy and an army. *This constitutes the start of the (III.B.3) vici section of the Trickster sequence unfolding in Fedot's story line.*
161		⇅					Fedot's armed forces launched a counter-attack. *The magical forces act as Fedot's friends/helpers here.*
162	⇅						The king, seeing his troops were outnumbered and his army captured or fleeing, tried to halt the attack. *At first, Fedot's forces overwhelm the king's forces. The king's troops fleeing rather than standing their ground, and the king's misplaced confidence in his own abilities to muster his troops and defeat Fedot both link to the Trickster step in his story line here. There's an unfolding triple structure to the 159–162 pair for the king, in which the troops flee, he tries to rally them, but he fails.*
163	(↑) ⇄))	↓					The king went to the front himself but failed to muster his troops. *The king's troops scatter or are captured and the king fails to rally them to his call. This nested Trickster structure is significant, as it shows that it's ultimately the internal trickster that defeats the king.*

Part	King	Fedot	Wife	Steward	Shmat Razum	Merchants	Outline
164	(⌐↑⌐)	⇑⌐					He was killed. *Fedot's forces win the battle. This concludes the (III.B.3) vici section of both the third-level subsection, and of the overarching structure in his unfolding story line, bringing the (III) section to a close here for him. The large-scale Quest structure which started for him at part 72 is now complete. In the king's story line, his death and the loss of his kingdom form a tragic culminating Transformation structure which completes the Call and Response-type Variation 2 structure which has been unfolding from part 154 up to this point in his story line.*
165	⌐	(↓⌐)					The people asked Fedot to rule over them. *Fedot's nested structure here appears in response to the people's request. From their perspective, he's thus acting in the capacity of friend/helper in their story line. For the people, a Quest structure is implied; for Fedot and his wife, I see it as a Transformation structure in their story lines, which could be expanded to a Call and Response Variation 2 structure.*
166							Fedot agreed.
167		↑⌐	(↑↑)⌐		⌐		Fedot became king; his wife became queen. *From both Fedot's perspective and his wife's, this final structure which spans parts 165–166 forms a culminating Transformation structure revealing the story structure which has unfolded for Fedot from part 72 to be a composite, expanded Call and Response-type Variation 2 structure.*
168	☐	☐	☐	☐	☐	☐	[Closing]

KEY:

at 108–123, 141–148: Fedot Quest 3 – 'Go I know not where and fetch I know not what'.

at 72–107: Fedot Quest 3 – Extended friend/helper sequence.

at 126–164: Shmat Razum's path to restoring order via Fedot.

at 54–59: Fedot's and the sailors' intersecting pair of story lines.

at 55–59: Fedot's and the king's intersecting pair of story lines.

[...] frame structures within which substructures are nested.

((...)) substructures. *Italicised sequences indicate implied events.*

**11. Can you condense (← ←) or (← → ←), to (←); (→ →)
or (→ ← →) to (→) and/or (⇌ ← ⇌) to (⇌) without losing
essential information? If you can, then do.**

The trick here is to condense the story structures outlined by the narrative to their 'bare bones' forms while still retaining their quality so they can be intuited visually at a glance.

If one were to reduce the Trickster Variation structure by condensing (← → ←) to (←) and (⇌ ← ⇌) to (⇌), it would go from this:

⊐⌐←→←⇌←⇌⌐⊐

to this:

⊐⌐←⇌⌐⊐.

Interestingly, this is distinct from the other story structures identified. The methodology has an internal logic. As Spencer-Brown notes, 'when I was wrong, the theorem was always right'.[15] Whether or not this proves to be the case with this application is up to us to establish by testing it out in practice.

In the analyses of the individual characters' story lines below, where formally identical or similar patterns have been reduced to a single iteration, a superscript number has been added to show how many iterations are contained within the condensed form. Square brackets indicate larger scale sequences, bold brackets nested sequences within those, and normal brackets sequences embedded within those. Normal brackets are sometimes used to indicate implied sequences in structures. This allows triple forms (generated by an underlying Dynamic Revelation structure) and dual or quadruple forms (generated by an underlying duple structure) to be easily distinguished, as in the following:

⊐⌐[((←→)←⇌((←→)←⇌←⇌)] which reduces to ⊐⌐[((←⇌)³]
and
⊐⌐[(←→←⇌←⇌)(←→←⇌←⇌)] which reduces to ⊐⌐[((←⇌)⁴]

We'll follow each of the main characters' story lines and break them down into logical sections. They'll appear first in full form, then in compressed form. Once the first section is introduced, subsequent sections will be highlighted when they're first introduced (usually in grey) and will then be built on sequentially.

The algebraic notation is simply there to denote the ebb and flow of the energetic pulse that story follows in each character's story line.

The king

The king's character and situation are set out at the start. He's unmarried (←) and has hunters who regularly supply him with food. The latter forms a Quest sequence. The various sequences are numbered K_n for ease of reference, with segments relating to each element and their reductions shaded in grey in each case. Numbers below each scribed line relate to the steps outlined in the table above, with a brief summary of the main events the parts cover.

K1   □⌐←(←→)

1–4: The king's unmarried; he needs and gets game (obtained by his hunters).

In the K1 sequence, the implied condensation of the (←→) pair from three pairs to one 'bare bones' pair points to a possible underlying Transformation structure. Is there some kind of transgression against the natural order here? Although this isn't explicit in the narrative, the king's love for Fedot who 'almost never misses' is taken as a clue to the potential for there being an excessive culling of natural resources. Although I haven't done this here, the two (← ←) steps can be condensed to a single step, strengthening the transgressive sense, something we'll come back to at the end of the analysis.

K2   □⌐←(←→)[((←→)←⇌((←→)←⇌←⇌))]
□⌐←(←→)[(←⇌)³]

32–35: Meets steward; desires and gets carpet (paying over the odds).

The king's story line really takes off when he meets the steward (K2). They're in the custom of dining together, which indicates an implied $(\leftarrow \rightarrow \leftarrow)$ sequence: a need to eat, leading to them sitting down to a meal together, condensing to $(\leftarrow)$ with no loss of basic content.

When the steward offers to show the king the new marvel he's acquired, the beauty of the carpet he's bought astounds the king. $(\rightleftharpoons)$. The presence of magic in the story points to a Threshold Structure here, with the most obvious pattern being the Trickster Variation structure. In this structure, two characters on separate quests meet, a cognitive dissonance is set up; there's a switch from one character's story line to the other, and a sequence unfolds which ends in a Transformational Twist which resolves the cognitive dissonance. It fits. The king's quest to acquire the carpet involves a Quest nested within a Trickster structure (a variation on the standard sequence presented in chapter 12). The $((\leftarrow \rightarrow)\leftarrow \rightleftharpoons (\leftarrow \rightarrow)\leftarrow \rightleftharpoons \leftarrow \rightleftharpoons)$ condenses to $((\leftarrow \rightarrow)\leftarrow \rightleftharpoons)$, marked with a superscript 3 to indicate the number of $(\rightleftharpoons)$ steps included here, then condenses again to give a single $(\leftarrow \rightleftharpoons)^3$ sequence.

Interestingly, in the symbolic notation above, the $(\leftarrow \rightleftharpoons)$ sequence is preceded by a decreasing number of $(\leftarrow)$ or $(\rightarrow)$ steps: first 6, then 3, then 1, showing the suspense leading up to the exchange.

K3 $\Box \daleth \leftarrow (\leftarrow \rightarrow)[(\leftarrow \rightleftharpoons)^3][(\leftarrow \rightarrow \leftarrow \rightleftharpoons ((\leftarrow \rightarrow)\leftarrow \rightleftharpoons \leftarrow \rightleftharpoons))]$
$\Box \daleth \leftarrow (\leftarrow \rightarrow)[(\leftarrow \rightleftharpoons)^3][(\leftarrow \rightleftharpoons)^3]$

38–42: Sees steward is down; finds out it's because of a beautiful woman; visits her behind the steward's back; falls in love; decides to marry her.

Although the qualities of the $(\rightleftharpoons)$ K3 steps are slightly different compared to those in K2 for the king, structurally, this section matches the sequence outlined in K2 exactly and reduces in the same way. The sequence could be seen as a *veni, vidi* sequence, each part of which culminates in some form of magic (the carpet, the stag), which leads to a more extended *vici* sequence with the magical appearance of the palace preceding the king's death, bringing his story line to a tragic end. We're not there yet, though.

K4   □ ⌐ ← (← →) ⟨ [(← ⇌)³] [(← ⇌)³] [(← → ← → ← →)] [(← →)] ⟩
         □ ⌐ ← (← →) ⟨ [(← ⇌)³] [(← ⇌)³] [(← →)³] [(← →)] ⟩

43–48: Orders steward to find a plan to get rid of Fedot; once told of it, orders it be executed.

Carets (⟨ ⟩) have been added to the K4 sequence above to mark the internal cohesion of this sequence in the king's story line. The sequence culminates in a new Transformation structure which balances the first and points to the dynamism of the triple structure formed by two triple $[(← ⇌)^3]$ sequences followed by a Quest sequence, distinguished from a Transformation structure with a superscript 3. In the light of an underlying Dynamic Revelation structure, the sequence (a nested sequence in the larger overarching story line) clearly follows a nested *veni, vidi, vici* pattern which will ultimately turn out to be tragic for the king.

The carpet, an object created by means of magic, introduces Fedot's wife vicariously to the king; he then comes face to face with her and sets off on a quest to find a plan to get rid of Fedot, which he orders to be put in place. In the short term, he's gained a carpet. Shortly, he'll gain a stag with golden horns. Ultimately, what he most desires is Fedot's wife. He doesn't get her. Not only will he lose her, but he will lose his life and the kingdom as well. It doesn't end well for him. For now, the move, which goes against the sanctity of Fedot's marriage and against his respect for Fedot whom he 'loved … more than all his comrades', is a clear transgression against the natural order. I considered whether or not there was a Trickster structure unfolding in the king's story line with respect to the steward (in parts 43–47) but dismissed this as the king isn't concealing his motives from the steward – he's simply using positional power to blackmail the steward into acting against his own interests and in service of the king's.

The king is behaving tyrannically, but the story structure still follows a Quest for him. The Trickster structure only unfolds in the king's story line where it intersects with Fedot's.

K5　$\square\urcorner\leftarrow(\leftarrow\rightarrow)\langle[(\leftarrow\rightleftharpoons)^3][(\leftarrow\rightleftharpoons)^3][(\leftarrow\rightarrow)^3][(\leftarrow\rightarrow)]\rangle$
$\langle[(\leftarrow\rightarrow\leftarrow\rightleftharpoons\leftarrow\rightleftharpoons)(\leftarrow\rightarrow\leftarrow\rightleftharpoons\leftarrow\rightleftharpoons)]$
$\square\urcorner\leftarrow(\leftarrow\rightarrow)\langle[(\leftarrow\rightleftharpoons)^3][(\leftarrow\rightleftharpoons)^3][(\leftarrow\rightarrow)^3][(\leftarrow\rightarrow)]\rangle$
$\langle[(\leftarrow\rightleftharpoons)^4]$

49–59: Summons Fedot and sends him on an impossible 'stag' quest; appoints him captain of an unseaworthy vessel; Fedot successfully completes the quest.

A caret ($\langle$) is added to K5 here to mark the start of this sequence which initiates Fedot's quests and culminates with the king's death at the end of the story. The sequence of the two Trickster structures condenses to one, and the structures ultimately reduce to two steps: the king attempts to get rid of Fedot but fails.

K6　$\square\urcorner\leftarrow(\leftarrow\rightarrow)\langle[(\leftarrow\rightleftharpoons)^3][(\leftarrow\rightleftharpoons)^3][(\leftarrow\rightarrow)^3][(\leftarrow\rightarrow)]\rangle$
$\langle[(\leftarrow\rightleftharpoons)^4][(\leftarrow\rightarrow\leftarrow\rightarrow\leftarrow\rightarrow)(((\leftarrow\rightarrow)\leftarrow\rightleftharpoons(\leftarrow\rightarrow))][(\leftarrow\rightarrow\leftarrow\rightarrow\leftarrow\rightarrow)$
$((\leftarrow\rightarrow)\leftarrow\rightleftharpoons(\leftarrow\rightarrow)\leftarrow\rightleftharpoons(\leftarrow\rightarrow)\leftarrow\rightleftharpoons))]$
$\square\urcorner\leftarrow(\leftarrow\rightarrow)\langle[(\leftarrow\rightleftharpoons)^3][(\leftarrow\rightleftharpoons)^3][(\leftarrow\rightarrow)^3][(\leftarrow\rightarrow)]\rangle$
$\langle[(\leftarrow\rightleftharpoons)^4][(\leftarrow\rightarrow)^3(((\leftarrow\rightleftharpoons(\leftarrow\rightarrow))][(\leftarrow\rightarrow)^3(\leftarrow\rightleftharpoons)^3)]$

60–82: Orders steward to come up with new plan to get rid of Fedot; sends Fedot on impossible 2nd quest and gives him money; orders steward to bring Fedot's wife to the palace; tries to get Fedot's wife to marry him, but she refuses and transforms into a bird.

The visual reduction afforded by the methodology shows that the first grey-shaded ($\leftarrow\rightarrow$) pair in the reduced form in K6 provides a potentially interesting hinge, with four Trickster-type steps directly to either side. A clear Revelation structure can be traced through the first three Trickster-type steps in the K6 sequence: 'I sent Fedot on his impossible quest in order that I might be able to come near his wife; I asked my steward to bring her to the palace so I could see her; I proposed to her so I could complete my conquest ...' but what the king didn't anticipate was the magical power that Fedot's wife had. The structure follows von Franz's '1,2,3,bang!' pattern discussed in chapter 11, giving an interesting Call and Response-type Variation 2 structure. The expectation of the structure mirroring further is fulfilled in the next sequence.

K7 $\Box\daleth \leftharpoonup(\leftarrow\rightarrow)\langle[(\leftarrow\rightleftharpoons)^3][(\leftarrow\rightleftharpoons)^3][(\leftarrow\rightarrow)^3][(\leftarrow\rightarrow)]\rangle$
$\langle[(\leftarrow\rightleftharpoons)^4][(\leftarrow\rightarrow)^3(((\leftarrow\rightleftharpoons(\leftarrow\rightarrow))][(\leftarrow\rightarrow)^3(\leftarrow\rightleftharpoons)^3)]$
$[((\leftarrow\rightarrow)\leftarrow\rightleftharpoons((\leftarrow\rightarrow)\leftarrow\rightleftharpoons(\leftarrow\rightarrow \leftarrow\rightleftharpoons(\leftarrow\rightarrow)\leftarrow\rightleftharpoons)))(\leftarrow\rightarrow)]\rangle\daleth\Box$
$\Box\daleth\leftharpoonup(\leftarrow\rightarrow)\langle[(\leftarrow\rightleftharpoons)^3][(\leftarrow\rightleftharpoons)^3][(\leftarrow\rightarrow)^3(\leftarrow\rightarrow)]\rangle$
$\langle[(\leftarrow\rightleftharpoons)^4][(\leftarrow\rightarrow)^3(((\leftarrow\rightleftharpoons(\leftarrow\rightarrow))][(\leftarrow\rightarrow)^3(\leftarrow\rightleftharpoons)^3)]$
$[(\leftarrow\rightleftharpoons)(\leftarrow\rightleftharpoons)^3(\leftarrow\rightarrow)]\rangle\daleth\Box$

154–168: Notices castle; finds out that Fedot and his wife have built it and are living there. Orders their destruction; sees his armies decimated by Fedot's troops. Goes to try to rally them and defeat Fedot and his troops; fails; is killed.

The end subtly mirrors the beginning. An outer ($\leftarrow\rightarrow$) pair at the end of K7 balances that at the start. It's preceded here by two structures with ($\rightleftharpoons$) steps. While there are two triple sequences at the start, there are two quadruple sequences at the end (formed by two 1+3 Trickster-type sequences). The three initial Trickster Awe or Trickster steps of these (actioned by the king's seeing the castle, by him being told of Fedot's return, and by the magical appearance of Fedot's forces when he was expecting his positional power and might would be able to get rid of Fedot) are all resolved by a single Transformational Twist (the king's defeat).

The sequence can thus essentially be seen to be made up of three pairs, subtly balancing the pair of triple sequences at the start and pointing to a pair of variations on the Call and Response structure – one at the start, one at the end. The initial one starts with a Transformation structure; the final one ends with a balancing one. The methodology clearly reveals this connection between the opening and closing Transformation structures, and points to a subtle underlying qualitative structural connection at a level beyond the intrinsic *a priori* connection that exists in any story between the initial and final states in a character's story line. Moreover, each ($\rightleftharpoons$) pair links to the intersection of two characters' story lines – king/Fedot; king/Fedot's wife; king/steward, with a Call and Response-type structure traceable through each pairing, one of the features which makes the story structure of this narrative particularly interesting to study, particularly in relation to the ways in which the Transformation structure acts as a 'hinge'.

The precise nature o'f this connection between transgression against the natural order and the attempt to restore balance typical of the Transformation structure will be shown when we examine Fedot's story line and the role of the native population in bringing things to a harmonious close at the end of the story. For now, it's time to examine the other main characters' story lines, starting with Fedot's.

Fedot

F1   ⊐⌐[((←→)((←→←→←→←→)(←⇌(←→)←⇌)(←⇌))(←→))]
⊐⌐[((←→)((←→)³(←⇌)²(←⇌))(←→))]

> 1–17: Fedot sets out to hunt, sees a bird. The bird speaks and commands him to follow its instructions. He does so and the bird transforms into a beautiful woman who proposes marriage, to which Fedot agrees.

The first two steps in F1 (Part 6) form a 'problem/journey' pair in a Quest structure. Next, in parts 7–11, he spots, shoots and is about to kill the bird. His hunting skills are his 'friends/helpers'. In parts 12–13, the structure his story line follows shifts from Quest to Trickster Variation, and a triple (←⇌) sequence unfolds. Is this a Trickster structure in the Fedot/king relationship? Or is it simply an (as yet) unfulfilled Quest structure? The narrative implies that he continues to provide the king with game. Should he have brought the bird-woman to the king? Doing so could have meant that he would have had to present her to the king, refuse marriage to her himself, thus rejecting the idea that she would be his 'God-given wife'. None of these things happen; neither he nor his wife seem wracked with guilt; neither hide from the king. They just move in different social spheres. Thus, I see the king/Fedot section as following a Quest structure, the completion of which is implied. The Fedot/Wife section unfolds as Trickster Variation-type structure, with the 'Huh?!' quality of the cognitive dissonance of their first meeting being resolved in an 'Ah!' through a nested Trickster Variation rather than a Quest. The sequence ends in a Transformation structure, making this a Call and Response-type Variation 2 structure, with Trickster Variation rather than Quest underpinned by a Dynamic Revelation structure in it.

F2 $\Box\neg[((\leftharpoonup\to)((\leftharpoonup\to)^3(\leftharpoonup\rightleftharpoons)^2(\leftharpoonup\rightleftharpoons))(\leftharpoonup\to))]$

$[((\leftharpoonup\to)(\leftharpoonup\to(\leftharpoonup\to)\leftharpoonup\to(\leftharpoonup\to)\leftharpoonup\to)(\leftharpoonup\to))(\leftharpoonup\to\leftharpoonup\rightleftharpoons\leftharpoonup\rightleftharpoons))(\leftharpoonup\to)]$

$\Box\neg[((\leftharpoonup\to)((\leftharpoonup\to)^3(\leftharpoonup\rightleftharpoons)^2(\leftharpoonup\rightleftharpoons))(\leftharpoonup\to))]$

$[((\leftharpoonup\to)(\leftharpoonup\to)^3(\leftharpoonup\rightleftharpoons)^2)(\leftharpoonup\to)]$

18–31: Fedot finds hunting tiring. His wife helps him by making a carpet for him to sell and giving him instructions on how to get the best price for it. Following her instructions, he negotiates a sale with the king's steward which leaves Fedot and his wife far richer than they were.

The condensed F2 sequence shown above is not the final version. I've left it in this form to demonstrate the working process and the particular advantage of this methodology.

In the reduced form above, there seems to be an implied parallelism related to the reduced sequence outlined in F1, which is short of a $(\leftharpoonup\rightleftharpoons)$ pair. In checking this against the narrative, I found that, when scribing the sequence, I'd conflated the merchants' Trickster Awe step which occurs when they came across the carpet with the steward's Trickster Awe step. This is perhaps understandable, as I didn't scribe the merchants story line that flows through this part of the story in the table, as they're secondary characters. Nevertheless, when retracing the sequence of events in the story structure in chronological order, and comparing the structural patterns which emerged from the analysis, I could pinpoint the 'missing' step and the parallelism of the structure was revealed. The map is not the territory. The methodology simply facilitates the analysis of the underlying pattern that flows through the story and conversely when used to inform the creation or retelling of a story, it can help writers and story spinners to avoid plot holes. Without the merchants' Trickster Awe step, the notation reveals a rather large hole. Including it results in the following compressed pattern for F2, and shows the internal qualitative symmetry in the story structure so far:

$\Box\neg[((\leftharpoonup\to)((\leftharpoonup\to)^3(\leftharpoonup\rightleftharpoons)^2(\leftharpoonup\rightleftharpoons))(\leftharpoonup\to))]$

$[((\leftharpoonup\to)(\leftharpoonup\to)^3(\leftharpoonup\rightleftharpoons)^3\quad)(\leftharpoonup\to)]$

F3 $\square\neg[((\leftarrow\rightarrow)((\leftarrow\rightarrow)^3(\leftarrow\rightleftharpoons)^2(\leftarrow\rightleftharpoons))(\leftarrow\rightarrow))][((\leftarrow\rightarrow)(\leftarrow\rightarrow)^3(\leftarrow\rightleftharpoons)^3)(\leftarrow\rightarrow)]$

$[((\leftarrow\rightarrow\blacksquare(\leftarrow\rightarrow\leftarrow\rightarrow((\blacksquare)(\blacksquare)(\blacksquare)(\blacksquare))(\blacksquare)\blacksquare)))]$

$\square\neg[((\leftarrow\rightarrow)((\leftarrow\rightarrow)^3(\leftarrow\rightleftharpoons)^2(\leftarrow\rightleftharpoons))(\leftarrow\rightarrow))][((\leftarrow\rightarrow)(\leftarrow\rightarrow)^3(\leftarrow\rightleftharpoons)^3)(\leftarrow\rightarrow)]$

$[((\leftarrow\rightarrow\blacksquare(\blacksquare)^3(\leftarrow\rightleftharpoons)^3)]$

49–59: The king orders Fedot to bring him the stag with the golden horns alive or face death. His wife helps him fulfil the king's request. He tricks the incompetent sailors the king's provided him with, turns the unseaworthy vessel around and returns in record time, his quest complete.

In F3, the initial black shaded pair of ($\leftarrow\rightleftharpoons$) steps has two triple resolutions. The grey set relates to the places where Fedot's story line intersects with the sailors'; the black set relates to where his story line intersects with the king's.

F4 $\square\neg[((\leftarrow\rightarrow)((\leftarrow\rightarrow)^3(\leftarrow\rightleftharpoons)^2(\leftarrow\rightleftharpoons))(\leftarrow\rightarrow))][((\leftarrow\rightarrow)(\leftarrow\rightarrow)^3(\leftarrow\rightleftharpoons)^3)(\leftarrow\rightarrow)]$

$[((\leftarrow\rightarrow\leftarrow\rightleftharpoons(\leftarrow\rightleftharpoons)^3(\leftarrow\rightleftharpoons)^3)][(\leftarrow\rightarrow)\leftarrow\rightleftharpoons(\leftarrow\rightarrow\leftarrow\rightleftharpoons$

$\square\neg[((\leftarrow\rightarrow)((\leftarrow\rightarrow)^3(\leftarrow\rightleftharpoons)^2(\leftarrow\rightleftharpoons))(\leftarrow\rightarrow))][((\leftarrow\rightarrow)(\leftarrow\rightarrow)^3(\leftarrow\rightleftharpoons)^3)(\leftarrow\rightarrow)]$

$[((\leftarrow\rightarrow\leftarrow\rightleftharpoons(\leftarrow\rightleftharpoons)^3(\leftarrow\rightleftharpoons)^3)][\leftarrow\rightleftharpoons^2$

65–68: The king orders Fedot to 'go I know not whither [and] bring [him] back I know not what' or face death. Fedot returns to his wife and complains that the misfortunes he faces are a consequence of her beauty.

In the F4 sequence, there's an opening which mirrors the opening of the structure that unfolded in F3. The intersection between Fedot's story line and those of the king and the sailors is analogous in what follows to the ways in which Fedot's story line intersects directly with those of his wife and the king. His wife returns, transforms, spins her story, and they end up ruling as a couple. Fedot's second quest for the king also contains three sequences with iterations of the ($\leftarrow\rightleftharpoons$) sequence – Fedot's instruction to Shmat Razum to build a magical palace on his return, his unleashing of his magical troops, and his defeat of the king (F7).[16]

F5   [(←→(←→)←→←→)

72–75: IA – Fedot gets money (from the king), 2 gifts (from his wife) and leaves.

(←→←←→←←→)

83–101: IB – He arrives at a castle, and the inhabitants, who turn out to be related to his wife, find a frog guide for him.

(←→←←→←←→)]

102–107: IC – Fedot's frog guide leads him to the cave where he witnesses Shmat Razum being summoned and providing two old men with food.

The F5 sequence reduces qualitatively to a series of nested Quest structures:

F5 $\square\urcorner[((\leftarrow\rightarrow)((\leftarrow\rightarrow)^3(\leftarrow\rightleftharpoons)^2(\leftarrow\rightleftharpoons))(\leftarrow\rightarrow))][((\leftarrow\rightarrow)(\leftarrow\rightarrow)^3(\leftarrow\rightleftharpoons)^3)(\leftarrow\rightarrow)]$
$[(\leftarrow\rightarrow\leftarrow\rightleftharpoons(\leftarrow\rightleftharpoons)^3(\leftarrow\rightleftharpoons)^3)][\leftarrow\rightleftharpoons^2[(\leftarrow\rightarrow)^3]$

F6   [((←→(←→←→←→)←→))

108–113: IIA – Fedot commands Shmat Razum and invites him to dine with him and then to enter into his service. When Shmat Razum agrees, he orders him to clear up and leaves the cave.

((←→)(←→)(←→))

114–119: IIB – Fedot, the frog, and Shmat Razum return to the bird-wife's family's castle.

(((←→)(←→)(←→))
(((←→)(←→)(←→))(←⇌←⇌←⇌))
(((←→)(←→)(←→))))]

120–125, 126–134, 141–148: IIC – When Fedot tires on the journey back to his homeland, Shmat Razum carries him over a deep sea and orchestrates a plan through which Fedot acquires three magical objects after they work together to trick a group of merchants. Shmat Razum then transports Fedot to his homeland.

As noted in the table at 125, the expansion of the grey-shaded (←→) step at 122 for Fedot indicates a significant aspect of his character development.

As a result of Fedot agreeing to follow Shmat Razum's plan, the magical objects he obtains give him power – something not particularly touched on in the narrative that's revealed through the process of analysis. It's even more significant to note, therefore, that even after Fedot has acquired these 'objects of power', he expresses more concern about Shmat Razum than he does about having them. As things turn out, Shmat Razum provides him with a safe and swift lift home. Nevertheless, his magical navy could have transported him, although it would presumably have taken them longer. Although Fedot summons the garden and troops with almost dismissive nonchalance, he appears more affected by Shmat Razum's disappearance. The significance is heightened when we recall that Shmat Razum means the 'destruction of reason'. The key point at which Fedot is carried into the air at top speed by Shmat Razum and he loses his cap implies a moment of enlightenment and a connection to higher faculties. Shmat Razum is associated with this state of enlightenment and for Fedot to value Shmat Razum above the magical objects which bring him material power says a lot.

The F6 sequence condenses to three condensed Quest structures, an extended triple structure featuring Trickster steps, in which Fedot acquires the magical objects which empower him, and a Quest structure which brings him home, helped by Shmat Razum.

F6 $\square\urcorner[((\leftarrow\rightarrow)((\leftarrow\rightarrow)^3(\leftarrow\rightleftharpoons)^2(\leftarrow\rightleftharpoons))(\leftarrow\rightarrow))][((\leftarrow\rightarrow)(\leftarrow\rightarrow)^3(\leftarrow\rightleftharpoons)^3)(\leftarrow\rightarrow)]$
$[(\leftarrow\rightarrow\;\leftarrow\rightleftharpoons(\leftarrow\rightleftharpoons)^3\;(\leftarrow\rightleftharpoons)^3)][\leftarrow\rightleftharpoons^2(\leftarrow\rightarrow)^3[((\leftarrow\rightarrow)^3(\leftarrow\rightleftharpoons)^3(\leftarrow\rightarrow))]$

This mirrors the second part of F4 and F5, essentially Quest type, Trickster type, Quest type, with 'type' being a generic reference to a family of structures. Quest type includes Quest and Transformation structures; Trickster type includes Trickster and Trickster Variation structures. One is led to expect a third iteration of this sequence, which is what one gets in F7/F8, with the final $(\leftarrow\rightarrow)$ sequence being a Transformation structure which brings the story to a close.

F7 $[((\leftharpoonup\rightarrow)(\leftharpoonup\rightarrow)((\leftharpoonup\rightarrow)\leftharpoonup\rightleftharpoons\leftharpoonup\rightleftharpoons))$

149–153: IIIA – Fedot asks Shmat Razum to build him a palace on the shore. Fedot then adds a garden through magical means; while he is admiring his garden, his wife returns as a bird and transforms into human form again.

$(\leftharpoonup\rightarrow$

159: IIIB – Fedot sees the king's troops advancing to attack him.

$\leftharpoonup\rightleftharpoons\leftharpoonup\rightleftharpoons)]$

160–164: IIIC – He creates a magical army and navy and launches a counter-attack in which the king's hostile army members are dissipated and the king's killed after he enters the fray to try to rally them.

F7 condenses to two Quest types, and two Trickster types:

F7 $\sqcup\sqcap[((\leftharpoonup\rightarrow)((\leftharpoonup\rightarrow)^3(\leftharpoonup\rightleftharpoons)^2(\leftharpoonup\rightleftharpoons))(\leftharpoonup\rightarrow))][((\leftharpoonup\rightarrow)(\leftharpoonup\rightarrow)^3(\leftharpoonup\rightleftharpoons)^3)(\leftharpoonup\rightarrow)]$
$[(\leftharpoonup\rightarrow \leftharpoonup\rightleftharpoons(\leftharpoonup\rightleftharpoons)^3(\leftharpoonup\rightleftharpoons)^3)][(\leftharpoonup\rightarrow) \leftharpoonup\rightleftharpoons (\leftharpoonup\rightarrow)(\leftharpoonup\rightarrow \leftharpoonup\rightleftharpoons[(\leftharpoonup\rightarrow \leftharpoonup\rightarrow \leftharpoonup\rightarrow)^3]$
$[((\leftharpoonup\rightarrow)^3(\leftharpoonup\rightleftharpoons)^3(\leftharpoonup\rightarrow))][(\leftharpoonup\rightarrow)^2(\leftharpoonup\rightleftharpoons)^4])]$

This sequence fulfils two functions: firstly, it provides a much-extended third pair of steps in the Trickster structure which started at part 64 (F5), when the king summoned Fedot and sent him off on his second quest, not expecting him to return – in fact, deliberately seeking to send him to his death. By returning successfully, Fedot turns the tables on the king by fulfilling his supposedly impossible task; secondly, it provides a response to the attack the king launches on Fedot. Up to that point, there's nothing in the narrative to suggest that Fedot isn't planning to fulfil his duty and complete his second quest as he did the first. The king, however, who should be a friend/helper to Fedot behaves unequivocally as an enemy/hindrance towards him. He acts out of extreme rage, in response to the perceived 'insolence' and his shock at experiencing the audacity that anyone dare 'to build a castle on [his] land without [his] permission'. Instead of behaving like a true king, in the best sense of that office, he conducts himself like a tyrant at best; a spoilt child at worst.

As a result, Fedot chooses to defend himself. In doing so, he turns the tables on the king in a final showdown. Fedot's armies act as his friends/helpers and follow a nested Quest structure in their story line. Their defeat of the king and his death link to the last ($\leftarrow\rightleftharpoons$) pair here. Interestingly, the triple ($\leftarrow\rightleftharpoons$) pattern unfolds in both the king's story line and Fedot's in this section. In an initial *veni* sequence, Fedot puts Shmat Razum's power on show. Following this, there's a *vidi* sequence in which the king sees the castle and garden and Fedot sees the king's army advancing towards him on the offensive. Following this, a final *vici* sequence sees the king conquered and Fedot victorious.

The sequence for the king is mapped in K7 in his story line. Whose side one thinks the members of the king's forces are on determines whether the last sequence (parts 163–164) in Fedot's story line is seen as a Quest structure, which would give a final F7 sequence that matches the previous F6 sequence in form more closely or as a Trickster structure, as in the above interpretation. The difference hinges on whether the attackers are seen as enemies/hindrances or tricksters. I see their loyalty being to the king, and thus antagonists to Fedot. I see their reason for 'fleeing' as a simple wish to survive leading them to defect rather than to be taken prisoner rather than a wish to avoid fighting Fedot whom they see as 'one of theirs'. The issue is made simple when one separates the army's relationship to the king from their relationship to Fedot. In relation to the king, they're engaged in a Trickster structure; in relation to Fedot, they're engaged in a (tragic) Quest structure. In terms of analysis, it makes sense to interpret the king's army as being linked to his story line, which is the approach I've taken here.

F8   ($\leftarrow\rightarrow$)⅂□

165–168: Fedot is asked by the people to become their king. He accepts.

In F8, a final Transformation sequence brings Fedot's story line and the story to a conclusion:

F8 ⊐⌐[((←→)((←→)³(←⇌)²(←⇌))(←→))][((←→)(←→)³(←⇌)³)(←→)]
[(←→ ←⇌(←⇌)³ (←⇌)³)][(←→) ←⇌ (←→)(←→ ←⇌[(←→ ←→ ←→)³]
[((←→)³(←⇌)³(←→))][(←→)²(←⇌)⁴])](←→)⌐⊐

There's a distinct Call and Response Variation 2 feel to Fedot's story line, which begs the question as to what the inciting incident might be that brings about the unfolding of the story in which his story line unfolds.

The Call and Response structure is a Threshold structure which hinges on and reveals the dynamics which govern the intrinsic link between two dimensions of being, variously referred to as the natural and the supernatural; the physical and the metaphysical; the actual and the real. The natural order contains both on many levels – from the human being to the social structure in which human beings operate to the cosmic order which that reflects. The Call and Response structure reveals that when a (binary) transgression against the natural order occurs in one dimension, it activates a (ternary) reactive and balancing response in the other.

In this story, the Transformation structures in the king's story line relate to key elements – the hunt, the plan to send Fedot on a quest to find the stag with the golden horns, the plan to get rid of Fedot and wed his wife, and the launching of the direct attack on Fedot at the end. They're associated with his position as a king and justify the Quest structures condensing to Transformation structures. When they do, they reveal that his power, rather than flowing along Creation Myth structure lines transgresses against the natural order.

When linking this to the fact that the overarching story is resolved by the people's request that Fedot become their new king, we can connect the end with the beginning and find an implied unity that flows through the entire story. The people's appearance at the end points to a triple transgression embodied by the person of the king: firstly, the stated problem of his not being married and his transgression towards Fedot's wife, resolved by Fedot ascending the throne with his wife as consort; secondly, a transgression against his subjects relating to the way in which he treats Fedot and his steward, resolved by Fedot having no need to abuse or mistreat his staff, and by his record of positive regard towards Shmat Razum; and lastly, the king's transgression against nature relating to hunting and view of land use which unfolds gradually through the story and unleashes the final salvo which backfires on him and leads to his death, resolved by Fedot's creation of a magical garden which heralds the return of his wife, symbolising harmony.

The wife's story line raises unanswered questions: Why does she appear? Why does she accept Fedot's ungrateful remark? Why is she economical with the truth at the end? Where does she go when she transforms into a bird to escape from the king? If she can transform into a bird herself, why does she need Fedot to facilitate her transform at the beginning?

Fedot's wife

Fedot's wife is an intriguing character. At first glance, her role seems to be that of Fedot's friend/helper. She marries him, helps him practically and magically; she and her family are instrumental in helping Fedot fulfil the 'impossible' quests set for him by the king. Able to evade the king's advances, she returns to Fedot when he completes his second quest, and is elevated to the rank of queen at the end. But where does she come from? Why does she so confound Baba Yaga? And why does she appear in the first place?

The initial sequence in her story line is interpreted as a Variation 1 pattern, composed of an initial Transformation structure (the wound, which comes out of nowhere for her, being an excess of evil).

W1a $\Box \urcorner [(\leftarrow\rightarrow)((\leftarrow\rightarrow)(\leftarrow\rightarrow\leftarrow\rightarrow\leftarrow\rightarrow)(\leftarrow\rightarrow))]$

1, 7–17: A bird is injured by a shot to her wing; when picked up by the hunter who shot her, she instructs him to take her home, and follow her instructions to gain a reward, which he does. She transforms into a beautiful woman, reveals she is his 'God-given wife' and they marry.

However, this could be just a problem for her, one she may well have foreseen and invited (although this isn't stated in the narrative), and the marriage could be the Transformation. I wondered about the W1 sequence following a Variation 2 pattern, with the wound as the initial problem:

W1b $\Box\neg[(((\leftarrow\rightarrow\leftarrow\rightarrow(\leftarrow\rightarrow)^3))(\leftarrow\rightarrow))]$

The Transformation structure is linked to an excess of good or evil. Fedot's capture of the bird is positive, but not excessively so. For the bird, it's excessively evil. The event's swiftness and its magical threshold quality indicate a Transformation structure. I feel, therefore, that the sequence fits a Call and Response Variation 1 pattern, condensing to:

W1 $\Box\neg[(\leftarrow\rightarrow)((\leftarrow\rightarrow)(\leftarrow\rightarrow)^3(\leftarrow\rightarrow))]$

However, the $((\leftarrow\rightarrow)^3(\leftarrow\rightarrow))$ sequence (spanning 12–17) does have the quality of a nested Call and Response Variation 2 structure.

W2 $\Box\neg[(\leftarrow\rightarrow)((\leftarrow\rightarrow)(\leftarrow\rightarrow)^3(\leftarrow\rightarrow))]$
$[((\leftarrow\rightarrow)(((\leftarrow\rightarrow)(\leftarrow\rightarrow)(\leftarrow\rightarrow))((\leftarrow\rightarrow)(\leftarrow\rightarrow\leftarrow\rightarrow\leftarrow\rightarrow)))(\leftarrow\rightarrow))]$
$\Box\neg[(\leftarrow\rightarrow)((\leftarrow\rightarrow)(\leftarrow\rightarrow)^3(\leftarrow\rightarrow))]$
$[((\leftarrow\rightarrow)(((\leftarrow\rightarrow)^3)^2)(\leftarrow\rightarrow))]$

18–31: When Fedot finds hunting tiring and unrewarding financially, she sends him on several quests to source supplies which she uses to conjure up a carpet through the use of magic and sends him to market giving him instructions on how to sell it, which he does successfully, enabling them to live more comfortably.

The W2 sequence starts off with the problem of how hard Fedot has to work for relatively little reward and the formulation of a plan to deal with this. A Quest structure 'problem/journey' pair unfolds:

a. $[((\leftarrow\rightarrow)(((\leftarrow\rightarrow)(\leftarrow\rightarrow)(\leftarrow\rightarrow))((\leftarrow\rightarrow)((\leftarrow\rightarrow)(\leftarrow\rightarrow\leftarrow\rightarrow\leftarrow\rightarrow)))(\leftarrow\rightarrow))]$

In an extended 'friend/helper' section in the overarching Quest structure, Fedot acts as one 'friend/helper' by gathering the materials his wife needs to create the carpet. Once the materials are gathered, a new problem arises, which is that of the need to create something using them. The sequence loops back, with the magical helpers acting, in their turn, as 'friends/helpers'.

Parts 19–24 in the wife's story line expand to three Quest structures:

b1. $[((\leftarrow\rightarrow)(((\leftarrow\rightarrow)(\leftarrow\rightarrow)(\leftarrow\rightarrow))((\leftarrow\rightarrow)(\leftarrow\rightarrow\leftarrow\rightarrow\leftarrow\rightarrow)))(\leftarrow\rightarrow))]$

The exchange with the magical helpers (24–27), which involves a clear threshold crossing, expands to a Call and Response Variation 1 structure:

b2. $[((\leftarrow\rightarrow)(((\leftarrow\rightarrow)(\leftarrow\rightarrow)(\leftarrow\rightarrow))((\leftarrow\rightarrow)(\leftarrow\rightarrow\leftarrow\rightarrow\leftarrow\rightarrow)))(\leftarrow\rightarrow))]$

When Fedot goes to market, sells the carpet, and returns with the funds (a nested structure extends through his story line here), a final 'meeting with enemy/hindrance' sequence in the wife's Quest structure is completed; their standard of living improves:

c. $[((\leftarrow\rightarrow)((\leftarrow\rightarrow)(\leftarrow\rightarrow)(\leftarrow\rightarrow))((\leftarrow\rightarrow)(\leftarrow\rightarrow\leftarrow\rightarrow\leftarrow\rightarrow)))((\leftarrow\rightarrow))]$

Interestingly, the nesting pattern seems to be specific to the wife's story line.

W3 $\Box\urcorner[((\leftarrow\rightarrow)((\leftarrow\rightarrow)(\leftarrow\rightarrow)^3(\leftarrow\rightarrow))]$
  $[((\leftarrow\rightarrow)((\leftarrow\rightarrow)(\leftarrow\rightarrow)(\leftarrow\rightarrow))((\leftarrow\rightarrow)(\leftarrow\rightarrow\leftarrow\rightarrow\leftarrow\rightarrow)))(\leftarrow\rightarrow))]$
  $[(\leftarrow\rightarrow)\leftarrow\rightleftharpoons(\leftarrow\rightarrow)\leftarrow\rightleftharpoons[\leftarrow\rightarrow\leftarrow\rightarrow\leftarrow\rightarrow]$
  $\Box\urcorner[((\leftarrow\rightarrow)((\leftarrow\rightarrow)(\leftarrow\rightarrow)^3(\leftarrow\rightarrow))]$
  $[((\leftarrow\rightarrow)((\leftarrow\rightarrow)(\leftarrow\rightarrow)(\leftarrow\rightarrow))((\leftarrow\rightarrow)(\leftarrow\rightarrow\leftarrow\rightarrow\leftarrow\rightarrow)))(\leftarrow\rightarrow))]$
  $[(\leftarrow\rightleftharpoons)^2[\leftarrow\rightarrow]^3$

37, 41, 51–53: She encounters the steward who leaves her, lovestruck; she encounters the king who also leaves her, lovestruck. When Fedot tells her the king has sent him on an 'impossible' quest, she helps him find a way to make the impossible possible through magical means.

The W3 sequence features two Trickster-type openings (both relating to unresolved Trickster Awe steps in the steward's and the king's story lines). In condensed form, these are surrounded with an extra set of brackets. A nested Quest structure follows for the wife in her capacity as Fedot's friend/helper.

W4 $\Box\neg[(\leftarrow\rightarrow)((\leftarrow\rightarrow)(\leftarrow\rightarrow)^3(\leftarrow\rightarrow))]$
$[((\leftarrow\rightarrow)((\leftarrow\rightarrow)(\leftarrow\rightarrow)(\leftarrow\rightarrow))((\leftarrow\rightarrow)(\leftarrow\rightarrow\leftarrow\rightarrow\leftarrow\rightarrow)))(\leftarrow\rightarrow))]$
$[(\leftarrow\rightleftharpoons)^2(\leftarrow\rightarrow)^3((\leftarrow\rightarrow\leftarrow\rightleftharpoons((\leftarrow\rightarrow\leftarrow\rightarrow\leftarrow\rightarrow)(\leftarrow\rightarrow)(\leftarrow\rightarrow)))$
$\Box\neg[(\leftarrow\rightarrow)((\leftarrow\rightarrow)(\leftarrow\rightarrow)^3(\leftarrow\rightarrow))]$
$[((\leftarrow\rightarrow)((\leftarrow\rightarrow)(\leftarrow\rightarrow)(\leftarrow\rightarrow))((\leftarrow\rightarrow)(\leftarrow\rightarrow\leftarrow\rightarrow\leftarrow\rightarrow)))(\leftarrow\rightarrow))]$
$[(\leftarrow\rightleftharpoons)^2(\leftarrow\rightarrow)^3((\leftarrow\rightleftharpoons(\leftarrow\rightarrow)^3)$

66–74: Fedot tells her that the king has sent him on another 'impossible' quest – this one even more demanding than the first and blames his fate on her beauty. She seeks help from her magical helpers, but they're unable to help. She tells Fedot to secure money from the king. She gives him two magical gifts and sends him on his way.

The W4 sequence contains a third Trickster Awe step. Previously, the two steps in W3 were intersections with the steward's and the king's story lines. This time, the intersection is with the king's story line via Fedot's. This hints at an overarching Call and Response Variation 2 structure which is unfolding. We are, however, left with a question: Why does she accept the ungrateful remark Fedot makes to her so readily when he tells her about the king's second quest?

W5 $\Box\neg[(\leftarrow\rightarrow)((\leftarrow\rightarrow)(\leftarrow\rightarrow)^3(\leftarrow\rightarrow))]$
$[((\leftarrow\rightarrow)((\leftarrow\rightarrow)(\leftarrow\rightarrow)(\leftarrow\rightarrow))((\leftarrow\rightarrow)(\leftarrow\rightarrow\leftarrow\rightarrow\leftarrow\rightarrow)))(\leftarrow\rightarrow))]$
$[(\leftarrow\rightleftharpoons)^2(\leftarrow\rightarrow)^3((\leftarrow\rightleftharpoons((\leftarrow\rightarrow)^3)$
$((\leftarrow\rightarrow\leftarrow\rightleftharpoons\leftarrow\rightleftharpoons)((\leftarrow\rightleftharpoons)(\leftarrow\rightarrow\leftarrow\rightarrow\leftarrow\rightleftharpoons))$
$\Box\neg[(\leftarrow\rightarrow)((\leftarrow\rightarrow)(\leftarrow\rightarrow)^3(\leftarrow\rightarrow))]$
$[((\leftarrow\rightarrow)((\leftarrow\rightarrow)(\leftarrow\rightarrow)(\leftarrow\rightarrow))((\leftarrow\rightarrow)(\leftarrow\rightarrow\leftarrow\rightarrow\leftarrow\rightarrow)))(\leftarrow\rightarrow))]$
$[(\leftarrow\rightleftharpoons)^2(\leftarrow\rightarrow)^3((\leftarrow\rightleftharpoons(\leftarrow\rightarrow)^3)((\leftarrow\rightleftharpoons)^4$

78–82: She's brought to the king by the steward and is proposed to by the king. When she rejects his proposal, she's threatened by him. In response, she transforms into her bird form and flies away.

The W5 sequence contains further Trickster Awe steps for the wife, in a Trickster Variation structure followed by a Trickster Variation-type sequence resolved by a sequence underpinned by a Revelation structure. Again, a large-scale variation on a Call and Response structure with embedded Trickster-type steps in it.

W6 $\square\neg[(\leftarrow\rightarrow)((\leftarrow\rightarrow)(\leftarrow\rightarrow)^3(\leftarrow\rightarrow))]$
$[((\leftarrow\rightarrow)((\leftarrow\rightarrow)(\leftarrow\rightarrow)(\leftarrow\rightarrow))((\leftarrow\rightarrow)(\leftarrow\rightarrow\leftarrow\rightarrow\leftarrow\rightarrow)))(\leftarrow\rightarrow))]$
$[(\leftarrow\rightleftharpoons)^2(\leftarrow\rightarrow)^3((\leftarrow\rightleftharpoons(\leftarrow\rightarrow)^3)((\leftarrow\rightleftharpoons)^4(\leftarrow\rightarrow)(\leftarrow\blacksquare))(\leftarrow\rightarrow)]\neg\square$

152–168: She flies back to Fedot, who has returned and created a magical garden around the magical castle he suggested Shmat Razum build; she transforms. They exchange stories. She's made queen after the king's defeat and after the people ask Fedot to be their king.

In the final sequence in this analysis of the wife's story line, part 153 provides a Transformational Twist which balances out the Trickster Awe steps where the wife's and the king's story lines intersect (at 80–82) and the Trickster Awe step in the intersection of the wife's and Fedot's story lines (at 68).

When Fedot's wife returns to him, she spins a story, but her story line doesn't follow a Voyage and Return structure. While she may have been forced into her transformation, she still has the power to transform and fly away. She still has agency here.

So why does she depend on Fedot's intervention to transform in the beginning given that she can do so herself when she flees the king and when she returns to Fedot? And why, as noted in the table (at 153), is she economical with the truth with regards to how long she has been 'flying in forests and groves as a blue dove'?

Where does she go to when she escapes from the king?

Why does she appear as a bird in the first place?

Despite the presence of several nested Call and Response Variation 2 structures in the opening, the predominant structure in the wife's story line seems to be a Call and Response Variation 1 structure; that of Fedot's, a Call and Response Variation 2 structure – something which we'll return to shortly. For now, it's time to look at the steward's story line.

The steward

As noted above, the steward's story line peters out disappointingly in the narrative. However, when working through the analysis of his story line, I noticed something which suggested a reading that reveals a possible underlying subtext as a result of engaging with the methodology, perfectly supported by the narrative. The insight is revealed at the end of this analysis of the steward's story line.

S1 $\Box\neg[((\leftarrow\rightarrow)\leftarrow\rightleftharpoons\leftarrow\rightleftharpoons))$
$\Box\neg[((\leftarrow\rightleftharpoons)^2)$

1, 30–31: The steward, passing by the market, notices a crowd. He stops to investigate and ends up buying a magnificent carpet which he finds out is made by Fedot's wife.

The S1 sequence opens with a Trickster Variation structure and has the feel of a final Transformation linked to a state of an excess of good in the steward's acquisition of the magical carpet.

S2 $\Box\neg[((\leftarrow\rightleftharpoons)^2)[((\leftarrow\rightarrow)\leftarrow\rightarrow((\leftarrow\rightarrow)\leftarrow\rightleftharpoons\leftarrow\rightleftharpoons))]$
$\Box\neg[((\leftarrow\rightleftharpoons)^2)[((\leftarrow\rightarrow)^2(\leftarrow\rightleftharpoons)^2)]$

32–35: The steward shows the king the carpet and ends up selling it to him for a profit, determining to order a better one for himself.

In the S2 sequence, we have a Trickster Variation structure which is resolved by a nested Trickster structure.

S3 $\Box\neg[((\leftarrow\rightleftharpoons)^2)[((\leftarrow\rightarrow)^2(\leftarrow\rightleftharpoons)^2)$
$[((\leftarrow\rightarrow)\leftarrow\rightleftharpoons(\leftarrow\rightarrow\leftarrow\rightleftharpoons(\leftarrow\rightleftharpoons)))(\leftarrow\rightarrow)]]]$
$\Box\neg[((\leftarrow\rightleftharpoons)^2)[((\leftarrow\rightarrow)^2(\leftarrow\rightleftharpoons)^2)[((\leftarrow\rightleftharpoons)^3)(\leftarrow\rightarrow)]]]$

36–43: The steward visits Fedot's house, sees his wife and is completely lovestruck by her. He tells the king about her and the next thing he knows, the king orders him, on pain of death, to devise a plan so that Fedot can be done away with in order for the king to marry Fedot's widow.

In the S3 sequence, we reach the close of an overarching structure that's been unfolding in the steward's story line. Another Trickster Variation structure provides the third of the series, followed by a

Transformation structure. Both of the Transformation structures are tragic for the steward; both are indirectly linked to Fedot's wife – firstly through the carpet; secondly through the king's infatuation with her.

S4 $\Box\neg[((\leftarrow\rightleftharpoons)^2)(\leftarrow\rightarrow)[((\leftarrow\rightarrow)^2(\leftarrow\rightleftharpoons)^2)[((\leftarrow\rightleftharpoons)^3)]]][(\leftarrow\rightarrow\leftarrow\rightarrow\leftarrow\rightarrow)$

      $\Box\neg[((\leftarrow\rightleftharpoons)^2)(\leftarrow\rightarrow)[((\leftarrow\rightarrow)^2(\leftarrow\rightleftharpoons)^2)[((\leftarrow\rightleftharpoons)^3)]]][(\leftarrow\rightarrow)^3$

44–47: The steward is helped by Baba Yaga and tells the king how to do away with Fedot.

Can this Quest structure reduce to a Transformation structure? It makes one wonder about the scribing of S2 in its condensed form. There's a strong feeling of a triple variation on a Call and Response Variation 2 structure, with three *veni, vidi, vici* sequences comprising Trickster Variation plus Transformation structures leading to a final Transformation structure (an excess of evil, in the form of Baba Yaga, balancing out the excess of good, in the form of the wife – in relative terms) up to this point. The final structure acts as a hinge point, serving as a culmination for both and potentially a launching point for the next sequence.

S5 $\Box\neg[((\leftarrow\rightleftharpoons)^2)[((\leftarrow\rightarrow)^2(\leftarrow\rightleftharpoons)^2)[((\leftarrow\rightleftharpoons)^3)]][(\leftarrow\rightarrow)]]][(\leftarrow\rightarrow)^3$

      $[(\leftarrow\rightarrow(\leftarrow\rightarrow\leftarrow\rightarrow\leftarrow\rightarrow)$

      $\Box\neg[((\leftarrow\rightleftharpoons)^2)[((\leftarrow\rightarrow)^2(\leftarrow\rightleftharpoons)^2)[((\leftarrow\rightleftharpoons)^3)]][(\leftarrow\rightarrow)]]][(\leftarrow\rightarrow)^3$

      $[(\leftarrow\rightarrow(\leftarrow\rightarrow)^3$

60–64: The steward, whose first plan failed, is once more summoned by the king and asked to devise a better plan on pain of death. Once more, he delivers a plan devised by Baba Yaga, who acts as his friend/helper.

The S5 sequence starts with a pair of steps indicating a problem and a journey. Expanded, it covers the summons by the king, the steward's arrival in answer to the summons, and his departure to fulfil the king's request to find a plan to get rid of Fedot that actually works. The central part involves his quest to find a second plan. In this, Baba Yaga acts as his friend/helper. His return with the plan completes the tripartite structure.

I've left the initial pair, as it provides a mirror to the hinge pair which appears at the end of the S3 sequence, with the two quests involving Baba Yaga seeming to form the first two of a triple sequence. This, as we see from the S6 sequence below, is left unresolved.

S6 $\Box\neg[((\leftarrow\rightleftharpoons)^2)[((\leftarrow\rightarrow)^2(\leftarrow\rightleftharpoons)^2)[((\leftarrow\rightleftharpoons)^3)(\leftarrow\rightarrow)]]][(\leftarrow\rightarrow)^3$
$[(\leftarrow\rightarrow(\leftarrow\rightarrow)^3[(\leftarrow\rightarrow(\leftarrow\rightarrow)\neg\Box$

76–78, 168: The steward is tasked by the king to bring Fedot's wife to the palace, which he does.

The S6 sequence definitely has a tragic feel to it. Once more, the steward acts in the king's interests and against his own. While he comes into the presence of Fedot's wife, he does so having been brought into the king's confidence, and he brings the 'clever woman' into the king's presence, perhaps intuiting that she'll have the power to outwit the king – but this is just speculation. The narrative is left open-ended and his story line ends enigmatically. The mirrored parallelism in the first and second pairs of bracketed sections is interesting to note. The lack of parallelism across the entirety of the remaining part of the steward's story line is significant – what if the triple Trickster-type steps had been mirrored after the hinge point that occurs directly after them? At first glance, the fact that they're not mirrored might be seen to reflect significantly on the cultural ethos – this is no early modern master-servant *commedia dell'arte*-inspired story. This comes from a tsarist epoch of domination and repression. The weakness in the steward's character serves to highlight the king's autocratic stance and it's in the king's story line and in Fedot's that the Trickster-type steps are found, again pointing to an underlying philosophical question about the true nature of kingship. However, we know from experience that stories which follow Trickster structures often appear in cultures of repression and/or oppression, and often do so in a covert manner. As parallelism has featured in other characters' story lines, it's worth exploring this further. We've already noted that the steward acknowledges that Fedot's wife is a 'clever woman'. Is it beyond the bounds of reason to imagine the sequence which unfolds in the steward's story line at S6 to be a Trickster structure? Much depends on the conversation he has with the bird-wife on the way. The methodology thus becomes a tool which allows deeper insight into individual characters' motivations, and encourages closer reading of the narrative, which in this case, is left open-endedly bivalent – perhaps deliberately so.

Shmat Razum

Shmat Razum's story line also peters out at the end, and it isn't clear how his story line and Fedot's continue from there. There's a sense that something magical happens in their flight over the ocean, bringing out innate qualities in Fedot which, despite his tenacity and perseverance in his attempt to fulfil the king's quest, only surface when he leaves the earth and is whisked through the air. His story line unfolds as follows:

SR1 $\square\urcorner[(\leftarrow\rightarrow)(\leftarrow\rightarrow)(\leftarrow\rightarrow)(\leftarrow\rightleftharpoons\leftarrow\rightleftharpoons)]$
$\square\urcorner[(\leftarrow\rightarrow)^3(\leftarrow\rightleftharpoons)^2]$

1, 106–112: Shmat Razum is summoned by two men who order him to serve them food and drink, then clear up. When the men leave, Fedot (who has observed what has happened from his hiding place) summons him, orders him to serve him food and drink, invites him to dine with him, surprising Shmat Razum, who agrees to leave the men and serve Fedot instead.

While the initial pair can be seen to be a compressed Quest structure, I see it more as a nested Transformation structure. While Shmat Razum acts as the merchants' friend/helper the appearance and disappearance of the furnishings and meal for the merchants has all of the qualities of the threshold crossing associated with the Transformation structure. Interestingly, the characters map to different dimensions of being. Is there an imbalance in the 'supernatural' dimension related to how Shmat Razum feels he's being treated by the two merchants? Does this link to Fedot's appearance (via an extended Call and Response structure) in a threshold crossing from Fedot's dimension to Shmat Razum's that takes on a Revelation structure at 108–112?

SR2 $\square\neg[(\leftarrow\rightarrow)^3(\leftarrow\rightleftharpoons)^2][((\leftarrow\rightarrow)(\leftarrow\rightarrow)(\leftarrow\rightarrow))(\leftarrow\rightarrow)]$
$\square\neg[(\leftarrow\rightarrow)^3(\leftarrow\rightleftharpoons)^2][(\leftarrow\rightarrow)^3(\leftarrow\rightarrow)]$

113–119: He clears up, responds to Fedot's call and accompanies him back to his mother-in-law's castle, where Fedot has him entertain the family and demonstrate his powers.

In SR2, Shmat Razum's story line follows a Call and Response-type Variation 2 structure. However, there are two Revelation sequences within this which differ in quality. While Shmat Razum's story line intersects with Fedot's via a Trickster Variation-type structure, it intersects with the merchants' via a Trickster structure, with a back story implied—but not revealed—by the narrative. They have a thirty-year history. What's the story there? What incentive might Shmat Razum have for leaving them so readily? It makes one wonder—how should magical helpers be treated? Is there a rule book?

It's interesting to trace the qualities of a Revelation structure unfolding in the larger-scale elements here, as shown by the square brackets (which indicates an unfolding Call and Response-type Variation 2 structure). If SR1 is the *veni* sequence, then seeing SR2 as the *vidi* sequence makes complete sense – it's the first time Fedot has drawn on Shmat Razum's powers in the presence of others, and the first time that others have seen the power that Shmat Razum puts at Fedot's service; the power that Fedot, in turn, puts at the service of his in-laws, and of the frog, who has helped him on his quest.

Thus, the SR2 sequence sheds light on the SR1 sequence. These two sequences can be viewed through the lens of the methodology as part of a larger unfolding Revelation sequence. This larger sequence can then be seen to link to Fedot's sense of wonder, and to his growing realisation of the potential power that Shmat Razum can afford him. It's a powerful driver and provides yet another piece of evidence which links Shmat Razum and Fedot's intuitive powers that, up to now, have lurked below the threshold of his awareness, but are about to surface, as we're will see as the next (*vici*) section of Shmat Razum's story line unfolds.

SR3 $\square\neg[(\leftarrow\rightarrow)^3(\leftarrow\rightleftharpoons)^2][(\leftarrow\rightarrow)^3(\leftarrow\rightarrow)^3][(\leftarrow\rightarrow((\leftarrow\rightarrow)\leftarrow\rightarrow\rightleftharpoons$
$((\leftarrow\rightarrow)\leftarrow\rightleftharpoons((\leftarrow\rightarrow)\leftarrow\rightleftharpoons((\leftarrow\rightarrow)(\leftarrow\rightarrow)(\leftarrow\rightarrow))(\leftarrow\rightarrow)\leftarrow\rightleftharpoons)))\leftarrow\rightarrow)]$
$\square\neg[(\leftarrow\rightarrow)^3(\leftarrow\rightleftharpoons)^2][(\leftarrow\rightarrow)^3(\leftarrow\rightarrow)^3]$
$[(\leftarrow\rightarrow(\leftarrow\rightleftharpoons(\leftarrow\rightleftharpoons)^2((\leftarrow\rightarrow)^3\leftarrow\rightleftharpoons)\leftarrow\rightarrow)]$

121–148: Shmat Razum carries Fedot over the ocean, then creates a 'golden arbor' where Fedot can rest and 'acquire a fortune' by trading Shmat Razum for three magical items. When merchant ships appear, he provides a feast for them. After the deal is struck, he lets the merchants believe he'll serve them 'in faith and in truth'. He serves a meal for them but then abandons them and returns to Fedot, leaving them without the goods they had traded, without his services and (by dematerialising the island) without any clear way of seeking restitution or justice. At Fedot's request, Shmat Razum transports him almost instantaneously back to his homeland.

There are two key elements in this section. First, the stand-alone $(\leftarrow\rightarrow)$ section (121–123) which forms an important symbolic hinge. It's the sequence in which Shmat Razum carries Fedot across the sea at top speed, losing his hat as a result. Second, an unfolding complex nested Trickster-type sequence with respect to the band of passing merchants which condenses to a simple 'meeting with friend/helper' pair, in which Shmat Razum acts as 'friend/helper' to Fedot (124–142). The sequence spanning 121–142 forms a Call and Response-type Variation 1 structure for him. As mentioned previously, Fedot's increasing agency in becoming master of his own fate and accepting control of the magical and metaphysical elements he's been handed is noteworthy. Within this sequence, there are two nested triple series of structures. The Quest structures at 137–142 condense to a single sequence, and occur as a stand-alone unit within the larger triple Trickster-type structure which frames them (as indicated by the bold brackets and increasingly darker shading added in to the sequence). This leads to a final Quest structure (which can possibly be taken to be a Transformation structure, given the swift and impetuous quality of the event) in which Shmat Razum carries Fedot back to his homeland (144–148). This sequence follows a Call and Response-type Variation 2 structure and forms a *vici* sequence in the larger overarching unfolding structure which goes across SR1–3, although there's more to come. Reflecting on what this might mean sheds light on the fact that Fedot is now coming into his own. He's embracing his link with Shmat Razum and taking full advantage of it. One might interpret his tricksterish approach towards the merchants either as fair game or as unjust behaviour. To what extent are magic and duplicity essential qualities of a true ruler? There's no clear answer in the narrative, which isn't a moralised telling, nor even in the story, which leaves the question open-ended.

SR4 $\square\urcorner[(\leftarrow\rightarrow)^3(\leftarrow\rightleftharpoons)^2][(\leftarrow\rightarrow)^3(\leftarrow\rightarrow)^3]$
$[(\leftarrow\rightarrow((\leftarrow\rightleftharpoons((\leftarrow\rightleftharpoons)^2((\leftarrow\rightarrow)^3\leftarrow\rightleftharpoons)))\leftarrow\rightarrow)][(\leftarrow\rightarrow)]\urcorner\square$

150, 167–168: Shmat Razum builds a magnificent palace at Fedot's request.

This section of Shmat Razum's story line takes on added significance when seen as a structure which comes at the end of the overarching sequence of Call and Response-type structures, and showing that his entire story line through the narrative follows a Call and Response-type Variation 2 pattern. The final structure serves as a bridge between the magical world and the actual world in which the tsar exists, and provides (predictably) an excessive result – here, an excess of good in the form of the sumptuousness of the palace, which spurs the king to attack and leads to his demise and the subsequent elevation of Fedot to the position of king, with his wife at his side. The part Shmat Razum plays during their accession and reign is unclear; there is no clear end point to his story line, so the final mark is indicated in grey.

Once more, the methodology serves to highlight hidden relationships between Shmat Razum and Fedot. It begs that we reflect, once again (as in the case of Fedot's wife, the other main magical character in the story), on the inciting incident, or initial condition which gives rise to the counterbalancing act at the end. By definition, with the appearance of a supernatural character with the power to do good (Shmat Razum), we expect the inciting incident to be one of an excess of evil. Shmat Razum, however, is capable of doing both good and evil. He has no hesitation in abandoning the merchants he has served for thirty years; he has no compunction in

coming up with the idea of tricking the merchants out of their goods
to help Fedot on his quest. Perhaps this points to an initial situation
which is morally ambiguous, which matches his use of trickery in
the form of evil masquerading as good to achieve evil ends. Viewing
the king's acts and the related appearance of both the bird-wife
in this light and in terms of the appearance of Shmat Razum is a
potentially productive exercise and will be explored shortly.

The final story line to explore before that, however, is that of the
merchants who are tricked by Shmat Razum.

The merchants

While we've noted that the merchants' story line follows a tripartite
structure, the precise structure of this is yet to be analysed. Is it a
standard Trickster-type structure? What can it tell us about their
characters?

M1 $\Box\urcorner[((\leftarrow\rightarrow)\leftarrow\rightleftharpoons(\leftarrow\rightarrow)\leftarrow\rightleftharpoons(\leftarrow\rightarrow)\leftarrow\rightleftharpoons((\leftarrow\rightarrow)\leftarrow\rightleftharpoons(\leftarrow\rightarrow)\leftarrow\rightleftharpoons))]$
    $\Box\urcorner[(\leftarrow\rightleftharpoons)^3(\leftarrow\rightleftharpoons)^2]$

> 1, 126–136: The merchants see an island and recognise it as 'a marvel'. They
> land, are welcomed by Fedot and regaled magically by Shmat Razum. They
> propose to trade one of three magical items they carry for him, but Fedot will only
> exchange Shmat Razum for all three. The merchants agree and the exchange is
> made. When they ask Shmat Razum whether he will serve them 'in faith and in
> truth', he leads to believe he will.

Here, three Trickster Variation structures are initiated, but they're
resolved with a conventional Trickster structure. An interesting
result of isolating the merchants' story line is that while the island
appears out of Shmat Razum's wish to trick the merchants, he simply
acts as Fedot's friend/helper. The initial three Trickster Variation
structure sequences hinge mainly on intersections between the
merchants' story line and Fedot's, while the Trickster structure
involves a direct intersection between the merchants' story line and
Shmat Razum's. Again, the methodology brings this distinction to
the fore very clearly and provides a way of distinguishing these
subtle differences in how the characters' story lines intersect.

M2 $\square\neg[(\leftarrow\rightleftharpoons)^3(\leftarrow\rightleftharpoons)^2][((\leftarrow\rightarrow)(\leftarrow\rightarrow)(\leftarrow\rightarrow\leftarrow\rightleftharpoons\leftarrow\rightleftharpoons)]\neg\square$
   $\square\neg[(\leftarrow\rightleftharpoons)^3(\leftarrow\rightleftharpoons)^2][((\leftarrow\rightarrow)^2(\leftarrow\rightleftharpoons)^2)]\neg\square$

137–147, 168: The merchants return to their ship with Shmat Razum. They order him to treat their crews to food and drink, which he does. They get drunk and fall asleep. When they wake up, they call on Shmat Razum to provide them with more drink, but 'no one answered, no one served them'. They come to terms with the fact that he has abandoned them, they've lost their magical items, and the island has disappeared, so they hoist sails and leave.

In M2, there's a tripartite sequence formed by three Quest structures, the first two (137–140) standard; the third (145), tragic. These are followed by what is, for them, a tragic Trickster structure (146–147). Once again, the Trickster structure involves an intersection between Shmat Razum's story line and the merchants'. It starts to unfold, at the level of story structure, when Shmat Razum abandons them. This happens at some point between the time when they fall into a drunken stupor and when they wake up and realise he's abandoned them. Their realisation of this fact (and of their losses) which forms the Transformational Twist is what gives this final Trickster structure in their story line its tragic quality.

The merchants' story line has some hidden symmetry in it. The two triple Trickster Variation/Quest structure sequences can both be seen to follow a Call and Response-type Variation 2 structure, both resolving in final Trickster structures. The two Trickster structures—one standard, one tragic—balance each other out. Whether or not the merchants' paths ever cross Fedot's again isn't stated in the narrative. It's tempting to see them reappearing in the story of Tsar Saltan, and this story being latticed with that one, but this is pure conjecture.[17]

12. Analyse the overarching structure of the entire story based on the dominant pattern which results using the 18 story structures currently identified as a guide.

In looking at the story as whole, subdivided into four sections outlined as follows, some interesting parallels are revealed.

Section 1: 1–17
From the set-up to Fedot's marriage

Wife:	Fedot:
Call and Response Variation 1	Call and Response Variation 2
Excess of evil at the beginning	*Excess of good at the end*
(king's excesses)	*(marriage)*

Section 2: 18–31
From the point at which Fedot is 'overworked and underpaid' to the transformation of his financial state the sale of the magical carpet his wife made to the royal steward, the deal being negotiated by him following her advice

Wife:	Fedot:
Call and Response Variation 1	Call and Response Variation 2
Excess of evil at the beginning	*Excess of good at the end*
(lots of work, little money)	*(sale of carpet - hinge leading to king)*

The parallelism is based on shared Call and Response structures. As outlined in chapter 11, an excess of evil typically results in the appearance of a supernatural being that embodies goodness (angel, fairy godmother, etc.) and an excess of good in the appearance of a demonic character. Here, the common structures point to a connection between the characters, supporting a reading that sees the magical wife appearing in the form of a bird in response to the king's excesses.

The above sequence could therefore be reduced to a single condensed Transformation structure.

From there, another interesting parallelism emerges:

Section 3a: 32–164
From the meeting which leads to the king seeing the carpet to his demise in battle against Fedot's magical troops

Section 3b: 127–147
From the point which leads to the merchants spotting the magical island to their realisation that they've been tragically duped

King:	Merchants:
Trickster Variation x 2, Tragic Trickster	Trickster Variation x 2, Tragic Trickster

The second sequence (labelled 'Section 4' here) is nested within the larger overarching ('Section 3') sequence, but they match. Both lead to a gain for Fedot. But what initiates each of the sequences? The reason that the carpet is created goes back to Fedot's accepting his wife's offer to 'make them rich'. The island is created because Fedot accepts Shmat Razum's offer to make him a 'golden arbor' where he can 'rest … and acquire a fortune'. The appearance of the carpet leads to its sale which helps Fedot and his wife improve their lot; the appearance of the island leads to the trade which leaves Fedot in possession of the merchants' magical items. Both section 3a and section 3b reduce to a Revelation structure underpinning three sequential Trickster-type sequences; both sections end with tragic Trickster structures. The king is tricked out of his ability to defeat Fedot when his armies desert him and he loses his life; the merchants lose their items when Shmat Razum leaves them and dematerialises the island. Fedot, however, remains in possession of both magical forces and his life when he becomes king. This connection points to a subtle thread which links to the philosophical point of the true meaning of kingship and again points to the inciting incident of the king's excessively negative starting point which is implied throughout but not explicitly stated. It's not about material goods or positional power – although it raises questions about the use of force; ultimately, it's about wisdom, balance and harmony, and about the wise channelling of power which might just be true magic.

As noted above, the final elevation of Fedot and his wife to the status of king and queen balance out the initial imbalance of the old king's excesses, providing a final Transformation structure (at 165–167), forming **section 4**. Paired hinge points featuring magical events indicate key threshold crossings: the bird-wife's appearance and the marriage; the reason for the appearance of the carpet and its acquisition by the king; the merchants' loss of their magical items and Shmat Razum's return to Fedot; Fedot's elevation to kingship (through the aid of magic). Ultimately, the entire story can be reduced (rather dramatically) to the following:

$$\square\daleth[(\leftarrow\rightarrow)\leftarrow\rightleftharpoons)^3(\leftarrow\rightarrow)]\daleth\square$$

This final reduced scribed version of the story line shown above does look like a bunch of algebraic symbols that could stand for countless other stories, and other interpretations are, of course, possible. However, they'll arguably reduce to a similar pattern. If they don't, the interpretations will still shed light on the energetic flow of the story's underlying structure, as informed by the methodology. This is what happens when we condense a character's story line down to its basic 'bare bones' form and condense the story lines down to an overarching story structure through which we can classify a story. The algebraic version is ultimately based on and complements the narrative version. They are simply different ways of viewing the elements of the story. Neither version is a substitute for the other. Both are valid on their own terms. The reduction condenses the story, but it doesn't need to result in a paucity of insight. Rather, the contrary is the case, for the condensation allows us to see the underlying pattern the symbols fall into and compare it to one of the 18 story structures revealed through this methodology, each of which has its own particular quality. The ability to do this can shed light on the inner workings, dynamics, and energy of the story structure(s) to inform the telling and appreciation of the story and give us an insight into how it relates to the concerns of its time which gave rise to it and which it reflects. Moreover, it can happen (as it does in this case) that a story will reveal a variation on one of the story structures outlined in this methodology, or a novel composite structure, or even a hitherto unidentified structure which is not simply a variation on or a combination of the structures outlined so far, but sufficiently self-contained and distinctive enough to merit classification as a stand-alone structure in its own right.

In this case, the story line gravitates towards variations on the Call and Response structure. There's a Dynamic Revelation structure underpinning groups of three story structures with Trickster steps – either Trickster structures (which involve one character deliberately duping the other) or Trickster Variation structures (which involve a shift from 'Huh?!' to 'Ah!').

What does this condensation reveal? What can we learn from it?

Beyond what I've already mentioned, the essence of the Call and Response structure, is that it's a Threshold structure which connects two dimensions of being: the natural and the supernatural; the physical and the metaphysical; the actual and the real. Both appear on many levels – in our composition as human beings; in the social structures in which we operate; in the cosmic order which that reflects and of which it is a part. The Call and Response structure shows is that when a (binary) transgression against the natural order occurs in one dimension, it activates a (ternary) reactive and balancing response in the other. This dynamism is central to the unfolding of the story, and provides its justification.

We see this in the Transformation structures in the king's story line which relate to key elements – the excessive love of hunting, the plan to send Fedot on a quest to find the stag with the golden horns, the plan to get rid of Fedot and wed his wife, and the launch of the direct attack on Fedot at the end. He has positional power as a king. His word must be obeyed. It justifies us condensing the associated Quest structures to Transformation structures. And yet, this reveals that his power, rather than flowing along Creation Myth structure lines, transgresses against the natural order.

When linking this to the fact that the overarching story is resolved by the people's request that Fedot become their new king, we can connect the end with the beginning and find an implied unity that flows through the entire story.

The people's appearance at the end points to a triple transgression embodied by the person of the king: firstly, his stated problem of not being married and his transgression towards Fedot's wife, solved by Fedot ascending the throne with his wife as consort; secondly, a transgression against his subjects relating to the way in which he treats Fedot and his steward, solved by Fedot having no need to abuse or mistreat his staff, and by Fedot's record of positive regard towards Shmat Razum; and lastly, the king's transgression against nature relating to hunting and view of land use which unfolds gradually through the story and unleashes the final salvo which backfires on him and leads to his death, resolved by Fedot's creation of a magical garden which heralds the return of his wife, symbolising harmony.

13. Note any questions or variations that result from your analysis when compared to the 18 story structures currently identified.
Some characters' story lines raise unanswered questions:

- Why does the bird appear?
- Why does Fedot's wife accept his ungrateful remark?
- Why is she economical with the truth at the end?
- Where does she go when she transforms into a bird to escape from the king?
- If she can transform into a bird herself, why does she need Fedot to facilitate her transform at the beginning?
- And how come the king is unaware of Fedot's wife's magical powers? After all, the steward is told about them by Baba Yaga – does this point to a hidden Trickster structure in relation to how his story line intersects with the king's that should be taken into account?

This story is a complex extended story. The characters' composite story lines are formed of a number of story structures which can still be clearly identified and the Revelation structure can be traced through a variety of Quest and Trickster structure sequences. Nevertheless, there are no major variations, showing that the methodology is robust enough to handle such analyses. Moreover, it has the potential to reveal subtleties which can add insights into the deeper meaning of a story and further research in applying the methodology will add further insights to what it can bring to the study of complex stories. For instance, whether such variations are typical of a certain type of story, or region, or time frame.

There are potentially answers to these questions to be found when exploring other stories which have been linked to this one through motif-based classification.

The story is classified as an ATU 465 type tale in the Aarne-Thompson-Uther motif classification system (The Man persecuted because of his beautiful wife). Afanas'ev records four variants of the story, and gives eight versions across these. The story analysed here is listed as the first variant. In other versions, there are three quests involving the capture of a sheep with a golden head and a sow with golden bristles before the third and final quest. In the second, the hunter meets his wife by observing a bird laying aside her golden wings which he captures. She claims him as her husband, and tells her sisters (who were with her) to fly off and inform their mother. She builds a palace for their wedding, and tells him to go and apologise to the king for having done so. He's followed by a flock of magical birds which he offers to the king and asks him for his forgiveness. The king asks to meet his wife, falls in love, and commands his boyars to find a similar beauty. They're advised by a drunkard not to bother, but to get rid of Fedot by sending him on an impossible quest to find the stag with the golden horns. Fedot fulfils the quest with his wife's help. The cycle repeats: the king sends him on a second impossible quest to fetch a mare and 70 stallions that frolic in a forbidden meadow. Again, he fulfils the quest with his wife's help. When he's sent to find 'I know not what' by going 'I know not where', his wife gives him a ring which rolls in front of him and leads him to his mother-in-law's house. From there, the story unfolds as the first variant does.

In the third variant, a soldier called Tarabanov, returning from the wars, comes across an enchanted castle with no doorway. He climbs up the wall and enters via a balcony, eats, drinks, and falls asleep. Twelve swans fly in, strike the floor with their wings, remove them, and transform to beautiful young women; one of them suspects that a stranger has been there, but the others ignore her. Hers are the wings that Tarabanov captures, and only agrees to give them back if she'll be his wife; she agrees, gives him a hundred roubles and tells him to buy silk. He does, but spends ten kopecks on a pint of beer, which doesn't make her happy. She creates three carpets which are sold to a merchant who sells them to the king who wants to meet the woman who created them, falls in love, and is advised by one of his generals to send the soldier to the end of the world to look for the servant 'Saoura' who lives in his master's pocket. The wife gives the soldier a magical ring which guides him to a hut where he meets 'Saoura'. He observes him serving a meal, commands him to do the same, and orders him to serve him from then on. He brings 'Saoura' to the king, who's furious at his success. The general advises the king to send Tarabanov to the next world and bring back news of the king's dead father. The wife advises him to take the general with him, which he does and they set off, guided by the ring. They find the king's father bound and tormented by devils. Tarabanov asks the devils to release him. When they do, he tells them to bind up the general temporarily and torment him instead. The king's father gives Tarabanov a three-part message for his son: Say mass for me; don't mistreat the people; don't mistreat the armed forces. He gives Tarabanov a key as proof they've met. Tarabanov and the general return, the key and the scars on the general's body being proof they've accomplished their mission. The king recognises the key as one to a secret cabinet which his father always carried in his pocket and had been buried with him. He gives up trying to secure Tarabanov's wife, and order is restored.

In the last variant, a merchant's son is so incompetent at running the business after his father's death that the king stamps his forehead so everyone knows not to do business with him, but rather simply offer him food and drink out of charity. The young man takes to the road and finds an old woman who lives in a hut. She advises him to go to a big house which overlooks a lake. He finds it abandoned, but there's a table set with food which he helps himself to. That evening, 33 girls arrive. One of them suspects someone has broken in, but the others ignore her. When they're asleep, the young man siezes the girl's dress, which gives him power over her. Her sisters escape by transforming into birds. He agrees to give her back her dress on condition that she marry him. She agrees. She leads him to an underground cellar with chests of copper coins, silver coins, and gold and pearls. They take enough gold and pearls to establish themselves in the young man's homeland. The king asks to meet his wife and grants them right to settle and live their peacefully. In this version, it's the king's adviser, who envies the young man's success, who tells the king that the young man has been boasting that he can go 'I know not where and find I know not what'. The king calls the young man's bluff, and when he protests, he threatens that he'll deprive him of his wife unless he fulfils the quest. His wife gives him a towel and he sets off. He reaches Baba Yaga's hut. Baba Yaga recognises the towel as her niece's. She gives the young man a dog to guide him. He eventually reaches a town called 'Nothing' and enters a deserted palace there. That evening, a man 'as tall as a fingernail with a beard as long as an arm' enters and is waited on by an invisible servant called 'Nobody'. The invisible servant ends up in the young man's service. On the return journey, they meet a man with a magical club that can kill anyone – the club is exchanged for 'Nobody'; its previous owner is killed and they move on. Next, the young man acquires a magic musical instrument (a gusli) in exchange for 'Nobody'. Again, the club gets rid of the previous owner. The gusli enables the young man to raise a fleet of warships to attack the king but agrees to call off the attack if the king orders that his adviser have an arm and a leg amputated. This is done. Understandably, the adviser isn't too happy. He consults a witch who tells him to convince the king to send the young man 'beyond three times nine countries, into the three times tenth kingdom' to bring back a magic storytelling cat. He succeeds with the help of magical objects his wife supplies him with. The king challenges the storytelling cat to scare him; the cat attacks him. The young man agrees to call off the cat if the king orders that the adviser be buried alive. The king agrees. The young man, his wife, 'Nobody', and the cat move into the palace where they live out their days in peace.

There are over 70 Russian versions of the story known, 8 Ukrainian, and 7 Belarusian ones. Similar tales are found in Latvia, Bashkir, and Kazakhstan.[18] The ATU index contains variations recorded in Ireland, America (in Spanish and French), Turkey, India, and China. Marzolph & van Leeuwen note the presence of versions in Japan and China that date back to the 7th C CE.

From the variants, the steward's character is seen to have more depth; Baba Yaga, as the wife's aunt brings the question of balance between good and evil in both the immanent and metaphysical realms to the fore. Of particular interest is the specific advice given to the king from his deceased father in variant three which makes explicit the king's transgression against people, and office. Where the variant brings in a spiritual duty, the version we've looked at in depth here focuses on his duty towards preserving the natural order – a difference that may show the imposition of a Christian gloss on a pre-Christian version of the story.

The story can be linked to both the story of *Swan Lake* (from Russia) and the story of *The Children of Lir* (from Ireland). There are significant differences in events and relationships between characters, however. In the former, although the narratives can vary, it's fair to say that Siegfried's antagonistic relationship to Rothbart is very different to the subservient relationship that exists between Fedot and the king. Siegfried and Odette's story has a tragic ending, whereas Fedot and his wife triumph over the king.

The Irish story is very different – the swans can't be changed back for 900 years; when they do transform, it's not through an act of kindness enabling them to enjoy life, but from an act of defiance which brings their lives to an end. Despite the differences, the instinctive feeling of there being a link between these stories is confirmed by a structural analysis, for all three stories start and end with an extreme act of transgression (Transformation structure), unfold through a Trickster-type sequence underpinned by a Revelation structure and end with a final Transformation structure. The commonalities can be easily seen by an application of the methodology outlined here. Another story which follows this pattern is the story of *Kate Crackernuts*. The links here may well point to similarities in the dynamics of how the societies in which they were told and emerge from function – both in terms of revealing something about how we might view and tell the history of these periods, but also in terms of illuminating common aspects, thus potentially telling us something new about them and about how human beings come to terms with the social and cultural situations in which they find themselves, storying as they are storied.

There's also the potential of seeing this as part of a larger latticed oral corpus of stories, based on the clear allusion to the bird-wife's back story, her connection with Baba Yaga, and the potential hinge role that the merchants might play, linking their presence in this story to other stories.

Other

The illustration of the cave included in the body of the text emerges from the social setting it was composed in and adds a gloss to the story, but is part of the narrative presentation, and is secondary to the analysis of the story structure presented here.

NOTES

1   Aleksandr Afanas'ev, *Russian Fairy Tales,* translated by Norbert Guterman (New York: Pantheon Books, 1945), 504–520.

2   Note the 'unusual' complex structure here.

3   See chapter 11.

4   I feel that the magical servants' story line follows a Call and Response Variation 2 structure, with the final Transformation structure coming at the crossover point at which the magically created carpet is transferred from the intangible dimension of the spirit world to the tangible dimension of the world in which Fedot and his wife operate.

5   Although the merchants face a dilemma, I identify their story structure as a Trickster Variation structure. A Trickster Variation structure is closed, and a Dilemma structure open-ended. In this case, the merchants' dilemma isn't left for the story seekers to resolve; it's resolved within the story once the steward appears.

6   Charting the carpet's story line is an experience which may prove both interesting and fruitful.

7   See chapter 11.

8   There's no indication in the narrative as to why Fedot mentions her beauty – for all we know he has no idea of how the steward or the king feel about his wife, nor are we told how she took his remark, although her first reaction was to agree. She acknowledged that he/they faced a long task with an unknown outcome, but she was more knowledgeable about the journey, and more confident than he was, invoking prayer and sleep as friends/helpers (nested Quest) which gave her time to summon her magical helpers. We know from the narrative that Fedot went to sleep which means he didn't stay up all night worrying. To what extent his sleep was troubled or untroubled is unclear. All we know is that he slept. My interpretation is informed by the information presented in the narrative.

9   If he's merely making a statement of fact (which is how his wife seems to take it – at least on the surface, and there are a variety of interpretations possible here), then a Quest structure would unfold. I read Fedot's state of mind here as displaying some form of cognitive dissonance, hence this reading.

10   Part 73 is a nested Quest which is secondary to the unfolding of the main structure.

11   The bird-wife's gifts of the ball of string and handkerchief, although not scribed as independent characters here, seem to follow a Revelation structure – after they appear, the ball then vanishes (at least it isn't seen on the outside of the palace), and the handkerchief, when seen ushers in a turning point: appearance conquers any doubt regarding Fedot's identity and the whereabouts of his bird-wife.

12   While the loops in the mother-in-law's story line have an underlying Revelation structure to them, there's also a sense of two journeys (clockwise, then anticlockwise) round the Chinese Circular Structure here. In the first, the creatures are summoned but she's still 'divided' from the answer. The journey the giants facilitate is a 'separation' and the appearance of the frog a 're-integration'. In the second, they're no longer 'separated' from their home, and the solution to the frog's problem provided by the jug eliminates their 'division' from the task, allowing Fedot to 'emerge' into a new clockwise cycle marking the start of the next structure in his composite story line. The mother-in-law's story line is essentially an extension of the bird-wife's role as friend/helper to Fedot.

13   This step and step 153 potentially complete the cognitive dissonance in his 'insult' step at the start of his second quest for the king at step 49.

14   This shouldn't be confused with the coronation rite which marks the couple's change in status. This later, separate sequence of events would follow a Quest structure underpinned by a Revelation structure.

15   George Spencer-Brown, "An Introduction to Reductors," unpublished manuscript, December 1992, PDF file.

16   These are 124–134, 149–153, and 159–164.

17   Alexander Pushkin, *The Tale of Tsar Saltan,* translated by Louis Zellikoff, illustrated by Ivan Bilibin (Moscow, USSR: Progress Publishers, 1968).

18   Wikipedia, s.v. "Va je ne sais où, rapporte je ne sais quoi," last modified 3 March, 2021, 02:1, https://fr.wikipedia.org/wiki/Va_je_ne_sais_où,_rapporte_je_ne_sais_quoi.

APPENDIX 2

WAYS OF MAPPING STORY

Just as there have been attempts to visualise logical relationships, there have also been attempts to visualise the forms that stories and narratives follow. Back in the 19th Century, Gustav Freytag gave us a visualisation of the structure of Greek tragedy that has become known as 'Freytag's pyramid'.[1]

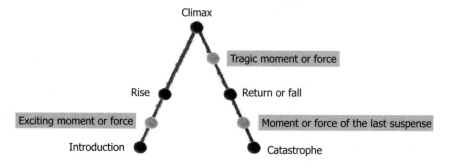

It's an interesting blend of static and dynamic elements, the four main elements he identified as 'Introduction', 'Climax', 'Return or fall' and 'Catastrophe' being the static 'landing points' of a tragedy; the other three all containing the word 'force' in them, as well as the word 'moment'. While 'moment' could be seen to imply a static point, it's primarily a point in time, rather than a point in space which is being described – the dynamic aspect here is primary. The relationship is intrinsic to the diagram which is built using points and lines.

In his book, *The Morphology of the Folktale*, the Russian narrative theorist Vladimir Propp proposed a system of assigning letters to 31 thematic 'functions' which he found in the folk tales he examined. While not every one of these functions was present in every folk tale, he found they always appeared in the same order. His system works, but it's relatively complex. The French anthropologist and structural analyst, Claude Lévi-Strauss later pointed out that Propp

had come up with a way of symbolising four basic variations on a
central theme which governed the structure of the archetype 'from
which all the wondertales have been derived, at least in Russia'.

By integrating all the typical formulae a canonical formula is
obtained:

$$\text{A B C}\!\uparrow\!\text{D E F G} \quad \frac{\text{H J I K}\!\downarrow \text{Pr--Ps}^\circ\,\text{L}}{\text{L M J N K}\!\downarrow \text{Pr--Rs}^\circ} \quad \text{Q Ex T U W}^*$$

from which the four fundamental categories are easily drawn,
corresponding respectively to:

1. First group + upper group + last group.
2. First group + lower group + last group.
3. First group + upper group + lower group + last group.
4. First group + last group.

The American researcher Jay Edwards, who was particularly
interested in Afro-American Trickster Tales bases his analysis on
Lévi-Strauss's approach, writing:

> Lévi-Strauss states:
> it seems that every myth (considered as the aggregate of all its
> variants) corresponds to a formula of the following type:
>
> $Fx(a):Fy(b)::Fx(b):Fa-1(y)$
>
> Here, with two terms, a and b, being given, as well as two
> functions, x and y, of these terms, it is assumed that a relation of
> equivalence exists between two situations defined respectively
> by an inversion of *terms* and *relations*, under two conditions:
> (1) that one term be replaced by its opposite (in the above
> formula, *a* and *a-1*); (2) that an inversion be made between
> the *function value* and the *term value* of two elements (above,
> *y* and *a*).[2]

He pits this system against Bremond's (in terms of 'Valences'), to propose a comparatively complex system of syntactical analysis of Value Oriented Actions in Trickster Tales.

As a writer, however, I've not found these approaches useful, and the work, based on Propp's motifs, is limited in terms of motifs by the specific data set of stories he was looking at.

The Lithuanian philologist and narrative theorist, Algirdas Julien Greimas tried to visualise the energetic flow of stories using a method based on logical relationships derived from the work of Aristotle.[3]

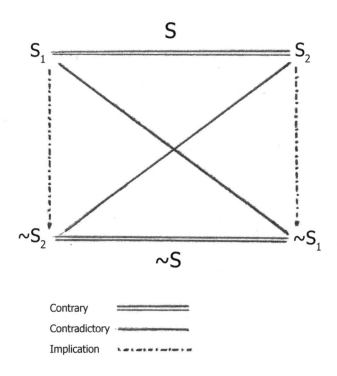

In his square of opposition, 'S' denotes an abstract quality, which makes sense, as all abstract qualities have contraries, whereas concrete ones don't. Think of the scale that goes from 'good' to 'evil'. However, there's no equivalent contrary to 'tree'. For Greimas, the opposition is an abstract moral opposition.

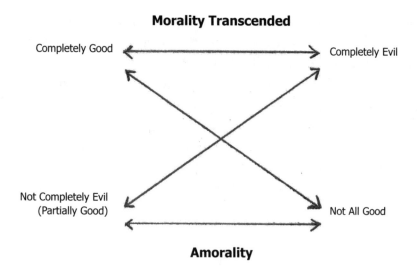

Greimas' square of moral opposition (akin to Blake's moral law) has its roots in the work of Claude Chabrol, who attributes the square of opposition to Apuleius.[4] Where Greimas fixes contraries in the transcendent and the ignominious (another morally opposed pair which fails to transcend its own binary structure), Chabrol is more nuanced, and admits cognitive dissonance. Where Greimas fixes, Chabrol dynamises. His square becomes a hexagon, where the modal possibility of 'Either all or none' (a state as yet undetermined in quality) appears at the zenith and that of 'Neither all nor none'/ 'some are and some aren't' (another undetermined state – which is it?) at the nadir. The vertical movement through the diagram, whether ascending or descending, fits the Revelation structure perfectly. Descending from a state of doubt at U, clarity is reached by seeing either A or E as being true, allowing the truth value (true, false, indeterminate) of the remaining elements to be established. The extent to which it reflects the dynamics of the Creation Myth structure is an interesting question worth pursuing.

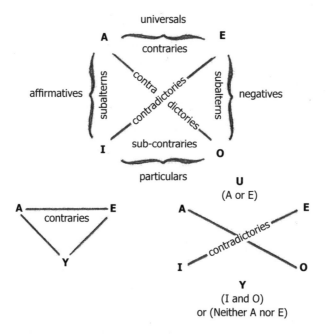

Chabrol, in turn, references Robert Blanché's work.[5] Both of these authors posit logical propositions in their diagrams (*x* is good, for example), whereas Greimas only focuses on the term (e.g., goodness), and implies the logical proposition.

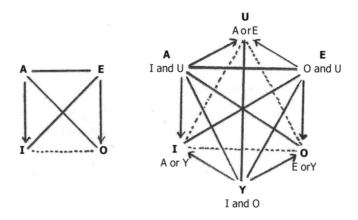

Key to propositional patterns:
A = universally affirmative (All *a* is *b*)
E = universally negative (No *a* is *b*)

I = partially affirmative (Some *a* is *b*)
O = partially negative (Some *a* is not *b*)
U = either universally affirmative or universally negative
    (Either all *a* is *b* or no *a* is *b*)
Y = both partially affirmative and partially negative
    (Some *a* is *b* and some *a* is not *b*)

Interestingly, in trying to define the elements of a narrative grammar, Greimas resorts to unidirectional and bidirectional arrows to indicate a (presupposed) positive or negative tendency and contradiction respectively. When the paths of the arrows are followed around Blanché's outline clockwise or anticlockwise, we see an inherent (←→) oscillatory movement. Ultimately, none of these two-dimensional mappings come close to the potential there is in exploring how Spencer-Brown's work, mapped to Shea Zellweger's Logical Garnet, might be applied in this kind of approach to narrative analysis.[6] Greimas' theory, as far as I can make out, has not been widely applied in a way which isolates individual characters' story lines, nor has it revealed the patterns which define distinctive story structures.

There are various renditions of Campbell's 'hero's journey', many of which revolve around a circle.

Whereas Campbell identifies 17 elements in his outline of the so-called 'hero's journey' structure, many diagrams, such as the example given here, based on the source on Wikipedia, are oversimplified. However, the horizontal division of space into upper and lower areas points to a dualism of contraries as being essential to this type of story (linking to Greimas' work) and the points along an arc which loops back to its starting point developing Freytag's more linear treatment of points along a pair of ascending/descending lines.

A simpler circular diagram from Madeleine L'Engle's *The Rock That Is Higher,* while elegant, is so reductive that beyond pointing to the unity in which a binary ebb and flow of events exists, serves only as an indication of the basic elements of story. 'The plot of Oedipus', she writes, 'has often been called the perfect plot, and it can be diagrammed, as can any other masterpiece, in the following way: Draw a circle and put a line down the middle. The left half of the circle is marked *C*, for complication. The right half of the circle is marked *R*, for resolution. Now surround the circle with another circle. The left side of this outside circle is marked *D*, for discovery, and the right side *P*, for peripety.'

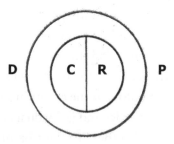

French anthropologist Denise Paulme's approach to visualising story structure, unlike the work of the theorists outlined above, does focus on structure at the level of *story* more.[7] Her classification includes the following structures:

1. Ascendant
2. Descendant
3. Cyclical
4. Spiral
5. Mirrored
6. Hourglass
7. Complex

Her work has a parallel in the analyses of non-linear structures explored by Jane Alison in her book, *Spiral, Meander, Explode.*

When looking at a non-linear structure, one should always remember that the story seeker's story line will always follow a Linear structure, and this will flow in counterpart to the way in which the story structure is presented in non-linear narrative form, a process which the methodology outlined in this book allows for.

Neither Paulme nor Alison, unfortunately, go beyond using visual forms as analogies to narrative structures. Where used (and they're used sparsely), any diagrams they supply are provided as rough guides. While their analyses work in terms of describing approaches to plot patterning, they don't map the relationships between plot pattern and underlying story structure.

Other authors have turned to line graphs in seeking to visualise the overarching shape of a narrative, the horizontal axis lending itself to mapping events over time, and thus potentially to mapping story structure, and the vertical axis to the binary pulsation of 'fortunate'/ 'unfortunate' events that unfold. If the events in a narrative were to be arranged in chronological order and individual characters' story lines charted in relation to each other, it might be of some use, but the approach doesn't allow any room for dealing with the expansion and contraction that is part and parcel of how story works. Kurt Vonnegut is one writer who takes this approach.[8] His work is entertaining; Janet Burroway's is more serious, but like the other theorists mentioned above, they both fail to map individual characters' story lines, so while their line graphs work as rough guides, as do those in Victoria Lynn Schmidt's work,[9] I've found them to be of limited use in practice.

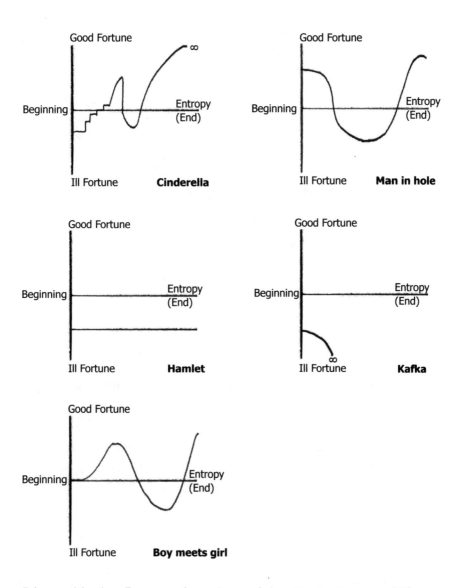

It's notable that Burroway's analysis of the *Cinderella* story differs from mine, focusing initially on 'the basic conflict: Cinderella's mother has died, and her father has married a brutal woman with two waspish daughters.' I find Burroway's attempt to indicate a secondary dynamic ebb and flow of energy criss-crossing a primary story line that indicates the flow of time against which all of the principal characters in the story are fitted leaves much to be desired.[10]

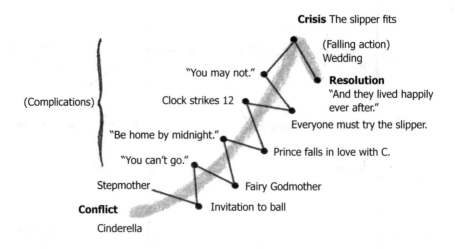

By contrast, Robert McKee attempts to visualise both relationships between characters and the dynamic pulsation of story structure in his work through illustrative diagrams.[11] However, the number of diagrams needed to illustrate the various points he wishes to make, and the emphasis on conflict (inner, personal, extra-personal) make for unnecessary complexity. The diagrams he uses to describe three 'grand categories' of 'Controlling Ideas' are no different, in essence, to the three types of barb presented in this work ($\rightarrow$), ($\leftarrow$), and ($\rightleftharpoons$), but the diagrams, unlike Spencer-Brown's symbols, present quite a few problems where issues relating to expansion and contraction have to be dealt with.

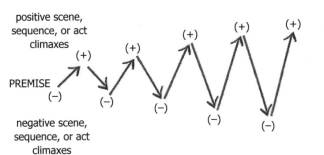

positive scene,
sequence, or act
climaxes

PREMISE

negative scene,
sequence, or act
climaxes

LAST ACT CLIMAX
IDEALISTIC
CONTROLLING
IDEA

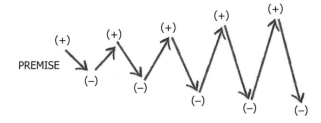

PREMISE

LAST ACT CLIMAX
PESSIMISTIC
CONTROLLING
IDEA

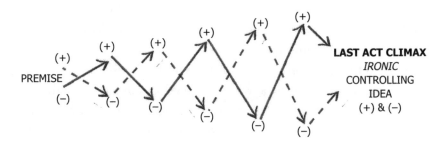

PREMISE

LAST ACT CLIMAX
IRONIC
CONTROLLING
IDEA
(+) & (−)

One approach which does deal successfully with expansion and contraction is Randy Ingermanson's *Snowflake Method*.[12]

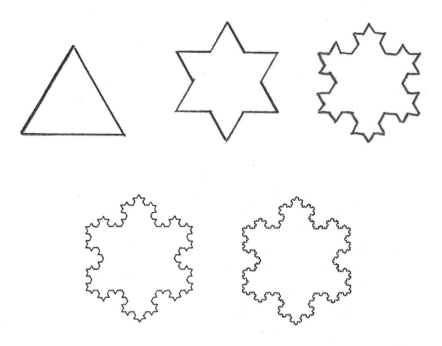

The approach to expansion and contraction, although masterful in terms of the potential for the visualisation to represent story or narrative structure, is only applied to plot patterning. Moreover, the expansion of each line happens in a 1:4 ratio, rather than the 1:3 ratio used in the methodology outlined in this book.

Although it may take a while to develop familiarity with the structures revealed by Spencer-Brown's notation, the facility with which it allows structures to expand and contract indefinitely, its ability to indicate linear and dynamic aspects of the way in which story 'stories', and its ability to shed new light on the ways in which story structures connect to each other clearly show its significant advantages over other systems of visualising the inner workings of story.

NOTES

1   Based on Gustav Freytag, *Freytag's Technique of the Drama: An Exposition of Dramatic Composition and Art,* translated by Elias J. MacEwan (Chicago, IL: S. C. Griggs & Company, 1895), 115, https://archive.org/details/freytagstechniqu00frey/page/114/.

2   Jay D. Edwards, *The Afro-American trickster tale: A structural analysis*, FPG Monograph Series, Vol. 4 (Bloomington, IA: Folklore Publications Group, Indiana University, 1978), 16–17.

3   Based on Algirdas Julien Greimas, *On Meaning: Selected Writings in Semiotic Theory,* translated by Paul J. Perron & Frank H. Collins (Minneapolis, MN: University of Minnesota Press, 1987), xiv–xv, 49.

4   Claude Chabrol, "Structures Intellectuelles," *Social Science Information* 6, no. 5 (1967): 205–209, at 206–208.

5   Robert Blanché, *Structures intellectuelles: essai sur l'organisation des concepts* (Paris: J. Vrin, 1966), 56.

6   The unidirectional arrows are shown in Greimas, *On Meaning*, 66. For more information on Shae Zellweger's logical garnet, see the *Logic Alphabet Project* website at http://www.logic-alphabet.net.

7   Denise Paulme, *La mère dévorante: essai sur la morphologie des contes africains*, Bibliothèque des Sciences Humaines (Paris: Gallimard, 1976), 134.

8   Based on Kurt Vonnegut, *Shape of Stories* Lecture, 4 February, 2004. The Case College Scholars Program. YouTube: GOGru_4z1Vc; "Here is a lesson in creative writing," in *A Man Without a Country*, New York, NY: Seven Stories Press, 2005.

9   Victoria Lynn Schmidt, *Story Structure Architect: A Writer's Guide to Building Dramatic Situations and Compelling Characters* (Cincinnati, OH: Writer's Digest Books, 2005), 29, 34, 39, 45, 50, 55, 61–62, 69, 75–76, 94.

10 Based on Janet Burroway, Elizabeth Stuckey-French, and Ned Stuckey-French, *Writing Fiction: A Guide to Narrative Craft* (Chicago, IL and London: University of Chicago Press, 2019), 135–136.

11 Robert McKee, *Story: Substance, Structure, Style, and the Principles of Screenwriting* (New York: ReganBooks, 1997), 123.

12 Randy Ingermanson, "The Snowflake Method For Designing A Novel," *Advanced Fiction Writing,* 2022 https://www.advancedfictionwriting.com/articles/snowflake-method/.

APPENDIX 3

RAGS TO RICHES – A REVERSAL?

What would happen if you set out to create a story which is the inverse of the Rags to Riches structure?

What this means is rather than following the Rags to Riches structure, defined as

$$\square\,\urcorner \rightarrow \hookleftarrow \rightarrow \hookleftarrow \rightarrow \hookleftarrow \rightarrow \urcorner\,\square,$$

we replace each of the steps with a step in the opposite direction:

$$\square\,\urcorner \hookleftarrow \rightarrow \hookleftarrow \rightarrow \ldots \hookleftarrow \urcorner\,\square.$$

Rather than starting with a heroine in a positive situation who meets with a reversal of fortune, let's say we start with an unfortunately repressed heroine, who is liberated by the fortunate (in this case) death of her parents (more interesting if they're repressively saintly), giving her the freedom and financial independence she has never had while they were alive. For the next step, an external agent of change would need to act (perhaps against her will) to reveal something which changes her view of her circumstances, seeing them as unfortunate. Returning to her previous condition in an altered state of consciousness, she decides she is even more fortunate than before … because she's not affected … not really …

We've reached the ellipsis … What happens next?

Does this story work for you? How does it differ from the way in which you respond to the *Cinderella* story?

Whatever you feel, why is it you think that this story engenders this particular reaction in you?

How do you feel you want to finish it?

And what about the grey shaded arrow after the ellipsis … what does it point to? What does the above example suggest to you?

APPENDIX 4

LIST OF STORY STRUCTURES

1 The Quest structure

Steps	Symbols	Structure
1	⊐	[Opening]
2	⌐	Initial situation (set-up: who, when, where – character and setting)
3	←	Problem
4	→	Journey
5	←	Meeting with ...
6	→	... friend/helper
7	←	Meeting with ...
8	→	... enemy/hindrance
9	⌐	Final situation (outcome/resolution)
10	⊐	[Closing]

2 The Transformation structure

Steps	Symbols	Structure
1	⊐	[Opening]
2	⌐	Initial situation (set-up: who, when, where – character and setting)
3	←	Transgression against the natural order
4	→	Restoration of natural order
5	⌐	Final situation (outcome/resolution)
6	⊐	[Closing]

3 The Rags to Riches structure

Steps	Symbols	Structure
1	⊐	[Opening]
2	⌐	Initial situation (set-up: who, when, where – character and setting)
3	→	Positive condition
4	←	Problem (that usually 'comes out of the blue') resulting in a state of **subversion**
5	→	Journey
6	←	Journey thwarted, meeting with …
7	→	… friend/helper (positive transformation often achieved by means of an external, often supernatural force)
8	←	**Reversion** to previous state <u>in an altered state of consciousness</u> Nested Quest structure involving a Saviour character starts
9	→	Nested Quest structure involving a Saviour character ends
10	⌐	Final situation (outcome/resolution)
11	⊐	[Closing]

4 The Death and Rebirth structure

Steps	Symbols	Structure
1	⊐	[Opening]
2	⌐	Initial situation (set-up: who, when, where – character and setting)
3	←	Problem (lack)
4	→	Lack fulfilled
5	←	There's a price to pay
6	→	There are attempts to avoid paying the price
7	←	The attempts fail, the price is exacted, there's a **submersion** Nested Quest structure involving a Saviour character starts
8	→	Nested Quest structure involving a Saviour character ends
9	⌐	Final situation (outcome/resolution)
10	⊐	[Closing]

5 The Trickster structure

Steps	Symbols	Structure
1	⊐	[Opening]
2	⌐	Initial situation (set-up: who, when, where – character and setting)
3	←	Problem
4	→	Journey
5	←	Meeting between ...
6	⇌	... the two characters (one is tricked or duped by the other)
7	←	Meeting between ...
8	⇌	... the two characters (the previously duped character tricks the other)
9	⌐	Final situation (outcome/resolution)
10	⊐	[Closing]

6 The Trickster Variation structure

Steps	Symbols	Structure
1	⊐	[Opening]
2	⌐	Initial situation (set-up: who, when, where – character and setting)
3	←	Problem
4	→	Journey
5	←	Meeting between ...
6	⇌	... the two characters which sets up a cognitive dissonance (Trickster Awe step)
7	←	Meeting between ...
8	⇌	... the two characters which resolves the cognitive dissonance (Transformational Twist)
9	⌐	Final situation (outcome/resolution)
10	⊐	[Closing]

7 The Revelation structure

Steps	Symbols	Structure	Example (attr. Julius Caesar)
1	⊓	Rumour/doubt	veni (I came)
2	⌐	Verification: confirmation/refutation	vidi (I saw)
3	⊐	Assertion/denial (statement or action which cancels doubt)	vici (I conquered)

8 The Call and Response structure (Variation 1, with initial Transformation structure)

Steps	Symbols	Structure		
1	⊓	[Opening]		
2	⌐	Initial situation (set-up: who, when, where – character and setting)		
3	←	State of lack	}	**Transformation structure** (with resolution not achieved)
4	→	State of excess		
5	←	**Quest structure** Problem	⊓	**Revelation structure** Rumour/doubt (*veni* step)
6	→	Journey		
7	←	Meeting with …	⌐	Verification: confirmation/refutation (*vidi* step)
8	→	… friend/helper		
9	←	Meeting with …	⊐	Assertion/denial (*vici* step) (statement or action which cancels doubt)
10	→	… enemy/hindrance		
11	⌐	Final situation (outcome/resolution)		
12	⊓	[Closing]		

9 The Call and Response structure (Variation 2, with final Transformation structure)

Steps	Symbols	Structure		
1	⊔	[Opening]		
2	¬	Initial situation (set-up: who, when, where – character and setting)		
3	↼	**Quest structure** Problem	⊔	**Revelation structure** Rumour/doubt (*veni* step)
4	⇀	Journey		
5	↼	Meeting with ...	¬	Verification: Confirmation/refutation (*vidi* step)
6	⇀	... friend/helper		
7	↼	Meeting with ...	╗	Assertion/denial (*vici* step) (statement or action which cancels doubt)
8	⇀	... enemy/ hindrance		
9	↼	State of lack	}	**Transformation structure** (with resolution not achieved)
10	⇀	State of excess		
11	¬	Final situation (outcome/resolution)		
12	⊔	[Closing]		

10 The Chinese Circular Structure

Steps	Seasons	Elements	Yin/Yang	Structure
1	Earth	Balance	☯	[Opening]
2	Spring	Wood	– – ——	Initiation/emergence
3	Summer	Fire	—— ——	Division
4	Autumn	Metal	—— – –	Separation
5	Winter	Water	– – – –	Completion
6	Earth	Balance	☯	Re-integration/ re-formation/ re-centring

11 The Ki-Shō-Ten-Ketsu structure

Steps	Symbols	Structure
1	⊐	[Opening]
2	⊓	Introduction (ki) 'to rise/start'
3	→	Development (shō) 'to continue'
4	⇌	Twist (ten) 'to turn/change'
5	⊓	Synthesis (ketsu) 'to unite/join'
6	⊐	[Closing: new state of oscillation from which a new structure can emerge]

12 The Open-Ended Ki-Shō-Ten-Ketsu structure

Steps	Symbols	Structure
1	⊐	[Opening]
2	⊓	Introduction (ki) 'to rise/start'
3	→	Development (shō) 'to continue'
4	⇌	Twist (ten) 'to turn/change' (a contrast is presented to an audience for debate so they can find a way of reconciling it)
5	⊓	Synthesis (ketsu) 'to unite/join' (a means of reconciliation is arrived at collectively through discussion)
6	⊐	[Closing: new state of oscillation from which a new structure can emerge]

13 The Koan structure

Steps	Symbols	Structure
1	⊐	[Paradoxical opening which is actually a closing]
2	⊓	Koan presented
3	⇌	Paradox which sets up a cognitive dissonance
4		Resolution of paradox leading to enlightenment
5	⊐	[Paradoxical closing which is actually an opening]

14 The Dilemma structure

Steps	Story Spinner	Story Seeker	Structure
1	⊐	⊐	[Opening]
2	⌐	⌐	Initial situation (set-up: who, when, where – character and setting)
3	←		Problem
4	→		Journey
5	←		Crossroads/paradox
6	⇌	⇌	The story seeker(s) is/are presented with a dilemma, which becomes ...
7		←	... their problem (nested Quest)
8		→	The discussion they have involves individual and collective powers of reasoning (→ ← → implied) ...
9	←	←	... which help them reach an outcome or resolution, which they turn to the story spinner to present, leading to the ...
10	⇌	⇌	... eventual resolution of the dilemma, which links to ...
11	⌐	⌐	... a new state of balance in the social order
12	⊐	⊐	[Closing]

15 The Riddle structure

Steps	Story Spinner	Story Seeker	Structure
1	⊐	⊐	[Opening]
2	⌐	⌐	Substance alluded to but not stated
3	⇌	⇌	Attributes listed, creating a cognitive dissonance
4	⌐	⌐	Riddle solved by resolving the cognitive dissonance
5	⊐	⊐	[Closing]

16 The Voyage and Return structure

Steps	Symbols	Structure
1	☐	[Opening]
2	⌐	Initial situation (set-up: who, when, where – character and setting)
3	←	Problem
4	→	Translation to a different dimension of being
5	←	Problem (of return to origins)
6	→	Solution to both problems (3, 5) usually via nested Quest and other structures
7	←	Return to origin
8	→	Resolution of initial problem
9	⌐	Final situation (outcome/resolution)
10	☐	[Closing]

17 The Perpetual Motion structure

Steps	Symbols	Structure
1	☐	[Opening]
2	⌐	Initial situation (set-up: who, when, where – character and setting)
3	←	Problem
4	→	Journey which results in a new ...
5	←	... problem
6	→	Journey which results in a return to the original ...
...	←	[... problem ... the cycle loops from step 3 to step 6 perpetually][1]

18 The Creation Myth structure

Steps	Symbols	Structure
1	☐	[Opening]
2	⌐	Character(s) emerge(s)
3	→	An unfolding proceeds ...
...	...	[... and continues to unfold in perpetuo ...]

Classification of Threshold and Non-Threshold structures

Threshold Structures	Non-Threshold Structures
Transformation	Quest
Trickster Variation	Trickster
Death and Rebirth	Perpetual Motion
Rags to Riches	Voyage and Return
Call and Response (2 Variations)	Ki-Shō-Ten-Ketsu
Revelation	Open-Ended Ki-Shō-Ten-Ketsu
Chinese Circular Structure	Dilemma
Koan	Riddle

Creation Myth

Classification of structures by initial step

⊐	⊓	⟵	⟶	⇌
Revelation	The Chinese Story Structure	Quest Transformation Death & Rebirth Trickster Call and Response (2 Variations) Trickster Variation Dilemma Voyage & Return Perpetual Motion	Ki-Shō-Ten-Ketsu Open-Ended Ki-Shō-Ten-Ketsu Creation Myth	Riddle Koan

Classification of Linear story structures by endings

Closed	Open-Ended	No Clear Ending
Quest Transformation Rags to Riches Death and Rebirth Trickster Trickster Variation Call and Response (2 Variations) Ki-Shō-Ten-Ketsu Voyage and Return	Dilemma Open-Ended Ki-Shō-Ten-Ketsu Koan Riddle	Perpetual Motion Creation Myth

NOTE

1 Steps 3, 4 and 5, 6 of the Perpetual Motion structure form two pairs of moves. Each pair can be expanded to a Quest structure. The number of pairs can be extended, but the last will always lead back to the first.

BIBLIOGRAPHY

'Attâr, Farîd-od-Dîn. *The Canticle of the Birds*. Edited by Diane de Selliers. Translated by Dick Davis and Afkham Darbandi. Commentary by Michael Barry. Paris: Diane de Selliers, 2013.

Abbott, H. Porter. *The Cambridge Introduction to Narrative*. 3rd ed. Cambridge: Cambridge University Press, 2021.

Adams, Richard. *Watership Down*. New York: Scribner, 2005.

Adler, Mortimer J. *Great Ideas from the Great Books*. Rev. ed. New York: Washington Square Press, 1969.

———. "Duty." In *A Syntopicon: An Index to the Great Ideas*. Vol. 1. The Great Books of the Western World. Vol. 2, 358–365. Chicago: Encyclopaedia Britannica, 1952.

Aeschylus. *The Seven Against Thebes*. Edited by The Reverend James Davies. London: Virtue Brothers, 1864. https://books.google.co.uk/books?id=Z9oIAAAAQAAJ.

Afanas'ev, Aleksandr. *Russian Fairy Tales*. Translated by Norbert Guterman. New York: Pantheon Books, 1945.

Albanese, Massimiliano. "MAZZUOLI, Giovanni, detto lo Stradino." In *Dizionario Biografico degli Italiani*. Rome: Istituto della Enciclopedia Italiana, 2008. http://www.treccani.it/enciclopedia/mazzuoli-giovanni-detto-lo-stradino_(Dizionario-Biografico)/.

An, Liu. *The Huainanzi*. Edited by John S. Major, Sarah A. Queen, Andrew Seth Meyer, Harold D. Roth, Michael Puett and Judson Murray. New York; Chichester: Columbia University Press, 2010.

———. *Jing Shen: The Vital Spirits, A Translation of Huainanzi Chapter 7*. Translated by Deena Freeman, Alan Hext, and Sandra Hill. London: Monkey Press, 2010.

The Arabian Nights: Tale of 1001 Nights. Translated by Malcom C. Lyons and Ursula Lyons. London: Penguin Classics, 2008.

The Arabian Nights Entertainments. Edited by Andrew Lang. London, New York and Bombay: Longmans, Green & Co., 1898. https://archive.org/details/arabiannightsen00fordgoog.

Arājs, Kārlis, Alma Medne. *Latviešu pasaku tipu raditajs* (The Types of the Latvian Folktales). Riga: Zinatne, 1977.

Areopagite, Dionysius the. *On the Divine Names and the Mystical Theology*. Translated by Clarence Edwin Rolt. London: Society for

Promoting Christian Knowledge, 1920. https://archive.org/details/dionysiusareopag00dion/.

Aristotle. *Aristotle: On Poetics*. Translated by Seth Bernardete and Michael Davis. South Bend, IN: St Augustine's Press, 2002.

———. *Rhetoric*. Translated by C. D. C. Reeve. Indianapolis, IN: Hackett, 2018.

———. *The Categories; On Interpretation; Prior Analytics*. Translated by Harold P. Cooke and Hugh Tredennick. Cambridge, MA: Harvard University Press, 1962.

———. *The Metaphysics*. Translated by Hugh Tredennick. Vol. 1. London: W. Heinemann; New York: G. P. Putnam's Sons, 1933.

Aristotle, Longinus, Demetrius. *Poetics. Longinus: On the Sublime. Demetrius: On Style*. Edited and translated by Stephen Halliwell, W. H. Fyfe, Donald Russell, W. Rhys Roberts, and Doreen C. Innes. Cambridge, MA; London, England: Harvard University Press, 1995.

Ashliman, D. L. "The Education of an Ox." *Folklore and Mythology Electronic Texts*. 1999–2014. https://www.pitt.edu/~dash/type1675.html.

———. "Nasreddin Hodja: Tales of the Turkish Trickster." *Folklore and Mythology Electronic Texts*. 16 May 2009. https://pitt.edu/~dash/hodja.html#walnuts.

———. "The Tar-Baby." *Folklore and Mythology Electronic Texts*. 2014–2018. https://www.pitt.edu/~dash/type0175.html.

———. "Trickster Wives and Maids." *Folklore and Mythology Electronic Texts*. 1999–2013. https://www.pitt.edu/~dash/type1741.html.

———. "What Should I Have Said (or Done)?" *Folklore and Mythology Electronic Texts*. 2000–2010. https://www.pitt.edu/~dash/type1696.html#england.

Asquith, Clare. *Shadowplay: The Hidden Beliefs and Coded Politics of William Shakespeare*. New York: PublicAffairs, 2005.

Atsma, Aaron J. "Gorgones & Medousa." *Theoi Project*. 2000–2017. https://www.theoi.com/Pontios/Gorgones.html.

Austin, James H. *Zen and the Brain: Toward an Understanding of Meditation and Consciousness*. Cambridge, MA and London, UK: MIT Press, 1999.

Aziz, Muhammad Ali. *Religion and Mysticism in Early Islam: Theology and Sufism in Yemen. The Legacy of Ahmad Ibn ʿAlwān*. London and New York: I. B. Tauris, 2011.

Baháʼuʼlláh. "Súriy-i-Haykal." In *Baháʼí Reference Library: Writings of Baháʼuʼlláh*. Edited by Shoghi Effendi. 2019. Accessed 14 June 2019.

https://www.bahai.org/library/authoritative-texts/bahaullah/summons-lord-hosts/3#719232199.

———. "The Tablet of the Houri." Translated by Juan R. I. Cole. 22 July 1996. http://www-personal.umich.edu/~jrcole/houri.htm.

Bal, Mieke. *Narratology in Practice.* Toronto, Buffalo, London: University of Toronto Press, 2021.

———. *Narratology: Introduction to the Theory of Narrative.* 4th ed. Toronto: University of Toronto Press, 2017.

———. *On Storytelling: Essays in Narratology.* Sonoma, CA: Polebridge, 1991.

Bally, Charles, Albert Riedlinger, Ferdinand de Saussure, and Albert Sechehaye. *Course in General Linguistics.* London: Duckworth, 1983.

Bancks, Tristan. "Beyond the Hero's Journey: 'Joseph [Campbell] is my Yoda (1).'—George Lucas (1)." *Australian Screen Education* 33 (Spring 2003): 32–34. https://go.galegroup.com/ps/anonymous?id=GALE%7CA112130487.

Barthes, Roland. "An Introduction to the Structural Analysis of Narrative." *New Literary History: On Narrative and Narratives* 6, no. 2 (Winter 1975): 237–272. https://doi.org/10.2307/468419.

Bascom, William. *African Dilemma Tales.* The Hague: Mouton, 1975.

———. *African Folktales in the New World.* Bloomington, IN: Indiana University Press, 1992.

Bashō, Buson, and Issa. *The Essential Haiku: Versions of Bashō, Buson, & Issa.* Edited and translated by Robert Hass. Hopewell, NJ: The Ecco Press, 1994.

Baum, L. Frank. *The Wonderful Wizard of Oz.* Chicago and New York: George M. Hill, 1900.

Benardete, Seth. *Socrates' Second Sailing: On Plato's "Republic".* Chicago: University of Chicago Press, 1992.

"Beowulf." In *The 'Southwick Codex,'* 132r–201v. The British Library. Cotton MS Vitellius A XV.

"Beowulf, Diacritically Marked Text of." *Beowulf on Steorarume,* June 2005. Edited and translated by Benjamin Slade. https://heorot.dk/beo-intro-rede.html.

Berensmeyer, Ingo. "'Twofold Vibration': Samuel Beckett's Laws of Form." *Poetics Today* 25 (3): 465–495.

Bessonov, A G. Bashkirskie narodnye skazki (Bashkirian Folktales). Ufa: Bashgosizdat, 1941.

Blake, William. *Blake: Complete Writings.* Edited by Geoffrey Keynes. London:

Oxford University Press, 1969.

Blanché, Robert. *Structures intellectuelles: essai sur l'organisation des concepts*. Paris: J. Vrin, 1966.

Boethius. *Consolation of Philosophy*. Translated by Joel C. Relihan. Indianapolis, IN: Hackett, 2001.

The Book of the Thousand Nights and a Night (Supplemental Nights). Edited by Leonard C. Smithers. Translated by Sir Richard Francis Burton. Vol. 11. London: H. S. Nichols, 1897. https://archive.org/stream/bookthousandnigh11burt.

Booker, Christopher. *The Seven Basic Plots: Why We Tell Stories*. London and New York: Continuum, 2005.

Bouissac, Paul. "Saussure's Legacy in Semiotics." In *The Cambridge Companion to Saussure*, edited by Carol Sanders, 240–260. Cambridge: Cambridge University Press, 2006.

Brandreth, Gyles. *1000 Jokes: The Greatest Joke Book Ever Known*. London: Carousel, 1980.

Briggs, Kathleen, ed. *A Dictionary of British Folk-Tales in the English Language*. Vol. 2, Part A. London: Routledge, 1970.

Brooke, Arthur. "Romeus and Juliet." *Shakespeare Navigators*, 1 February 2021. https://www.shakespeare-navigators.com/romeo/BrookeIndex.html.

Brown, Dayle L. *Skylore from Planet Earth: Stories from Around the World – The Moon*. Bloomington, IN: AuthorHouse, 2012.

Burch, Michael R. *The Best Limericks of All Time: A Brief History of the Limerick, with Definitions and Examples*. n.d. Accessed 5 May 2021. http://www.thehypertexts.com/The Best Limericks of All Time.htm.

Burns, Kevin, dir. *Lost in Space Forever*. 1998; Los Angeles: Emmett Street Films et al. https://www.imdb.com/title/tt0244630/.

Burroway, Janet. *Writing Fiction: A Guide to Narrative Craft*. 4th ed. New York: HarperCollins, 1996.

Burroway, Janet, Elizabeth Stuckey-French, and Ned Stuckey-French. *Writing Fiction: A Guide to Narrative Craft*. Chicago and London: University of Chicago Press, 2019.

Butler, Robert Olen. *From Where You Dream: The Process of Writing Fiction*. New York: Grove, 2005.

Cahill, David. "The Myth of the 'Turn' in Contrastive Rhetoric." *Written Comunication* 20, no. 2 (2003): 170–194.

Calder, Andrew. *Molière: The Theory and Practice of Comedy*. Atlantic Highlands, NJ: Athlone Press, 1996.

Campbell, Joseph. *The Hero with a Thousand Faces.* Princeton and Oxford: Princeton University Press, 2004.

Campbell, Kimberley Hill, and Kristi Latimer. *Beyond the Five-Paragraph Essay.* Portland, ME: Stenhouse, 2012.

Carroll, Lewis. *The Annotated Alice: The Definitive Edition.* Edited by Martin Gardner. Illustrated by John Tenniel. London: Penguin, 2001.

Casey, Peter J. *What Hollywood's Addiction to The Hero's Journey is Doing to the Broadway Musical (Parts 1, 2).* 10 April 2015. https://majortominor. wordpress.com/2015/04/10/what-hollywoods-addiction-to-the-heros-journey-is-doing-to-the-broadway-musical/#comments.

Cashford, Jules. *From Thoth to Mercurius.* Ilford, Somerset: Kingfisher Art Productions, 2017.

———. *Mnemosune: The Great Memory.* [Ilford, Somerset:] Kingfisher Art Productions, 2013.

Chabrol, Claude. "Structures Intellectuelles." *Social Science Information* 6, no. 5 (1967): 205–209.

Charlip, Remy. *Fortunately.* New York: Aladdin, 1993.

Cho, Jai Hee. "A Study of Contrastive Rhetoric between East Asian and North American Cultures as Demonstrated through Student Expository Essays from Korea and the United States." PhD diss., Bowling Green State University, 1999. http://faculty.fullerton.edu/jcho/dissertation. htm.

Clagett, Marshall. *Ancient Egyptian Science Volume I: Knowledge and Order.* Tome 1. Philadelphia: American Philosophical Society, 1989.

Clarke, Bruce. *Posthuman Metamorphosis: Narrative and Systems.* New York: Fordham University Press, 2008.

Connell, Del, and Dan Spiegle. *Space Family Robinson.* New York: Gold Key Comics, 1962–1982.

Conrad, Leon. "A Veil of Mystery: English 16th and 17th Century Woven and Embroidered Textile Bookbindings." *Academia.edu.* April 2005. https://independent.academia.edu/LeonConrad/Thesis-Chapters.

———. "Analysis of Genesis I using the Chinese Circular Structure." Unpublished manuscript, last modified 20 February 2022. PDF file.

———. "Analysis of The Story of Sidi-Nouman." Unpublished manuscript, last modified 20 February 2022. PDF file.

———. "Analysis of two versions of the story of 'The Three Little Pigs'." Unpublished manuscript, last modified 20 February 2022. PDF file.

———. "Laws of Form – Laws of Narrative – Laws of Story." In *Laws of*

Form: A Fiftieth Anniversary. Series On Knots & Everything. Vol. 72.
Edited by Louis H. Kauffman, Fred Cummins, Randolph Dible, Leon
Conrad, Graham Ellsbury, Andrew Crompton, and Florian Grote, Ch.
21. Singapore: World Scientific, 2022.

———. "Laws of Form/Laws of Logic (Paper)." *Academia.edu*. 2016. https://
www.academia.edu/12103235/Laws_of_Form_Laws_of_Logic.

———. "Laws of Form–Laws of Logic (Talk)." Delivered to Alternative
Natural Philosophy Association (ANPA), 2016. https://www.
academia.edu/31080884/Laws_of_Form_-_Laws_of_Logic_-_
ANPA_2016.

———. "Roots, shoots, fruits: William Blake and J M Robertson: two
key influences on George Spencer-Brown's work and the latter's
relationship to Niklas Luhmann's work." *Kybernetes* 51, no. 5 (2022):
1879–1895.

———. "The Chinese Circular Structure." 2 parts. Unpublished manuscript,
last modified 18 and 2 June 2020 respectively. PDF files.

———. "The Unknown Storyteller," filmed 10 August 2019 by West
Den Haag in Liverpool, England. https://www.youtube.com/
watch?v=GZJdlhG0z78.

Conrad, Leon, and Aristel Škrbić. "TEDx Talk: The Magic of Words," filmed
3 December 2013 in London. *YouTube*. https://www.youtube.com/
watch?v=HYit3MYAoqM.

Cox, Marian Roalfe. *Cinderella; three hundred and forty-five variants of
Cinderella, Catskin, and Cap o'Rushes, abstracted and tabulated,
with a discussion of mediaeval analogues, and notes*. London: David
Nutt for the Folk-Lore Society, 1893. https://archive.org/details/
cinderellathreeh00coxmuoft/.

Cronk, Nicholas. "Aristotle, Horace, and Longinus: The Conception of Reader
Response." In *The Cambridge History of Literary Criticism*. Vol. 3,
The Renaissance, edited by Glyn P. Norton, 199–204. Cambridge:
Cambridge University Press, 2006.

Csikszentmihalyi, Mihaly. "TED Talk: Flow, the Secret to Happiness,"
filmed February 2004. *TED*. https://www.ted.com/talks/mihaly_
csikszentmihalyi_flow_the_secret_to_happiness.

d'Huy, Julien. "L'Aquitaine Sur La Route d'Oedipe? La Sphinge Comme Motif
Prehistorique." *Société d'études et de recherches préhistoriques des Eyzies*
61 (2012): 15–21.

da Porto, Luigi. *Romeo and Juliet*. Translated by Maurice Jonas. London: Davis

& Orioli, 1921. https://archive.org/details/romeojulietphoto00dapo/page/n9.

da Porto, Luigi, Matteo Bandello, and Pierre Boaistuau. *Romeo and Juliet Before Shakespeare: Four Early Stories of Star-crossed Love.* Toronto: Centre for Reformation and Renaissance Studies, 2000.

Daly, Peter M. *The English Emblem and the Continental Tradition.* New York: AMS Press, 1988.

Deacon, Terence W. "Emergence: The Hole at the Wheel's Hub." In *The Re-Emergence of Emergence: The Emergentist Hypothesis from Science to Religion*, edited by Philip Clayton and Paul Davies, 111–150. Oxford and New York: Oxford University Press, 2006. https://doi.org/10.1093/acprof:oso/9780199544318.001.0001.

Defoe, Daniel. *The Life and Strange Surprizing Adventures of Robinson Crusoe, of York, Mariner.* 3rd ed. London: W. Taylor, 1719.

Dundes, Alan, ed. *Cinderella: A Folklore Casebook.* New York: Garland, 1982.

Dye, David S. *How to Teach the Five-Paragraph Essay.* Mesquite, NV: Model Citizen Enterprises, 2005.

Edwards, Jay D. *The Afro-American trickster tale: A structural analysis.* FPG Monograph Series, Vol. 4. Bloomington, IA: Folklore Publications Group, Indiana University, 1978.

Elea, Parmenides of. *Fragments.* Translated by David Gallop. Toronto: University of Toronto Press, 1991.

Eliot, T. S. "East Coker." *Four Quartets.* June 2000. http://www.davidgorman.com/4Quartets/2-coker.htm.

Foreman, Michael. *Fortunately, Unfortunately.* Minneapolis, MN: Andersen, 2011.

Foster, Richard. *Patterns in Thought: The Hidden Meaning of the Great Pavement of Westminster Abbey.* London: Jonathan Cape, 1992.

Freystetter, Josef. "Zeit in Form: Ein Strukturvergleich von Laws of Form und Genesis 1,1 - 2,4a." PhD diss., Universität Witten/Herdecke GmbH, 2020.

Freytag, Gustav. *Freytag's Technique of the Drama: An Exposition of Dramatic Composition and Art.* Translated by Elias J. MacEwan. Chicago: S. C. Griggs & Company, 1895. https://archive.org/details/freytagstechniqu00frey.

Friedlander, Walter J. *The Golden Wand of Medicine: A History of the Caduceus Symbol in Medicine.* Contributions in Medical Studies, Vol. 35. Westport, CT: Greenwood, 1992.

Genette, Gerard. *Narrative Discourse.* Oxford: Blackwell, 1979.

Graham, Paul. "A Version 1.0." *PaulGraham.com.* October 2004. http://paulgraham.com/laundry.html.

———. "The Age of the Essay." *PaulGraham.com.* September 2004. http://paulgraham.com/essay.html.

Graves, Robert. *The Greek Myths.* London: Penguin, 2011.

Greimas, Algirdas Julien. "Elements of a Narrative Grammar." *Diacritics* 7, no. 1 (Spring 1977): 23–40.

———. *On Meaning: Selected Writings in Semiotic Theory.* Translated by Paul J. Perron and Frank H. Collins. Minneapolis, MN: University of Minnesota Press, 1987.

Greimas, Algirdas Julien, and François Rastier. "The Interaction of Semiotic Constraints." *Yale French Studies: Game, Play, Literature* 41 (1968): 86–105.

Griswold, Eliza, and Seamus Murphy. "Landays." *Poetry Foundation.* Accessed 30 October 2018. https://static.poetryfoundation.org/o/media/landays.html.

Guénon, René. *The Essential René Guénon: Metaphysics, Tradition, and the Crisis of Modernity.* Edited by Ed Herlihy. Bloomington, IA: World Wisdom, 2009.

Haven, Kendall. *Story Proof: The Science Behind the Startling Power of Story.* Westport, CT: Libraries Unlimited, 2007.

Hawhee, Debra. *Bodily Arts: Rhetoric and Athletics in Ancient Greece.* Austin, TX: University of Texas Press, 2004.

Hawhee, Debra, and Sharon Crowley. *Ancient Rhetorics for Contemporary Students.* New York: Pearson Longman, 2004.

Heiner, Heidi Anne. *Cinderella Tales from Around the World.* N.p.: SurLaLune Press, 2012.

———. *History of Cinderella.* 1998–2021. https://www.surlalunefairytales.com/a-g/cinderella/cinderella-history.html.

Henderson, Harold G. *Haiku in English.* Rutland, VT and Tokyo, Japan: Charles E. Tuttle Company, 1997.

Hesiod. *Theogony.* Translated by Martin Litchfield West. Oxford and New York: Oxford University Press, 1988.

Heywood, Simon. "Silver Threads of Fear: Restoring the agency of female protagonists in Jewish women's storytelling traditions." In *Strategies of Silence: Reflections on the Practice and Pedagogy of Creative Writing,* edited by Moy McCrory and Simon Heywood, 34–42. London:

Routledge, 2021.

Heywood, Simon, and Shonaleigh Cumbers. "War and the Ruby Tree: The Motif of the Unborn Generations in Jewish Women's Story-Telling." In *War, Myths, and Fairy Tales*, edited by Sara Buttsworth and Maartje Abbenhuis, 219–237. Singapore: Palgrave Macmillan, 2017. https://doi.org/10.1007/978-981-10-2684-3_10.

Higginson, William J. *The Haiku Seasons: Poetry of the Natural World.* Tokyo, New York and London: Kodansha International, 1996.

Hill, Sandra. *Chinese Medicine from the Classics: A Beginner's Guide.* London, UK: Monkey Press, 2014.

Hill, Simon. "The best texting games." *Digital Trends.* 15 July 2019. https://www.digitaltrends.com/mobile/best-texting-games/.

Hoca, Nasreddin. *The Turkish Jester, or the Pleasantries of Cogia Nasr Eddin Effendi.* Translated by George Borrow. Ipswich: W. Webber, 1884; Project Gutenberg, 2005. http://www.gutenberg.org/files/16244/16244-h/16244-h.htm.

Huang, Alfred. *The Numerology of the I Ching.* Rochester, VT: Inner Traditions International, 2000.

Ichiki, Tadao. *Suggestive Brevity: Haiku into the World.* Kyoto: Biseisha, 1985.

Javitch, Daniel. "The Assimilation of Aristotle's Poetics in Sixteenth-Century Italy." In *The Cambridge History of Literary Criticism.* Vol. 3, *The Renaissance*, edited by Glyn P. Norton, 53–65. Cambridge: Cambridge University Press, 2006. https://doi.org/10.1017/CHOL9780521300087.006.

Jeffers, Herrick. *Once Upon A Time, They Lived Happily Ever After.* Melbourne Village, FL: Herrick Jeffers, 1997.

Joseph, Sister Miriam. *The Trivium.* Philadelphia: Paul Dry Books, 2002.

Kaminski, Michael. *The Secret History of Star Wars: The Art of Storytelling and the Making of a Modern Epic.* Kingston, Ontario: Legacy Books Press, 2008.

Kanda, K. C. *Masterpieces of Urdu Ghazal From 17th to 20th Century.* New Delhi: Sterling Paperbacks, 1995.

Kant, Immanuel. "What Is Enlightenment?" 1784. Translated by Mary C. Smith. http://www.columbia.edu/acis/ets/CCREAD/etscc/kant.html.

Kappraff, Jay. *Beyond Measure: A Guided Tour through Nature, Myth, and Number.* Singapore: World Scientific, 2002.

Karlgren, Bernhard. "The Book of Documents." *The Museum of Far Eastern Antiquities Stockholm* 22 (1950): 1–82.

Kauffman, Louis H. "Laws of Form and Form Dynamics." *Cybernetics & Human Knowing* 9, no. 2 (2002): 49–63.

Keats, John. *Selected Letters.* Edited by Robert Gittings. Oxford: Oxford World's Classics, 2002.

Keene, Donald. *The Winter Sun Shines In: A Life of Masaoka Shiki.* Columbia, MA: Columbia University Press, 2013.

———. *World Within Walls: Japanese Literature of the Pre-Modern Era, 1600–1867.* New York: Grove, 1978.

Kelly, Lynne. *Knowledge and Power in Prehistoric Societies.* Cambridge: Cambridge University Press, 2015.

———. *The Memory Code: Unlocking the Secrets of the Lives of the Ancients and the Power of the Human Mind.* London: Atlantic, 2017.

Kern, Martin. "Creating a Book and Performing It: The 'Yao lüe' Chapter of the 'Huainanzi' as a Western Han 'Fu'." In *The 'Huainanzi' and Textual Production in Early China*, edited by Sarah A. Queen and Michael Puett, 124–150. Leiden: E. J. Brill, 2014. https://doi.org/10.1163/9789004265325_006.

Keys, James [George Spencer-Brown]. *Only Two Can Play This Game.* Bath: Cat Books, 1971.

———. *Only Two Can Play This Game.* Toronto, New York and London: Bantam, 1974.

Kipling, Rudyard. "Just So Stories." 1912; Project Gutenberg, 23 May 2010. http://www.gutenberg.org/files/32488/32488-h/32488-h.htm.

———. *Something of Myself.* New York: Doubleday, Doran & Company, 1937.

Kitāb Alf Laylah Wa-Laylah (version al-al-Ṭab'ah 1). Cairo: al-Maṭba'ah al-'Āmirah al-'Uthmānīyah, 1885. https://archive.org/details/McGillLibrary-rbsc_isl_arabian-nights_kitab-alf-laylah-wa-laylah_PJ7711A521885_v1-2-15548.

Krämer, Hans Joachim. *Plato and the Foundations of Metaphysics: A Work on the Theory of the Principles and Unwritten Doctrines of Plato with a Collection of the Fundamental Documents.* Edited and translated by John R. Catan. Albany, NY: SUNY Press, 1990.

Kroeker, Allan, dir. *Star Trek: Voyager, Endgame.* 2011; New York: Paramount Network Televison. https://www.imdb.com/title/tt0394911.

Kunze, Don. "Triplicity in Spencer-Brown, Lacan, and Poe." In *Lacan and the Nonhuman.* Edited by Gautam Basu Thakur and Jonathan Michael Dickstein, 157–176. Cham: Palgrave Macmillan, 2018.

Lahad, Mooli. "Story-making: An Assessment Method for Coping with Stress."

In *Dramatherapy: Theory and Practice 2*. Edited by Sue Jennings, 150–163. London: Routledge, 1992.

———. "Six Part Story Revisted: The Seven Levels of Assessment Drawn from the 6PSM." In *The "BASIC PH" Model of Coping and Resiliency: Theory, Research, and Cross-Cultural Application*. Edited by Mooli Lahad, Miri Shacham, and Ofra Ayalon, 47–60. London: Jessica Kingsley, 2013.

Lahad, Mooli, and Ofra Ayalon. "BASIC Ph: The Story of Coping Resources." In Community Stress Prevention. Vol. 2. Israel: Kiryat Shmona, Community Stress Prevention Centre, 1997.

Laney, Dave. *African Starlore*. 2006. http://sirius-c.ncat.edu/ EthiopianEnochSociety/Africa-Star/.

Lang, Andrew. *The Green Fairy Book*. New York: A. I. Burt, n.d. Accessed 20 February 2022. https://archive.org/details/greenfairybook00langiala/.

Laozi. *Tao Te Ching: A New English Version*. Translated by Stephen Mitchell. New York: Harper & Row, 1988.

Lawlor, Robert. *Sacred Geometry: Philosophy and Practice*. London: Thames & Hudson, 2002.

Leeming, Joseph. *Riddles, Riddles, Riddles: Enigmas and Anagrams, Puns and Puzzles, Quizzes and Conundrums*. Mineola, NY: Dover, 2014.

Legman, Gershon. *The Limerick*. New York: Random House, 1988.

Lichtheim, Miriam. *The Old and Middle Kingdoms*. Vol. 1, Ancient Egyptian Literature: A Book of Readings. Berkeley, CA: University of California Press, 2006.

Livo, Norma J. *Tales to Tickle Your Funny Bone: Humorous Tales from Around the World*. Westport, CT: Libraries Unlimited, 2007.

Ma, Y. W., and Joseph S. M. Lau. *Traditional Chinese Stories: Themes and Variations*. New York: Columbia University Press, 1978.

Marzolph, Ulrich, and Richard van Leeuwen. *The Arabian Nights Encyclopedia*. 2 vols. Santa Barbara, CA: ABC-CLIO, 2004.

Maynard, Senko K. *Japanese Communication: Language and Thought in Context*. Honolulu, HI: University of Hawaii Press, 1997.

McDermott, Phil. *Transformations: Stories to Tell in the Classroom*. Alresford: Liberalis Books, 2015.

McKee, Robert. *Story: Substance, Structure, Style, and the Principles of Screenwriting*. New York: ReganBooks, 1997.

Mitchell, Stephen. *The Second Book of the Dao*. New York: Penguin, 2009.

Monzani, Patrizia and Beate Kunath, dirs. *The Moon and his two Wives*. 2002; Chemnitz: Chemnitzer FIlmwerkstatt e.V. https://www.youtube.com/

watch?v=7EHKZdUphGQ.

Nasr, Seyyed Hosein. "Scientia Sacra." In *The Underlying Religion: An Introduction to the Perennial Philosophy*, edited by Martin Lings and Clinton Minnaar, 114–140. Bloomington, IN: World Wisdom, 2007.

Nylan, Michael. "Translating Texts in Chinese History and Philosophy." In *Translating China for Western Readers: Reflective, Critical, and Practical Essays*, edited by Ming Dong Gu and Rainer Schulte, 119–148. Albany, NY: SUNY Press, 2014.

Opoku-Agyemang, Kwadwo, and Rogers Asempasah. "Theorising the ambiguous space: The narrative architecture of the dilemma tale as an interpretive frame for reading Morrison's B." *Asemka* (2006): 164–178. https://www.scm.uni-halle.de/gsscm/online_papers/online_papers_2006/morrisons_beloved/?lang=en.

Osho. "Zen: The Path of Paradox, Vol. 2." *Internet Archive.* n.d. Accessed 23 January 2018. https://archive.org/details/zen-the-path-of-paradox-volume-2/.

Ovid. *Metamorphoses.* Translated by Anthony S. Kline, 2000. 2nd ed. N.p.: Poetry in Translation, 2000. https://www.poetryintranslation.com/klineasovid.php; http://ovid.lib.virginia.edu/trans/Ovhome.htm#askline.

Painter, William. "Romeo and Juliet". In *The Palace of Pleasure: Elizabethan Versions of Italian and French Novels from Boccacio, Bandello, Cinthio, Straparola, Queen Margaret of Navarre, and Others.* Vol. 2, Tome 2. Edited by Joseph Jacobs. 3 January 2011; Project Gutenberg. http://www.gutenberg.org/files/34840/34840-h/34840-h.htm#novel2_25.

Paulme, Denise. *La mère dévorante: essai sur la morphologie des contes africains.* Bibliothèque des Sciences Humaines. Paris: Gallimard, 1976.

Pausanias. *Phocis, Ozolian Locri.* From Pausanias: Description of Greece in Four Volumes, Vol. 3. Translated by William Henry Samuel Jones. Cambridge, MA: Harvard University Press; London: W. Heinemann; 1965. http://www.perseus.tufts.edu/hopper/text?doc=Paus.+10.24.

Peck, Russell A. *The Cinderella Bibliography.* In *A Robbins Library Digital Project.* Accessed 16 November 2018. http://d.lib.rochester.edu/cinderella.

Pinault, David. *Story-Telling Techniques in the Arabian Nights.* Leiden: E. J. Brill, 1992.

Planck, Max. "Interviews with Great Scientists VI: Max Planck." *The Observer.* 25 January 1931. https://www.newspapers.com/search/#lnd=1&query=Interviews+with+Great+Scientists+VI%3A+Max+Planck&t=1000.

Plato. *Philebus.* From Plato in Twelve Volumes, Vol. 8. Translated by Harold

N. Fowler. Cambridge, MA: Harvard University Press; London: W. Heinemann, 1925. http://www.perseus.tufts.edu/hopper/text?doc=Perseus%3Atext%3A1999.01.0174%3Atext%3DPhileb.%3Asection%3D11a.

———. *Symposium*. From Plato in Twelve Volumes, Vol. 3. Translated by W. R. M. Lamb. Cambridge, MA: Harvard University Press; London: W. Heinemann, 1967. http://www.perseus.tufts.edu/hopper/text?doc=Perseus%3Atext%3A1999.01.0174%3Atext%3DSym.%3Asection%3D172a.

———. *Timaeus*. From Plato in Twelve Volumes, Vol. 9. Translated by W. R. M. Lamb. Cambridge, MA: Harvard University Press; London: W. Heinemann. 1925. https://www.perseus.tufts.edu/hopper/text?doc=Perseus%3Atext%3A1999.01.0180%3Atext%3DTim.%3Asection%3D17a.

———. *The Republic of Plato*. Translated by Allan Bloom. New York: Basic Books, 1991.

Plutarch. *Moralia*. Translated by Frank Cole Babbitt. Vol. 5. Cambridge, MA; London: Harvard University Press, 1936. http://www.perseus.tufts.edu/hopper/text?doc=Perseus%3Atext%3A2008.01.0243.

Polti, Georges. *The Thirty-Six Dramatic Situations*. Translated by Lucile Ray. Franklin, OH: James Knapp Reeve, 1924. https://archive.org/details/thirtysixdramati00polt/.

Pound, Ezra. *ABC of Reading*. London: Faber and Faber, 1991.

Propp, Vladimir. *Morphology of the Folktale*. 2nd ed. Austin, TX: University of Texas Press, 2005.

Pullman, Philip. *Dæmon Voices: Essays on Storytelling*. Edited by Simon Mason. Oxford: David Fickling, 2017.

———. *His Dark Materials*. London: Scholastic, 2001.

———. *Perverse, All Monstrous, All Prodigious Things*. Sheffield: National Association for the Teaching of English (NATE), 2002.

Pushkin, Alexander. *The Tale of Tsar Saltan*. Translated by Louis Zellikoff, illustrated by Ivan Bilibin. Moscow, USSR: Progress Publishers, 1968.

Reichel, André. "Snakes all the Way Down: Varela's Calculus for Self-Reference and the Praxis of Paradise." *Systems Research and Behavioral Science* 28, no. 6 (2011): 646–662. https://doi.org/10.1002/sres.1105.

The Rigveda: The Earliest Religious Poetry of India. Translated by Stephanie W. Jamison and Joel P. Brereton. Vol. 3. New York: Oxford University Press, 2014.

Robbins, Jerome and Robert Wise, directors. *West Side Story.* 1961; Los Ange-
    les: United Artists.

Roberts, Gillian. *Adam and Evil: An Amanda Pepper Mystery.* New York:
    Ballantine, 1999. http://books.google.co.uk/books?id=iEWwLwQ_
    ExsC.

Robertson, Rt Hon John Mackinnon. *Letters on Reasoning.* 2nd ed. Revised
    with additions. London: Watts, 1905.

Rojas, Martin M. *How to Write Like a College Student.* N.p.: CreateSpace
    Independent Publishing Platform, 2014.

Rooth, Anna Birgitta. *The Cinderella Cycle.* New York: Arno, 1980.

The Sacred Books of China: The Texts of Confucianism. 2nd ed. Edited by Max
    Müller. Translated by James Legge. Vol. 3. Oxford: Clarendon, 1899.
    https://archive.org/details/sacredbooksofchi12conf/page/n9.

Saiber, Arielle. *Giordano Bruno and the Geometry of Language: Literary and
    Scientific Cultures of Early Modernity.* Aldershot and Burlington, VT:
    Ashgate, 2005.

Samuels, Richard S. "Benedetto Varchi, the Accademia degli Infiammati and
    the Origins of the Italian Academic Movement." *Renaissance Quarterly*
    29, no. 4 (Winter 1976): 599–634. https://doi.org/10.2307/2860034.

Sanders, Carol, ed. *The Cambridge Companion to Saussure.* Cambridge:
    Cambridge University Press, 2004.

Schaberg, David. *A Patterned Past: Form and Thought in Early Chinese
    Historiography.* Cambridge, MA: Harvard University Press, 2002.

———. "Remonstrance in Eastern Zhou Historiography." *Early China* 22
    (1997): 133–179.

Schmidt, Victoria Lynn. *Story Structure Architect: A Writer's Guide to Building
    Dramatic Situations and Compelling Characters.* Cincinnati, OH:
    Writer's Digest Books, 2005.

Schwaller de Lubicz, René Adolph. *The Temple of Man.* Translated by Deborah
    Lawlor and Robert Lawlor. Rochester, VT: Inner Traditions
    International, 1998.

Scots, Mary Queen of. *Letters of Mary Queen of Scots and Documents
    Connected with her Personal History.* Edited by Agnes Strickland.
    Vol. 2. London: Henry Colburn, 1843. https://archive.org/details/
    lettersofmaryque02mary/.

Selcraig, Bruce. "The Real Robinson Crusoe." *Smithsonian Magazine on
    Smithsonian.com.* July 2005. https://www.smithsonianmag.com/
    history/the-real-robinson-crusoe-74877644/.

Shakespeare, William. *Romeo and Juliet*. In *The Arden Shakespeare, Third Series*, edited by René Weis, 1125–1158. London: Bloomsbury, 2012.

Skinner, Richard. *Writing a Novel: Bring Your Ideas to Life the Faber Academy Way*. London: Faber & Faber, 2018.

Snake Jokes. 2018. http://jokes4us.com/animaljokes/snakejokes.html.

Snodgrass, Adrian. *Architecture, Time and Eternity: Studies in the Stellar and Temporal Symbolism of Traditional Buildings*. 2 vols. Delhi: P. K. Goel for Aditya Prakashan, 1990.

Spain, Peter of. *Syncategoreumata*. Translated by Joke Spruyt. Leiden: E. J. Brill, 1992.

Spencer-Brown, George. "An Introduction to Reductors." Unpublished manuscript. December 1992. PDF file.

———. *Laws of Form*. Leipzig: Bohmeier Verlag, 2011. First published 1969 by George Allen and Unwin (London).

———. *Laws of Form*. New York: Dutton, 1979.

———. *Laws of Form*. Ashland, OH: BookMasters, 1994.

Star Trek: Voyager. 1995–2001. https://www.imdb.com/title/tt0112178/?ref_=fn_al_tt_1.

Tetlow, Adam. *The Diagram: Harmonic Geometry*. Glastonbury, Somerset: Wooden Books, 2021.

Towler, Solala. *The Spirit of Zen: Teaching Stories on the Way to Enlightenment*. London: Watkins, 2017.

Trimble, Michael. *Why Humans Like to Cry: Tragedy, Evolution and the Brain*. Oxford: Oxford University Press, 2012.

Tymieniecka, Anna-Teresa. "Life's Primogenital Timing: Time Projected by the Dynamic Articulation of the Onto-Genesis." In *Life: Phenomenology of Life as the Starting Point of Philosophy*. 25th anniversary publication. Book 3, edited by Anna-Teresa Tymieniecka. Dordrecht: Kluwer Academic Publishers, 1997.

———. *The Fullness of the Logos in the Key of Life: Book 1. The Case of God in the New Enlightenment*. Vol. C of Analecta Husserliana: The Yearbook of Phenomenological Research. Dordrecht: Springer, 2009.

van Gennep, Arnold. *Rites of Passage*. Chicago, IL: Chicago University Press, 1959.

Van Zile, Susan. *Mastering the 5-Paragraph Essay: Mini-Lessons, Models, and Engaging Activities That Give Students the Writing Tools They Need to Tackle—And Succeed On—The Tests*. New York: Scholastic, 2006.

von Franz, Marie Louise. *An Introduction to the Psychology of Fairy Tales*. Irving,

TX: Spring Publications, 1978.

Vonnegut, Kurt. "Here is a lesson in creative writing." In *A Man Without a Country*. New York: Seven Stories Press, 2005.

———. "Shape of Stories." Lecture for The Case College Scholars Program, 4 February 2004. https://www.youtube.com/watch?v=GOGru_4z1Vc.

Warner, John. *Why They Can't Write: Killing the Five-Paragraph Essay and Other Necessities*. Baltimore, MD: Johns Hopkins University Press, 2018.

Waters, T. E. "On Narrative Structure: Kishōtenketsu and Obokuri-Eeumi." *Serpent Scribbles* (blog). 29 January 2013. http://blog.tewaters. com/2013/01/on-narrative-structure-kishotenketsu.html.

Whitman, Walt. *Complete Poetry and Collected Prose*. New York: Library of America, 1982.

Williams, Duane. *The Linguistic Christ – Understanding Christ as the Logos of Language: The Metaphysical Etymology of Heideggerian Linguistics*. Lewiston, NY: Edwin Mellen Press, 2011.

Williamson, Craig. *A Feast of Creatures: Anglo-Saxon Riddle Songs*. The Middle Ages Series. Philadelphia, PA: University of Pennsylvania Press, 2011.

Wittgenstein, Ludwig. *Tractatus Logico-Philosophicus*. Translated by D. F. Pears and B. F. McGuinness. London and New York: Routledge Classics, 2001.

World Kigo Database (blog). "WKD . . . Welcome !." Updated 4 January 2022. https://worldkigodatabase.blogspot.com/.

Womersley, David. "The 'Da Vinci Code' of Shakespeare Scholarship." Review of *Shadowplay: The Hidden Beliefs and Coded Politics of William Shakespeare*, by Clare Asquith. *The Social Affairs Unit*, 5 December 2005. https://web.archive.org/web/20170315013411/http://www. socialaffairsunit.org.uk/blog/archives/000685.php.

Wyss, Johann David. *The Swiss Family Robinson*. 1812; Salt Lake City, UT: Pink Tree Press, 2000; Project Gutenberg, 2000. http://www.gutenberg.org/ cache/epub/3836/pg3836-images.html.

Yates, Frances A. *Theatre of the World*. London: Routledge & Kegan Paul, 1969.

Yi Jing. Translated by Wu Jing-Nuan. Washington, DC: The Taoist Center, 1991.

Yorke, John. *Into the Woods: How Stories Work and Why We Tell Them*. London: Penguin, 2013.

INDEX

451–4; *Barbara* syllogism, 300;
perennial or classical syllogistic,
300

marks (⊐), (⌐), (⌐), ( ), in
Linear structures, 5, 30, 48,
148, 222, 285–6; in Dynamic
structures, 6, 10–11, 149–50,
192, 286; and poetic forms, 335
metaphor, 103–4, 108, 115–17, 318
monomyth, xv, xxiii, 29, 267–9,
278, 456; initiation in, 268–71;
return in, 268–71; separation in,
268–71

narrative(s), 4, 35, 41–2, 47, 248,
261, 267, 278, 289–91, 298–9,
315–17; defined, xxi–xxiv
nesting, 320–1
Non-Threshold structures, 11–12,
307–8, 343, 353

Open-Ended structures, 213–15,
219–25, 287–8, 304, 308; and
poetic forms, 335, 352–3, 429–30
Open-Ended Ki-Shō-Ten-Ketsu
structure, 220–1, 287, 303–4;
and Chinese Circular Structure,
273, 355–60; and poetry, 335,
353–4, 355–60
openings: of poems 335, 355; of
stories, 5, 27–30, 40, 253
oscillation, 30, 38, 454; states of,
10–11, 208n12, 253, 296; in
Chinese Circular Structure,
192, 199; in Perpetual Motion
structure, 263, 264n7, 299; of
steps, 38

oxymoron, 104, 117

parable, 224, 241–2, 306
paradox, 22n2, 104, 170, 221, 223,
226n3; and category corrections,
140–2; and category mistakes,
125, 128, 136, 139; in haiku,
355, 359; and tragedy, 125, 128,
136, 139
Paulme, Denise, 455–6
perennial philosophy, xviii
Perpetual Motion structure,
259–60, 271, 288, 299; and
Chinese Circular Structure, 271;
as expansion of Transformation
structure, 299; and ghazals, 350–
2; oscillation in, 263, 264n7,
299; and Revelation structure,
262
Pinault, David, 330
Planck, Max, 205
Plato, 19, 22n2–3
plot holes, 291, 415
plot patterns, xxiv, 4, 41, 248, 254,
289, 291, 298, 315–24, 456, 460
plot twists, 315
poetic forms: English sonnets,
345–9; ghazals, 332, 350–2;
haikus, 331–2, 350, 354–60;
Italian sonnets, 349; landays,
332, 350, 352–4; limericks,
332, 336–44; rubaiyat, 331;
villanelles, 331
poetry, xix, 96, 104, 217, 323, 324,
329–60; metre in, 332–4;
rhyme in, 341–2; rhythm
in, 334–41; and Threshold
structures, 335, 343–4, 353